contemporary influences in early childhood education

Second Edition

ELLIS D. EVANS

University of Washington

HOLT, RINEHART AND WINSTON, INC.
New York   Chicago   San Francisco   Atlanta
Dallas   Montreal   Toronto   London   Sydney

To Jennifer and Alicia, my daughters,
who have brought to life the beauty
of early childhood and now the
further excitement, charm, mystery,
and promise of middle childhood

Library of Congress Cataloging in Publication Data

Evans, Ellis D.
    Contemporary influences in early childhood education.

    Bibliography, each chapter
    1. Education, Preschool—United States—1945–
I. Title.
LB1140.2.E9   1975   372.21'0973   74–16007
ISBN 0–03–089584–7

*Cover photo by Alan Keimig. Courtesy of Muckleshoot
Tribal Head Start, Auburn, Washington.*

preface

The second edition of this book has been prepared largely in response to the rapid developments occurring in early childhood education since 1970. Much of the original book remains valid and timely. But during the past four years some profound shifts and reassessments in major ideas, policies, and practices concerning early education in America have materialized. These changes provide the substance for many segments of this new version of the book. And, much more now is known about early education as a result of the sheer volume of study which has been conducted since the first edition was written.

Readers familiar with this earlier version will note that both its organization and content have been modified. As a result, I believe new research information is better conveyed and salient issues are more sharply delineated. The strong empirical research orientation established in the first edition remains a distinguishing feature of the text. If anything, the documentation is more thorough than before in order to satisfy personal and professional standards of scholarship. The resultant chapter bibliographies can also serve as a springboard for serious students who wish to develop further their fund of in-depth knowledge about psychology and early education.

More specifically, this revised edition differs from its predecessor in four ways. First, a "new" opening chapter has been written in order to summarize recent significant changes in the field and to establish a conceptual background for subsequent chapters. Second, a chapter has been written to portray the wide range of approaches specific to language education in early childhood and some important issues associated with the increasingly popular language emphasis in early educational programming. Third, this revision contains an expanded discussion of infant and parent education, together with new data about children's educational television. And fourth, the final chapter of this edition is more conceptually detailed with respect to major issues. It also deals to a greater extent with matters related to research in early childhood education.

The only major segment of the original book not included in this revision concerns research and theory about perceptual-motor training for young children. Briefer sections about some early education programs (e.g., the new nursery school, the early training project) also have been omitted. These omissions are due primarily to space restrictions and should not be taken to indicate a lack of concern about the place of these programs in the overall early education picture. In the case of perceptual-motor training, few, if any, points made in the original edition have been contradicted by recent research. Interested readers may wish to review those comments before taking up the current edition. As for other omissions, I can only say that selectivity in reporting is inevitable in a book of this kind. To review all programs of note in early education would require a volume of encyclopedic proportions. In general, I have preferred to concentrate upon programs which I know about in depth and which can be taken to illustrate more general classes or categories of programs.

It is notable that since the first edition of this book appeared in print, early childhood education professionals have come increasingly to support a definition of such education as "group settings which are deliberately intended to effect developmental changes in children in the age range from birth to the age of entering the first grade."[1] Clearly, this definition can be taken to include nursery schools, kindergartens, and most day care centers whose functions are not limited to minimum physical caretaking. Accordingly, I have made greater reference to the day care literature in this second edition. However, the magnitude of this literature made it impossible for me to do justice to advances in day care, much less to the issues of import which pervade every major aspect of the day care scene in America. Readers concerned principally with day care practices, problems, and research will therefore have to turn elsewhere for a comprehensive discussion. Furthermore, I still believe that early childhood education legitimately can encompass primary grade schooling. Consequently, space in this edition has been reserved for discussions of programs that extend beyond the first grade and into the mainstream of elementary schooling.

As in the first edition, many persons have provided me with wide-ranging assistance in the preparation of the text. Without their help, the book would still be languishing in a state of disarray, both technically and conceptually. To the following persons, then, I wish formally to express my sincere gratitude: J. Myron Atkin, Wesley Becker, Harold Bessell, Margaret Bland, Barbara Calabrese, Daisy Dawson, Rheta DeVries, Margo Fitzgerald, Harry Guay, Mary O. Haller, Norris Haring, Alice Hayden, Ronald Henderson, Alice Honig, Margaret Johnston, Constance Kamii, Shari Nedler, Peter Rinearson, Irving Sigel, James O. Smith, Joseph Stevens, Jr., Robert Tostberg, Nancy Van Arsdale, David Weikart, and Aline Wolf. Thanks are also due to my critic reviewers, whose efforts were coordinated by John Tugman; and especially to my wife, Cindy, whose immeasurable contributions include moral support, just criticisms, and manuscript typing. Finally, I wish to express my appreciation to the many editors and publishers of professional literature who have given their consent to quote important passages from published materials.

Ellis D. Evans

Seattle, Washington
September 1974

---

[1] Katz, L. Early childhood education as a discipline. *Young Children*, 1971, *26*, 82.

contents

Photograph courtesy of Camera Craft, Seattle, Washington.

changing
patterns
of early
education

For most of us, the decade of the 1960s brings to mind international conflict, political assassinations, urban crises, student dissent, moon walks, a growing sense of urgency about ecology, and the onset of liberation movements. Less sensational but significant in its own way was a stirring of educational and psychological thought that continues to swirl in the 1970s. This thought, together with a social catalyst known as the War on Poverty, served to energize a renaissance within early childhood education. This was not an overnight occurrence. But certain patterns of philosophical discourse and empirical research jelled during the early sixties to nourish society's view of young children's educational needs. Among these patterns were new concepts of the nature of psychological development during infancy (Kessen, 1963), an overhaul of concepts of motivation (White, 1959), creative insights into children's thought processes and the variables that affect them (Piaget, 1961), a heightened understanding of learning and language performance associated with social class differences (Bernstein, 1961), new interpretations of the structure of knowledge and the relationship of early to later learning (Bruner, 1960), the effects of early stimulation on brain structure and chemistry (Kresh, 1969), an apparent shift in socialization practices toward a greater emphasis on children's achievement training (Bronfenbrenner, 1961), and new data from the study of human intelligence (Stott and Ball, 1965).

The cumulative impact of these and other patterns of research and scholarly discussion provided a credible psychological rationale for educating children under six years of age. Of course, early childhood education had existed for many years (see Chapter 2). But the marshalling of scientific data facilitated a much more serious view of the importance of such education. It also supplied a firmer basis for an expenditure of vast sums of federal monies, many of which went to finance experimental programs for children from poverty backgrounds. The name of the game was "early intervention"—education for four-year-olds with more than occasional interest in programs for even younger children (see Chapter 8). In the discussion that follows, an attempt is made to portray some forces which contributed to the unprecedented concern for children's cognition which dominated the 1960s. Next to be examined are some major outcomes of the early intervention movement, all of which have implications for our conceptualization of early childhood education in the seventies. The final section is reserved for an overview of major issues in early education. These issues are, for the most part, timeless, although their intensity may vary with changing social conditions.

EARLY INTERVENTION: A PSYCHOLOGICAL PERSPECTIVE

The Move to Cognitive Enrichment

Most generally, *cognition* refers to the processes by which children acquire knowledge and thinking skills and utilize them in problem solving. We are concerned here with a growth of conviction among psychologists about the crucial role of environmental stimulation in children's cognitive development. An appropriate exemplar of the move to study cognitive enrichment during the early childhood years is the work of psychologist William Fowler. Fowler's early analytic review (1962a) of the gaps in our understanding of early cognitive learning (and the reasons for these gaps) led to several important conclusions. One was that the potential of the preschool years for maximizing cognitive development had never been fully exploited in American education. Another conclusion was that the early years are better than those later in the developmental sequence for building conceptual learning sets, interests, and habit patterns, and that early learning can facilitate learning which occurs later.[1]

This elaborate review of research on early learning was followed by a general proposal to promote early conceptual development through a series of learning sequences tailored to the cognitive abilities of preschool children (Fowler, 1965). At the heart of this proposal is the task of devising sequential levels of complexity that progress from perceptual to classification activities. Fowler's general teaching strategy requires an atmosphere

---

[1] Tangible evidence of Fowler's orientation to systematic cognitive stimulation is his study of process variables in a two-year-old child's learning to read (Fowler, 1962b).

of "play-game activities" coordinated with children's problem-solving capacity. A further refinement of this cognitive-stimulation approach has appeared in the form of a developmental curriculum for disadvantaged children (Fowler, 1966). Its main features are psychocognitive diagnosis procedures and the precise programming and pacing of "simulation sequences."

A concept of developmental learning as the basis for analyzing and arranging educational experience for young children has continued to dominate Fowler's subsequent professional contributions. In one, for example, the problem of timing in forms of deprivation-stimulation is examined (Fowler, 1970). Another contribution is a three-year study of infant care based upon developmental learning principles and practices, the details of which are discussed in Chapter 8. In still another paper, Fowler (1971) has discussed the role of structured guidance in facilitating children's cognitive development. After reviewing much research, including his own infant development program, Fowler concludes that

> on a broad plane our findings generally support the notion of the equal, indeed essential, value of both symbolic, guided cognitive orientations and self-propelled free play and flexible approaches toward early child care and education. The implications of our research to date suggest that, far from being uneconomic, integrated cognitive-interpersonal approaches to child rearing foster the development of competence, autonomy, and personality development in children from many social backgrounds (Fowler, 1971, p. 35).[2]

This conclusion represents a balance of viewpoints that are too often phrased in adversative terms: free play versus structured academic learning; or a child-centered, learning by self-selection and self-pacing approach versus a tightly structured, authoritarian, and didactic approach to childhood education. As will be seen, such false dichotomies do much to distort and confuse thinking about early learning in school settings.

Educational Policy Commitments As balanced as Fowler's programming may be, his continued work is cited primarily to exemplify a growing commitment to the value of stimulating cognitive development in systematic ways. This commitment, established during the sixties, neither was nor is today shared by all professional early childhood educators. Yet cognitive development has become the watchword for many researchers and practitioners. This value orientation has represented a shift away from the more traditional nursery school (and to some extent, kindergarten) emphasis upon social-emotional development (see Chapter 2). This shift has been formalized in many ways, including the issuance of policy statements from high-level professional organizations. Consider, for instance, the following excerpt from the introductory statement of the powerful

[2] Reprinted with permission from *Young Children*, Vol. XXVII, No. 1, October 1971. Copyright © 1971, National Association for the Education of Young Children, 1834 Connecticut Ave., N.W., Washington, D.C. 20009.

Educational Policies Commission (1966) in a document entitled *Universal Opportunity for Early Childhood Education:*

> The development of intellectual ability and of intellectual interest is fundamental to the achievement of all the goals of American education. Yet these qualities are greatly affected by what happens to children before they reach school. A growing body of research and experience demonstrates that by the age of six most children have already developed a considerable part of the intellectual ability they will possess as adults. Six is now generally accepted as the normal age of entrance to school. We believe this practice is obsolete. All children should have the opportunity to go to school at public expense beginning at the age of four (p. 1).

Similarly, the Research and Policy Committee of the Committee for Economic Development (1971) has made public the following position:

> Preschooling is desirable for all children, but it is a necessity for the disadvantaged. Without it, there is little possibility of achieving equality in education. . . . only a massive effort to establish both public and private preschool educational programs will provide the preparation in motivation, intellectual capacities, and physical skills essential to success in achieving total basic literacy (reading, writing, and computation) (pp. 35–37).

This committee has also advocated federal support for free day care centers at which children as young as two years of age would be eligible for "educational experience and enrichment."

These two policy statements do not necessarily imply a subsidiary role for emotional development or the full cultivation of children's total capabilities. But these committees' joint concern for children's intellectual-academic life is clear. Both statements are based on the idea that earlier organized school experience will result in greater intellectual gains than would otherwise be likely (to say nothing of this avenue as a means to attack educational inequalities). And, again, support for this idea has been drawn largely from data published by researchers in developmental and educational psychology. Such data have been synthesized by Bloom (1964) and Hunt (1961). The latter authority has integrated both classical and new data from the study of intellectual development and its measurement. Hunt's framework permits a basic reinterpretation of the concept of human intelligence. Basically, Hunt's thesis is a challenge to the traditional idea that intelligence is fixed or predetermined by genetic forces. Instead, Hunt argues that intelligence is a network of central neural processes and information-processing strategies, which is affected significantly by the kinds of encounters a child has with his environment.

Bloom's summary and analysis (1964) of longitudinal data concerning intelligence has led him to infer that the rate of intellectual development is at its point of highest acceleration during the child's early years. This inference is coupled with the notion that growth variables are most

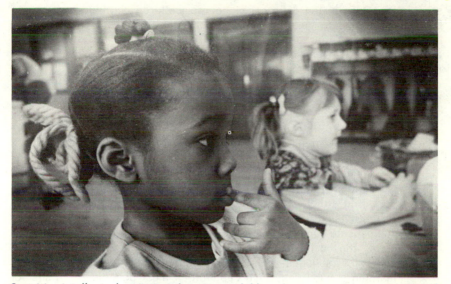

Cognitive intellectual activities for young children have come to occupy a much more central role in many contemporary approaches to early education. This child in a Project Follow Through classroom has paused to consider a concept classification task. Photo by Peter Rinearson.

affected by environmental intrusions (variations) during the period of most rapid acceleration. Therefore, Bloom argues that the greatest payoff from environmental stimulation—at least in terms of intellectual growth—will come from the child's experiential base during the first four to six years of life.

It should be noted that many problems and issues are associated with this line of thinking: the true nature of intelligence, how intelligence is measured, how environmental interactions may differentially influence intelligence at different points in development, and the validity of research data upon which any generalization about intellectual development is based. Such matters will be raised in later sections of this book. Moreover, the concept that the early years represent a critical formative period for all subsequent intellectual growth has been seriously questioned by authorities in developmental psychology. Kagan (1973), for example, has extrapolated from research on Guatemalan children to make the point that early intellectual deprivation is not an overwhelming obstacle to normal development. His argument has been extended to the idea that intellectual deprivation may be reversible, even within the average classroom.

Basic Assumptions for Early Intervention

The continual emergence of psychoeducational controversies makes it difficult to say what is the truth about intellectual development and its stimulation. Despite the debates, of course, children continue to grow, to be socialized, and to be educated for better or worse. It seems safe to say, however, that the dominant body of thought about early development and education revolves around the importance of early experience in the total span of human development. Certainly, this idea is central to the overall rationale for educational intervention at the preschool level, as indicated by the following assumptions (Blank, 1970; Sigel, 1973):

1. Children are, by nature, malleable and their growth and development can be modified extensively in a variety of directions.
2. The earlier one can effect a plausible intervention, the better.
3. The manipulation of early experience will influence subsequent psychological functioning. This influence can be salutary or *hindering.* In either case, cumulative development is involved.
4. The provision of qualitatively sound experience can mollify or compensate for basic lacks in children's environments. Such lacks define the basis on which experiences can be built. Furthermore, since the school's scholastic emphasis demands certain basic learning capabilities, such capabilities must become the focus for early intervention.
5. Children who fail to reap the benefits of planned intervention are likely to develop in ways that are counterproductive to extant social-educational conditions. Or, since a high-level capacity for symbolic (cognitive) activity is one of man's greatest strengths, children who manifest disorders in cognitive performance are failing to achieve their human potential. Thus, resources must be marshalled to prevent or remediate such disorders.

Compensatory Education

Such assumptions about early education, however valid, set the stage for an intervention movement that became virtually synonymous with the term *compensatory education*—education to "compensate" for real or perceived lacks in the total environment of many children. These children were almost exclusively children of the poor. They also were frequently children from racial-ethnic minorities. Thus, whereas prior to about 1965, prekindergarten education was largely the province of affluent children, it became an attempt to provide better opportunities for great numbers of so-called disadvantaged children. A psychological rationale was firmly molded—largely around the *cumulative deficit* hypothesis—and political conditions were ripe for improved educational and other services for the poor and oppressed. The cumulative deficit hypothesis was implicit in the initial rationale for early intervention. According to this hypothesis, experiential deficiencies induce growth deficits that interfere progressively with subsequent growth processes, learning, and motivational development (Ausubel, 1964; Deutsch, 1964; Jensen, 1966). Thus, a hierarchical arrangement of developmental phenomena is presumed. Data pertinent to the hypothesis include school failure rates among poor children and research on the effects of environmental deprivation and enrichment upon measured intelligence and language development. (See Schultz and Aurbach, 1971, for a critical examination of the cumulative deficit hypothesis.)

Compensatory education programs collectively represented two historically innovative components (Beilin, 1972). First, as mentioned above, formal and semiformal educational programs were introduced at ages below that at which most children begin kindergarten or first grade. Second, as will become more evident throughout this book, the focus of early education was substantially modified from a socialization–mental health function to a cognitive-stimulation approach. Despite the rhetoric for change, resistance was encountered by the new advocates of early cognitive education (Beilin, 1972). The economics of early intervention were questioned on the grounds that existing resources could be more satisfactorily improved than could a blueprint for an entire preschool system be translated into reality. The modified curriculum focus was resisted largely by the early childhood education establishment, whose tradition was steeped in the mental health–socialization point of view.

Regardless of the initial economic and philosophical resistance, the outcome of compensatory programs is clear: a massive educational experiment in the form of Project Head Start (see Chapter 2) joined by myriad smaller-scale intervention programs, subsidized mostly by governmental funds. Considering Head Start activity as a whole, the curriculum shift away from traditional early education practice was slow and complex. Perhaps the critical factor was a change in attitude to accept greater accountability for the impact of early education upon intellectual development.

Criticisms of Compensatory Education

Several streams of criticism regarding the theory and practice of compensatory education have since begun to flow (Bernstein, 1972; Nimnicht, 1973b). For some, it is illogical to speak of "compensatory" education when most of the recipients had not been offered an adequate educational environment in the first place. In other words, these critics argue that low-income minority children have been forced to accept all the shortcomings of public education: inadequate facilities, unstable teaching faculties, excessively large classes. This argument is perhaps less relevant when the clients for compensatory education are *preschool* children. However, preschool compensatory education followed by unimproved public school experience would hardly seem worth the effort.

A second criticism is that the concept of compensatory education has drawn attention to the wrong dimension of the problem. This means that too many professionals have been distracted by the presumed defects of poor families. Instead, these professionals should have been looking more critically at the internal organization of the school and its general climate for learning.

A third criticism, perhaps more widely discussed, is rooted in the classic and seemingly unsolvable dilemma of heredity versus environment in intellectual development. As summarized by Jensen (1969), the argument is that heredity accounts for as much as 80 percent of intelligence, as indicated by IQ (intelligence quotient). Consequently, environmental manipulations are unlikely to affect in any profound way children's intellectual achievement status. To this contention have been added various claims about genetically determined racial-ethnic differences in measured intelligence. To say that much passionate disagreement surrounds this viewpoint is a supreme understatement, although no one seriously denies that heredity does act as a major force in the course of intellectual development. At issue, again, is the nature and modifiability of intellectual capabilities, about which an entire literature has evolved. (See, for example, Bayley, 1970, and Guilford, 1973.)

A final criticism is directed not at the alleged impotency of compensatory education to produce respectable gains in intellectual competence, but at the methods of intervention, including the use of IQ gain to determine program effectiveness. This stream of criticism includes charges that compensatory education personifies an "institutional racism" in American social science and educational circles (Baratz and Baratz, 1970); that compensatory education is based upon a social pathology model which assumes that children of poverty and racial minorities are basically inferior. Even the basic right of educators to intervene has been challenged (Sroufe, 1970). Some authorities (e.g., Nimnicht, Johnson, and Johnson, 1973) have acknowledged the validity of such criticisms to the point of actively redesigning their early education strategy for two different groups of children: those whom the schools fail because the children do not fit the ubiquitous white, middle-class pattern; and those who are a product of genuine environmental deprivation. The latter group includes children whose environment does not provide the bare essentials—food, shelter, health, and adult attention—necessary for unstunted development.

And so changes occur. Sometimes the changes are minor or trivial. Other radical changes are often slow in coming. But changes do occur. In the next section some of the more visible outcomes of the early flirtations with intervention programs for young children are examined. Some results are enormously important. Others, more than anything else, reinforce some of the basic good sense that many educators have demonstrated through the years. Taken together, these outcomes continue to pave the way for a deeper probing of contemporary influences in early childhood education.

SOME MAJOR OUTCOMES OF THE EARLY INTERVENTION MOVEMENT

Modified Expectancies about the Effects of Early Education on Children

As indicated above, several changes in our collective thinking about early intervention and compensatory education have occurred during the past several years. It should become clear in later chapters that the measured impact of such intervention efforts upon children's intellectual growth has not often confirmed the optimistic predictions made during the sixties. It can be said that the experience of the past decade has jolted many expectations about what can be realistically accomplished under the circumstances faced by most early childhood educators. Few such educators are now likely to deceive themselves about the magnitude of the overall lasting intellectual-academic gains which can be attributed to preschool programs.

Hindsight is a remarkable phenomenon. Several national authorities (e.g., Akers, 1972; Zigler, 1973) maintain in retrospect that early intervention was oversold. Others (e.g., Nimnicht, 1973a) argue that in many parts of the country far too great a burden was placed on children to respond to crash and often short-lived intervention efforts by educators. Regardless of the past, we are now well into a period of consolidation, introspection, and more critical examination of the premises, intents, and procedures of early intervention programs. Accordingly, professionals appear more modest, even humble, about the enormous complexity of early education problems. Simple solutions are not forthcoming. Early childhood education is decreasingly seen as a panacea for society's ills, despite the fact that such education historically has been viewed by many as a means of social reform (Lazerson, 1972). More comprehensive interrelated social programs now seem to hold greater promise for change than singular efforts at preschool education. True, it can (and has) been argued that the great early cognitive-stimulation experiment has yet to be attempted on a mass scale (Medinnus, 1970). This argument is based on the premise that Head Start, for instance, did not (and still does not) comprise systematic cognitive education. Often more encouraging, however, have been data from smaller-scale, intensively structured and organized programs that suggest impressive immediate gains in terms of their stated goals (Edwards and Stern, 1970; Weikart, 1972). Examples of such programs appear in later chapters.

The humble spirit in early education has possibly been dampened even further by a broad frontal attack on inequalities in education (Jencks, et al., 1972). The essence of this argument, supported by reams of standardized test data, is that the quality of an educational experience— measured in terms of expenditures per pupil, structural arrangements, teacher characteristics, or any other index taken to indicate equality in educational opportunity—has little, if any, bearing on the cognitive development and even the eventual earning capacity of an individual. What can make a difference, it is claimed, are factors such as initial socioeconomic standing, motivation, and other personal-social characteristics of children. Even luck, chance, and fate have been brought into the picture. In other words, it is claimed that the long-term effects of education are fairly uniform, regardless of what goes on in schools. This claim would presumably include any organized effort at preschool education. Schools, therefore, should be evaluated not on the basis of cognitive-intellectual impact, but on how satisfying a place children and teachers find them to be (Jencks et al., 1972).

Predictably, this viewpoint has its critics. The logic, methodological features, interpretations of data, and proposals for change reflected in *Inequality: A Reassessment of the Effect of Family and Schooling in America* (Jencks et al., 1972) have all been well roasted (for example, by Ellena, 1973). If nothing else, existing data clearly show that the quantity of educational experience can make a difference in postschool success, including further options for self-development (Levin, Guthrie, Kleindorfer, and Stout, 1971). Yet the Jencksonian viewpoint adds to the sobering effect of unrealized hopes about the extent to which early education can influence intellectual development.

Perhaps because of the lack of confirming evidence of any lasting impact of early intervention upon intellectual development, many childhood educators have backed away from an extreme and often narrow concern with cognitive outcomes at the preschool level. There are, of course, numerous programs which continue a vigorous and rather strict formal emphasis upon cognitive activities—if not on empirical then on philosophical grounds (Bereiter, 1972). Generally speaking, however, the early education enterprise seems more balanced in terms of its basic priorities. Having been little influenced by the cognitive ground swell, some program builders maintain now, as always, a stronger affective emphasis. Examples of both value positions are examined at various points in this book.

As program emphases have been tendered, so has the obsession with measurable long-term cognitive effects as an inviolable condition for program justification. The idea that short-term outcomes are good has begun to take hold. Early childhood programs have their unique contributions to make within the total scope of developmental education, as do programs for older children, adolescents, and young adults. More apparent now is the sensible view that the accomplishment of carefully selected immediate objectives has merit. If educators at each successive grade level worked to ensure the best possible experience for children within a coordinated hierarchical curriculum, perhaps the harsh trial of early childhood education could be further softened.

Renewed Appreciation of Home-Related Factors: Nutrition and Parental Support

However profound and lasting the impact of any educational program may be, the power of home-related factors as mediators of such impact must be recognized. Surely, some prerequisites must be met for any early education program to succeed. Foremost among these prerequisites are adequate nutrition, beginning in the period of prenatal development, and consistent home support and stimulation of children by their parents or caregivers (Gordon, 1971; Read, 1972).

First, consider nutritional factors. Unfortunately, malnutrition is often a telling accompaniment of poverty status. Exact statistics are unknown, but even severe malnutrition—including protein-calorie deprivation—can be observed in the United States. Such malnutrition often is implicated

as a factor in impaired mental development. No known educational program has much chance of overcoming the effects of early and prolonged
malnutrition. Even children who may not suffer chronic malnutrition, but
are simply hungry a great deal of the time, are poor prospects for the
best educational services.

Fortunately, many preschool programs include a minimal food service.
This can be a fairly effective weapon against hunger, at least during
school hours. The more serious problem, however, involves children whose
nutritional care has been below minimally acceptable levels prior to
their entry into a preschool or early school program. For more extended
discussions of nutritional variables on brain development and learning,
see Coursin (1972) and Foster (1972).

Obviously, parental responsibility and resources are involved in providing adequate nutritional care. Equally obvious is the fact that parental
influence extends beyond nutrition and general caretaking activities. Much
evidence has accumulated to dramatize the potential impact of parental
support, encouragement, the modeling of learning strategies, general verbal
stimulation, reinforcement for autonomous behavior, and achievement
training upon children's responsivity in formal school settings (McCandless
and Evans, 1973). In fact, the preschool programs that seem most effective
nearly always include a systematic means for eliciting and maintaining
parental involvement (see Chapter 8).

The salient influence of parents on children in early intervention
programs should come as no surprise. Many early childhood educators—
especially those associated with home and family life cooperative nursery
schools—have long believed in the importance of parental support and
education. Active parental involvement—with the ultimate goal of en-
hancing the family's ability to respond to its children—is increasingly seen
as a given in any intelligent approach to early childhood education (Nimnicht, Johnson, and Johnson, 1973).

Sensitivity to Cultural Differences

As we have seen, a fundamental premise of compensatory education
was that certain cognitive and motivational deficits characterized most
"disadvantaged" children, predisposing them to early and cumulative school
failure. Accordingly, compensatory education was an attempt to make up
for these deficits. One dangerous undercurrent of thinking about the disadvantaged child as deficit ridden was a reinforcement of ethnocentrism
regarding any deviation from the white middle-class norm. Certainly
ethnocentrism did not color the teaching patterns of all educators. But
a prevailing attitude seemed to equate cultural *differences* with cultural
deficiencies (Cole and Bruner, 1972). The results of a shift in thinking
about this matter can now be observed. Ethnic, racial, or social class
differences are increasingly seen as differences to be respected and
accommodated to in the schools, not as deficiencies invariably tied to
poverty or purported social disorganization.

The early intervention movement begun in the 1960s has contributed much to a renewal of sensitivity about, and appreciation for, the value of cultural pluralism in education. Photo courtesy of Camera Craft, Seattle, Washington.

The several traditions that established precedent for this shifting viewpoint have been articulated by Cole and Bruner (1971). Briefly, these authorities maintain, as do others (e.g., Meichanbaum and Turk, 1972), that cultural deprivation is a special case of cultural difference. This difference is manifest when a child must cope with demands to perform in ways that are inconsistent with his previous cultural experience. Hence, if the term *deficit* is at all useful, it should apply to a child's performance, not necessarily his learning ability or competence. A particularly good example of this distinction between performance and competence comes from the study of language development and education, as will be discussed in Chapter 4.

With the above distinction in mind, Cole and Bruner (1971) reject the cumulative deficit hypothesis on three grounds. The first involves the "doctrine of psychic unity" (Kroeber, 1948). Briefly, this means that different conclusions about man's existence can be reached depending upon the way one organizes his experience. Ultimately, all ways of organizing experience are arbitrary. The dominant view of "cultural deprivation" probably is an artifact of the way the majority culture experience is organized.

Second, Cole and Bruner maintain, with others (such as Labov, 1970), that all peoples are basically equivalent in their functional linguistic ability. One therefore cannot legitimately attribute less intellectual ability than is necessary for the complex development of language to any ethnic, racial, or cultural group.

And, third, Cole and Bruner are critical of the dominant "situation-bound" nature of most psychological experimentation and study. In other words, they claim that psychologists (and social scientists in general) too often overlook the complex interplay among cultural-social variables that influences children's behavior differently in different situations and at different points in time. Again, the argument is that groups labeled as culturally deprived possess underlying basic competencies equivalent to those present in the mainstream of the dominant culture. Performance differences are a function of various situations or contexts in which competencies are expressed.

Two important implications are contained in this set of ideas. First, Cole and Bruner invite recognition and acceptance of the idea that educational difficulties can be analyzed in terms of cultural differences (as opposed to learner pathology). They maintain that this change in outlook among teachers, for example, could lead to a more positive attitude toward minority group school children. If so, these children would benefit in many ways. Of course, more than acceptance of the "cultural differences" interpretation is needed: teachers must also become proficient in their understanding of their pupils' minority cultures and the ways in which these cultures are similar to and different from the teacher's own cultural background.

A second implication for Cole and Bruner is that the right road to education for minority group children does not force teachers to attempt to create new cognitive structures in their pupils. Instead, more skillful procedures for transferring existing skills to classroom activities are needed. This is an intriguing point, fraught with philosophical overtones. If agreement on the point is reached, it will mean that specific and valid ways for achieving skills transfer must be identified. This has yet to be done, but Cole and Bruner effectively communicate the idea of better adapting instruction to the needs and school-entering skills of young children.

Cole and Bruner may exaggerate cultural differences by failing to acknowledge basic commonalities among children from all walks of life. It should be noted, however, that other authorities have formed their thinking along similar lines on the basis of sound research evidence. Rohwer (1971), for example, disagrees with the notion that *inherent* racial- or social class-related deficiencies exist among poor black children. He believes that such children enter school with somewhat "less developed" learning tactics than do their white economically advantaged peers and that this difference typically is most marked during the kindergarten year. Rohwer suggests that while poor black children often improve their skills nearly to the point of equality by first grade, these skills are not as well honed for some modes of receptive and active learning as for others. He also points out that many impoverished black children are less adequate in their essential classroom skills mastery than in their abilities to operate in more informal settings such as the playground or ghetto streets. (This is consistent with Cole and Bruner's point about situational relativity.) Rohwer then reasons that such children will require training in elaborative learning techniques in order to engage and refine their capacity for imaginative conceptual activity through concrete, explicit, and specific instructional procedures. This recommendation for direct systematic instruction is not totally compatible with Cole and Bruner's position, yet both viewpoints reinforce the idea of differences versus inevitable cultural deficiencies.

The shift in thinking from deprivation to cultural difference has been accompanied by a much greater sensitivity among educational leaders to the needs of children from *all* minority group settings. In the early stages of the 1960s intervention movement, the poverty-stricken American black child seemingly occupied most of the attention from researchers and educators alike. In fact, generalized essays on the "disadvantaged child" (e.g. Reissman, 1962), were dominated by references to the low-socio-economic-status black child in the urban ghetto. Running a distant second, in terms of sheer amount of educational and psychological literature, was the child from a Spanish-speaking background. Almost nothing was established about children from other minority groups. Fortunately, a greater spectrum of study and program building regarding various minority group children can now be observed. Bilingual-bicultural curricula have emerged (see Chapter 4). Helpful and enlightening resource materials are now more available about exceptional groups of children—including migrant workers' children, American Indian children, Mexican-American children, Asian-American children, and poor children from isolated, rural settings—all of whom have unique and common educational needs (Albertson, 1971; Combs, 1971; Forster and Arnaud, 1968; Heathman and Nafziger, 1969; Holland, 1969).

The trend toward greater recognition and appreciation of cultural pluralism appears well established and increasingly likely to promote cultural diversity and relevance in early childhood education.

The Advent of Curriculum Models

Values of pluralism and choice alternatives are further reflected in Project Follow Through. Initiated full scale in 1968 as a part of the federal compensatory education design, Project Follow Through provides a variety of educational planning guidelines for kindergarten and primary grade education. An early assumption underlying this project was that such planning could promote a more sustained pattern of the initial, although modest, gains shown by Head Start children (see Chapter 2). In a real sense, Project Follow Through is an extension of Head Start, because of its orientation to children from low-income families for whom comprehensive services are provided. Instruction, medical and dental health, nutrition, psychological and social services, and provisions for staff development and career advancement for paraprofessionals from the community, who are engaged in the delivery of services to children are all included.

A distinctive aspect of Project Follow Through, however, is the principle of *planned variation*. That is, project participants are encouraged intentionally to devise a wide range of curricular activities and instructional strategies consistent with various philosophies of child growth and education. These activities and strategies take the form of *curriculum models*. A curriculum model can be thought of as an ideal representation of the essential philosophical and pedagogical components of a grand educational plan. This representation usually is descriptive—in graphic or narrative form—and serves as a basis for action on the part of its advocates (Spodek, 1973). Initially, fourteen different models for Project Follow Through education were created. By 1970–1971, twenty-two models were operational. This meant that the ideal of pluralism had finally been translated into action, albeit on a comparatively small and experimental scale (approximately 78,000 children in 4000 classrooms during 1971–1972). Implicit in the principle of planned variation are three beliefs: (1) judicious, competent experimentation is basically a good thing; (2) there is no one best way to educate all children; and (3) community choice in the selection of alternative educational approaches can increase the probability of successful early education.

Similarities and Differences among Models Conceptually, the twenty-two Follow Through models have similarities and differences in their basic features, stated philosophy, and actual practice (Maccoby and Zellner, 1970). The following summary of similarities and differences is included to highlight two important concepts: first, any competently designed approach to early education can reflect considerable agreement, even among persons with diverse preferences and beliefs; and second, honest differences in beliefs about child development and education do exist and provide a healthy latitude in which educational alternatives can be sought.

Similarities According to Maccoby and Zellner (1970), six points of theoretical agreement are reflected in the planned variation strategy. One is a mutual commitment among model builders to the idea of readiness for learning: Start where the learner is. This means that education must begin at the child's level at the point of program entry. Normally, some relevant assessment of children's capabilities is made, and program adaptations are made according to the results of such assessment. Second, model builders agree that every attempt should be made to individualize instruction within the limits of available educational resources. This means a strong emphasis upon both individual and small-group instruction with frequent adult-child interchange. Third, it is presumed that children, including those who come from impoverished backgrounds, *can* and *will* learn the essentials from a curriculum if the "right" conditions for learning are established. In other words, if learning fails to occur, the materials and techniques of instruction are faulty, not the child. It should be noted that uniform agreement does not exist among model builders concerning the right conditions for learning. This will become more apparent in later chapters as alternative frames of reference for early education are examined.

A fourth point of general agreement is that successful programs must have sufficiently clear goals to provide direction and consistency in educational planning and curriculum delivery. Authorities do not always agree, however, on the degree of precision with which objectives must be stated, nor upon the means for assessing the extent to which objectives —particularly short-range ones—have been reached. At issue is a criterion for judging program effectiveness, a controversy dramatized by the contrasts of behavioral analysis (Chapter 3) with open education (Chapter 7).

Fifth, most model builders agree that a "core" of school-appropriate behaviors—of which all children must eventually be capable if classroom instruction is to succeed—can be identified. These behaviors include attentional responses, capacity for task-orientation (versus disruptiveness or distractibility) and motivation to learn academic content.

Finally, there is a consensus that children should feel good about what they do in school. A positive attitude toward school and self must dominate. This requires, it is believed, that success experiences should override failure; punishment and coercion should give way to encouragement and meaningful incentives. Thus, we can note attention to children's affective development—to helping them have self-confidence, positive self-esteem, and freedom from fear (see Chapter 8). Every attempt is also made to make learning interesting and consistent with a child's cultural background.

Differences   Differences among Project Follow Through models generally reflect the educational philosophies and theories of learning that provide their base.[3] To illustrate, a rough grouping of models into four categories can be made (Maccoby and Zellner, 1970). One category includes programs that are designed specifically according to principles of behavior modification (see Chapter 3). The position taken is that education is, or should be, a process of establishing precise behavioral objectives (outcomes of instruction stated in terms of what pupils actually can be observed to do), providing systematic strategies for the presentaton of academic material, and reinforcing (rewarding) children for desired behavior. Examples of such programs are the behavioral analysis approach (Chapter 3) and DISTAR (Chapter 4).

A second category is programs organized to facilitate broad, general cognitive development, including structures for logical thought. Technology often reflected in the first category of programs is tempered in favor of less stringent academic objectives and more child-initiated activities.

[3] Cowles (1971) provides a concise summary of four prevalent interpretations of children's learning and development: behavioral-environmental, cognitive-transactional, psychosexual-personality, and normative-maturational. See Brameld (1956) for a lucid overview of dominant educational philosophies.

Structure exists, but in a fluid, flexible framework. Education is seen essentially as a means to support and enhance the normal, stage-related evolution of cognitive processes. Examples of such programs are summarized in Chapter 5.

Programs geared toward the ideal of "self-actualization" comprise a third category. Children's self-determined goals usually take precedence over goals predetermined by adult authorities. Test performance, for example, is applicable only to the extent that a child himself chooses to master the test content. Education is viewed as a process of fostering children's natural curiosity and providing a wide range of age-appropriate experience in a loosely organized nurturant atmosphere. Under these conditions, it is reasoned that children will have the opportunity to become competent in ways that are important to them. In many ways, this approach captures the essence of traditional nursery school practice (see Chapter 2). But many programs under the banner of "open education" also fit comfortably into this orientation (see Chapter 7).

Finally, there exist programs that emphasize more directly than the others the concept of client-controlled education. Their advocates argue that any educational program must be responsive and directly accountable to the community it serves. Curriculum design comes through the exercise of community decision-making power, rather than from professional educators. As a result, and perhaps partly by chance, many programs in this grouping are oriented strongly toward ethnic-cultural-linguistic identities. These orientations, of course, are not exclusive to client-controlled education. But at issue is the locus of power or authority for determining educational needs, consolidating educational resources (materials and staffing), and evaluation criteria. Additional comment about client-controlled education is reserved for Chapter 8.

Other Differences   In addition to the foregoing categories, other broad philosophical or theoretical differences can be observed. One is the degree to which systematic attempts at parent involvement are undertaken; another is the nature of research and evaluation strategies that are utilized. Still another is the degree to which *pupil product criteria* (tangible pupil outputs such as test scores) are preferred indicators of program effectiveness to criteria that deal with *process variables* (e.g., the nature, frequency, and quality of teacher-pupil, pupil-pupil, and pupil-learning materials transactions).

To conclude this section, the educational alternatives established by Project Follow Through can be arranged along several important and related continua: (1) stated philosophy of education and view of the learning process, (2) nature of educational objectives (extent of traditional academic emphasis and degree of prescriptive diagnostic and instructional procedures), (3) extent to which pupil initiative, individual choice of activities, and general learner autonomy are encouraged, (4) amount of teacher direction and control, (5) scope of cultural-linguistic activities provided, and (6) the degree and type of client control or parent involvement. It is appropriate here to mention that Project Follow Through has been subjected to a national evaluation action contracted by the federal government with the Stanford Research Institute in Palo Alto, California. In addition, program sponsors carry out their own unique evaluation practices. Specific data from these two types of evaluation programs are not easily obtained.[4] However, preliminary and general reports indicate that observable (real) differences exist among Follow Through models in both their implementation and children's classroom behavior (Stanford Research Institute, 1972). Perhaps more significant is that Follow Through seems generally to be achieving its basic objectives; children in the project tend to excel as compared to similar children in regular public school classrooms (Stanford Research Institute, 1972).

Two final points about Project Follow Through warrant attention. The first concerns this writer's enthusiasm for the idea of planned variation and educational alternatives. Project Follow Through has demonstrated not only that genuine and feasible alternative models can be developed but that they can be translated into practice. This has established an important precedent for organized variety in public school education.

The second point is cautionary. One may question the wisdom of expecting a given model to be universally applicable, regardless of the specific community in which it is operationalized. In other words, the same model may work well in one community and fail miserably in another due to peculiar social conditions. Further, no model works on its own. The persons who implement the model surely must be competent and believe in the approach to education that is taken. It is unlikely that even the best of master educational plans can succeed with a mediocre and/or a psychologically resistant staff. Finally, a model may hamper its own "exportability" due to vague guidelines or too loose organization.

Rise of Concern for Master Plans of Early Experience

On the heels of model building and experimentation for kindergarten-primary education has come a gush of recommendations—and in some cases, legislative programs—for broader, community-coordinated child care and educational services for America's young. Two avenues of social action must be discussed here: the growing concern and support for comprehensive day care services and the genesis of major task force efforts to regenerate public early childhood education at the statewide level.

Developmental Day Care   Traditionally, day care centers and homes have been custodial—places for children of working parents where the accent is upon meeting children's basic physical needs. The times are changing. Custodial day care gradually is giving way to a broad services approach. A long-standing distinction between "child-keeping" and teach-

---

[4] See Soar and Soar (1972) for an example of Follow Through evaluative research wherein observational procedures are creatively utilized to assess classroom process variables in relation to children's cognitive growth.

ing programs, for instance, is becoming dissolute (Robinson and Robinson, 1972). It is now fashionable to speak of *developmental day care*, a much expanded concept of service to children that includes an educational component, diagnostic services, medical and social services, and a nutritional program (Feeney, 1973). Given today's social, political, and economic conditions, there are few who would argue against comprehensive day care services. The children of working mothers alone represent an overwhelming group in need of supplemental care: roughly half of all American mothers of preschool and school-age children are employed full-time outside of the home (Zigler, 1972). The issue is that educators have tended to see themselves and the schools as separate from day care. Only recently have they begun to show much interest in day care problems. By the same token, day care personnel have formerly shown little initiative in coordinating their efforts with those of the educational establishment. And so it goes, although both education and day care have the common goal of fostering wholesome development among young children (Caldwell, 1971).

Many respected authorities with professional day care and education identities are now sounding out the service needs, problems, and possible directions for planning and implementing developmental day care programs (e.g., Fein and Clarke-Stewart, 1973; Nimnicht, 1973b). Legitimate concerns about what desirable things may not, or what undesirable things may, occur in day care settings have been expressed (Kagan and Whitten, 1970). Issues range from the impact of group versus home care (see Chapter 9); licensing standards; training competent day care workers; evaluation; facilities; legislation; and a host of others that should not be minimized (Wells, 1971).

Nevertheless, it is apparent that the momentum for comprehensive day care services is gathering. Equally apparent is that the conceptualization of day care services reflects a considerable range of leadership responsibilities (Grotberg, 1972). This range includes state departments of education, regional or local organizations coordinated to build from an existing base of services toward greater comprehensiveness and quality (e.g., "4 Cs," or Community Coordinated Child Care, which is under the auspices of the Office of Child Development). In some cases, a corporate enterprise has been commissioned by state governments to establish the groundwork for a delivery system of child care (e.g., the State of Pennsylvania).

Persisting problems for day care during the seventies will undoubtedly be the design of successful procedures for parent participation and the extension of services to all children, not just those from low-income families (Grotberg, 1972). While day care is definitely on the increase, there is still not enough of it, and, with some exceptions, it remains costly even to low-income consumers (Bereiter, 1972). Staffing and providing all necessary resources for a meaningful educational component in day care is sure to increase the cost. This cost factor and other reasons of a philosophical nature lead some authorities (e.g., Bereiter, 1972) to continue their resistance to a full marriage of education and day care. Perhaps the ultimate issue is the meaning of education. It appears that the intervention movement of the sixties has prompted a greater sensitivity among educators to day care in general. This sensitization has clearly resulted in some basic rethinking about the relationship of early childhood education to systems of day care. As this book is written, however, much work remains to be done to effectively orchestrate day care and early education practices.

The Task Force Phenomenon   Related to the idea of comprehensive developmental child care services is the work of specialists in child development and education to recommend master plans for statewide early childhood education. Such work is typically done at the request of state boards of education and/or superintendents of public instruction with more or less tacit approval or encouragement from state legislatures. Possibly the best example of such work is the report of the State of California task force on early childhood education (1972). Briefly, a team of twenty-five distinguished professionals submitted to California's Superintendent of Public Instruction a set of recommendations and implementation guidelines for the plan. All features of the plan did not receive unanimous endorsement from the task force personnel themselves. Some of the key ingredients are opportunity for voluntary public education for four-year-olds; utilization of parent volunteers, provision for inter-age tutorial experiences; early identification, diagnosis, and remediation of learning disabilities; low (1–10) adult-child ratio in the classroom; provision of extra-school experiences; and the use of team teaching procedures. Primary schools have been conceived as "community centers" wherein all existing public and private educational, physical, social, and psychological services are coordinated to meet children's needs. The total product has become more than just a paper plan for early childhood education beginning at age four and extending through age eight. The report also led to the passage in late 1972 of state legislation to implement the plan. And lively debate continues to surround the entire package.

The debate associated with the California plan is concisely summarized by the contrasting views of Lewis (1973) and Moore (1973). Defense of the plan, as legislated, revolves around a humanistic educational philosophy and encouraging data from successful, smaller scale early childhood programs across the country (Lewis, 1973). In contrast, it is charged that the plan's rationale is actually more intuitive than empirical and, in the final analysis, signifies a highly politicized endeavor (Moore, 1973). Fear is expressed that formalized early education will result in academic force-feeding rather than in a general stimulation approach; that premature introduction of academic activities, especially reading, will lead to physiological damage (e.g., myopia); and that home-based education is far superior to institutionally based programs, especially in view of the emotional needs of very young children (Moore, 1973).

Students of early childhood education need to weigh carefully the arguments both for and against massive public education for four-year-olds. As an assist, data pertinent to the California debate will be included at points in this book. But one cannot escape a confrontation with the ethical and philosophical aspects of such debates. The key issue is what kind of education is best for young children. Once this issue is plucked from the stream of educational thought, many others follow in its wake (see the last section of this chapter). Meanwhile, the California plan can be viewed as a firm step beyond the lip service paid to early childhood education in many sections of the country. It is concrete evidence of a reasoned commitment to the basic worth of integrated educational and child care services for the young.

The Evaluation Imperative

Any generalizations about the value of the California plan for children are unlikely to materialize in the near future. But evaluation—the assessment of merit—is a fundamental dimension of the plan. Throughout the entire intervention period of the 1960s the necessities and advantages of evaluation as a basic component of any programmatic approach to early education were strongly reinforced. Unfortunately, then (and even to some extent now) many educators were faced with the task of designing and implementing evaluation strategies without sufficient time, training, and resources to satisfy themselves or others. Consequently, weak or faulty evaluation procedures were commonplace. Often, evaluation was an afterthought or inadequately planned in terms of seeking data necessary for valid decision making. It seems safe to say, however, that a new consciousness about and receptivity to the values of evaluation now pervade the field of early childhood education. In some cases, of course, providing for evaluation is a matter of simple survival: intervention programs, for instance, rarely are funded initially, much less continued, in the absence of purposeful evaluation proposals and, eventually, real data about impact. But now educators must take the initiative in determining the validity of their intervention procedures. This is especially true when what is at stake is the educational welfare of children, to say nothing of the general knowledge about intervention that can be gained and shared with other professionals.

The activities undertaken by early childhood program evaluators can be referred to as *evaluation research*. Evaluation research has as its purpose the measurement of program effects against the goals that the program has been designed to accomplish (Weiss, 1972). Note that four key elements are contained within this definition. Measuring program effects is a matter of *research methodology*. Effects refer to *program outcomes*. A comparison of effects with program goals calls for the use of clearly defined *criteria for judging a program's success*. The use of evaluation data for decision making and program improvement accentuates the *social purpose* of evaluation (Weiss, 1972). In addition, evaluation in its broadest sense also involves a process of and criteria for determining the worth, adequacy, and ethical qualities of program goals.

Program goal evaluation is explored more fully in Chapter 9, as are other concepts of research in early education. Meanwhile it is desirable to keep in mind that evaluation research is intended to be of practical use to educators in decision making, policy formulation, and the like. Often evaluation research will extend beyond the immediate, pragmatic level to deal with basic theoretical concerns about the role of certain kinds of experience in children's development and about how evaluation data may affect basic conceptualizations about developmental processes. Regardless, the questions that constitute evaluation research activity are generally derived from programs. Any answers to these questions usually require judicious interpretation by program evaluators for reasons that will become evident in the next few pages. The context for such evaluation activity generally is a social action setting wherein complicating factors or obstacles to the ideal evaluation are encountered. Such obstacles can arise from logistical problems, interpersonal conflict, methodological compromises, and political and economic restraints. In this respect, evaluation research is often a more arduous and tentative undertaking than is basic research conducted in controlled, laboratory settings. Like most laboratory research, however, evaluation research is anchored in empiricism—observed fact. Since evaluation research is a dominant theme of this book, more than just a passing nod is given here to its basic components. In the section that follows, the idea of *empirical verification* is developed. In this way, a more comprehensive perspective within which to interpret subsequent references to evaluation data may be presented.

Empirical Verification   As indicated above, the empirical verification of an intervention program may involve determining (1) the degree to which a program is effective or successful in meeting its own stated goals and/or (2) how well goals are achieved by children within one program as compared to one or more other programs. The latter question deals with *comparative evaluation*, which requires that the objectives of programs being compared be similar enough so that common measurements can be taken across programs. What distinguishes the direct, empirical verification approach from other forms of evaluation is an explicit reference to observable, measurable, and, hence, quantifiable outcomes. Quantification generally implies magnitude—how much of something has been achieved or performed. Occasionally, however, the question is simply whether or not a given objective has been reached by what percentage of children in a program.[5] To reiterate, then, the reference point in empirical verification is a program's demonstrated effectiveness as evidenced by observable, measurable behaviors. These behaviors usually are specified cognitive skills and abilities, language skills, and attitudes and emotionally

---

[5] The terms *goal* and *objective* both appear in this paragraph. In common parlance, goal refers to a long-range outcome while an objective is a shorter-range, more immediate outcome. In this discussion, however, the two terms are used interchangeably.

based responses (affective behaviors). Observable teacher and parent behaviors also serve as criteria outcomes in many evaluation designs.

Formative and Summative Evaluation Two related kinds of basic evaluation activity have come to characterize thorough investigations of early education programs: *formative* and *summative* (Scriven, 1967). These terms are used repeatedly in the chapters to follow and are therefore defined here. It has been this writer's experience that most students conceptualize evaluation as an attempt to assess and make judgments about the worth or quality of a program at its completion. Thus, one evaluates a course of instruction at semester's end; a kindergarten program is evaluated at the end of the school year; an experimental parent education program is evaluated at its terminal point; and so on. This is *summative evaluation*: evaluation to "sum up" the total impact of a given program, the final achievements of children in a program, and the like. Generally speaking, summative evaluation implies a product orientation, i.e., some form of tangible evidence to indicate change.

In contrast is another equally important kind of evaluation activity, particularly pertinent where new programs are being developed: *formative evaluation.* Formative evaluation can be thought about as "in-process" evaluation, an activity that is performed in various stages of program evolution. The process orientation of formative evaluation involves a careful and periodic assessment of variables such as instructional techniques, the adequacy of learning materials, program setting, and aspects of teacher behavior. Formative evaluation may also be conducted to determine how well children are doing in a given subcomponent of instruction or in a specific content area. In this way, diagnosis and necessary and feasible program modifications can be made while there is still time and before a program deteriorates irreversibly.

Both formative and summative evaluation can serve unique functions in a total program evaluation activity. Utilized in concert, these two kinds of evaluation can provide valuable information about the improvement and ultimate validity of an educational program. Many programs discussed in this book have incorporated and profited from such evaluation. For example, preliminary summative evaluation data about the impact of "Sesame Street" on child viewers have been made public and are discussed in Chapter 8. Less often discussed is the extensive sequence of formative evaluation activity that occurred before "Sesame Street" was broadcast. The achievement of one "Sesame Street" programming standard required a series of format modifications so that children would watch a specific episode for 90 percent of the total potential viewing time, even though they could have watched a competing picture slide show. This sort of "distractor" study comprised an integral part of the early "Sesame Street" formative evaluation.

To summarize, both formative and summative evaluation can be used in the service of more informed and objective decision making. Ordinarily such decisions will be made in relation to one or more of the following criteria: to continue or discontinue a program, to seek improvement in program strategies and procedures, to add or drop specific program components, to initiate similar programs in other settings, to apportion resources among competing programs, and to accept or reject a program approach or theory (Weiss, 1972).

Basic Problems in Empirical Verification   Four basic problems are confronted by persons involved in early education program evaluation (Messick and Barrows, 1972). The first involves a selection of variables, characteristics or behaviors as evaluation criteria. Normally, this requires a specification of what outcomes signify the stated purposes of a given program. To meet the demand for empirical verification, the aims, goals, or objectives of a program must be translated into measurable terms. In practice, the specification of a wide range of outcomes is usually involved: child behaviors (e.g., IQ change, achievement test performance, sensory discrimination skills, observed independence in problem-solving situations, self-reports of fearfulness or liking of school), teacher behaviors (e.g., demonstrated skill in classroom management, desirable use of prompting and feedback techniques, concrete evidence of planning and adapting instruction), and parent behaviors (e.g., self-reports of satisfaction with their child's program and progress, observed degree of program participation). Even broader community service changes may be included as in the Kirschner report discussed in Chapter 2.

Sophisticated thinking about evaluation is not limited simply to expected or desired outcomes. Evaluation may include the monitoring of a wide variety of *possible* effects, effects that are unanticipated, unintended, or even adverse. For example, a program may successfully raise the arithmetic achievement among its young participants. But if one side effect of such achievement is a high degree of pupil anxiety about arithmetical activity, the program's instructional methods may be suspect. Unless steps are taken to monitor possible side effects, they are likely to go undetected. Thus one could unwittingly continue a self-defeating instructional strategy. A related problem is that evaluation plans are often built around excessively narrow outcomes or objectives or that one's choice of measurements is limited by the value system of a program builder-evaluator (Glick, 1968). Furthermore, *a lack of agreement on evaluation* criteria among various authorities has interfered with finding answers to questions about the impact of preschool education (Weikart, 1972). This disagreement usually springs from deep-seated philosophical differences about program goals or objectives and the means for securing evidence of change in children's behavior. Such conflict is closely tied to the long-standing schism between behavioristic and natural growth theories of child development and the educational process, a schism that will appear in various ways throughout this book.

Philosophical conflicts notwithstanding, the more usual methodological problem in evaluation is that program outcomes are stated in such general, ambiguous terms that they fail to provide explicit points of reference for empirical assessment (Stern, 1968). Consider, for example, the difficulties faced in evaluating the extent to which a program "facilitates self-actualization among young children," or "promotes greater proficiency in logical thinking skills." Most educators view these as worthy goals, but for any meaningful evaluation of program impact a more precise specification of "self-actualization" and "logical thinking skills proficiency" is mandatory.

A second problem of empirical evaluation is how adequately one is able to measure the criterion variables once they are selected and clearly stated. This introduces the complex problem of selecting or devising appropriate measurement tools as well as conducting the assessment procedure itself. Criteria for selecting measurement tools include the validity and reliability of the behaviors or variables that such tools are intended to measure. Practicality also is important and necessitates a careful consideration of factors such as cost, ease of administration, and time and staff requirements. One problem of the early intervention movement was sorely conspicuous: a lack of suitable tools to measure many of the desired outcomes of new programs. Consequently, evaluators often resorted to limited measures such as general intelligence scales because they were the best tool available or because "everyone else is using them, too." In response to critical measurement needs, specialists quickly began to develop new, ostensibly more suitable measures of varied program outcomes. The resultant mushrooming of tests, scales, observational systems, checklists, and questionnaires has expanded greatly the supply of available tools. Unfortunately, many are still inadequately field tested, and caution must be exercised in their use.[6] Even with a greater variety of experimental measures upon which to draw, evaluators continue to rely most heavily upon children's scores from traditional achievement tests as indicators of program worth. Aside from serving as narrow or limited measurement criteria, achievement test scores are usually obtained from children in formal, even artificial, situations by adults whose only contact with the children may be for testing purposes. It can be argued that such conditions may not be adequate for gathering meaningful data about program impact or worth. In fact, the common tendency to equate measurement with testing delimits the important measurement function in evaluation. Increasing use of direct observation techniques and other alternatives to formal testing for purposes of evaluation research is now being made (Evans, 1974).

A third problem of empirical verification is whether, or to what extent, observed effects, changes, or outcomes can legitimately be attributed to the specific instructional methods or intervention tactics that comprise a given program. In other words, if desired changes occur in the way children behave during their educational experience, how sure can the investigator be that the changes are produced solely or primarily by the

---

[6] See Evans (1974) for an expanded discussion of measurement tools, their selection, and use, as well as an annotated bibliography of recently developed measures of young children's behavior. Early results of comprehensive efforts to evaluate preschool and kindergarten tests are also now available to consumers (Hoepfner, Stern, and Nunmedal, 1971). Another basic source of information about tests that are referred to in this book is the well-known series of *Mental Measurements Yearbooks* edited by Oscar K. Buros.

program and not by some other set of factors? For example, can normal maturational processes be ruled out as a source of change? Are program effects confounded by or in any way a function of the children's extra-program experiences? Does the activity of merely taking a test influence children's future performance on that test? Are program effects influenced by any biases in the initial selection of children for a program and/or withdrawal by children from that program? If a yes answer to these questions cannot be ruled out by a program evaluator, then there is no assurance that the program produces change. In a phrase, this is a problem of determining the *internal validity* of a program.

Controlling or eliminating threats to the internal validity of a program is a matter of research methodology discussed in detail elsewhere (Campbell and Stanley, 1963). Controlling internal validity also involves the design of an evaluation activity and the interpretation of any measurements that are taken. For the moment, however, we are emphasizing an essential evaluation task: a valid demonstration of the degree to which prescribed treatments are effective in achieving stated outcomes. As suggested earlier, the priority question may be the extent to which one treatment is more or less effective than other treatments in attaining certain objectives (comparative evaluation). Recently, another question has come into play: is *trait-by-treatment* or *aptitude-treatment* interaction occurring? (Berliner and Cohen, 1973). This question about interaction concerns the extent to which the same program may yield different results for different children, i.e., children who differ in selected cognitive and personal-social attributes. For example, a program may have a greater or lesser impact upon children with delayed language and who are high in dependency or anxiety than, say, upon their more secure and autonomous peers who are advanced in language development. Generally speaking, trait-by-treatment interaction analysis is not yet common in the evaluation of early education programs. But it could be a promising trend, especially in the exploration of different methods for children who fail to respond positively to conventional intervention procedures. Ultimately, the study of trait-by-treatment interaction may help us better to solve the problem of matching in constructive ways the characteristics of children with the characteristics of programs.

Finally, the problem of *generalizability*, or degree of *external validity*, can be posed: how broadly can the results of an educational experiment be generalized or extended beyond the children with which the experiment dealt? Normally, the answer to this question will depend upon a cluster of factors: sampling procedures (e.g., what and how many children participate in a program and how they are selected), extent of treatment replicability (e.g., how detailed and explicit is a written version of the treatment or curriculum), and the nature of the evaluation procedure. Other problems of external validity include the much discussed "self-fulfilling prophecy" and the well-known "Hawthorne effect." The former means that "an expectation, belief or prediction held by a participant in any event is a factor working toward fulfillment of the prediction" (English and English, 1958, p. 487). Thus, a teacher who expects that a child will fail or that a program will succeed may subtly behave in ways that facilitate a confirmation of these expectancies. Self-fulfilling prophecies seem to materialize to one degree or another in many educational settings, although their dynamics are poorly understood (McCandless and Evans, 1973).

The Hawthorne effect is perhaps a more serious threat to program generalizability; it refers to a subject's behavior change simply as a function of knowledge that he is participating in an experimental program. Without some means to rule out this possibility, an evaluator can be deceived about the effects of an experimental program upon its participants. Generalizability is therefore limited: children may react to experimental arrangements differently in the original experimental setting than will other children who experience the same arrangements in future nonexperimental settings. As will be seen, the results of much early education evaluation research cannot be generalized because of weaknesses in the control of factors that contaminate external validity. This is perhaps one reason why an initially effective program may become progressively less effective over time in the same setting or may fail to produce equivalent results in a different context.

Issues related to generalizability will vary in intensity according to one's basic approach to evaluation or the ultimate purpose for which evaluation is performed. For example, a distinction was made earlier between evaluation for theory making in early childhood education and evaluation for local policy formulation or organizational decision making. In the former case, wide generalizability is a fundamental objective; in the latter case, generalization may be secondary, if important at all. In any case, it is good to recognize that the "further removed the application of a program or policy is from the data which support its value, the more vulnerable it is to failure or to differential effectiveness as different types of students and conditions are brought under consideration" (Messick and Barrows, 1972, pp. 279–280).

In summary, four classes of problems mark the empirical verification approach to evaluation: (1) specification of evaluation criteria, (2) the accuracy and reliability of criterion measurements, (3) the degree to which program outcomes can be attributed to program inputs, and (4) the generalizability of results. These problems are highlighted throughout this book in relation to evaluation research on early education programs. Presently, it is enough to reemphasize that evaluation has come to occupy an increasingly prominent role in early childhood. A major reason for this prominence is the greater sense of accountability and investigative spirit that was engendered by the 1960s intervention movement.

Guidelines for the Conceptual Analysis of Early Education Programs

We have stressed the idea that evaluation is the assessment of merit. As such, evaluation requires criteria, or standards from which merit can be assessed. For the empiricist, the basic standard is observed fact—

what can be seen to occur during and at the terminus of an educational program. But evaluation often goes beyond the standard of observed occurrence to include a set of basic "goods," a priori values, or important dimensions upon which programs may vary. Thus, a program can be systematically analyzed and in a broad sense, evaluated, according to specified rationalized criteria. This activity is known as *conceptual analysis*. In some cases, conceptual analysis is performed to determine the degree to which a program incorporates some desirable or relevant feature. In other cases, its purpose is to ascertain whether or not a program meets the specifications of a conceptual blueprint or master plan. In either case, a set of value judgments is made about what are the most important criteria, or standards. Additional purposes of conceptual analysis include (1) specifying the basic ways in which various programs are alike or different and (2) seeking a more thorough understanding of the consequences for children that may result by selecting one program for application instead of another (Elliot, 1971).

Guidelines for conceptual analysis are partly a response to pressures for selecting and evaluating new programs of early education which lack a sufficient empirical verification data base. But the method of conceptual analysis has become an increasingly popular and insightful means for examining programs, traditional and experimental alike. Gordon (1972), for example, has devised an analytic schema based upon instructional theory. His commitment is to the notion that an organized theory of instruction should provide the meat for a thorough examination of a given program's suitability for children and teachers. Three interrelated criteria provide the framework for analysis: a specification of program goal characteristics, the characteristics of pupils for whom the program is designed, and the characteristics of the setting in which instruction occurs. Other schema for conceptual analysis are based upon dimensions of program content (Lay and Dopyera, 1971), multiple program components (e.g., objectives, methods, structuredness, theoretical orientation, modes of interaction; Mayer, 1971), and "master guidelines" (including administrative-organizational requirements and evaluation methods; Elliot, 1971).

In order both to illustrate more concretely the conceptual analysis approach and provide cues for forthcoming program commentary, the five-dimension schema of Parker and Day (1972) will be summarized here. The reader should find that familiarity with such a schema provides a set of tools with which to think more specifically about early childhood education curriculum analysis and evaluation.

Dimensions for Conceptual Analysis   The first dimension for conceptual analysis of programs according to Parker and Day (1972) concerns basic foundations for curriculum development. Two criteria are proposed: (1) the degree to which a formal theory of child development influences curriculum design; and (2) the extent to which empirical research data are central to the conceptualization of a given program. By combining these criteria a "continuum of possibilities" can be formulated, which ranges from a curriculum grounded in a formalized theoretical base that enjoys strong empirical support to a curriculum that presumably reflects neither theoretical nor empirical backing. Such could be the case with an atheoretical or eclectic program in which true exploratory experimentation is being conducted. It appears to this writer, however, that few contemporary published curricula neglect or avoid both theoretical referents and pertinent research literature. To be sure, early nursery school curricula gave no strong evidence of organized theoretical frameworks, save vague and scattered references to concepts of psychoanalytic personality theory and Deweyian philosophy (see Chapter 2). Neither did such curricula have many empirical roots, perhaps because early education activity research itself was barely under way in the early 1920s. Eventually, this picture changed somewhat (see Chapter 2). Curricula that claim definite theoretical alignments and a respectable research orientation may be represented by those discussed in connection with Piagetian thought (see Chapter 5).

A second dimension for conceptual analysis concerns the goals and objectives of a program. Goals refer to global long-term aims that constitute major areas of curriculum emphasis (e.g., healthy self-image, development of perceptual motor skills, positive attitude toward learning). Objectives typically are more precise, specific, and hopefully observable descriptions of behavioral outcomes (e.g., ability to classify like objects according to their physical and functional characteristics, ability to perform imitative speech responses, skill in eye-hand coordination). Objectives serve more readily to guide the actual instructional process and its evaluation to an ongoing basis.

For Parker and Day (1972), program analyses and comparisons can be made in terms of three features of goals and objectives: (1) the degree to which objectives are explicit or operationalized for assessment, (2) the breadth of objectives across various aspects of child learning and development, and (3) the extent to which educational *process* or *content* factors are emphasized. Five interrelated, although somewhat distinct, areas for the categorization of main program objectives can be noted: sensory motor skills, cognition, language, socioemotional development, and academic content. All five areas, by the way, are pertinent to the *breadth* of program objectives (number 2 above). As shall be seen, programs do vary enormously in their main objectives. The DISTAR curriculum (Chapter 4) is almost exclusively geared to language and academic content objectives. In contrast, the Montessori method (Chapter 6) early accents various sensory-motor skills as a foundation for later cognitive-academic tasks. The Human Development Program (Chapter 8) is an attempt to highlight the socioemotional components of learning. These are but a few examples. The reader is encouraged to keep in mind this second dimension of conceptual analysis as still more programs are reviewed in later chapters.

Although Parker and Day make no reference to the relationship between goals and objectives, such a linkage (or its lack) should be a part of a thorough conceptual analysis approach to program selection or evaluation. In particular, a rationale for coordinating immediate objectives and long-term goals is often weak or missing in various curricula (Stern, 1968). If so, problems for empirical evaluation usually follow, especially in regard to decisions about choice of measurement tools and the interpretation of longitudinal data. However, the root issue for a conceptual analysis or any other approach to program evaluation is probably *why* certain goals and objectives are preferred over others. This issue cuts across the earlier discussed dimension of basic foundations for curriculum development as well.

A third dimension of conceptual analysis can be summarized by the term *implementation.* This term refers both to the way in which a curriculum is presented and the organizational qualities of the classroom environment: grouping practices, the arrangement of materials, and content sequencing tactics, for example. To illustrate this dimension more specifically, three aspects of implementation can be reviewed. One is the nature of the instructional format in a program. Instructional format can range from direct presentation strategies through active games to exploratory or discovery learning, wherein varying levels of structure may be encountered by the child. Related to this aspect of implementation is the role of the teacher, for again the notion of structure is central. Structure can be thought about in terms of a continuum from highly preformulated and tightly organized procedures for instruction and evaluation (e.g., DISTAR, Chapter 4) to near total teacher autonomy where only very broad, abstract ideas about curriculum development and execution are provided (e.g., the Education for Continuing Growth Plan, Chapter 7). Finally, parent participation is considered in the implementation phase of program analysis. Three forms of parent participation may serve as reference points: (1) parental familiarity with program content and techniques (minimal participation); (2) involvement by parents for the purpose of becoming more thoroughly educated about children in general and their own children in particular; and (3) participation in actual decision making about the educational program for children. The latter relates to the idea of client-controlled education previously discussed in the section on curriculum models in this chapter. Concepts of parental participation are discussed more thoroughly in Chapter 8.

Parker and Day's fourth dimension of conceptual analysis (1972) concerns the capacity of a program to initiate and sustain intrinsic motivation (learning for its own sake; learning for the sheer enjoyment of activity, exploration, and competence building) and/or the provision of (and perhaps reliance upon) supplementary motivational techniques such as contingent material (tokens, gold stars, toys) or social reinforcement (praise, recognition, approval). In any case, a rationale for utilizing one sort of motivational technique or another should be present. This concern for motivation can be extended to the teacher as well: growth opportunities for staff that are inherent in a program, the basic challenges to staff that a program creates, and the provision for teacher recognition. Issues related to motivation are perhaps best illustrated by the bedrock of reinforcement procedures underlying behavioral analysis (Chapter 3) in contrast to the idea of open education (Chapter 7).

The fifth, and final dimension for conceptual analysis according to Parker and Day (1972) is a program's potential for successful exportation. This goes beyond the dissemination of a program's results to its actual implementation in different geographic regions with different children and staffs. Several requirements can be specified, including clearly communicable statements of philosophy and a written curriculum that describes (and *prescribes* to varying degrees) both the materials and methods of instruction. Strong provisions for teacher training and for assessing training effectiveness are also vital considerations. It is timely to mention here that Project Follow Through models collectively are an example of this export function. Program sponsors, in effect, have maintained the responsibility for seeing that their models were appropriately implemented in various sections of the country where applicable. Understandably, the logistics of this affair were (and are) complex. Tightly organized approaches (e.g., behavior analysis, Chapter 2; Englemann-Becker, Chapter 4) seemingly are more consistently similar from one setting to another as compared to less structured approaches (e.g., TEEM, Chapter 4; EDC model, Chapter 7). This should not be interpreted as criticism, merely as indicative of an issue in exportability.

In summary, five dimensions upon which early education programs may vary can be used for a conceptual analysis of any program: basic foundations for curriculum development, goals and objectives, implementation, motivational capacity, and exportation. The schema for conceptual analysis summarized here is but one of many useful approaches. However, the ideas encapsulated by Parker and Day (1972) provide a frame of reference to which we will return periodically in the remainder of this book.

SUMMARY OF MAJOR ISSUES

A discussion of early childhood published several decades ago identified three interrelated issues faced by those who assume responsibility for children's education: what, when, and how (Anderson, 1947). As the reader already may have surmised, these issues are no less critical today than they were in the 1940s. The issue of *what*, as mentioned earlier, concerns the content of a program. Clearly, and as evidenced by following chapters, a wide range among programs can be observed. This range involves several dimensions including both type of content and the rationale for a structure of content for children's learning encounters.

The *when* issue in early childhood education concerns timing, or the sequential management of experiences appropriate to the developmental process. This issue cannot be separated from the problem of content for it involves a determination of what experiences are most appropriate at what points in time. Both issues raise the broader philosophical question of long-range goals for early education. Other problems related to timing concern the stability of early learning and possible hazards of beginning "too early" or "too late" (Robinson and Robinson, 1968) and the extent to which behavior—particularly intellectual and school achievement behavior—can be "boosted" by early intervention programs (Jensen, 1969). We have already seen that a considerable amount of puzzlement and controversy is associated with these problems.

Fused to the issues of content and timing is the issue of *how*. This involves a set of questions concerning methodology valid for early childhood education, whatever the purposes of such education might be. Teaching methods suitable at one stage of development may not be suitable at earlier or later stages. Methods which contribute to early mastery may not be appropriate for longer-term objectives (Robinson and Robinson, 1968). The variety of methods applied to early childhood education is remarkable. Varied also is the quality of research performed to assess the validity of such methods.

To the above triad may be added a fourth issue, one which concerns *who will prosecute* programs of early childhood education. This issue has two facets. First, there is the problem of what qualifications (standards) an individual should (must) demonstrate prior to actual involvement with children where educational purposes are professed. (This subsumes a number of other problems, including the nature of pre-service training and teacher selection procedures.) A second major facet of the who problem concerns the assessment of in-service teaching effectiveness and reliable measures for the removal of individuals who may be judged unsuitable in relation to established objectives of early childhood education. Related to this second notion is the type of teaching role prescribed by a given program.

A fifth issue or problem involves *where* a program for early childhood education is conducted. In American education it has been taken for granted that formal education best takes place in a special setting away from the home where groups of children homogeneous in chronological age are established. Subissues related to the where problem include the age at which group instruction is begun, the degree to which homogeneity in grouping is practiced, group size, and the nature and organization of the physical facilities and space provided for children.

Early childhood education program builders inevitably make decisions about the problems of what, when, how, who, and where in one way or another. These decisions reflect variations in philosophy, psychological conceptions of child development and learning, availability of personnel, and the formulation of day-to-day practices. But perhaps the most overriding question relevant to the five issues above is the why question. For example, as a given program is reviewed one may ask: Why this content as opposed to something else? Why is a set of experiences provided at a given point in time? Why is this method of execution or technique preferred over other possible methods or techniques? Why are certain teaching skills established as more imperative than others?

The why question serves to point up several traditional and emerging conflicts of early childhood education theory. A conflict of longstanding involves two diverse views of education. One holds that education should be preparation for the future; the momentary needs and interests of children may receive secondary consideration. In contrast is a view of education based upon the immediate needs and interests of children where concern for subsequent responsibilities and societal demands is de-emphasized (Anderson, 1947). The first view most clearly amplifies a curriculum based upon an analysis of what society requires generally in order for one to operate "successfully" according to broadly defined adult roles. The second view assumes that a full and complete daily existence during childhood is the best insurance for successful adulthood. The writer does not mean to establish a false dichotomy in making this distinction. Most educators generally agree that the issue is not an either-or matter and that discussions of the issue are frequently oversimplified. It is apparent, however, that this distinction generates a great deal of debate among adults who think that they know best what kind of experiences children should have. Frequently, this debate centers on a *product-oriented* versus a *process-oriented* concept of education and appears in different guises throughout the early education literature.

Within the discipline of developmental psychology there exists a conflict parallel to this debate in early childhood education: a schism between heritors of "naturalistic, indigenous growth" theories of development and the "cultural competence" or "environmental determination" point of view. Supporters of the "natural growth" viewpoint believe that maximum socialization benefits can be reaped by providing children with an enriched, benign, accepting, permissive, informal educational environment. The highest value is placed upon the need for children to express their creative growth forces. It is through such expression that children's self-development can be nurtured and developmental-maturational sequences provide whatever cues may be important for self-actualization. Innate factors (maturational processes which unfold in a predetermined manner) provide the basis for cultivating complete and integrated growth patterns, including the child's mental structure. In contrast, supporters of the "cultural competence" school place a greater emphasis upon the shaping power of experience; collective teaching forces are therefore assumed to play collectively a stronger role. Skill development and mastery of the environment are seen as the means to achieve positive growth; children need to be helped in systematic ways by trained pedagogues if children are to develop their maximum potentials. Response pattern development in children is primarily determined by the structure and association of events in their environment (Kohlberg, 1968). Again, the difference in these two conceptions is more a matter of degree than of a dichotomy. Whether one view is more correct than the other is largely a matter of conjecture—if, in fact, either of them is (McCandless, 1967).

As broad orientation, however, these views are the basis of many issues that pervade contemporary early childhood education, including the degree to which specific content and teaching techniques are stressed.

While most traditional early childhood education practices in America, at least nursery-kindergarten practices, seem to have mirrored the "natural development" position (see Chapter 2) many of the new intervention programs of the 1960s, took for their direction the systematic achievement of cultural competence. Some have now evolved as a constructive blend of traditional and experimental programs. Theoretical foundations for interactionism-based (cognitive-developmental) approaches now exist and are discussed later in this book, most specifically in Chapter 5.

To summarize, the strong commitment by many educators to early childhood education has for many years been based on the belief that children will be more likely to realize their developmental potential with such educational experience than without it. But only recently has the search for a better yield from early educational programs involved a careful examination of cognitive behavior. As Kohlberg (1968) suggests, a principal contribution to this search has been a growing awareness among educators that differences in early academic achievement among children are due less to formal schooling functions than to children's general background of preschool experience and the personal characteristics they develop during the early years of life. Yet basic schisms in educational and psychological thought have continued to affect program development, particularly at the preprimary level. Hopefully these theoretical conflicts among adults do not occur at the expense of children. Possibly the superordinate issue is what specific experiences are best for individual children at what points in time rather than what one approach or set of experiences is best for all children simultaneously and at a uniform point in the developmental sequence. This issue, like those summarized above, has a good many psychological and philosophical overtones which are sounded in this book.

REFERENCES

Akers, M. Prologue: the why of early childhood education. In I. J. Gordon (ed.), *Early childhood education*. Chicago: University of Chicago Press, 1972, 1–12.

Albertson, E. *ERIC materials concerning migrant and Indian education*. Toppenish, Wash.: Center for the Study of Migrant and Indian Education, 1971.

Anderson, J. The theory of early childhood education. In N. Henry (ed.), *Early childhood education*. Chicago: University of Chicago Press, 1947, 70–100.

Ausubel, D. How reversible are the cognitive and motivational effects of cultural deprivation? *Urban Education*, 1964, Summer, 16–37.

Baratz, S., and J. Baratz. Early childhood intervention: the social science basis of institutionalized racism. *Harvard Educational Review*, 1970, 40, 29–50.

Bayley, N. The development of mental abilities. In P. Mussen (ed.), *Carmichael's manual of child psychology*. (3rd Ed.) Vol. 1. New York: Wiley, 1970, 1163–1210.

Beilin, H. The status and future of preschool compensatory education. In J.

Stanley (ed.), *Preschool programs for the disadvantaged.* Baltimore: The Johns Hopkins Press, 1972, 165–181.

Bereiter, C. An academic preschool for disadvantaged children: Conclusions from evaluation studies. In J. Stanley (ed.), *Preschool programs for the disadvantaged.* Baltimore: The Johns Hopkins Press, 1972, 1–21.

Berliner, D., and L. Cohen. Trait-treatment interaction and learning. In F. Kerlinger (ed.), *Review of research in education.* Vol. 1. Itasca, Ill.: F. F. Peacock, 1973, 58–94.

Bernstein, B. Social structure, language, and learning. *Educational Research*, 1961, *3*, 163–176.

Bernstein, B. A critique of the concept of 'compensatory education.' In A. Passow (ed.), *Opening opportunities for disadvantaged learners.* New York: Teachers College, 1972, 70–83.

Blank, M. Assumptions underlying preschool programs. *Journal of Social Issues*, 1970, *26*, 15–33.

Bloom, B. S. *Stability and change in human characteristics.* New York: Wiley, 1964.

Brameld, T. *Philosophies of education in cultural perspective.* Hinsdale, Ill.: The Dryden Press Inc., 1956.

Bronfenbrenner, U. The changing American child: a speculative analysis. *Journal of Social Issues*, 1961, *17*, 6–18.

Bruner, J. *The process of education.* Cambridge, Mass.: Harvard University Press, 1960.

Caldwell, B. Day care: pariah to prodigy. *Bulletin of the American Association of Colleges for Teacher Education*, 1971, *24*, 1–6.

Campbell, D., and J. Stanley. Experimental and quasi-experimental designs for research on teaching. In N. Gage (ed.), *Handbook of research on teaching.* Skokie, Ill.: Rand McNally, 1963, 171–246.

Cole, M., and J. Bruner. Cultural differences and inferences about psychological processes. *American Psychologist*, 1971, *26*, 867–876.

Cole, M., and J. Bruner. *Preliminaries to a theory of cultural differences.* In I. J. Gordon (ed.), *Early childhood education.* Chicago: University of Chicago Press, 1972, 161–180.

Combs, E. Florida's early childhood learning program for migrant children. *Young Children*, 1971, *26*, 359–363.

Coursin, D. Nutrition and brain development in infants. *Merrill-Palmer Quarterly*, 1972, *18*, 177–202.

Cowles, M. Four views of learning and development. *Educational Leadership*, 1971, *28*, 790–795.

Deutsch, M. Facilitating development in the preschool child: social and psychological perspectives. *Merrill-Palmer Quarterly*, 1964, *10*, 249–263.

Educational Policies Commission. *Universal opportunities for early childhood education.* Washington, D.C.: Government Printing Office, 1966.

Edwards, J., and C. Stern. A comparison of three intervention programs with disadvantaged preschool children. *Journal of Special Education*, 1970, *4*, 205–214.

Ellena, W. (ed.). *Christopher Jencks in perspective.* Arlington, Va.: American Association of School Administrators, 1973.

Elliot, D. Guidelines for the analysis and description of early childhood programs. *Educational Leadership*, 1971, *28*, 812–820.

English, H., and A. English. *Dictionary of psychological and psychoanalytical terms.* New York: McKay, 1958.

Evans, E. Measurement practices in early childhood education. In R. Colvin (ed.), *Preschool education: theory and practice.* New York: Springer, 1974.

Feeney, S. Child care debate: key question. *Compact*, 1973, July-August, 25–26.

Fein, G., and A. Clarke-Stewart. *Day care in context.* New York: Wiley, 1973.

Forster, J., and E. Arnaud. Disadvantaged Mexican-American children and early educational experience. Austin, Tex.: Southwest Educational Development Corporation, 1968.

Foster, F. Nutrition and educational experience: interrelated variables in children's learning. *Young Children*, 1972, *27*, 284–288.

Fowler, W. Cognitive learning in infancy and early childhood. *Psychological Bulletin*, 1962, *59*, 116–162. (a)

Fowler, W. Teaching a two-year-old to read: an experiment in early childhood learning. *Genetic Psychology Monographs*, 1962, *66*, 181–283. (b)

Fowler, W. A study of process and method in three-year-old twins and triplets learning to read. *Genetic Psychology Monographs*, 1965, *72*, 3–89.

Fowler, W. The design of early developmental learning programs for disadvantaged young children. *IRCD Bulletin*, 1966, *1A*, 1–4.

Fowler, W. Problems of deprivation and developmental learning. *Merrill-Palmer Quarterly*, 1970, *16*, 141–162.

Fowler, W. On the value of both play and structure in early education. *Young Children*, 1971, *27*, 24–36.

Fowler, W. A developmental approach to infant care in a group setting. *Merrill-Palmer Quarterly*, 1972, *18*, 145–176.

Glick, J. Some problems in the evaluation of preschool intervention programs. In R. Hess and R. Bear (eds.), *Early education.* Chicago: Aldine, 1968, 215–221.

Gordon, I. J. *Parent involvement in compensatory education.* Urbana, Ill.: University of Illinois Press, 1971.

Gordon, I. J. An instructional theory approach to the analysis of selected early childhood programs. In I. J. Gordon (ed.), *Early childhood education.* Chicago: University of Chicago Press, 1972, 203–228.

Grotberg, E. Institutional responsibilities for early childhood education. In I. J. Gordon (ed.), *Early childhood education.* Chicago: University of Chicago Press, 1972, 317–338.

Guilford, J. P. Theories of intelligence. In B. Wolman (ed.), *Handbook of general psychology.* Englewood Cliffs, N.J.: Prentice-Hall, 1973, 630–643.

Haskett, G. Research and early education. *American Psychologist*, 1973, *28*, 248–256.

Heathman, J., and A. Nafziger. Migrant education: a selected bibliography. *ERIC: ED 028 011*, 1969.

Hoepfner, R., C. Stern, and S. Nunmedal, (eds.). *CSE-ECRC preschool/kindergarten test evaluations.* Los Angeles: Center for the Study of Evaluation, University of California at Los Angeles, 1971.

Holland, N. A selected ERIC bibliography on the evaluation of urban American Indian and Mexican-American children. *ERIC: ED 029 935*, 1969.

Hunt, J. McV. *Intelligence and experience.* New York: Ronald, 1961.

Jencks, C. et al. *Inequality: a reassessment of the effect of family and schooling in America.* New York: Basic Books, 1972.

Jensen, A. Cumulative deficit in compensatory education. *Journal of School Psychology*, 1966, *4*, 37–47.

Jensen, A. How much can we boost IQ and scholastic achievement? *Harvard Educational Review*, 1969, *39*, 1–123.

Kagan, J. Late starts are not lost starts. *Learning*, 1973, *2*, 82–85.

Kagan, J., and P. Whitten. Day care can be dangerous. *Psychology Today*, 1970, *4*, 36–41.

Kessen, W. Research in the psychological development of infants: an overview. *Merrill-Palmer Quarterly*, 1963, *9*, 83–94.

Kohlberg, L. Early education: a cognitive-developmental view. *Child Development*, 1968, *39*, 1013–1062.

Kresh, D. Psychoneurobiochemeducation. *Phi Delta Kappan*, 1969, *50*, 370–375.

Kroeber, A. *Anthropology*. New York: Harcourt, 1948.

Labov, W. The logic of nonstandard English. In F. Williams (ed.), *Language and poverty*. Chicago: Markham, 1970, 153–189.

Lay, M., and J. Dopyera. *Analysis of early childhood programs: a search for comparative dimensions*. Urbana, Ill.: ERIC Clearinghouse on Early Childhood Education, 1971.

Lazerson, M. The historical antecedents of early childhood education. In I. Gordon (ed.), *Early childhood education*. Chicago: University of Chicago Press, 1972, 33–54.

Levin, H., J. Guthrie, G. Kleindorfer, and R. Stout. School achievement and post-school success: a review. *Review of Educational Research*, 1971, *41*, 1–16.

Lewis, E. The real California report: a new approach to education. *Phi Delta Kappan*, 1973, *54*, 558–559.

Maccoby, E., and M. Zellner. *Experiments in primary education: aspects of Project Follow Through*. New York: Harcourt, 1970.

Mayer, R. A comparative analysis of preschool curriculum models. In R. Anderson and H. Shane (eds.), *As the twig is bent: readings in early childhood education*. Boston: Houghton Mifflin, 1971, 286–314.

McCandless, B. R. *Children: behavior and development*. New York: Holt, Rinehart and Winston, 1967.

McCandless, B., and E. Evans. *Children and youth: psychosocial development*. Hinsdale, Ill.: The Dryden Press Inc., 1973.

Medinnus, G. Head Start: an examination of issues. In G. Medinnus and R. Johnson (eds.), *Child and adolescent psychology: a book of readings*. New York: Wiley, 1970, 411–421.

Meichanbaum, D., and L. Turk. Implications of research on disadvantaged children and cognitive training programs for educational television: ways of improving Sesame Street. *Journal of Special Education*, 1972, *6*, 27–42.

Messick, S., and T. Barrows. Strategies for research and evaluation in early childhood education. In I. J. Gordon (ed.), *Early childhood education*. Chicago: University of Chicago Press, 1972, 261–290.

Moore, R. Further comments on the California report. *Phi Delta Kappan*, 1973, *54*, 560–561.

Nimnicht, G. Speech delivered at conference on early childhood education. Olympia, Wash., October 18, 1973. (a)

Nimnicht, G. Where are we going with day care? In G. Nimnicht and J. Johnson, Jr. (eds.), *Beyond compensatory education*. Washington, D.C.: Government Printing Office, 1973, 152–160. (b)

Nimnicht, G., and J. Johnson, Jr. (eds.). *Beyond compensatory education*. Washington, D.C.: Government Printing Office, 1973.

Nimnicht, G., J. Johnson, Jr., and P. Johnson. A more productive approach to education than 'compensatory education' and intervention strategies. In G. Nimnicht and J. Johnson, Jr. (eds.), *Beyond compensatory education*. Washington, D.C.: Government Printing Office, 1973, 27–49.

Parker, R., and M. Day. Comparisons of preschool curricula. In R. Parker (ed.), *The preschool in action*. Boston: Allyn and Bacon, 1972, 466–508.

Piaget, J. The genetic approach to the psychology of thought. *Journal of Educational Psychology*, 1961, *52*, 275–281.

Read, M. The biological bases: malnutrition and behavioral development. In I. J. Gordon (ed.), *Early childhood education*. Chicago: University of Chicago Press, 1972, 55–70.

Reissman, F. *The culturally deprived child*. New York: Harper & Row, 1962.

Research and Policy Committee of the Committee for Economic Development. *Education for the urban disadvantaged: from preschool to employment*. New York: Committee for Economic Development, 1971.

Robinson, H., and N. Robinson. The problem of timing in preschool education. In R. Hess and R. Bear (eds.), *Early education*. Chicago: Aldine, 1968, 37–51.

Robinson, H., and N. Robinson. A cross-cultural view of early education. In I. J. Gordon (ed.), *Early childhood education*. Chicago: University of Chicago Press, 1972, 291–216.

Rohwer, W., Jr. Learning, race, and school success. *Review of Educational Research*, 1971, *41*, 191–210.

Schnur, J. Migrant education: a synthesis of current research. *ERIC: ED 042 936*, 1971.

Schultz, C., and H. Aurbach. The usefulness of cumulative deprivation as an explanation of educational deficiencies. *Merrill-Palmer Quarterly*, 1971, *17*, 27–39.

Scriven, M. The methodology of evaluation. In B. O. Smith (ed.), *Perspectives of curriculum evaluation*. American Educational Research Association Monograph Series on Curriculum Evaluation. Skokie, Ill.: Rand McNally, 1967, 39–83.

Sigel, I. Developmental theory and preschool education: issues, problems, and implications. In I. J. Gordon (ed.), *Early childhood education*. Chicago: University of Chicago Press, 1972, 13–32.

Sigel, I. *Contributions of psychoeducational intervention programs in understanding of preschool children*. Unpublished manuscript, State University of Buffalo, New York, 1973.

Soar, R., and R. Soar. An empirical analysis of selected Follow-Through programs: an example of a process approach to evaluation. In I. J. Gordon (ed.), *Early childhood education*. Chicago: University of Chicago Press, 1972, 229–260.

Spodek, B. *Early childhood education*. Englewood Cliffs, N.J.: Prentice-Hall, 1973.

Sroufe, L. A methodological and philosophical critique of intervention-oriented research. *Developmental Psychology*, 1970, *2*, 140–145.

Stanford Research Institute. *A preliminary guide to Follow Through: a progress report on the national evaluation: 1969–1971*. Menlo Park, Calif.: Stanford Research Institute, 1972.

State of California. *Report of the task force on early childhood education*. Sacramento, Calif.: California State Department of Education, 1972.

Stern, C. Evaluating language curricula for preschool children. *Monographs of the Society for Research in Child Development*, 1968, *33*, Serial No. 124, 49–61.

Stott, L., and R. Ball. Infant and preschool mental tests: review and evaluation. *Monographs of the Society for Research in Child Development*, 1965, *30*, Serial No. 101.

Weikart, D. Relationship of curriculum, teaching, and learning in preschool education. In J. Stanley (ed.), *Preschool programs for the disadvantaged*. Baltimore: The Johns Hopkins Press, 1972, 22–66.

Weiss, C. *Evaluation research: methods of assessing program effectiveness.* Englewood Cliffs, N.J.: Prentice-Hall, 1972.

Wells, A. Day care: an annotated bibliography. *ERIC: ED 068 199*, 1971.

White, R. Motivation reconsidered: the concept of competence. *Psychological Review*, 1959, *66*, 297–323.

Zigler, E. Child care in the seventies. *Inequality in Education*, 1972, *13*, 17–28.

Zigler, E. Project Head Start: success or failure? *Learning*, 1973, *1*, 43–47.

Photo by Peter Rinearson.

2

*the
mainstream
of early
childhood
education*

INTRODUCTION

In Chapter 1, the recent history of early and often specialized intervention efforts was discussed, together with some major outcomes of the past decade's experience with education for young children. Ideas put forth throughout that discussion can now serve as a fulcrum for the present chapter in which more long-standing concepts of early childhood education are examined. Additionally, an attempt will be made to show more fully how these concepts relate to the broad spectrum of contemporary intervention practices. At some risk, these enduring concepts can be thought of as mainstream influences in early education. Certainly, their effect upon kindergarten and nursery school practices in America has been profound, and it is these practices that occupy much of this chapter's spotlight. Eventually, many of these enduring concepts helped to break the ground for Project Head Start, also discussed in this chapter. A mixture of old and new is now apparent in many of the current models for early education, and an overview of the "developmental-interaction" point of view about such education will complete the present chapter. The orientation to issues established in Chapter 1 will continue, along with appropriate references to evaluative research.

KINDERGARTEN AND NURSERY
SCHOOL PRACTICE

Early childhood education in the mainstream often is described by the terms *traditional programs* or *conventional practice*. As popular as these terms may be, they are suspect, if not misleading. The variety of activities under the umbrella of kindergarten-nursery education both historically and presently makes generalization about what is "traditional" or "conventional" nearly impossible. It seems fair to say, however, that certain persistent currents of thought have pervaded the mainstream of American early childhood education. These currents take the form of dominant philosophical and pedagogical commitments among the majority of early childhood educators.

To illustrate, three thematic commitments can be said to have shaped the course of early education in this country (Lazerson, 1972). One, the *ethic of social reform*, was mentioned briefly in the previous chapter. This ethic refers to a tenacious expectation among childhood educators that early schooling will affect positively both the general quality of American child-rearing practices and children's long-range social mobility by providing a foundation for subsequent school success. As was seen in Chapter 1, the ethic of social reform was implicated in the compensatory education movement, but has been battered more than mildly by the pungent accounts of Jencks et al. (1972), Jensen (1969), and Moore and Moore (1972), to name a few.

A second thematic commitment of mainstream early education has been to *freedom for children to learn* in flexible, child-centered, benevolent environments. This ideal is accompanied by the hope that elementary school practices which are allegedly more prevalent, depersonalized, and authoritarian will be abandoned in favor of those championed by child welfare advocates. In other words, it has been thought that a beginning overhaul of rigid public school classrooms can be gained if early educators model a more permissive approach to education and show how positive its results can be. According to Lazerson (1972), this "move from below" to effect change at upper school levels more often than not has been a frustrating experience for leaders in preschool education. This writer tends to agree—with the qualifying note that negative criticism of public school practices is frequently exaggerated, if not fabricated. Further, there is some evidence (see Chapter 7) that open approaches to education are gaining more acceptance in this country, even though no one knows for sure whether they are any more or less effective for children's academic and social development.

Related to the concept of freedom to learn is a third influence in mainstream early education: a belief in childhood as a unique, precious, and critical period for affective development. As one consequence of this belief, traditional early education programs often have been dominated by free play and attention to aesthetics. Children's affinity and presumed "need" for play have aroused much spirited argument between those who believe that school is properly a *child development experience* and those who see the role of the kindergarten (and certainly the primary grades) as primarily to inculcate culturally valued *academic skills*. Resultant issues are examined more fully later in this chapter. Meanwhile, let us consider the kindergarten movement in education.

Kindergarten

History The tap roots of contemporary early childhood education extend clearly to European thinkers such as J. A. Comenius (1592–1670), J. J. Rousseau (1712–1778), and J. H. Pestalozzi (1746–1827), all of whom championed the rights of children. But out of the chaotic life of Frederick Froebel (1782–1852) came perhaps the first solidified approach to the education of young children. Froebel's attention to the "preschool child" and the training of young, single women to teach young children were contributions of lasting importance.

Having derived his educational principles from the observation of children, Froebel formulated a philosophy built upon the spontaneous, self-sustaining nature of children. Play and the cultivation of children's spiritual feelings were considered paramount. Then-unfamiliar educational materials, such as geometric blocks (used to teach form and number concepts), musical activities, and games systematized through play constituted the core of Froebel's kindergarten.[1] The child's "natural tendency" to play and dance in circles with other children was capitalized upon by Froebel to cultivate the child's imagination.

Froebel's child-centered orientation has persisted among his successors and provides, at least in theory, the backbone of modern nursery and kindergarten practices. It was not, however, until several years after Froebel's death that the concept of kindergarten as a matter of regular public school experience was formalized.

A primary agent in this formalization was Susan Blow (1843–1916), whose early educational experiments at the kindergarten level took place in St. Louis, Missouri, shortly after the Civil War. Susan Blow's ideas were tailored directly from the Froebellian approach—particularly from the spontaneous self-activity and specific curricular activities advocated by Froebel. Shortly after the Missouri experiments, a department of kindergarten was established by the National Education Association (NEA) in 1874.[2] This move was followed by a significant NEA recommendation that kindergarten programs be included as a regular part of the public school enterprise. As the thinking of John Dewey (1859–1952) gathered support around the turn of the century, philosophical and pedagogical controversy

---

[1] *Kindergarten* is the German word for *garden of children* and thus portrays the original analogy of children as garden plants to be nurtured carefully.

[2] Earlier programs were evident in the United States, although they were essentially private operations. An exception was a brief experience with public school kindergarten in Boston in 1870.

over the purpose and content of kindergarten programs became strikingly apparent. Among the major figures involved were Dewey himself, Patty Smith Hall (a translator of Dewey's ideas into kindergarten–primary grade experiences), Susan Blow, a scattering of Montessori followers, and others. In retrospect, this early controversy seems to have anticipated that which currently flourishes in this country with respect to the content and nature of early childhood education.

Contemporary Status, Objectives, and Curriculum Patterns   In the United States a kindergarten program is generally restricted to five-year-old children who spend eight to ten months in activities which precede formal academic work (first grade). Most kindergartens are set up for half-day sessions. Not all school systems in this country support kindergartens, however, and severe restrictions on kindergarten offerings exist in others. Only thirty-eight of the United States, for example, provide state financial aid to kindergartens (*Young Children*, 1973). Despite this, survey data illustrate a remarkable increase in the number of eligible children enrolled in kindergartens during the past several decades. In 1949, for example, 960,000 children were official kindergarten participants; by 1966, over 2.4 million kindergarten enrollees were reported (Ream, 1969). In 1968, this figure had reached 3.1 million (Nehrt and Hurd, 1969) and had dipped only slightly by 1971 to 3,086,000 children (*Young Children*, 1973). This massive increase must be considered in relation to the number of children found in any given classroom, for overloading is generally considered detrimental to program quality. Large classes of over twenty-five children are directly antithetical to the principle of individual differentiation so basic to general kindergarten philosophy. That the enrollment fort is being held reasonably well is indicated by an average of twenty-six children per class in the kindergartens of some 1100 school systems (Ream, 1969).

Objectives of the kindergarten vary in their specific terminology but generally converge upon broad dimensions of growth including sociability, aesthetics, sensory-motor development, and achievement motivation. Headley (1965), for example, suggests that the function of the kindergarten is to assist the child toward the following objectives:

Friendliness and helpfulness in relationships with other children
Greater power to solve problems based in individual activities and
    group relationships
Respect for the rights, property, and contributions of other children
Responsiveness to intellectual challenge
Achievement of good sensory-motor coordination
Understanding of concepts necessary for the continued pursuit of
    learning
Responsiveness to beauty in all forms
Realization of individuality and creative propensities

In this kindergarten classroom, children are encouraged to experiment with colors and express their individuality through art. Photo by Peter Rinearson.

The breadth and abstractness of these goals permit countless programmatic variations.[3] Thus the most unifying aspect of kindergarten programs may be the commitment among their personnel to the positive and total growth of children.

The general activities prescribed by kindergarten curricula—while often remarkably similar from one school district to another—seem to vary in the emphasis placed upon pre-academic training (specific academic "readiness" building) and the degree to which evaluation procedures are implemented. According to Headley (1965), roughly 40–50 percent of a typical kindergarten day is devoted to specific creative activities (art work, model building, and so on), music (singing, listening, and rhythmic activities), and language-based activities (story listening and telling, poetry, "group discussion" such as show and tell, and question-answer activities). The remaining time is distributed among self-care, free play, and rest periods. The flexibility of a kindergarten curriculum, however, enables a good teacher to infuse daily activities with ample doses of basic language, mathematical, science, and social studies concepts. In fact, both the

---

[3] Variation in content and quality, if nothing else, may be implied by statistics relevant to per-pupil expenditures in kindergarten. In 1967–1968, the average cost per pupil ranged from 150–800 dollars per academic year (Ream, 1969).

nursery school and kindergarten settings provide an extensive opportunity for a teacher to do one's own thing, at least in comparison to most upper grades where parameters typically are firmer. This freedom could simultaneously represent a boon and a hazard to young children. Nevertheless, the development of a positive attitude toward learning to serve the child as a foundation for future school learning is a central concern. Curriculum flexibility would seem to enhance progress toward this objective (Mager, 1969).

Curriculum Patterns   Close examination of any kindergarten curriculum usually reveals a potpourri of materials and techniques that are best described as *eclectic*, that is, combinations of activities that transcend any one philosophy or theory of educational psychology. In other words, unlike many approaches to early childhood education examined in this book, the kindergarten concept as it is applied in the public schools does not necessarily imply an articulated psychology of learning or philosophy of growth. Substantial use is made of a variety of commercially prepared materials whose widespread application is further evidence of eclecticism.

Eclecticism in kindergarten practice makes it difficult to categorize programs, although writers such as Davis (1963) maintain that broad differences in kindergarten-primary curriculum patterns may be identified. One such pattern, according to Davis, is based upon the *socialization* theory of instruction. The socialization pattern emphasizes the child's social behavior and development. Responsible group interaction, activities built from the interests of children, a permissive learning environment, social adjustment, and free play are among the guidelines for this approach. A second theme, the *developmental pattern*, is based upon "levels of experiences that permit growth to proceed at its normal rate and direction" (Davis, 1963, p. 35). Maturational readiness is considered within this pattern; education is geared primarily to assist the child toward an understanding of himself and his world. A recognition of children's self-regulatory mechanism of learning and growth leads developmental educators to encourage self-selection and self-pacing for children's educational activities. It is from this pattern that the now familiar plea for "education of the whole child" is strongly heard. A third blueprint for curriculum organization is the *instructional pattern*. In this pattern, the selection and sequencing of subject matter content are emphasized. Language and sensory-motor skills are singled out for major attention, although a concern for the child's socioemotional life is not precluded. *Content* (ideas and skill-building activities) is viewed as the best nutrient for total growth.

As Davis suggests, most kindergarten programs probably represent a fusion of all patterns. Variation is most likely a function of individual teachers' philosophies and competencies. Kindergarten curriculum development has been plagued, however, with the persistent problem of determining both quality and quantity of intellectual content (Robison and Spodek, 1965). Content-oriented childhood educators often are viewed with suspicion by those who feel such an emphasis implies a priority higher than children themselves. But a shift to content consideration defines a part of the revolution in early childhood education that began in the 1960s.

Perhaps in anticipation of pressures for a substantive reorientation in kindergarten curricula, Robison and Spodek (1965) have recommended a format for kindergarten practice under the flag of "new directions." These authorities attempt to demonstrate, by specific attention to content and organizational variables, how the substance of a curriculum can be made commensurate with the needs and cultural backgrounds of today's children. For Robison and Spodek, the selection of content comes from a structural analysis of major disciplines—geography, history, economics, social science, science, and mathematics—in which pivotal concepts in each are identified and interrelated in the service of economical and permanent learning for children. Only the "big ideas" are brought to kindergarten children. These ideas are translated through concrete manipulative experiences, dramatic play, and developmental language activities. From this base of big ideas, children go on to confront hierarchically more complex concepts, generalizations, and principles. This approach requires a teacher who has organizational and long-range planning skills, adeptness in conducting guided discovery learning activities, motivational power, and a self-concept as a resource person—a clarifier of ideas and experience—rather than as a pontificator. This redefined teaching role is technically complex and requires a sound insight into both the structure of knowledge and the psychology of learning. The implications of this conceptualization of the teacher have been specified elsewhere (Spodek, 1969).

The impact of the new directions described above and other positions (such as that of Leeper, Dales, Skipper, and Witherspoon, 1968) upon actual kindergarten practice is not easily determined. Statements of curriculum theory, program recommendation, and innovative ideas abound in the literature. One cannot readily assume that practices on the firing line are a direct outgrowth of practices advocated in the literature. We may observe no quarrel with the idea and general characteristics of good programs for young children. Yet we observe great variations in educators' concepts of what is "good" for children and their skills of implementation for early school programs.

Additional insights into actual kindergarten practice are conveyed by the extensive survey data of Ream (1969), a collection of information concerning enrollment, administrative policy, financing, and curriculum from 110 public school districts. Ream reports that where formalized procedures are found in a kindergarten curriculum, they are most likely to be associated with number concepts and reading readiness activities. The "exposure to experience" technique, rather than structural methods, is more often preferred for science and social studies. Curriculum areas least frequently included in the kindergartens of these districts were estimated to be language arts, music, and direct reading instruction. Health, physical education, and art activities, in contrast, were reported with great frequency. These survey data suggest that most districts lean toward informal learning experiences, a tendency consistent with most traditional views on the functions of kindergarten. One immediate question is whether the predominantly informal kindergarten experience makes a real difference in the subsequent academic and motivational development of the child.

Certainly the data above are not inconsistent with the viewpoint of Pratcher (1968), who looks to the kindergarten teacher to develop "creative patterns of readiness" among children. This would involve, for example, a unification of number readiness, reading readiness, and nature study in the kindergarten setting, where experiences would be arranged to allow each child to exercise initiative and originality *at his own pace.*

Other manifestations of this persuasion are found in materials widely circulated by the Association for Childhood International (Law, et al., 1966). Educators are warned that programs designed with a future orientation may too easily neglect children *as children.* Recommended for kindergarten curricula, therefore, are episodes of integrated experiences—social, aesthetic, emotional, and intellectual—which allow children to follow their natural growth patterns. These sentiments are also endorsed by Leeper et al. (1968), who view preparatory academics as subservient to the objective of helping children live "fully and richly" as *five-year-olds.* This latter objective demands of a teacher great skill and knowledge with respect to children's processes of growth and learning. A full and rich existence at any point in time seemingly would require that the child's needs be well met. Two things are therefore required: (1) valid means for the identification of children's specific needs, including teacher skill in applying these means, and (2) teacher skill in planning and executing activities which meet children's needs. The extent to which practicing kindergarten teachers are skillful in these areas is not clearly known, although it is likely that a wide range of individual differences in these skills would be observed.

More recently, standardized and prepackaged kindergarten programs have appeared. These are similar to *models* (as discussed in Chapter 1), but are specifically designed as commercial ventures. Typically, all necessary teaching materials—teacher's guides, workbooks, worksheets, manipulables, audiovisual aids—are included; and a teacher has but to become skilled in the execution of prescribed instructional activities. An example of prepackaging is the Open Court Kindergarten Program (Open Court, 1970). Ostensibly, this program supplements the "natural experience of childhood" by providing special learnings unlikely to occur at home. Thus, instruction in skills deemed useful for later schooling (basic scholastic skills) is programmed together with sequenced tasks for thinking skills and games for perceptual-motor skill refinement. The prescriptive portion of the program contains material for a one-and-one-half-hour teaching day:

Language development (20 minutes: 10 on letters and sounds, another
   10 on classification or basic vocabulary)
Counting and measuring (15 minutes)
Thinking skills (15 minutes)
Perceptual games and activities (10 minutes)
Social development and self-awareness (5–10 minutes), at intervals
Human understanding through literature (15–20 minutes)
Music (10 minutes)

The authors of Open Court assume that the remainder of a daily kindergarten session will be occupied by informal activities, including arts and
crafts, for which the packaged program does not provide. This is apparently out of respect for an individual teacher's tastes and talents, and the
varying cultural settings to which arts and crafts activities can wisely
be adapted.

At this writing, research evidence about the Open Court program
was unaccessible. Prospective adopters, however, hopefully will take the
initiative to seek evidence about the impact of this or any other commercially available prepackaged program. Attention should also be given
to a program's suitability for particular local applications. The community,
teacher, total school program, and especially the children involved should
be considered. A new core curriculum—Playway—is among the more
flexible packaged programs for local kindergarten adaptations (Davis,
Davis, and Hansen, 1973). Conceivably, any reasonably capable and motivated adult could implement such a prepackaged program. But is the
success of an educational program solely determined by a structure of
prescriptive learning materials? This question is examined more fully in
later sections.

Evaluative Research in the Kindergarten The most typical strategy
for kindergarten evaluative research has involved broad comparisons on
selected criteria of children who have attended kindergarten with children
who have not participated in a kindergarten. Outcomes immediately subsequent to the kindergarten experience have most often been assessed,
although one occasionally uncovers a study concerned with long-range
results. Many reviews of such comparative research have appeared in
the literature. Bricker and Lovell (1965), for example, have reviewed the
academic and social effects of kindergarten training. A majority of the
studies summarized by these writers dealt with global behavioral patterns,
such as "social adjustment." Several, however, indicated specific favorable
outcomes for kindergarten in longer-term reading skills such as improved
word recognition, word comprehension, and reading rate. Such data indicate that favorable outcomes can and do occur, but they do not mean that
such outcomes will necessarily occur in a given kindergarten setting.

Similar gross generalizations appear in other research reviews. Conway
(1968), for instance, has reported data that are favorable to the kindergarten experience for children, especially in private kindergartens where

smaller classes often prevail. More specific comparative evaluations have been made in connection with Project Follow Through. Stronger academic performances have been documented among disadvantaged children in a Follow Through kindergarten based upon token reinforcement procedures (see Chapter 3) as compared to their regular, non–Follow Through kindergarten peers (Miller, 1972). The traditional approach has also been contrasted with other alternative kindergarten curricula. In one study, the small-group personal and social behavior of children in a traditional classroom was rated generally more favorable (cooperative, alert, friendly) than was that of children in a "cognitive-structured" approach; children in a third classroom—a "creative-aesthetic" curriculum—were rated alternately aggressive and enthusiastic (Torrance, 1970). In an independent later study, children in the creative-aesthetic curriculum were observed as more skillful in question asking than were their traditional curriculum counterparts or first-grade children who had not participated in a pre-primary program (Torrance, 1972).

Though interesting, these data are difficult to interpret without complete knowledge of what constitutes one or another curriculum. In research reports, curricula are frequently described in very general terms, if at all. A consumer is left with the hazardous task of inferring the particulars. Perhaps it is most judicious, then, to derive from such studies only the generalization that different curricula can produce different results. The real issue involves deciding what results are desired in a given situation and then selecting the most valid means to achieve them.

It is tempting to agree with Bricker and Lovell (1965), who believe there is sufficient evidence to document the academic and social advantages of kindergarten education.[4] This confidence is apparently shared by society. No longer does the educational defense of the kindergarten seem to be a serious problem. Yet the absence of kindergarten programs in many school systems and the relatively low priority they apparently carry in others are testimony to the light regard in which kindergarten still is held among some segments of the general public. This light regard may be due, in part, to a general lack of understanding of kindergarten and its egregious function in a total school curriculum. In addition, school programs not clearly subject-matter based—as is often the case with kindergartens—fail to qualify as "educational" in some people's view.

Some Current Issues   Evaluators have generally treated kindergarten practice kindly. But several tormenting issues pervade the kindergarten literature. In Chapter 1, the issue of *what* goals and content a program should realize was mentioned. This issue clearly is applicable to kinder-

---

[4] These authorities have exercised selectivity in the choice of studies which appear in their review, which is a showcasing of research that demonstrates the capabilities of well-designed kindergartens for promoting behavior change. Not all comparative studies reveal advantages for kindergarten children; nor do all children respond favorably to a given program. The issue is not whether kindergarten can make a difference, but whether it will.

garten in general: How much and what kind of intellectual content and efforts at academic acceleration should be attempted? The what issue is exemplified by the controversy about "readiness" for reading and teaching reading at the kindergarten level (de Hirsch, Jansky, and Langford, 1966). And closely related is the issue of how to proceed with such teaching if an affirmative decision is made to incorporate formal reading instruction into the kindergarten year. This issue often takes the form of a debate between advocates of sight methods ("look and say") and those who champion a phonics approach (Chall, 1967). Most of the newer methods of reading instruction reflect a strong phonics orientation, but "the beat goes on," as one popular lyricist has written.

Issues surrounding the certification of kindergarten teachers aptly illustrate the *who* issue mentioned in Chapter 1. In theory, certification is believed to maximize the probability that minimum technical skills will be developed by teachers prior to actual kindergarten service. Most generally, certification requirements include special course work related to child development and some period of practice teaching under supervision. Even with such protective measures, society has no guarantee that all kindergarten teachers will be personally suited to work effectively with children. The most obviously maladjusted teacher candidates are usually prevented from entering the classroom, but screening procedures in teacher education are woefully inadequate. The issue is made more frustrating by (1) slow strides among educators toward a definition of the "effective" teacher and (2) a dearth of valid measurement devices to detect in advance unsuitable candidates for classroom teaching.

Recently there has been much ado about competency-based teacher education. Briefly, this means that even a preliminary certification for teaching requires a candidate to demonstrate an ability to promote desirable learning among pupils or at least exhibit teaching behaviors known to promote such learning. These competencies must be observable in actual instructional settings; the simple accumulation of college credits for entry into the profession is secondary, if even relevant. Space limitations preclude a full discussion of the complexities, issues, and implications of competency- or performance-based teacher education, but a fuller study of this trend is recommended (see, for example, McNeil and Popham, 1973, and *Phi Delta Kappan*, 1974).

Still other psychophilosophical issues in kindergarten practice can be identified: age of entry to kindergarten (McCandless, 1957), the full- versus half-day kindergarten (Gorton and Robinson, 1969), continuous admission plans (Jones, 1969), grouping for individual differences (Harris and Fischer, 1969), the early reader (Durkin, 1966), screening practices (Rogolsky, 1969), and general "school readiness" (Ames and Ilg, 1965). Because of its relevance to the whole of early childhood education, this last issue will be dealt with in Chapter 9. Finally, the persistent problem of compartmentalization in kindergarten practice should be mentioned (Headley, 1965). *Compartmentalization* refers to a tendency among teachers and curriculum developers to segment or isolate learning experiences in two basic ways: (1) within the kindergarten program and (2) in relation to the vertical progression of the subsequent primary grade curriculum. To some extent, compartmentalization has been created by some educators' failure or reluctance to consider the kindergarten as an integral part of the total school curriculum. It has been intensified by the recent thrust toward cognitive stimulation in preprimary programs. Solutions to the compartmentalization problem have been slow to come, and more will be said about this later.

Greater detail about kindergarten philosophy, practices, and issues is supplied by an enormous kindergarten literature. (See Weber, 1969, for a comprehensive overview and bibliography, and LaCoste, 1971, for a useful anthology of practical papers concerned with major elements of kindergarten programming.)

Nursery Schools

History   Nursery school education in the United States has a much more recent history than does kindergarten. Public nursery schools were first established in 1919 (F. Mayer, 1960), yet only a handful of nursery schools existed in the early 1920s. The first parent-cooperative nursery of record was formed by a group of Cambridge, Massachusetts, parents in 1923. With the gathering momentum of the child guidance movement in the late 1920s, nursery schools began to flourish. Several important centers for child study operated model programs, including the Gesell Child Guidance Nursery at Yale University, the Merrill-Palmer Institute in Detroit, Teachers College of Columbia University, and the Iowa Child Welfare Research Station at the University of Iowa. At such locations important child development and education research was initiated to pave the way for much of what came to pass in early intervention projects in the 1960s. Emergency legislation during the great depression, subsumed under Franklin Roosevelt's Works Progress Administration program, created a federal nursery school sponsorship. Further federal subsidization for nursery school education was given during World War II by the famous Lanham Act.[5]

By the mid-1960s close to 700,000 children were officially enrolled in public and private nurseries (excluding day care and Head Start programs, Schloss, 1967). By 1971, prekindergarten enrollment had reached over a million, with about 35 percent of this figure in public, as opposed to privately supported, programs (*Young Children*, 1973). Although the enrollment continues to rise, it is clear that children's nursery school experiences are not coextensive. Regardless of how the pie is divided, a piece which symbolizes the nursery school cannot be neatly cut. Nursery schools exist on the campuses of colleges and universities, in churches, homes, shopping centers, and civic buildings. Some are commercial, others

---

[5] See Frank (1962) for a succinct historical overview of the emergence of child study and family life education in the United States.

are nonprofit. Some require professional credentials, others do not. Some are exclusively parent-cooperative ventures, while others may exercise no apparent commitment to parental involvement. Some accommodate three-, four-, and five-year-olds; others accept four-year-olds only. Some are limited to half-day programs, others include a full day. Some schools convene two or three days a week, others utilize the full five-day week. In short, variation is the rule rather than the exception. Exceptional, however, is the sponsorship of nursery school programs by public school systems. During the 1966–1967 school year, nursery school programs were provided by only 148 public school systems, as compared to nearly 9800 that regularly mount kindergarten programs (Ream, 1968).[6]

Objectives and Contemporary Status   In theory, the objectives of the many thousands of nursery programs now in operation are not grossly dissimilar. Actual procedures, however, seem less uniform. The generality of the nursery school concept can be best illustrated by the following typical schedule of activities for American four-year-olds (Farwell, 1958; Green and Woods, 1965; Pitcher and Ames, 1964).

Arrival and health inspection	
Outdoor and/or indoor play	20–30 minutes
Toilet and clean-up	10 minutes
Music	10–20 minutes
Snack time	10–15 minutes
Rest (may include listening to records, looking at books, etc.)	15 minutes
Indoor free play	20–30 minutes
Story time; toilet and clean-up	15–30 minutes
Outdoor play and departure	

This schedule reflects several emphases commonly found in nursery schools. One is an accent upon basic socialization and the child's physical health needs. A second is the emphasis upon fantasy play to promote sensory-motor and emotional development. Nursery school educators have long reasoned that it is through organized and free play that a child learns to know himself, his capabilities, and the realities of his social existence. Play is also thought to provide a medium through which aesthetics and self-expression activities may be elaborated. Traditionally, most nursery school programs have not dealt in specific ways with the matter of academic readiness, although some attention usually is paid to the grooming of general sensory discrimination skills and social responses necessary for group learning activities.

---

[6] A better perspective on this figure is provided by a National Education Association report that identified a total of 19,369 United States public school districts in 1969–1970.

Relatively informal activities, such as clay modeling, have long been an integral part of nursery school programs everywhere. It is usually thought that activities such as that shown here will foster the development of perceptual-motor skills and general creativity. Photo by Peter Rinearson.

The binding force for most nursery programs is considered to be the rapport between the teacher and each child—a rapport capable of fostering self-confidence, security, and spontaneity within the child. Hence, the teacher-child ratio, as in the kindergarten, is by consensus viewed as a critical factor in nursery schools (Farwell, 1958). For example, it is generally advised that nursery groups should not exceed twenty children in schools for four-year-olds (and three to four less where two- and three-year-olds are involved). This assumes further that at least two teachers are available for constant supervision within such groups.

Another dominant belief about nursery school in the mainstream is that children should enjoy a learning environment as free as possible from restraint and direction. Consequently, children are provided with a supportive latitude as regards their specific activities. Respect for and accommodation to individuality are essential. Teachers usually assume responsibility for guiding music activities and informal discussion periods, but in many cases the most apparent evidence of planning and organization is represented by a teacher's selection of play equipment and the creation of art activity centers. Parent relations, including family life education activities, also receive systematic attention in the more comprehensive nursery programs.

Evaluative Research Concern for the influence of nursery school on children has most commonly been expressed in terms of global behaviors such as "improved" social skills, "greater" intellectual competence, or "increased" emotional adjustment. This concern automatically awakens a sleeping giant called by psychologists the *criterion problem*, i.e., determining specifically what defines a given behavior change and how it can be measured. An incisive review of nursery school research has resulted in several inferences germane to this problem (Swift, 1964). First, Swift believes that while studies of the global effects of nursery experiences are at times encouraging, they are frequently inconclusive. This inconclusiveness, Swift charges, is due to the failure of researchers to relate expected changes (e.g., sensory-motor, social, or intellectual) to specific program features thought to be relevant antecedents.[7] Second, most nursery studies suggest that effects depend largely upon the extent to which a program supplements (rather than duplicates) the experiences the children receive elsewhere. Third, Swift concludes that nursery programs depend for their effectiveness upon the skill of the individual teacher and the socioemotional climate in which activities are pursued. Swift implies that diffuse programs leave a substantial degree of potential effectiveness to chance. An overriding philosophical question, of course, is whether nursery school programs must justify their existence in terms of measurable outcomes. One might satisfy oneself with the notion that children's lives are being enriched and made more enjoyable (assuming a sound physical, psychological, and social environment). Yet as long as programs purport to accomplish growth objectives, the question of their validity is legitimate.

Swift's remarks (1964) are echoed in an independent review of nursery research by Sears and Dowley (1963), as the following quotation will demonstrate:

> It is clear that attendance at nursery school, in and of itself, does not radically alter personalities of children. The evidence suggests, but not strongly, that certain social participation skills are enhanced by a good nursery school experience and that in certain cases these effects can be observed several years later. Language and intellectual development may be influenced, apparently, particularly if the home or out-of-school environment of the child is meager in stimulating qualities. (Sears and Dowley, 1963, p. 850).

As for the difficulties faced in interpreting such research, these authorities further maintain that

> firm knowledge of the effect of teaching methods or roles cannot be gained without taking into account characteristics of the children toward whom the methods are directed. It is clear by now that a "method" cannot be abstracted from the interpersonal setting;

---

[7] See Thompson (1944) for a respectable early effort to counter this failure.

methods are employed by teachers having certain characteristics and they are directed toward children with certain characteristics. Shorn of these factors statements about a method (and its effects) must necessarily be stated in such tentative terms that they are of little value (Sears and Dowley, 1963, p. 859).

Thus is pinpointed an issue that includes the idea of trait-treatment interaction mentioned in Chapter 1; Sears and Dowley are concerned about the degree of matching or interrelationship between a method, the children involved, the teacher's skill, and the emotional climate in which learning takes place. This issue, among others, continues to stimulate research into educational strategies for young children.

The Swift (1964) and Sears and Dowley (1963) reviews obviously do not include studies about nursery school practices during the more recent intervention period described in Chapter 1. Of current interest are comparative studies of the more general and traditional nursery school programs and "new look" experimental programs. Overall, the results are mixed. In one study, comparable groups of disadvantaged children experienced two different preschool programs of seven months duration: a highly structured experimental curriculum designed to promote mastery of cognitive tasks and a more informal, conventional program for personal-social and motor development (Karnes et al., 1968). As indicated by measures of intellectual functioning, language abilities, perceptual development, and school readiness, the experimental program yielded significantly greater results. This and other studies have prompted Karnes and her colleagues to advocate the necessity of advance planning and systematic instruction if school-related skills are to be groomed and polished during the preschool years.

In a moderate contrast, Weikart (1972) reports that a unit-based traditional approach was equally effective in affecting intellectual development when compared to two other more cognitively oriented, structured, academic programs for three- and four-year-old children. In this case, *traditional* refers to instruction from an intuitive base with strong attention by teachers to the perceived needs of children as manifest from moment to moment during a school period. Documented program equivalence has prompted Weikart to believe that the operational conditions of an experimental project—cooperative interchange among skilled teachers who work together, staff commitment to the program itself, planning and self-evaluation by teachers—may be more "potent" influences upon program outcomes than is an explicit predetermined curriculum. Curriculum content is not dismissed. Rather, Weikart implies that basic cognitive training will occur inevitably when teachers are sensitive to the needs of children and rich in their repertoire of knowledge and communication skills. It is as if a set of "spontaneous forces" (qualitative aspects of interpersonal contact) are at work to produce the more salient effects of schooling (Stephens, 1967). Not to be overlooked in this comparative evaluation are (1) a strong home teaching component, rarely observed in earlier nursery school programs of the traditional type and

(2) a low (1–5) teacher-child ratio. It is possible that these factors, given teams of highly skilled classroom teachers and the excitement of an experimental project, can mediate the outcomes of most any type of preschool program.

Finally, the most typical pattern of findings about nursery school—or preschool experience of any kind—has been reported by Baker (1973). He refers to series of evaluations which collectively indicate the generally positive impact of public nursery school experience upon the conceptual and affective development of both economically advantaged and disadvantaged children. However, follow-up comparisons to similar children who lacked a nursery school background revealed that the gains did not persist. This negative finding again highlights the issue of sustained influence from early educational experiences. As indicated in Chapter 1, however, there seems to be more support for the idea that initial positive achievements are good in themselves. A value can also be placed upon the day-to-day enjoyment that children can derive from quasi-formal social and academic experiences at age four. Certainly, this is a humanistic view. The criteria for determining the worth of a nursery school program are at stake.

Preoccupation with lasting behavioral outcomes of nursery school can also result in failure to acknowledge less obvious contributions. Consider, for example, the opportunity provided by nursery school contact for specialists early to identify childhood problems. Or, as Westman, Rice, and Bermann (1967) have put it, the nursery school represents a "strategic output" for mental health screening and intervention. Westman and his colleagues' longitudinal research on 130 nursery schoolers disclosed that the early adjustment problems of these children tend to persist in later life. The most valuable data obtainable at the nursery level for predicting subsequent need for mental health service were teachers' judgments of the children's social relations, behavior eccentricities, and family relationships. This finding assumes that nursery school personnel will be sufficiently trained to discriminate valid adjustment problems; but the data indicate the potential of a nursery school setting for preventive mental health programs and early detection of emotional problems.

Some Representative Issues Many of the issues discussed in the previous segment about kindergarten apply to the nursery school as well. A concern for trained personnel and the significance attached to individual teacher skills, for instance, reminds us again of the who issue. Quality of teaching personnel is an immense issue in nursery school practice. Only minimal professional qualifications are required in many settings. State certification standards do not reach extensively into the fabric of nursery school education. By 1971, for example, only twenty states required certification of some kind for prekindergarten teachers (*Young Children*, 1973). In-service training facilities within nursery school operations are also usually limited. This leaves a great deal to the moral responsibility toward children felt by those who conduct nursery programs. The squeeze for qualified teachers and teacher aides resulting from personnel needs of Head Start and other federal programs has intensified training and selection needs. This issue is not being overlooked, as witness the work of organizations such as the National Association for the Education of Young Children. An oiling and attunement of the machinery needed for improved training procedures is also manifest in a World Organization for Early Childhood Education report (1966) about preparation opportunities and status of preschool teachers.

Related to issues of training and certification is the appropriate role for a teacher in the nursery school environment. Role definitions will be affected strongly by the goals or objectives of a nursery program, but some stylistic factors must be considered as well. Katz (1970), for example, has identified three broad role models which can be observed in preschools. One, the *maternal* model, places emphasis upon the security, safety, happiness, and comfort of children. In effect, the teacher is a mother substitute and takes over basic socialization functions while the child is away from home. A second model, the *therapeutic* role, is similar to the first, but makes a stronger and more deliberate effort to nurture mental health and promote "ego functioning." Tensions, conflicts, anxieties, and the like become the focus for teacher-child interaction. In contrast, the third model, the *instructional* role, stresses the deliberate transmission of knowledge. This latter role represents the strongest departure from traditional practice, particularly if the pursuit of academic objectives prevails: training testable skills, promoting conformity to public school classroom routine; and providing preliminary work with basic arithmetic, reading, and writing activities.

Much space could be devoted to a discussion of the possible effects and implications of different role models. For the present, it will be said only that the instructional role has grown in visibility, if not popularity, during the past several years. This has served to rankle and confuse supporters of the maternal and therapeutic models because of the basic philosophic schism involved and the greater status claimed by many protagonists of direct instruction. It is further maintained that many "new look" nursery educators fail to distinguish between school adjustment skills and achievement, on the one hand, and more basic problem-solving skills, learning strategies, and motivation for learning *in general*, on the other (Katz, 1970). The latter are appropriately intellectual activities and need not be slighted in a conventional nursery program.

Role conflicts are sure to persist, as is another basic issue: the role of play in nursery school (and to some extent, kindergarten) practice. During the sixties, in particular, the validity of assumptions underlying a heavy nursery school investment in play activities was challenged. One authority, for example, seriously questioned the appropriateness of fantasy play for most disadvantaged children on the grounds that they are ill equipped to profit from a play-oriented environment due to language and conceptual lacks (Deutsch, 1964). The rhetoric can too easily fall along polar extremes: a nursery school program should be either play based or not. When this polarization occurs, the distinction is both unfortunate and oversimplified.

More accurately at issue is the function of different types of play in relation to the child's total growth—cognitive, affective, and sensory-motor—and to what degree a given program depends upon play for its effectiveness (e.g., ratio of free play to teacher-directed activity). With respect to play functions, Almy (1966) has expressed serious concern over a sharp swing of the pendulum away from spontaneous play activities in many of the newer cognitive-based preschool programs. Almy's position exemplifies a long-standing conviction of nursery school authorities that self-initiated play is an indispensable stimulus to children's total development. A similar conviction is implied by Sigel (1965), who contends that a child's interaction with a physical world properly "adjusted to his size and relative fragility" will aid his growing sense of competence and mastery.

These thoughts about play are perhaps most explicitly supported at the theoretical level by Erik Erikson, an internationally recognized psychoanalyst. For Erikson (1963), personality development during the first six years of life involves the achievement of a basic sense of trust, autonomy, and initiative. The latter two "senses" are developed largely through volitional motor and social play, including fantasy role enactments, in a responsive environment. Erikson would perhaps agree with the *autotelic* principle of O. Moore and Anderson (1969), which states that the best learning takes place in an environment of safety, i.e., an environment conducive to free exploration without adverse physical or social consequences. This principle is at least implicit in general nursery school approaches. The assumption that its application and augmentation is constant across nursery schools, however, is less tenable.

At a more empirical level, Sutton-Smith (1967) has examined research which suggests tentatively a functional relationship between play (especially children's game activity) and cognitive development. Related studies (e.g., Humphrey, 1966) have supported the academic benefits of an active games approach to learning. These data support a type of play that extends beyond a random, nonpurposive level. Thus, a critical variable would be the way in which an environment is arranged for the occurrence of play activities. This notion finds indirect support in a perceptive review of cognitive-developmental theories (e.g., Dewey, Piaget, Vygotsky) and their implications for preschool education and intellectual stimulation strategies. In this review, Kohlberg (1968) concludes that for cognitive growth specific forms of stimulation or content (e.g., pre-academic and language training) may be subordinate to a *systematic formulation* of activities traditionally associated with the nursery school, including play, aesthetics, and social activities. If so, we can formulate as a criterion for the evaluation of an early education program the extent to which activities beyond the dimension of specific academic preparations are systematically incorporated into a child-centered curriculum.

The value of children's play and respect for its potential contributions to cognitive and affective development seem to have been generally re-established among early childhood educators in the 1970s. One contributing factor has been a more specific definition of a teacher's function as a stimulator of creativity in children's play and even as an active participant in particular kinds of play activities (Robison, 1971; Smilansky, 1971). Additionally, an impressive resurgence of interest in play and its effects has occurred in the psychological research literature (Herron and Sutton-Smith, 1971). There is not yet a consensus, however, about the conceptual parameters of play, much less a single coherent theory of play that can provide a foundation for curriculum development. Steps in this direction are indicated by the work of some authorities in cognitive-developmental theory (see Chapter 5). Further variety in educators' thinking about play within the framework of organized early childhood education is communicated in *Play: The Child Strives toward Self Realization* (Engstrom, 1971).

PROJECT HEAD START

With some exceptions, the traditional approach to nursery and kindergarten has been based upon a maturationist view of learning and development. That is, developmental stages are seen as determined primarily by genetic forces. Proper environmental nourishment is considered influential, but only with respect to the "relative ease" with which developmental stages unfold, the "fullness" to which they unfold, and the "particular shape which the more general developmental patterns take" (Cowles, 1971). As an example, the general pattern of language may be particularized to French, Portuguese, or Swahili; but the basic mechanism of development is physiological maturation. Educational programs constructed on this view call for a richly nurturant environment with little pressure from without to obstruct natural growth processes. The materials and requirements of any educational activity must be matched to children's level of "readiness" as indicated by unique self-expressive behavior and the general stage of development at which they exist.

This view, augmented modestly by developmental-interactionist thinking (see the last section in this chapter), seemed to dominate the origins of Project Head Start (Branche and Overly, 1971). Admittedly, the psychological brain trust behind Head Start exuded a strong message that the cognitive or intellectual development of many children would be qualitatively enriched or even accelerated by preschool experience. Initially, however, Head Start's approach meant that a general cultivation and fertilization service along the lines of existing nursery schools would be rendered to large numbers of educationally disadvantaged children. There was little recourse. It quickly became necessary to implement a multidimensional intervention program on a large scale with little precedent for deviation from prevalent nursery school practice. Neither were necessary staff and material resources fully available at the outset. Optimism mounted, however, from the idea that *earlier* intervention for total development would somehow reduce or eliminate the educational disadvantage that children of poverty seemed to face continually at regular school entry and beyond.

Head Start Centers are now integral parts of family life in areas where organized preschool experiences for children formerly were rare. These young males are participants in a Head Start program designed for an American Indian community in America's Pacific Northwest. By the mid-70s, some 10,000 American Indian children from 64 reservations in 19 states were being served by Head Start. (Photo by Alan Keimig, courtesy of Muckleshoot Tribal Head Start).

Beginning in 1965, the legislation for Project Head Start authorized a set of organized summer programs for children aged four and five whose socioeconomic status predicted their failure or marginal success in elementary school. Action programs were accomplished through federal grants to local community agencies whose responsibility was to guarantee that child, family, and community welfare would be maintained. Subsequent to the first summer's operation, Head Start programs came to encompass a full academic year prior to the children's formal school entrance. Variety—both in general services and levels of specificity in educational programming—was characteristic of Head Start from the beginning. However, general guidelines for operation applied to all local action programs. The following paragraphs are concerned with Head Start's guiding principles, the evaluative research about this important social experiment, and some broad, far-reaching contributions to society and its children that have thus far resulted from Head Start.

Guiding Objectives and Principles of Head Start

Seven objectives have guided the national Head Start program, including the many research and demonstration projects which have been conducted under federal auspices since 1965 (Grotberg, 1969):

Two Head Start children ponder a form discrimination task. Informal, small group learning activities such as these now are a basic aspect of most Head Start Center programs. Photo by Peter Rinearson.

1. Improving the child's physical health and physical abilities.
2. Helping the emotional and social development of the child by encouraging self-confidence, spontaneity, curiosity, and self-discipline.
3. Improving the child's mental processes and skills with particular attention to conceptual and verbal skills.
4. Establishing patterns and expectations of success for the child which will create a climate of confidence for his future learning efforts.
5. Increasing the child's capacity to relate positively to family members and others, while at the same time strengthening the family's ability to relate positively to the child and his problems.
6. Developing in the child and his family a responsible attitude toward society, and fostering constructive opportunities for society to work together with the poor in solving their problems.
7. Increasing the sense of dignity and self-worth within the child and his family.[8]

---

[8] Head Start is composed of six major parts: administration, education, social services, health services, parent involvement, and career development.

These objectives, prepared by a panel of child development authorities, are not dissimilar to those of conventional nursery and kindergarten programs. The breadth of such objectives, however, does allow for latitude in interpreting what activities will be undertaken in a given program.

The similarity of Head Start to traditional preschool programs of long standing is also apparent in the following format recommended for a Head Start center program (Project Head Start, Pamphlet No. 11).

Arrival, Independent Activity Period (Breakfast in some Centers)	8:00–8:45
Work-Play Activity Period, including:	8:45–10:00
Self-Directed Activities	
Dramatic Play	
Block-Building	
Creative Experiences with Unstructured Media (e.g., painting, clay modeling, and waterplay)	
Activities with Structured Media (e.g., games, puzzles, alphabet sets)	
Informal Experiences in Language, Literature, Music	
Transition (clean-up, snack)	10:00–10:15
Outdoor Work-Play	10:15–11:15
Clean-up	11:15–11:30
Lunch	11:30–12:30
Departure	
P.M. Program (In All-day Centers)	12:30–5:00
A typical afternoon program includes a nap, outdoor play, and miscellaneous activities such as cooking project, experiments with various classroom materials, book browsing, record listening, and game playing.	

Head Start guidelines early called for a limit of fifteen children per class. A 1–5 adult-child ratio was required; one teacher, one paid aide, and at least one volunteer parent are necessary to achieve this ratio. Variations exist, but these guidelines represent the generally accepted standard. Most programs operate three to four hours a day (e.g., from 9:00 to 1:00 P.M.) with a full-day program being the exception. Head Start guidelines require that each child attend his program for a minimum of fifteen hours a week.

A recognition that many things can occur within a general format has led some to assess the Head Start effort more specifically according to the operational principles apparent in actual Head Start classes. One of the few and early accounts was provided by the Educational Testing Service (Dobbin, 1966). From a morass of observational data involving some 1300 classes was formulated a seven-point conceptual pattern:

1. For young children the teaching-learning process must be intimately woven into the fabric of human social interaction.
2. Parents and the community at large should share with teachers the teaching process.
3. The probability that meaningful learning experiences can be arranged cooperatively by adults is vastly increased if planners are aware of the intellectual and emotional patterns of development characteristic of the early years.
4. Children learn best by doing, not just by being told.
5. Methods of known validity for reinforcing and encouraging children's total development are available and should be used.
6. A commonly overlooked but remarkably rich material for instruction is food.
7. The real test of Project Head Start is what happens to its children in the early grades immediately following Head Start.

As the reader can see, these points constitute a scrambling of philosophical and psychological principles. While possibly helpful to researchers, these points would have to be supplemented by a careful analysis of the activities in an individual Head Start classroom, including teacher behavior, to determine the extent to which they and additional principles are operational (Katz, 1970). In spite of general agreement among educational rationale for Head Start, uniform paper objectives, and selected common principles, a classification of Head Start programs was (and is) problematical. Among other things, this unclassifiability set the stage for difficulties in program evaluation. Early accounts of various program types can be consulted (e.g., Getzels, 1966; Gray and Miller, 1967). But variation in program quality was the rule, not the exception, and program changes were occurring in Head Start even as initial evaluation efforts were begun. And despite Head Start's emphasis upon the general welfare and social competence of children, evaluation more typically was concerned with the intellectual-academic aspects of the experiment. We can now examine Head Start research in more detail.

Head Start Research

In the beginning, two types of research activity were dominant within Project Head Start: descriptive and evaluative. The former activity has involved the search for general behavioral characteristics that may (1) differentiate Head Start children (or, more broadly, educationally disadvantaged children) from their more advantaged or privileged age-mates and (2) suggest implications for curriculum development and the design of special services. Evaluative research, of course, has assessed Head Start's merit. In recent years, these research activities have been embellished by efforts to develop better tools for measuring young children's developmental status and responsivity to intervention programs (Gotts, 1973).

Additional efforts have been directed toward the development of supplementary curriculum modules (content units) for use in Head Start classrooms (Boger, 1971). And further innovative research has been stimulated, some of which is discussed in the forthcoming section about the broader contributions of Head Start. For the present, however, the commentary is confined largely to the descriptive and evaluative activities.

Descriptive Studies   Great masses of data that describe the characteristics of educationally disadvantaged children have been published (Cazden, 1966; Hellmuth, 1967; Meichanbaum, 1972, D. Moore, 1971; Stodolsky and Lesser, 1967). Generally, this descriptive research has been designed to identify these children's behavioral deficits rather than their strengths. This research is based upon the fairly gross study of large numbers of children from diverse socioeconomic strata and ethnic groups. While generalizations thus derived may apply to many such children, they do not apply to all. Commonly reported deficiencies (Grotberg, 1969) among disadvantaged children include the following: (1) developmental language response patterns (e.g., vocabulary size, sentence length, and syntax), (2) logical reasoning skills (e.g., the ability to categorize concepts, deal with causal relations, and exercise sequential thought), (3) auditory discrimination skills, (4) attentional responses (e.g., high rates of attentional shifts, lowered persistence, and high motor impulsivity), and (5) selected social-emotional behaviors (e.g., greater dependency conflicts, lessened intellectual achievement responsibility, and less consistency in relationship with adults.

On the other hand, there is little evidence that memory skills or basic acquisitional skills of disadvantaged children are markedly different (Bereiter and Engelmann, 1966). Thus, many authorities are convinced that the primary issue is not a learning capacity deficit, but a deficit in the conceptual tools which facilitate learning (Jensen, 1968). Conventional public school encounters generally serve successively to magnify this problem in a vicious cycle. That is, the initial gap between a "disadvantaged" child's developmental status and the language-based tasks faced in school frequently increases due to incomplete learning. Furthermore, many authorities (e.g., Ginsburg, 1972) argue eloquently that many of the purported deficits of poor children are in large part an artifact of various tests and measurements utilized by research workers. This issue was partially addressed in Chapter 1 and is raised again in Chapter 4.[9]

At best, comparative descriptive data may assist toward more reasoned decisions about program planning. But there always remains the dual risk of overgeneralization and stereotyped perceptions among those who deal with the educationally disadvantaged. A serious problem

---

[9] The single most enlightened treatment of specific testing problems, especially language development in young low-income children, has probably been offered by Dickie and Bagur (1972).

in program planning is the possible failure of deficit-oriented teaching to capitalize upon the positive attributes such as the spontaneity and game skills which many disadvantaged children bring to the classroom.

Evaluation Research   As indicated in Chapter 1, a basic question in evaluative research is whether reliable differences can be observed in program children who subsequently participate in another form of program. A meaningful answer to this question applied to Head Start programs requires that comparisons be between children of similar background experience and cultural-ethnic identity. This requirement is not always met. In most evaluation studies, children in one Head Start program are compared to those in another or to children who are "stay homes." But Head Start classrooms are subject to variations both in teacher competence and group composition due to myriad demographic variables. As Wattenberg (1966) has remarked, research based upon gross categorizations is not unlike comparing baskets of oranges, pears, and grapefruit to baskets of pineapple, strawberries, and peaches. The fruit is grown in different areas and nurtured by different elements. Thus only rough tentative statements may legitimately be made concerning the effects of nurturance. This evaluative situation is further complicated by the frequently unproven validity of evaluation instruments and the frequently tacit assumption that something universal defines all Head Start programs. Given these and other methodological problems, any honest discussion about intervention program evaluation must be tentative.[10] With this caveat in mind, one representative study of early Head Start evaluation is briefly discussed. Thereafter, generalizations from the growing Head Start data are summarized, including the initial findings from Head Start's planned variation experiment.

The Westinghouse Study   Perhaps the most pivotal evaluative research in Head Start's brief history is a project known as the Westinghouse study (Cicirelli et al., 1969). The principal focus of this study was the intellectual and personal-social development of primary grade children with Head Start backgrounds. From a sample of 104 Head Start centers, children were chosen—all of whom were attending first, second, or third grade at the time of the study. This population included children whose Head Start experience was limited to one summer and those who had attended full-year programs. These Head Start children were then compared to a sample of "matched controls," i.e., children of the same age, grade, socioeconomic status, etc., who had not attended Head Start classes. Psychometric instruments were administered to all children to obtain data on language development, reading readiness, and academic achievement.[11] Projective techniques and teacher ratings were employed

---

[10] See Madow (1969) and McDavid (1970) for insightful comments about the basic evaluation difficulties inherent in early Head Start practice.

[11] Among the measures utilized were the Illinois Test of Psycholinguistic Abilities, the Metropolitan Readiness Test, and the Stanford Achievement Test.

to describe such affective characteristics as positive self-concept; desire for achievement; and attitudes toward school, home, peers, and society.

Comparative analyses of the Westinghouse data led to several tentative conclusions. First, no persistent gains in either cognitive or affective development were associated with summer Head Start programs. Second, while full-year programs appeared to result in improved reading readiness, affective measures did not indicate any advantage to Head Start children. This latter finding was somewhat qualified by a subanalysis based upon variables such as geographic location: more favorable patterns of affective development were detected among Head Start children from predominately black population centers in the southeastern United States and among Head Start children from ghetto areas in large cities. Third, whether from summer or full-year programs, Head Start children maintained through the early school years a below-average position on national norms for standardized tests of language development and scholastic achievement. More hopeful was a fourth finding: that parents of Head Start children strongly approved of the program and had been motivated to participate in many of its activities.

On balance, the Westinghouse data, limited as they were, did not promote much optimism about the longer range intellectual impact of Head Start. The absence of reliable affective growth was perhaps doubly disappointing. There is the strong possibility, of course, that certain changes did occur, but were not measured. Certainly the Westinghouse study did not address the medical and nutritional benefits to Head Start children. But, this massive study set the stage for a continuing debate about the impact of compensatory education. At first, this debate occurred at the level of methodological critique and rebuttal (e.g., Cicirelli, Evans, and Schiller, 1970; Smith and Bissell, 1970). The passage of time has now resulted in a sharper perspective on this debate: a head-on collision between two channels of thought about social action programs (Williams and Evans, 1972).

In one channel is the idea, basic to the War on Poverty of the sixties, that effective programs could be implemented full scale and would quickly result in significant life improvements among economically handicapped Americans. Head Start exemplified this hope: within its first year of operation, over a half-million children were served. The opposing channel of thought has come from the premise that objective data are a prime contributor to decision making. The more rigorous the evaluation of programs, the better can be the decisions about their continuation or modification. The Westinghouse study thus crystallized a conflict between hopeful social action for immediate returns and the sharp edge of reality so often revealed by evaluations. One outcome might have been to scrap Project Head Start and turn elsewhere for more productive experiments. This did not happen. Many other factors combined to sustain Head Start through its early crisis in accountability, including recommendations from the Westinghouse study itself. For example, the researchers suggested that "summer only" programs be abandoned in favor of more extended programs. These programs, in turn, should involve younger children, provide more varied teaching strategies, deploy remedial tactics for specific learning disabilities, and place a much heavier emphasis upon parental training. The Westinghouse recommendations cannot be given credit for fully shaping the subsequent course of Head Start. But these concepts, together with data from other federally supported compensatory programs, provided a basis for many landmark developments including parent-child centers, planned variation in Project Follow Through (and eventually Head Start itself), and a general loosening of the strong hold on early childhood education by supporters of the socialization model in traditional nursery school practice.

Since the early evaluative reports concerning Head Start, several timely reviews of the published evidence about preschool program effects on disadvantaged children and their families have appeared (e.g., Beller, 1973). These sources often are more helpful than singular evaluation studies. This is because the reviews are usually written to identify broad patterns of data suggested by the amalgamation of similar intervention impact studies. Ordinarily, more confidence can be placed upon generalizations based on greater, rather than smaller, quantities of comparable data. Working generalizations from later Head Start evaluative research now seem justified, if still tentative, and can be summarized by the five statements below (Beller, 1973; Haberman, 1972; Miller, 1972; Stearns, 1971). In each case, a term such as *advantage*, *better*, or *more positive* indicates aspects of learning or development measured immediately following a special program and sometimes remeasured one or more years thereafter.

1. For most children, and especially males, any type of Head Start program seems better than none.
2. Positive gains in academic-intellectual areas, when achieved within Head Start, usually dissipate when special services are terminated and children move on to "regular" programs. Even a K–1 Follow Through experience seems desirable for maintaining gains among children from conventional Head Start classes.
3. Upon formal school entry, Head Start children generally manifest a slight advantage over their non–Head Start peers in "school socialization," which includes adjusting to classroom routines, self-care skills, sharing behavior, and following teacher directives.
4. Only in unusually well-designed and executed programs for basic skill learning is the overall rate of disadvantaged children's educational development much accelerated. (Such programs have been rare within the mainstream of Head Start.)[12]

---

[12] It is notable that in a more recent report of general, overall Head Start effects, faster rates of growth in cognitive skill development—up to twice the "normal, expected" rate—have been documented (Marshall, 1973). In a phrase, Head Start helps kids. These data, however, include those provided by the planned variation experiment.

5. Disadvantaged children who achieve and maintain cognitive advantages more generally attend schools which have a low proportion of low-income children in the overall student body.

Again, it must be stressed that evaluation studies in Head Start have more often been of global comparisons: Head Start (whatever happens) versus no Head Start. Far too little research has been conducted regarding these questions:

> Which kinds of Head Start programs are effective with particular subgroups of children? With which children are no present programs working? What programs should be tried with Head Start "failures"? What designs for differential programming and child grouping will best serve the cause of compensatory early childhood education? How shall the schools respond differently to successful graduates of Head Start programs? (Gotts, 1973, p. 415).

Planned variation, of course, is one step in the search to find answers to such questions.[13] Hence, it is appropriate to refer here, if only briefly, to the planned variation experiment within Head Start.

The Planned Variation Experiment   Earlier in our discussion we noted that the planned variation approach within Head Start could be summarized by three major program categories: the pre-academic, cognitive discovery, and discovery approaches. Evaluation of the impact of these differential program emphases involved an assessment of the extent to which models actually were implemented in a given classroom. At issue was the congruity between a written curriculum and observable evidence of its execution by staff. Preliminary results have indicated that the pre-academic programs are generally implemented most successfully, cognitive discovery programs somewhat less so, and discovery programs the least (Bissell, 1973). Further observations have revealed frequent variance between published curricula descriptions and actual practice, although in areas of basic concern (primary goal domains) to different models, the curriculum orientations are manifest in children's activities. Teachers in all three model categories, however, have been observed over time to progress toward more realistic or accurate implementation. This calls our attention to the exportability criterion for program analysis (Parker and Day, 1972) first mentioned with all its implications in Chapter 1. Interestingly, evaluation data indicate that whatever is the specific model, when good implementation is realized, its general impact on children tends to be similar to other models and in a positive direction. Specific effects do

---

[13] Another example of the attempt to come to grips with the deeper questions about Head Start is the ETS-Head Start longitudinal study. Begun in 1969–1970, this is a six-year longitudinal study involving nearly 1900 children in four different geographic regions of the United States. It differs in important ways from the more usual comparative evaluation, with some valuable implications for educational planning and individual differences. See Shipman (1973) for details.

obtain, however, and (as one might expect) follow the pattern of selective emphasis upon various objectives and activities within programs. At the risk of oversimplification, we might say that one seems to pay his money and take his choice; final analysis in program selection is largely a matter of choosing what one values most for children or thinks children will profit most by. As yet, not many educators have given serious consideration to what children value most or believe is most important. With the possible exception of open education (see Chapter 7), adults continue to call the shots for better or worse. No one can deny the right of parents to seek whatever education they think is best for their children. But one wonders how free parents are to choose among alternatives, to say nothing of the rights of children themselves.

A final matter of planned variation evaluation in Head Start concerns the conditions of successful model implementation. From the box score to date, the following factors loom as most powerful: adequate facilities and resource materials, stable and well-organized model staffs, staff satisfaction with the consultant services of model sponsors, and belief in the value of the model content (Bissell, 1973). These and other data (e.g., Klein, 1973) suggest that teacher competence and morale are the most critical aspects of any meaningful educational service delivery. In fact, there is some evidence to suggest that ratings of model implementation may reflect more than anything a rater's sense of the degree of harmony that exists among the staff at a given site; but, oddly enough, little, if any, relationship is reported between perceived extent of model implementation and measured child outcomes within the planned variation experiment generally (Marshall, 1973).

Some Broader Contributions of Head Start

It would be easy to become preoccupied with the measured cognitive or affective impact of Head Start upon children. However, this would result in a narrow view of educational and social service programs. Many concerned educators, this writer included, believe strongly in the value of less direct and specific intellectual-academic benefits from Project Head Start. In Chapter 1, for example, the reintroduction of strong parental involvement and family life education within early childhood education at large was stressed as a major outcome of the 1960s early intervention movement. It became increasingly clear during the late sixties that program success is enhanced when intervention efforts are designed to involve parents actively and to educate them (Gordon, 1970; Klaus and Gray, 1968; McCarthy, 1969; Weikart and Lambie, 1968; and Willmon, 1969). In fact, the basic thrust of Head Start now seems aimed at reaching children through their parents, rather than at attempting to perform educational magic directly and exclusively upon children. More is said about this in Chapter 8.

Meanwhile, many other important but less heralded contributions of Head Start can be identified. For example, American educators had to take a long hard look at the learning patterns and instructional problems of children who had in the past been viewed as bad risks or incapable of academic progress. Evidence of this long overdue scrutiny is the explosion in the professional literature of data on disadvantaged children. The ideal of equal educational opportunity may be realized sooner now that educators have assumed a greater responsibility for these children.

A related point is that Head Start spurred a revolution still under way in the design of learning materials most suitable for children from varied social backgrounds. While new materials are not by definition more effective, there is reason to believe that action research will validate the increased value of many of these materials.

Another significant contribution is that Head Start has facilitated the earlier identification of children whose problems or mental and physical health might otherwise go unnoticed or unattended. Through 1971, for example, 35 percent of Head Start children were found to have identifiable physical defects of some kind; medical services were helpful to 75 percent of the affected children (Zigler, 1972).

Nor should the salubrious influence of Head Start in creating new careers for professional and paraprofessional personnel be underestimated. While it would be difficult to justify this contribution purely on economic grounds, opportunities for Head Start involvement have been extended to many people, including the economically disadvantaged. The problem is, of course, that this involvement must not occur at the expense of children's psychological development. Concern for the children's welfare leads to the issue of training procedures which guarantee quality staffing within various programs. Many of the disappointing early returns from Head Start research may very well have been due to "faculties" unprepared to deal with the complexities of compensatory education problems. Eventually, a career development and training program was initiated to involve Head Start, community action agencies, and institutions of higher learning. Its general intent—to provide longer-term training and career advantages for Head Start workers—has reportedly been realized in terms of improved Head Start staffing and expanded opportunities for self-development among adults. According to Zigler (1972), over 9000 persons from low-income and ethnic minority backgrounds have received college training as a result of their Head Start involvement. This training program—coupled with refined program performance standards and procedures for monitoring all phases of Head Start practice—has helped to affect positively the entire experimental enterprise. This is not to say that practice has made perfect; staffing problems are still crucial in many areas. Monitoring reports indicate a wide range of quality from good to poor in Head Start centers across the United States (Zigler, 1972).

A final contribution of Head Start is the extent to which community institutions have changed directly in response to Head Start practices or indirectly as a function of the project's presence in a given locale. One important survey, known as the Kirschner report (Kirschner Associates, Inc., 1970), has revealed at least four kinds of change in association with

Head Start: (1) greater involvement of the poor in making decisions about institutional policies that affect them; (2) greater employment opportunities within the public schools at the paraprofessional level; (3) increased emphasis upon the educational needs of poverty and minority groups; and (4) more adequate health services for the poor. These changes seem to be more pronounced in communities with Head Start centers than in communities without them. Marked differences in community attitudes and services have been observed, however, and much remains to be done before community leaders become more reliably responsive to their constituencies, especially the disenfranchised poor.

To conclude, it can be said that lessons from the birth and development of Head Start have been both invaluable and bittersweet. We have much to be encouraged about, but many problems and issues have to be worked out, particularly in evaluation. Overall, this writer believes that Head Start is among the most significant educational and social experiments in American history. Hopefully, it will remain a zestful experiment and not become a new orthodoxy or an overly encumbered, creaky, and unresponsive instrument of self-serving bureaucrats. As Zigler (1973) suggests, the continued vigor of Head Start will require many things, including more realistic expectations about educational intervention, a renewed commitment to broad social competence among children, and increased grass-roots participation in community service programs. To this list can be added the criterion of explicit accountability to consumers by representatives of federal, state, and local government officials, whose fiscal and political clout is a reckoning force in compensatory education programs.

A DEVELOPMENTAL-INTERACTION VIEWPOINT

One way to summarize the gradual blending of historical and contemporary thought about early childhood education in the mainstream is by an overview of the developmental-interaction viewpoint (Biber, Shapiro, and Wickens, 1971). Developmental interaction is most clearly linked to an evolution of educational thought over some fifty years at the Bank Street College of Education in New York City; but it can be generalized to much conventional practice. This viewpoint also has much in common with the forthcoming discussion of open education (Chapter 7) and Piagetian influences (Chapter 5) for at least two reasons: (1) an agreement that active interaction with the physical and social environment is the primary source of children's learning and (2) a consensus that development involves a stage-based reorganization of cognitive structures (Shapiro and Biber, 1972). But for Bank Street theoreticians, the developmental-interaction viewpoint also differs from a purist Piagetian perspective on two accounts. First, Bank Street theory gives more attention to characterizing and articulating a child's learning environment, with less concern for a theoretical accounting of children's response patterns and internal modes of cognitive organization. Second, Bank Street leaders seem more resolute about the interactive (rather than parallel) functions of cognitive and affective development. With this in mind, the term *developmental inter-action* is defined as follows:

> Developmental refers to the emphasis on identifiable patterns of growth and modes of perceiving and responding which are character-ized by increasing differentiation and progressive integration as a function of chronological age. Interaction refers, first, to the emphasis on the child's interaction with the environment—adults, other children, and the material world—and second, to the interaction between cognitive and affective spheres of development. The developmental-interaction formulation stresses the nature of the environment as much as it does the patterns of the responding child (Shapiro and Biber, 1972, pp. 59–60).

From this definition has been elaborated a set of profound, variously abstruse principles upon which the Bank Street educational program is based. Actually, the principles themselves (see Biber, Shapiro, and Wickens, 1971) are the result of a mixture of theoretical nutrients ranging from developmental psychology (Piaget, 1952; Werner, 1957) gestalt psy-chology (Wertheimer, 1959), developmental accounts of ego processes (Erikson, 1963; Freud, 1950; Rapaport, 1960), and educational psychology and philosophy (Dewey, 1963). In final form, this mixture is the yeast for an educational program focused on process. This means "providing the experiences that make it possible for children to try out, shift backward as well as forward, to create where necessary the opportunities for the kind of interaction that is essential for the assimilation of experience, the achievement of new integrations, and the resolution of conflict—in both the cognitive and emotional realms" (Shapiro and Biber, 1972, p. 68).

Goals for Education

This process orientation conceives of the school as a place to foster children's psychological development in the broadest possible sense. *Ego strength* (the child's ability to deal effectively with his environment); *autonomy* (including a sense of true individuality, creativity, and an ex-perimental attitude); and the *integration of thought, feeling, and action* (including self-understanding and empathy with others) are aims of the program. The goal of fostering psychological development can be broken down into several interrelated and general goals for education across the span of the preschool and elementary years (see Shapiro and Biber, 1972, pp. 62–63, for an example).

For early childhood in particular the idea of achieving a positive self-image as a learner and a sense of self-direction in learning is central to classroom practice. More specific objectives for individual children gener-ally are not predetermined, at least in theory. Rather, they evolve on the basis of a thorough and continuous analysis of each child's progress. Accordingly, varying methods of instruction also evolve. This requires that a teacher have command of a varied repertoire of teaching strategies from which to choose as the individual situation dictates. No system of extrinsic rewards for children's achievement is proposed; rather, motivation is seen to spring from the satisfactions of learning.

The Learning Environment

The process orientation cited above also provides a rationale for the design of a developmental-interaction educational environment. Again, the most important component is the teacher, whose job is to create a healthy climate for learning and to respond positively to the needs of children. Other environmental requirements are flexible arrangement of classroom equipment, a large variety of materials for learning, a rational system of controls built upon positive motivation and effective classroom management (rather than on power assertion and rules), a teacher-child relationship of mutual trust, an interweaving of work and play (particularly socio-dramatic and symbolic play), and a functional relationship between home and school. The latter refers to constructive teacher-parent interchange and to school experiences for children which are couched in the realities of life outside the classroom. Cognitive skills, for example, are thought to develop best within a context of "total life experience." For Bank Streeters, attempts to teach cognitive (and language) skills separately from such experiences constitute an unnatural instructional policy. Among other things, this means that a teacher must know the broader socio-cultural context for learning as well as each child's family situation.

Other aspects of Bank Street technique include (1) conventional language stimulation activities (reading to children, discussing books and pictures) and (2) an organization of springboard activities around central themes beginning with personal concrete experiences (cooking, pet, and plant care) and extending to broader community matters (food marketing, traffic control, sanitation). A transition from nondirective to directive teaching may occur, depending upon a teacher's evaluation of a child's current needs and interests; the approach in general, however, is unstructured.

Moreover, apart from minimum resource requirements, no one set or type of learning materials is advocated. As Gilkeson (1969) states, successful implementation of Bank Street technique assumes (depends upon) a "high level of autonomous professional judgment" among instructional personnel. To assist this judgment, certain basic materials are available: The *Bank Street Readers* (primers through grade three with a strong inner-city orientation), special language stimulation materials, and discovery learning materials. Cuisenaire Rods and the Nuffield Series materials (John Wiley and Sons) are recommended for mathematics. Teachers are encouraged to create their own materials and are free to select from among other commercially available materials according to their unique learning program. In fact, a set of *Early Childhood Discovery Materials* have been prepared at Bank Street College and are now published by Crowell-Collier-Macmillan.

It is notable that the developmental-interaction viewpoint is manifest in a Follow Through model that has served over a dozen school districts in the United States. For this purpose, five basic objectives for children have been established:

To develop a facility with abstract symbols (numbers and letters)
To develop thinking processes
To develop ordering processes such as understanding of variations in sizes, amounts, and conditions
To develop a sense of time
To develop a sense of change as it occurs in both natural and man-made forms in the immediate and larger environment

Compensatory measures are not a part of the model; educational goals for all children are the same, irrespective of cultural identity or social class. However, the Follow Through program sponsor, Elizabeth Gilkeson, maintains that disadvantaged children usually need first to "trust the predictability of the school environment and to learn the effects of their own actions within it before they are able to persist at and profit by their work" (Gilkeson, 1969, p. 10). If so, a heavy responsibility is placed upon the teacher, who must ensure a predictable environment and arrange for ample feedback to children regarding the consequences of their actions.

The developmental-interaction approach to early education places a high priority on the development of a positive attitude about learning within a flexible and varied format of child-centered activities. Photo by Peter Rinearson.

In summary, Bank Street teaching is the "disciplined practice of differentiation and particularization" (Gilkeson, 1969): a teacher, fully grounded in child development theory and subject matter, adapts the instructional process to individual children's needs. Adaption occurs through a combination of teacher assessments, mutual planning with parents, and hypothesis testing. The "essential core" of a preschool program in the Bank Street view is *support-guided play* (Biber and Franklin, 1967). Such play is based upon the principle of active exploration in a nurturant, safe, varied environment and the assumption of growth stages in the direction of increased differentiation and hierarchical integration. Instability in young children's behavior is interpreted as a function of conflict between impulse and reality demands. A tolerant acceptance by the teacher and the avoidance of pressure on children are seen as necessary conditions for constructive teacher-child relationships. Play and freedom to experiment provide the media through which skills such as categorizing, information gathering, and problem solving are thought to develop. Cooperative group projects are also conceived and built through play. Desired outcomes at Bank Street include an expansion of every child's world; a sensitization to and differentiation of sensory experience; the expression of fantasy and an understanding of reality; and improved ability to deal with social crises, felt problems, and frustrations (Minuchin and Biber, 1968). Bank Street philosophy and goals are considered appropriate for all children. Marked departures are not advised for disadvantaged children, except that the importance of a stable, predictable environment is stressed even more for them.

Evaluation

Evaluation of the developmental-interaction approach to early education relies heavily upon the data of direct observation; a much lighter emphasis is placed on the formal testing of skills and achievement. At Bank Street, in particular, a philosophy based upon the idea of progressive revision prevails. Evaluation is a process of analyzing observable changes in children, the curriculum, and the climate for learning in the service of continued improvement. For this purpose, two classes of techniques, or diagnostic tools, are utilized. One class involves systematic, highly differentiated observational techniques. A Child Behavior Observation form used at Bank Street, for example, covers six broad categories for data gathering in both formal and informal contexts for learning (including transitions and routines): the child gives information, explores and questions, uses representations and symbols, demonstrates self-awareness, demonstrates awareness of others and social reponsibility, and demonstrates autonomy. Program success, then, would be judged partly in terms of the extent to which children consistently behave satisfactorily along these and other lines which vary from time to time depending upon the situation. It is assumed that behavior patterns observed in the classroom will generalize to life outside the classroom.

The second class of techniques is comprised of various instruments to promote self-study among teachers, project staff members, and even parents. These take the form of sundry rating scales, checklists, and interview schedules that are still undergoing development. One, a "teacher assessment scale," is designed to promote teacher self-diagnosis periodically during a given school year. Another, the "analysis of communication in education," is an observational system for the purpose of gathering data about teacher-child and child-child classroom interaction patterns.

Taken together, these two classes of diagnostic tools evince a high priority for formative evaluation among educators with a developmental-interaction bent. A concern for process variables and faith in the judgmental abilities of internal staff members are basic to such evaluation. For summative evaluation data, standardized tests may be administered to children, but they are interpreted with utmost caution. At Bank Street, for instance, the Metropolitan Test Battery, the Screening Test for Academic Readiness, and the Spache Diagnostic Reading Test may be used. Collective summative evaluation data taken in Project Follow Through classrooms based on the Bank Street model are said to indicate consistently favorable progress as determined by degree of congruence with program objectives.

Actual data from Bank Street program evaluations are rarely available for public inspection. Thus, it is not possible for this writer to say much about the overall impact on children of a Bank Street version of developmental-interaction education. Certainly Bank Street personnel believe in what they do, and the approach has consistently appealed to large numbers of early childhood educators across the country. Relative weaknesses in empirical verification seem not to have detracted substantially from Bank Street's leadership role in early education. But this is not to say that Bank Street is without its distractors. This writer, for example, has heard classrooms in the Bank Street mold criticized for their "mystical qualities" and for being essentially "armchair operations." What motivates such criticism is a conjectural matter. The point is that each student of early childhood education should weigh carefully all alternative program models and arrive at an independent judgment based upon systematic critical analysis.

As indicated in Chapter 1, the method of conceptual analysis often can supplement, and under some circumstances substitute for, the method of empirical verification in program evaluation. Conceptual analyses of the child development or developmental-interaction approach have appeared in the literature. R. Mayer (1971), for example, has made comparative statements about interaction patterns, sequencing grouping, and verbal content variations among certain approaches to early education. As compared to a verbal-didactic model (DISTAR, Chapter 4), for instance, the child development model has much more child-child and child-materials interaction and significantly less teacher-child interaction, especially of the drill and recitation type. The point is that where type and quantity of interactions are valued, judgments about the appropriateness of a given model can be made accordingly. It is more difficult to state much about the quality of interactions without actual classroom observation.

Finally, the Parker and Day (1972) criteria for conceptual analysis can be applied to the developmental-interaction approach. According to the literature, the Bank Street curriculum is strongly influenced by formal child development theory, although a combination of theories prevails. The influence of empirical research literature on curriculum development at Bank Street is less clear. Goals and objectives, while generally broad in scope, are not consistently operationalized for precise measurement. On the other hand, a process orientation is clearly favored over an emphasis upon content skills and knowledge. Grouping of small numbers of children is very flexible, as are the arrangement of materials and strategies for sequencing the activities for learning. Other aspects of implementation—structure and parent participation—are comparatively low and moderate, respectively. The Bank Street approach would seem to be very high in its attempt to initiate and sustain motivation on intrinsic (versus extrinsic) grounds. The approach is certainly challenging and potentially rewarding to teachers in view of the nuclear role they must fulfill if the approach is to succeed. As for Parker and Day's fifth criterion, exportability, it seems to this writer that Bank Street must depend upon the selection and training of master teachers rather than upon a curriculum that is easily communicated and interpreted by adherents to this approach.

SUMMARY

Mainstream early childhood education in America has been described in this chapter in terms of evolutionary kindergarten and nursery school practices. Several themes have dominated these practices, including the ethic of social reform, child-centered schooling, and early childhood as a critical period for socioemotional development. Over time, a consensual kindergarten curriculum has taken shape—one heavily invested with creative activity, language stimulation, and general "school readiness" activities. Even so, variety in kindergarten curriculum patterns is commonplace, with specifics usually determined at the local school level and heavily dependent upon individual teachers. More recently, prepackaged programs, or kindergarten curriculum "models," have included a stronger prescriptive component of scholastic activities. Evaluation studies of kindergarten practice, although usually of a gross nature, seem at most to support the general purposes of the kindergarten and at least to call for a periodical reexamination of the longer-term impact of kindergarten upon children's development. Kindergarten practice also provides a medium within which to examine many basic issues in early childhood education—goals, content, methodology, and personnel matters—along with a number of specific policy issues, including admission guidelines, screening and early identification of learning problems, and grouping practices.

Much that can be said about the kindergarten applies also to

American nursery school practices. In personnel training, certification, and program content, for example, the issues that pervade nursery school education are even more intense than at the kindergarten level. The role and functions of fantasy play, in particular, have been a continual source of debate within the nursery school literature.

From the general body of educational and psychological thought about kindergarten and nursery school education, the conceptual superstructure for Project Head Start was largely developed. This massive and complex social experiment was first begun in 1965 and has since been a source of continuing controversy. Yet gradually, and despite early and severe challenges of its worth, Project Head Start has earned a place in this nation's mainstream of early childhood education. Among the contributions of this program are a vastly expanded research data base about children of poverty, the development and implementation of educational alternatives for such children (planned variation), and the provision of numerous other personal-social services at the broader community level.

Chapter 2 was concluded with a discussion of the developmental-interaction viewpoint in early education. This viewpoint represents a blend of traditional and contemporary thinking about the soundest way to approach young children for the purpose of fostering their total psychological development. Emphasis is placed upon the child's self-image and his self-direction in learning. The details of curriculum implementation require considerable teacher skill, including a continual assessment (albeit informal) of individual children's learning styles, interests, and problems. Both a preschool and a Project Follow Through model based upon the developmental-interaction viewpoint have been established at the Bank Street College of Education in New York City. Support-guided play is the core of the preschool program; a broad mixture of general cognitive-affective goals serves to shape the course of education at the kindergarten-primary level. Until more definitive evaluation occurs, little can be said about the overall impact of the Bank Street approach upon children's educational development. In the meantime, the method of conceptual analysis provides some basis for an assessment of this viewpoint. Finally, the strengths and weaknesses of the developmental-interaction approach rest in procedures for the selection, training, and continued education of master teachers.

REFERENCES

Almy, M. Spontaneous play: an avenue for intellectual development. *Bulletin of the Institute for Child Study*, 1966, *28*, No. 2.

Ames, L., and F. Ilg. *School readiness.* New York: Harper & Row, 1965.

Austin, G., B. Rogers, and H. Walbesser, Jr. The effectiveness of summer compensatory education: a review of the research. *Review of Educational Research,* 1972, *42*, 171–181.

Baker, G. The effectiveness of nursery school on affective and conceptual development of disadvantaged and nondisadvantaged children. *Developmental Psychology*, 1973, *9*, 140.

Beller, E. Research on organized programs of early education. In R. Travers (ed.), *Second handbook of research on teaching*. Skokie, Ill.: Rand McNally, 1973, 530–600.

Bereiter, C., and S. Engelmann. *Teaching the culturally disadvantaged child in the preschool*. Englewood Cliffs, N.J.: Prentice-Hall, 1966.

Biber, B., and M. Franklin. The relevance of developmental and psychodynamic concepts to the education of the preschool child. *Journal of the Academy of Child Psychiatry*, 1967, *6*, 5–24.

Biber, B., E. Shapiro, and D. Wickens. *Promoting cognitive growth: a developmental-interaction point of view*. Washington, D.C.: National Association for the Education of Young Children, 1971.

Bissell, J. Planned variation in Head Start and Follow Through. In J. Stanley (ed.), *Compensatory education for children, ages 2 to 8*. Baltimore: The Johns Hopkins Press, 1973, 63–108.

Blow, S. *Educational issues in the kindergarten*. New York: Appleton, 1904.

Boger, R. (chrmn.). Development of early childhood curriculum modules by the member centers of the National Institute for Research in Early Childhood. Symposium, presented at the meeting of the American Educational Research Association, New York, February, 1971.

Branche, C., and N. Overly. Illustrative descriptions of two early childhood education programs. *Educational Leadership*, 1971, *28*, 821–826.

Bricker, W., and L. Lovell. What research says about the advantages of the kindergarten. Eugene, Ore.: Eugene Committee for Preschool Education, 1965.

Cazden, C. Subcultural differences in child language. *Merrill-Palmer Quarterly*, 1966, *12*, 185–219.

Chall, J. *Learning to read: the great debate*. New York: McGraw-Hill, 1967.

Chow, S., and P. Elmore. *Early childhood education information unit: resource manual and program descriptions*. San Francisco: Far West Laboratory for Education Research and Development, 1973.

Cicirelli, V., et al. *The impact of Head Start. An evaluation of the effects of Head Start on children's cognitive and affective development*. Report to the U.S. Office of Economic Opportunity by Westinghouse Learning Corporation and Ohio University, Washington, D.C.: Government Printing Office, 1969.

Cicirelli, V., J. Evans, and J. Schiller. The impact of Head Start: a reply to the report analysis. *Harvard Educational Review*, 1970, *40*, 105–129.

Conway, C. A study of the public and private kindergarten and nonkindergarten children in the primary grades. *ERIC: ED 028 837*, 1968.

Cowles, M. Four views of learning and development. *Educational Leadership*, 1971, *28*, 790–795.

Davis, D. *Patterns of primary education*. New York: Harper & Row, 1963.

Davis, D., M. Davis, and R. Hansen. *Playway*. Minneapolis: Winston Press, 1973.

de Hirsch, K., J. Jansky, and W. Langford. *Predicting reading failure*. New York: Harper & Row, 1966.

Deutsch, M. Facilitating development in the preschool child: social and psychological perspectives. *Merrill-Palmer Quarterly*, 1964, *10*, 249–264.

Dewey, J. *Experience and education*. New York: Crowell-Collier-Macmillan, 1963 (originally published in 1938).

Dickie, J., and J. Bagur. Considerations for the study of language in young, low income minority group children. *Merrill-Palmer Quarterly*, 1972, *18*, 53–58.

Dobbin, J. Strategies and innovations demonstrated in Project Head Start. *Journal of School Psychology*, 1966, *4*, 9–14.

Durkin, D. *Children who read early.* New York: Teachers College, 1966.

Early childhood discovery materials. New York: Crowell-Collier and Macmillan, 1973.

Engstrom, G. (ed.). *Play: the child strives toward self-realization.* Washington, D.C.: National Association for the Education of Young Children, 1971.

Erikson, E. *Childhood and society.* (2nd ed.) New York: Norton, 1963.

Farwell, D. The nursery school program. In J. Leavitt (ed.), *Nursery-kindergarten education.* New York: McGraw-Hill, 1958, 51–94.

Freud, S. *The ego and the id.* London: Hogarth, 1950.

Foster, J., and N. Headley. *Education in the kindergarten.* (4th ed.) New York: American Book, 1966.

Frank, L. The beginnings of child development and family life education in the 20th century. *Merrill-Palmer Quarterly*, 1962, *8*, 207–227.

Fuller, E. *What research says to the teacher about the kindergarten.* Washington, D.C.: National Education Association, 1961.

Getzels, J. Preschool education. *Teachers College Record*, 1966, *68*, 219–228.

Gilkeson, E. *Bank Street approach to Follow Through.* New York: Bank Street College of Education, 1969.

Ginsburg, H. *The myth of the deprived child.* Englewood Cliffs, N.J.: Prentice-Hall, 1972.

Gordon, I. J. *Parent involvement in compensatory education.* Urbana, Ill.: ERIC Clearinghouse on Early Childhood Education, 1970.

Gorton, H., and R. Robinson. For better results—a full day kindergarten. *Education*, 1969, *89*, 217–221.

Gotts, E. Head Start research, development, and evaluation. In J. Frost (ed.), *Revisiting early childhood education.* New York: Holt, Rinehart and Winston, 1973, 409–420.

Gray, S., and J. Miller. Early experience in relation to cognitive development. *Review of Educational Research*, 1967, *37*, 475–493.

Green, M., and E. Woods. *A nursery school handbook for teachers and parents.* Sierra Madre, Calif.: Sierra Madre Community Nursery School Association, 1965.

Grotberg, E. *Review of research: 1965–1969.* Washington, D.C.: Project Head Start, U.S. Office of Economic Opportunity, 1969.

Haberman, M. Compensatory education: implications for teacher education. *ERIC: ED 066 435*, 1972.

Harris, B., and R. Fischer. Distortions in the kindergarten. *Young Children*, 1969, *24*, 279–284.

Headley, N. *The kindergarten: its place in the program of education.* New York: Center for Applied Research in Education, 1965.

Hellmuth, J. (ed.). *The disadvantaged child: vol. I.* Seattle: Special Child Publications, 1967.

Herron, R., and B. Sutton-Smith. *Child's play.* New York: Wiley, 1971.

Humphrey, J. An exploratory study of active games in learning of number concepts by first grade boys and girls. *Perceptual Motor Skills*, 1966, *23*, 341–342.

Jablonsky, A. Status report on compensatory education. *IRCD Bulletin*, 1971, 7, 1–21.

Jacobsen, L., et al. Effects of age, sex, systematic conceptual learning, acquisition of learning sets, and programmed social interaction on the intellectual and conceptual development of preschool children from poverty backgrounds. *Child Development*, 1971, *42*, 1399–1415.

Jencks, C., et al. *Inequality: a reassessment of the effect of family and schooling in America.* New York: Basic Books, 1972.

Jensen, A. Social class, race, and genetics: implications for education. *American Educational Research Journal*, 1968, *5*, 1–42.

Jensen, A. How much can we boost IQ and school achievement? *Harvard Educational Review*, 1969, *39*, 1–123.

Jones, D. A feasible plan for continuous admission. *Education*, 1969, *89*, 195–202.

Karnes, M., et al. An evaluation of two preschool programs for disadvantaged children: a traditional and a highly structured experímental approach. *Exceptional Children*, 1968, May, 667–676.

Katz, L. Teaching in preschools: roles and goals. *Children*, 1970, *17*, 43–48.

Klaus, R., and S. Gray. The early training project for disadvantaged children: a report after five years. *Monographs of the Society for Research in Child Development*, 1968, *53*, Serial No. 120.

Kirschner Associates, Inc. *A national survey of the impacts of Head Start centers on community institutions: summary report.* Report No. B89-4638. Washington, D.C.: Government Printing Office, 1970.

Klein, J. Making or breaking it: the teacher's role in model (curriculum) implementation. *Young Children*, 1973, *28*, 359–365.

Kohlberg, L. Early education: a cognitive-developmental view. *Child Development*, 1968, *39*, 1013–1062.

LaCoste, R. (ed.). *Early childhood series with focus on kindergarten.* Olympia, Wash.: Office of the State Superintendent of Public Instruction, 1971.

Law, N., et al. *Basic propositions for early childhood education.* Washington, D.C.: Association for Childhood Education International, 1966.

Lazerson, M. The historical antecedents of early childhood education. In I. J. Gordon (ed.), *Early childhood education*. Chicago: University of Chicago Press, 1972, 33–54.

Leeper, S., R. Dales, D. Skipper, and R. Witherspoon. *Good schools for young children.* (2nd ed.) New York: Crowell-Collier-Macmillan, 1968.

Madow, W. Head Start: methodological critique. In D. Hays (ed.), *Britannica Review of American Education*. Vol. 1. Chicago: Encyclopedia Britannica, Inc., 1969, 245–252.

Mager, R. *Developing positive attitude toward learning.* Palo Alto, Calif.: Fearon Press, 1969.

Marshall, M. Paper read at the meeting of the National Association for the Education of Young Children, Seattle, November, 1973.

Marshall, M., and P. Bentler. IQ increases of disadvantaged minority group children following an innovative enrichment program. *Psychological Reports*, 1971, *29*, 805–806.

Mayer, F. *A history of educational thought.* Columbus, Ohio: Merrill, 1960.

Mayer, R. A comparative analysis of preschool curriculum models. In R. Anderson and H. Shane (eds.), *As the twig is bent: readings in early childhood education*. Boston: Houghton Mifflin, 1971, 286–314.

McCandless, B. Should a bright child start to school before he's five? *Education*, 1957, 77, 1–6.

McCarthy, J. Changing parent attitudes and improving language and intellectual abilities of culturally disadvantaged four-year-old children through parent involvement. *Contemporary Education*, 1969, *40*, 166–168.

McDavid, J. Head Start's lesson for educational research: can we profit from experience? *Educational Perspectives*, 1970, *9*, 2–6.

McNeil, J., and W. Popham. The assessment of teacher competence. In R. Travers (ed.), *Second handbook of research on teaching*. Skokie, Ill.: Rand McNally, 1973, 218–244.

Meichanbaum, D., and L. Turk. Implications of research on disadvantaged children and cognitive training programs for educational television: ways of improving Sesame Street. *Journal of Special Education*, 1972, *6*, 27–42.

Miller, L. Experimental variations of Head Start curricula. Louisville, Ky.: University of Louisville, Department of Psychology, 1972.

Minuchin, P., and B. Biber. A child development approach to language in the preschool disadvantaged child. *Monographs of the Society for Research in Child Development*, 1968, *33*, Serial No. 124, 10–18.

Moore, O., and A. Anderson. Some principles for the design of clarifying educational environments. In D. Goslin (ed.), *Handbook of socialization theory and research*. Skokie, Ill.: Rand McNally, 1969, 571–613.

Moore, R., and D. Moore. The dangers of early schooling. *Harper's*, 1972, *245*, 58–62.

Moore, R. D. Language research and preschool language training. In C. Lavatelli (ed.), *Language training in early childhood education*. Urbana, Ill.: University of Illinois Press, 1971, 3–48.

Nehrt, R., and G. Hurd. *Preprimary enrollment of children under six: October, 1968*. Washington, D.C.: U.S. Office of Education, 1969.

Nuffield mathematics project. Published for the Nuffield Foundation, England, by John Wiley & Sons, 1967, 1968, 1969, 1970. (series)

Open Court. *An introduction to the Open Court kindergarten program*. La Salle, Ill.: Open Court, 1970.

Parker, R., and M. Day. Comparisons of preschool curricula. In R. Parker (ed.), *The preschool in action*. Boston: Allyn and Bacon, 1972, 466–508.

Phi Delta Kappan. Special issue on competency/performance-based teacher education, 1974, *55* (5), 290–343.

Piaget, J. *The origins of intelligence in children*. New York: International Universities, 1952.

Pitcher, E., and L. Ames. *The guidance nursery school*. New York: Harper & Row, 1964.

Pratcher, M. *Teaching in the kindergarten*. New York: Exposition Press, 1968.

Project head start daily program III. Pamphlet No. 11. Washington, D.C.: Department of Health, Education, and Welfare, 1967.

Rapaport, D. Psychoanalysis as a developmental psychology. In B. Kaplan and S. Wapner (eds.), *Perspectives in psychological theory*. New York: International Universities, 1960.

Ream, M. *Nursery school education, 1966–67*. Washington, D.C.: Research Division, National Education Association, 1968.

Ream, M. *Kindergarten education in public schools, 1967–68*. Washington, D.C.: Research Division, National Education Association, 1969.

Robison, H. The decline of play in urban kindergartens. *Young Children*, 1971, *26*, 333–341.

Robison, H., and B. Spodek. New directions in the kindergarten. New York: Teachers College, 1965.

Rogolsky, M. Screening kindergarten children: a review and recommendation. *Journal of School Psychology*, 1969, *7* (2), 18–27.

Schloss, S. *Nursery-kindergarten enrollment of children under six: October, 1966*. Washington, D.C.: U.S. Department of Health, Education and Welfare, 1967.

Sears, P., and E. Dowley. Research on teaching in the nursery school. In N. Gage (ed.), *Handbook of research on teaching*. Skokie, Ill.: Rand McNally, 1963, 814–864.

Shapiro, E., and B. Biber. The education of young children: a developmental-interaction approach. *Teachers College Record*, 1972, *74*, 55–79.

Shipman, V. Disadvantaged children and their first school experiences, ETS Head Start longitudinal study. In J. Stanley (ed.), *Compensatory education for children, ages 2 to 8*. Baltimore: The Johns Hopkins Press, 1973, 145–195.

Sigel, I. Developmental considerations of the nursery school experience. In P. Neubauer (ed.), *Concepts of development in early childhood education*. Springfield, Ill.: Charles C Thomas, 1965, 84–111.

Smilansky, S. Can adults facilitate play in children? Theoretical and practical considerations. In Engstrom, G. (ed.), *Play: the child strives toward self-realization*. Washington, D.C.: National Association for the Education of Young Children, 1971, 39–50.

Smith, M., and J. Bissell. Report analysis: the impact of Head Start. *Harvard Educational Review*, 1970, *40*, 51–104.

Spodek, B. Constructing a model for a teacher education program in early childhood education. *Contemporary Education*, 1969, *40*, 145–149.

Stearns, M. Report on preschool programs: the effects of preschool programs on disadvantaged children and their families. Washington, D.C.: Office of Child Development, U.S. Department of Health, Education, and Welfare, 1971.

Stephens, J. *The process of schooling*. New York: Holt, Rinehart and Winston, 1967.

Stodolsky, S., and G. Lesser. Learning patterns in the disadvantaged. *Harvard Educational Review*, 1967, *37*, 546–593.

Sutton-Smith, B. The role of play in cognitive development. In W. Hartup and N. Smothergill (eds.), *The young child*. Washington, D.C.: National Association for the Education of Young Children, 1967, 96–108.

Swift, J. Effects of early group experience: the nursery school and day nursery. In M. Hoffman and L. Hoffman (eds.), *Review of child development research*. Vol. 1. New York: Russell Sage, 1964, 249–288.

Thompson, G. The social and emotional development of preschool children under two types of educational programs. *Psychological Monographs*, 1944, Whole No. 528.

Torrance, E. Small group behavior of 5-year-old children under 3 kinds of educational stimulation. *Journal of Experimental Education*, 1970, *38*, 79–82.

Torrance, E. Influence of alternate approaches to pre-primary educational stimulation and question-asking skills. *Journal of Educational Research*, 1972, *65*, 204–206.

Tulkin, S. An analysis of the concept of cultural deprivation. *Developmental Psychology*, 1972, *6*, 326–339.

Vane, J., and W. Davis. Factors related to the effectiveness of preschool programs with disadvantaged children. *Journal of Educational Research*, 1971, *64*, 297–299.

Wattenberg, W. Review of trends. In W. W. Wattenberg (ed.), *Social deviancy among youth*. Chicago: University of Chicago Press, 1966, 4–27.

Weber, E. *The kindergarten: its encounter with educational thought in America*. New York: Teachers College, 1969.

Weikart, D. A traditional nursery revisited. In R. Parker (ed.), *The preschool in action*. Boston: Allyn and Bacon, 1972, 189–215.

Weikart, D., and D. Lambie. Preschool intervention through a home teaching program. In J. Hellmuth (ed.), *Disadvantaged child.* Vol. 2. Seattle: Special Child Publications, 1968, 437–500.

Werner, H. The concept of development from a comparative and organismic point of view. In D. Harris (ed.), *The concept of development.* Minneapolis: University of Minnesota Press, 1957.

Wertheimer, M. *Productive thinking.* (rev. ed.) New York: Harper & Row, 1959.

Westman, J., D. Rice, and E. Bermann. Nursery school behavior and later school adjustment. *American Journal of Orthopsychiatry,* 1967, *37*, 725–731.

Williams, W., and J. Evans. The politics of evaluation: the case of Head Start. In P. Rossi and W. Williams (eds.), *Evaluating social programs.* New York: Seminar Press, 1972, 247–264.

Willmon, B. Parent participation as a factor in the effectiveness of Head Start programs. *Journal of Educational Research,* 1969, *62*, 406–410.

World Organization for Early Childhood Education. *The preparation and status of preschool teachers.* Oslo, Norway: World Organization for Early Childhood Education, 1966.

Young Children, 1973, *28*, p. 288.

Zigler, E. Child care in the seventies. *Inequality in Education,* 1972, *13*, 17–28.

Zigler, E. Project Head Start: success or failure? *Learning,* 1973, *1*, 43–47.

Photo courtesy of Camera Craft, Seattle, Washington.

chapter

3

behavior
analysis
procedures

All educational strategies are designed to modify behavior in desired ways. This is true whether one seeks a gross objective such as "positive growth and adjustment" or a specific one such as "the ability to discriminate visually the letters of the alphabet." Where objectives are sought, behavioral change is implied. Since behavior never occurs in a vacuum, that is, it always occurs in an environmental context, an educator must attend to the characteristics of the environment which influence behavior. This chapter is concerned with environmental influences which affect the rate at which a learner progresses en route to a given objective. It is the systematic study and manipulation of such influences which characterizes a behavioral analysis approach to teaching and learning. This viewpoint provides a sharp contrast to the generally looser developmental-interaction approach to education discussed in the previous chapter.

Most generally, behavior analysis involves the application of principles and procedures for behavior modification where environmental conditions and events are systematically arranged in specific temporal relationships with specific behavior. These principles and procedures, independent of any subject matter content, have been developed through a system for the measurement of behavior change. This measurement system is designed to enable a teacher to identify environmental events which influence the acquisition, maintenance, strengthening, or disappearance of various types of responses or response patterns. This chapter explains behavior analysis principles and how they can be applied to the behavior of young children. Representative research data obtained through such application are also presented. This chapter concludes with an examination of some major issues associated with reinforcement principles and practices. In order to assist the reader toward an understanding of these principles, the conceptual system from which behavioral analysis procedures have been derived will first be described.

THE SYSTEM: BASIC CONCEPTS

Respondent and Operant Behavior

The technical system which encompasses principles of behavior analysis was born of laboratory experimentation in operant conditioning by B. F. Skinner (1938). Within the framework of associationistic S-R (stimulus-response) approaches to learning, Skinner early distinguished two classes of behavior: *respondent* and *operant*.[1] Respondent behavior is elicited unconditionally by some known and observable stimulus. For example, a strategically placed hammer blow immediately below one's kneecap results in the familiar knee jerk response—one's knee *responds* to the hammer blow stimulus. Respondent behavior is basically reflex behavior. It involves responses over which voluntary control is highly improbable.

In contrast, *operant* behavior is volitional. Instead of being elicited predictably by some known stimulus, an operant response is emitted voluntarily, presumably to produce some effect on the environment. In other words, one operates intentionally on the environment to effect some change or result. Consider a child who asks his mother for a nickel. His asking behavior (verbalization of request) represents an operant response. So would any further act he performed using the nickel, such as buying a candy bar. If the child is successful, that is, if he receives the nickel after asking, he has produced a change in his environment.

Unlike respondent behavior, operant behavior is not necessarily associated with a known antecedent stimulus. Rather, it is influenced by the consequences which follow the behavior. Operant behaviors do, however, usually become associated with an antecedent stimulus condition. When this occurs, the antecedent establishes the occasion for an operant response to occur. As such, the antecedent becomes the *cue* for the emission of an operant response; the antecedent does not elicit a response in the same sense as a hammer blow elicits a knee jerk.

---

[1] A third class, involving an overlap or interaction between operant and respondent behavior, has also been identified. This class will not be treated in this brief chapter. And, since most classroom behavior with which teachers deal is primarily operant, neither will the intricacies of respondent conditioning be examined here.

In the above example, consider that the child asks for a nickel only when he is near a candy machine. This suggests that the candy machine has taken on antecedent-cueing properties, i.e., the machine's presence is necessary to establish the occasion for nickel-asking behavior. The observed relationships between the cue (candy machine) and the response (nickel asking) would signal the development of a *discriminated operant* response. In other words, the child now makes a predictable response in the presence of a specific stimulus. This is due to his history of reinforcement—receiving a nickel—for making that specific response in the presence of that stimulus. It should be noted, however, that operant conditioning is concerned basically with providing a reinforcer after a response has occurred. A cue-response connection is not at issue; rather, it is the response per se which is strengthened by reinforcement. A legitimate description of operant conditioning can be made quite apart from the specifying stimuli which precede a response. Despite this methodological point, the essence of a teacher's job is the development of strong discriminant operants.

Reinforcement

For a discriminated operant to be developed and maintained over time, a *reinforcing consequence* is necessary. That is, a response emitted in the presence of a set of antecedent stimuli must be followed by a *reinforcing stimulus*. Consider once again our example above. If giving the child a nickel *after* he has asked for it increases the probability that he will emit the request again under similar circumstances, the nickel may be defined as a reinforcing stimulus.

The important features of operant conditioning is the relationship of an operant response (or series of operant responses) to its reinforcing stimulus (consequence). This relationship is said to be *contingent* if a reinforcing stimulus is presented when and only when the operant response is emitted. Reinforcement would thus depend upon the emission of a response. This concept is fundamental to the development and modification of behavior soon to be discussed under the rubric of *contingency management.* Finally, it must be noted that a stimulus which occurs subsequent to an operant response is a reinforcer *only* if the frequency of that operant response is maintained or increased over time. In other words, a reinforcer is determined by its effect upon response emission. Thus is defined an empirical concept of reinforcement (Bijou, 1964).

Positive and Negative Reinforcement   As behavior is conceived in terms of respondent and operant classes, so may reinforcement be classified. Although any consequent stimulus is a reinforcer if it increases response probability, two primary classes of reinforcers may be distinguished: *positive* and *negative*. Each involves a quite different method for the conditioning of operant behavior.

If a consequent stimulus, when added to a set of circumstances, increases or strengthens the probability of an operant response, the stimulus is defined as a positive reinforcer. To illustrate, consider a small child who picks a piece of cloth up from the kitchen floor and hands it to his mother. The mother responds immediately by patting the child's head. The child is then observed to repeat his picking-up response, although this time it is performed upon a small piece of paper. Again, a loving headpat from his mother follows. A third item, a crust of bread, is then picked up and delivered by the child to his mother, and still another head pat follows immediately. This observation plus the subsequent observation of similar kitchen behavior may permit the inference that headpatting (consequent stimulus) has taken on the properties of a positive reinforcer. This would be true, however, *only* if headpatting had an observed effect on the maintenance or increased frequency of the child's picking-up response. (Our original example involving a child and a candy machine also illustrates positive reinforcement). While this concept may appear very simple, parents and teachers frequently assume that certain events have "reward value" when they have none or may even have aversive properties. Thus, it becomes necessary to observe carefully any effects a presumed reinforcer has upon operant response strength. Positive reinforcement, then, refers to events which upon presentation strengthen the probability that an operant response will recur in the future. Recent data indicate a pattern effect of continued positive reinforcement in which initially small changes in response frequency are generally followed by more rapid accelerations (Lindsley, 1969). This means that the effects of positive reinforcement may not always be self-evident early in a response acquisition process. Its cumulative effect over time is the significant criterion.

Negative reinforcement must be distinguished from positive reinforcement. If an antecedent stimulus, when *removed from* a situation following the occurrence of an operant response, increases the probability of response occurrence, it meets the criterion for a negative reinforcer. For example, consider a mother who tweaks her child's ear until he picks up a piece of paper from the floor. If removal of the ear tweak increases the strength of picking-up behavior, ear-tweak removal (antecedent stimulus) becomes a negative reinforcer. Note also in this example that ear-tweak removal would be contingent upon the operant response of picking up the paper. Such circumstances could ultimately result in active avoidance learning, in which picking-up behavior would be executed in order to avoid an ear tweak. Perhaps a more cogent classroom illustration of negative reinforcement is the child who daily confronts a nagging, punitive teacher. If the teacher's nagging behavior, when directed toward this child, is (1) aversive to the child and (2) ceases only when he performs a given response (e.g., sitting quietly), the removal of the teacher's nagging may negatively reinforce that response. That is, the teacher's nagging increases the child's rate of responding (sitting still) because by so responding the child removes the teacher's reason for nagging.

Two additional concepts in the operant conditioning system warrant brief mention: *nonreinforcement* and *punishment.* Nonreinforcement refers to the absence of a reinforcing stimulus following an operant response. A withholding of reinforcement indefinitely, according to research-derived principles of behavior, leads gradually to the extinction of an operant response. That is, the no longer functional response is either dropped from the individual's response repertoire or is superseded by a more effective response (a response which *is* reinforced). For example, consider a kindergarten child who receives his teacher's full attention every time he tugs at her skirt. If teacher attention has the effect of maintaining or increasing the strength of the child's skirt tugging (operant response), such attention would be a positive reinforcer. Therefore, according to Skinner's position, failure to provide teacher attention (nonreinforcement) should have the effect of gradually decreasing the child's rate of skirt tugging. If the child ceases this behavior entirely, extinction would be assumed. To facilitate extinction one might find it necessary, however, to make teacher attention contingent upon behavior incompatible with skirt tugging. This would necessitate using teacher attention to reinforce constructive, nonskirt-tugging behavior.

Finally, *punishment*, as used in the operant conditioning vocabulary, refers generally to the application of an aversive stimulus after an operant has been emitted. Thus, a child may be spanked following the performance of a voluntary act judged inappropriate by his parents. Skinner has indicated that the effects of punishment are less predictable than the effects of reinforcement and require further investigation. Related study, however, shows the consequence of punishment to vary from no effect to a slight decrement of response strength to virtual suppression of the punished response, (as well as other types of responses in the punished organism's repertoire).[2] The application of punishment has yet to be shown effective in eliminating (or "stamping out") a response; and the side effects of punishment are typically quite undesirable. The preferred and most effective behavioral modification strategies are based upon positive reinforcement, nonreinforcement, and negative reinforcement. Although punishment is generally not advocated by those identified with behavioral analysis procedures, its contingent application has been studied in an attempt to decelerate hazardous and otherwise unmanageable childrens' behavior (Birnbrauer, 1968; Bucher and Lovaas, 1967; Tate and Baroff, 1966).

According to Lindsley (1969), punishment, if "effective," produces large initial changes in response frequency followed by successively smaller ones. One implication of this generalized pattern is that if behavior change does not occur quickly as a consequence of a systematically applied

---

[2] The literature on punishment is complex, and psychologists do not agree completely upon the definition of punishment. Among the most representative students of punishment and from whom the generalization above has been taken are Azrin and Holz (1966), Maier (1956), Skinner (1938), and Solomon (1964).

punishing condition, the condition should be abandoned. It is unlikely to have any significant effect if continued and may only serve to complicate an already unfortunate situation.

Types of Reinforcement   As we have noted, a reinforcer is broadly defined as any stimulus event following a response (consequent stimulus event) which increases the frequency with which that response occurs. Many types of consequent events are possible, although basic categories for them have been identified (Bijou and Sturges, 1959). These categories are consumables (such as food or drink), manipulables (such as toys), visual and auditory stimuli (such as pictures or music), social stimuli (such as attention from others), and tokens. Consumable reinforcers, although very powerful, have been used largely in animal research, and their contingent use is neither ethical nor practical in the classroom. The remaining four types, however, are clearly feasible for use in most classroom situations. In fact, with the possible exception of tokens, they have been used by teachers for centuries. In behavioral analysis, stress is placed upon the *systematic* (rather than random and unscheduled) use of such types. Social stimuli have been shown to be a particularly strong reinforcement, especially in relation to young children. This is significant because such stimuli (e.g., teacher attention, approval, and disapproval) occur as a matter of course in any classroom. As we shall see, studies of the systematic arrangement of social stimuli on children's classroom behavior represent a major class of behavior analysis research.

To the above five types of reinforcers may be added a sixth: high-strength behavior (Meacham and Wiesen, 1969). Briefly, high strength behavior refers to behavior that occurs "naturally" with a high frequency and can be used to reinforce behavior with lower natural frequencies. This notion will soon be clarified in reference to the *Premack principle* (Premack, 1959, 1965).

Reinforcement Schedules

Reinforcement can be either *continuous* or *intermittent.* In the first case, reinforcement would proceed each and every emission of an operant response. Data indicate that the acquisition of operant responses is expedited by continuous reinforcement (Ferster and Skinner, 1957). This suggests that continuous reinforcement is highly desirable in the early stages of learning. Teachers are advised to reinforce continuously children's new learning, to the extent that this tactic is practical.

Apart from carefully planned situations, continuous reinforcement is a rare phenomenon. More typical of real life situations is intermittent reinforcement, in which a reinforcing stimulus occurs only periodically. Skinner and his followers have explored two dimensions of intermittent reinforcement in detail. One dimension is the *interval* of time between one reinforcement and the next. An interval schedule of reinforcement based on time may be fixed or variable. A fixed-interval schedule is one in which reinforcement is delivered or obtained (following a specific response) at standard time intervals, whether every five minutes or every five days. A report card full of "As" received at the end of a six-week grading period might represent such a schedule, assuming that grades are a reinforcer. In contrast, a variable interval schedule involves nonstandard blocks of time, as in the case of reinforcement after two minutes, then twenty minutes, and so on. A strategy whereby a teacher periodically strolls about the classroom administering praise to industrious students engaged in seatwork could exemplify the variable interval schedule.

The second dimension of intermittent schedules is *ratio* reinforcement. Instead of time, the number of discrete responses performed constitutes the criterion for reinforcement. A fixed-ratio reinforcement schedule is one in which reinforcement follows the commission of a set number of responses. Reinforcements administered to a child after every tenth word he spells correctly, irrespective of time lapsed, would comprise a fixed-ratio schedule. In contrast, a *variable ratio* schedule involves reinforcement after a series of varying numbers of responses have been accomplished. For example, a child reinforced after spelling two words correctly and not again until he has emitted three correct responses, then four, and so on would be operating on a variable ratio schedule.

One of the most significant contributions of this approach to the study of behavior is the identification of reliable relationships between reinforcement schedules and operant response rates. Each of the four general types of schedules discussed above has predictable effects on the frequency with which operant responses are emitted. Various combinations of time and interval schedules can also be made to produce specific effects.[3] All of this carries profound implications for those who desire to systematically develop and maintain specific behaviors of children. Generally, fixed-ratio reinforcement is associated with fairly uniform response rates. Response rate is primarily a function of ratio size, and a pause in responding is often observed after a reinforcement. Uniform response rates are also associated with variable ratio schedules. Further, behavior established under the latter is usually strongly resistant to extinction. This is significant for teachers, since a major goal in most classrooms is the development of academic responses that will continue to be emitted at an efficient rate even when no reinforcement is available. Response rates may also be higher with variable ratio schedules because (1) reinforcements increase with a higher response output; and (2) by the very nature of the schedule, a higher rate is reinforced. Consequently, a high rate of response will most probably occur again.

Fixed-interval and variable interval schedules also result in typical response rate patterns. The former pattern generally involves an increase in response rate just prior to reinforcement and a decrease in rate immediately after, although rate is generally proportional to the interval

---

[3] Sixteen distinct schedules have been developed and validated by Ferster and Skinner (1957).

length. Many a classroom teacher has observed an analogous phenomenon. Consider, for example, a class whose study rate skyrockets immediately before each weekly test, only to drop dramatically upon completion of this task. Or consider the rapidity with which many children complete their classroom assignments as recess time nears, even when they have been given ample time to complete these assignments leisurely. This response phenomenon can generally be avoided by utilizing a variable interval schedule. A fairly stable or uniform response rate prevails under this second type of schedule; and behavior subject to a variable interval schedule is also highly resistant to extinction (Ferster and Skinner, 1957).

To summarize, the cardinal feature of ratio schedules is that reinforcement increases proportionately to the frequency with which responses are made. Hence, the higher the response rate, the more frequent the reinforcement. Conversely, as fewer responses are made, the probability of subsequent responding is lowered because of the decrease in reinforcement received—a phenomenon which may lead to a vicious cycle (Michael and Meyerson, 1962).

Moderate response rates are typical of variable interval schedules, but a principal characteristic of behavior reinforced by such schedules is its high degree of resistance to extinction. The vicious cycle problem is generally avoided as variable interval schedules tend to be self-corrective. In other words, a reduced response rate is raised by the reinforcement which will eventually come, and a higher response probability is again restored.

Finally, behavior maintained by intermittent reinforcement schedules, especially the variable ratio type, tends also to be strongly resistant to extinction. In other words, response frequency will persist for lengthy periods of no reinforcement. This generalization is implicit in the following comment made by a psychologist to a group of mothers concerned about the management of their preschoolers' persistent nagging behavior: "Remember, a single yes can undo a thousand no's!"

It is important to note that if reinforcers are intended to establish and maintain desired behavior, they must be scheduled on a *contingent* basis. Supplying a hungry child with a cookie every fifteen minutes regardless of how he behaves *does not* make a contingency. This fixed-interval procedure would tend only to reinforce the behavior emitted immediately prior to reinforcement. If, for example, a child happened to be picking his nose at that point in time, nose picking would probably be reinforced. Contingent reinforcement avoids chance conditions such as this.[4]

Behavior analysis researchers have been much more concerned with manipulating reinforcement schedules and contingencies to observe their effects than with explaining why such effects are obtained. In fact, the entire approach is descriptive. Causal inferences and explanations are

---

[4] See Stumphauzer and Bishop (1969) for an illustrative procedure concerning the contingent use of television viewing to modify children's behavior, e.g., thumb sucking.

typically avoided, since they are speculative and involve phenomena not directly observable. Perhaps the major behavioral principle is that any child will respond according to the reinforcements available to him. The task is to find valid reinforcers and schedule them appropriately in order to construct desirable response patterns in the child.

In principle, this approach may be likened to a tenet of long-standing in psychology: the *empirical law of effect*. This law—whose history extends formally back to Thorndike's laws of learning (1913)—indicates that "acts leading to consequences which satisfy a motivating condition are selected and strengthened, while those leading to consequences which do not satisfy a motivating condition are eliminated" (McGeoch, 1942, p. 574). In behavioral analysis, however, no assumption is made about internal motivating conditions or subjective feelings of satisfaction. Motivation is considered strictly from the standpoint of externally manipulative conditions. When a pattern of behaviors has been acquired to the point that it occurs predictably at a consistent rate under intermittent reinforcement, an individual gives the appearance of being "intrinsically motivated" to respond, or "self-motivated." Further, the behavioral approach emphasizes the contingent arrangement of consequences according to systematic schedules. This is one feature which differentiates the operant approach from other S-R psychologies. Another subtle modification of the law of effect has been made by Skinner, namely, that behavior is a function of consequences which have in the past followed behavior rather than a function of consequences which are going to follow behavior. The latter would introduce the notion of *expectancy*, a hypothetical phenomenon. Behavior analysis researchers, it must be stressed, restrict themselves to directly observable responses. It is reasoned that to do otherwise would involve a less than scientific approach to the study of behavior.

BEHAVIOR ANALYSIS IN EARLY CHILDHOOD EDUCATION

From an operant perspective, a classroom is considered to be an environment of stimuli which is capable of developing, maintaining, and changing the responses of a learner. This control is achieved by a systematic arrangement of cues (e.g., materials, equipment, and the teacher's behavior) and reinforcers. Thus, a learner operates within a context of stimulus events and becomes a product of those events under specific temporal arrangements.

Stimulus events may be considered in terms of independent variables, or factors which are manipulated in order to assess their effect on behavior and to capitalize upon their potential to change behavior. Responses are behaviors emitted by the learner which are influenced by specifiable stimulus events. By employing cueing and reinforcement procedures, a teacher becomes a virtual architect of classroom behavior. In other words, strategies are devised to condition in desired ways a child's operant behavior to the environmental setting which the classroom provides. We will now deal with the general procedures appropriate for such conditioning. While technical variations on the theme of behavioral analysis or operant conditioning exist (Lindsley, 1968; Lovitt, 1968), the strategy suggested by Reese (1966) will be used to illustrate the basic components necessary.

Basic Principles

(1)   **Specification of Final Performance**   If one is to arrange combinations which facilitate behavioral development, one must have clearly in mind what behavior is to be established. Two requirements are thus imposed: (1) a statement defining the desired terminal behavior and (2) a procedure for measuring the behavior. Thus, first must be solved the problem of specifying in observable terms the behavior that is desired. The idea of precision in specifying objectives was first introduced in Chapter 1. A behavioral objective is a necessary but not a sufficient condition to define the behavioral analysis approach. A second requirement—specifying a procedure for measuring the behavior—is critical to this technology. Several alternative measurement strategies may be employed; and aside from an acceptance of response frequency as a basic datum, complete agreement concerning their merits and validity is not apparent in the literature on operant conditioning. Nevertheless, if conditioning procedures are to be arranged, terminal objectives must be clarified empirically.

Desired terminal behavior may be comparatively simple and reflect immediate concerns, or it may be extremely complex and involve an extensive instructional task. Consider, for example, the difference between teaching children to clean up after finger painting and teaching them to read silently a grade-level primer at a demonstrated rate of speed and comprehension. (Additional examples of terminal behavior conceived in operant terms follow in the next section). Finally, while many objectives may be predetermined prior to initial behavioral assessment, goals and subgoals are frequently created only after such assessment.

(2)   **Assessment of Entering Behavior**   If procedures are to be instituted in order to help a child acquire stated terminal behaviors, one must have a starting point. In behavior analysis the best starting point is the child's response capabilities at the outset of training. This criterion is extremely important in order to ensure early success in a program, i.e., initially to provide a child with tasks which fall within his response repertoire at the point of entry. Entering behavior *must* be assessed if a teacher is to "start where the learner is" (readiness principle). Once a learner's position in relation to the broader objectives of a program has been determined, then a sequence of activities can be tailored for individualized instruction.

A variety of formal and informal procedures may be used for the assessment of entering behavior. Ordinarily, procedures are selected to reveal response deficits which must be considered in program planning. Psychometric tests are used less often than criterion measures of response capabilities. Direct continuous observation of a child is preferred in most situations (Werry and Quay, 1969). Also helpful are checklist procedures designed to inventory precisely what a child can and cannot do. In all cases, assessment procedures are selected in relation to objectives peculiar to the existing circumstances.

To illustrate, suppose a teacher is confronted with a child who exhibits a high rate of antisocial behavior (e.g., pushing, hitting, and commandeering the property of other children). If one's immediate objective is to decelerate such behavior, a first task would be to observe the frequency with which the antisocial responses occur *and* the conditions under which these responses occur. This task would be accomplished prior to the application of modification procedures and result in a *baseline* from which to gauge subsequent progress.[5] Only with a baseline from which to operate can one empirically determine the effectiveness of the modification procedures. If, on the other hand, one is concerned with academic responses such as counting from 1 to 100 or demonstrated skill in dealing accurately with rational concepts like "in between" and "middle-sized," a checklist might be used. In these cases, one would notate the child's initial span of counting responses and whether or not he responds correctly to tasks which require an understanding of object relations. This procedure would be preferred to the use of such global indicators of "readiness" as age or IQ, particularly for the purpose of planning educational activities.

Specific baseline statements may be conceived in several ways depending upon the criteria represented by terminal objectives. For example, a teacher may be concerned with a child's rate of arithmetic responses (e.g., correct performance of two-digit addition problems). This teacher could count such responses as they occur under a specified set of circumstances, in terms of (1) number correct and (2) number of errors committed. The specified circumstances could involve presenting the child with a list of twenty addition problems to solve within a period of ten minutes. Baseline would then be determined through this accounting procedure. Assume that in this hypothetical situation the child attempted only one problem and was in error. In terms of frequency, the child's *correct rate* could be described as zero; the teacher's task would then be to arrange conditions to increase the child's correct response rate. If the terminal objective is two correct addition responses per minute, conditions must be manipulated until such a rate is achieved. Once this has occurred the task changes to that of maintaining the child's rate.

Technically speaking, a rate statement is the only type of statement acceptable to a committed operant methodologist. In this writer's view, however, one is not required to meet this criterion in order to apply the basic conditioning strategy. For example, one may be interested in helping a child develop the ability to recite the Pledge of Allegiance to the Flag.

---

[5] In laboratory conditioning procedures, the term *baseline* generally refers to *operant level*, i.e., the strength of a response prior to the introduction of conditioning procedures.

Thoroughgoing classroom observational and continuous data-gathering procedures are an integral part of an applied behavioral analysis approach to early childhood education. The full scope of investigative and recording techniques, however, is more usually present in combined research- and service-oriented settings such as the University of Washington's Experimental Education Unit. Photo courtesy of Media Services, Experimental Education Unit, University of Washington.

The main concern here is that the child perform this response when appropriate. That he performs this verbal chain at x frequency per unit of time is not at issue. True, if instruction is successful, a child's rate has increased from none to one per school day, but whether the terminal objective needs to be stated in responses per unit of time is questionable. The critical aspect is that the objective be stated in terms of what the child is able to do and the conditions which come to control the recitation response.

To summarize, the assessment of entering behavior serves two important functions. The first is to provide behavioral data which may be used to determine a point of embarkation for instruction. The second is to provide a baseline for observation concerning the rate of progress and procedural effectiveness. This second point of strategy marks the beginning of a continuous cycle of data gathering characteristic of operant or behavioral analysis procedures. Ordinarily, every effort is made to graph the results of assessment. Graphic tabulations enable a teacher to examine the flow of behavior through a specified period of time. While variations in assessment methods occur, continuous data gathering is imperative for purposes of educational diagnosis, programming, and teacher decision making.

Structuring a Favorable Situation[6]   *Structuring a favorable situation* refers to the way in which the learning environment is arranged. Aspects of the environment (e.g., physical equipment, teacher behavior, learning materials) are arranged to maximize the probability of desired behavior and to minimize the likelihood of incompatible behavior. In other words, the cues to which the child will respond appropriately must be structured in relevant ways so that positive reinforcement can be administered. Applied successfully, this principle has a very broad implication for the motivation of behavior. If emission of correct responses early in a learning sequence can be facilitated, the frustration of failure and error may be reduced while success and self-confidence are bolstered.

Several levels of application of this principle can be noted. At a gross but important level is the arrangement of physical equipment in a nursery school or kindergarten classroom. Play materials would not be easily made available to children while they are engaged in pre-academic or academic activities. Otherwise, "play responses," or responses incompatible with desired academic responses, might accelerate because of teacher mismanagement.

A second level of application involves the ways in which teacher-child and child-child interaction are carried out. Suppose a teacher is working in the beginning stages of developing "cooperative social responses" among children. This broad aim might be reflected in a number of activities, including the self-selection of rhythm instruments for a music activity. If a teacher placed a box of instruments on the floor in the middle of a group of children the probability that children would "grab and fight over" the instruments (responses incompatible with social cooperation) might be increased. If, on the other hand, the teacher passes from child to child asking each to take an instrument in turn, the probability of uncooperative behavior is substantially lowered. More probable would be the emission of a desired social response which could be reinforced. It is important to note here a basic strategy characteristic in behavior analysis, a strategy nicely summarized by the old song, "Accentuate the positive, eliminate the negative." Avoided also are situations which may lead to the reinforcement of an undesirable response. In the above case, a child may be "reinforced" for grabbing behavior if his grabbing succeeds in gaining him a desired instrument.

A third level of application for the favorable situation principle is the arrangement of learning materials and feedback procedures. A careful

---

[6] "Structuring a favorable situation" may include or be preceded by a policy known as *adaptation*, that is, arranging events which have the effect of training an individual to behave so that conditioning may take place. For example, a child who will not stay in the classroom will not be available for conditioning until he has first become adapted to the classroom. Adaption procedures are described elsewhere (Reese, 1966).

ordering of the sequence of stimulus events where sufficient cues are present to prompt a response is necessary. Practices based upon this level are relevant for a wide variety of activities ranging from reading (Staats, 1968) to training for originality (Maltzman, 1960). Also important is the nature of the feedback given to a child concerning the adequacy of his response and what might be done to improve it if needed.

Attention to this third level of application has resulted in the extensive use of programmed materials among protagonists for behavior analysis.[7] The general features of programmed materials are threefold, although their collective objective is to make learning as efficient as possible. First, materials are arranged in a graduated sequence so as to elicit the continuous active response of a learner. In some cases, elaborate machinery is utilized. For example, a child may be required to press buttons which represent his answer to prerecorded oral questions, as in computer-assisted instruction. In contrast, a child may emit a marking or writing response to visually presented stimuli where no hardware is involved, as in a programmed workbook. The essential point is that a learner is constantly responding actively to carefully sequenced material.

A second major feature of programmed materials is that they provide for immediate confirmation or correction of a learner's response. In other words, the materials are designed so that a learner is informed or may inform himself immediately by checking the appropriate source whether or not his response is correct. A third feature of such materials is the opportunity they provide for individualization in terms of rate of progress. A learner may proceed through a programmed sequence as quickly or as slowly as he feels is necessary or most comfortable. Thus rapid learners and slow learners may proceed according to their own rate—the former being free to move ahead, the latter avoiding the frustrations of being pushed.

Programmed materials have been envisioned as one major solution to several problems inherent in most classroom settings (Skinner, 1968). Among Skinner's most serious criticisms include the relative infrequency with which learners are reinforced in school and the excessive delay between the time a behavior occurs and its reinforcement. Equally serious for Skinner are two additional problems: the aversive nature of many educational practices and the predominance of poorly sequenced curricula. In connection with the infrequency of learner reinforcement, Skinner (1954, 1968) has remarked that whether educators like it or not, most students today study to avoid the consequences of not studying. Even more striking he believes is the frequent apathy, withdrawal, and aggression of many school children—response patterns which he attributes to

---

[7] The use of programmed materials is by no means exclusive to behavior analysis procedures. The concept of programming has been applied in a wide variety of classroom settings by educators with diverse pedagogical orientations. It is true, however, that Skinner (1954) is generally credited with having provided a principal impetus to modern programmed material development and use.

the extensive use of aversive control techniques in most schools. With respect to curriculum sequencing, Skinner has maintained that many teachers feed material to students in such large unmanageable chunks that it contributes to inefficient and ineffective learning. For Skinner this practice establishes a "natural condition" for failure.

Another school problem identified by Skinner is the apparent tendency of teachers (and parents) to attend primarily to the undesirable behavior of children and to ignore the desirable. In effect, this tendency personifies a behavior change system based upon aversive control; there is little systematic reinforcement for "good" behavior, but ample punishment for "bad." Even casual observation tends to verify the insight of Skinner's critical contentions. Structuring a more favorable situation is a most acute requirement if many of the above problems are to be avoided.

Selection of Reinforcers Once a situation has been structured to maximize the probability that desired responses will occur, the next task is clear: to reinforce positively the responses when they occur. One must ensure, however, that the reinforcing stimulus serves to strengthen behavior. The reinforcing value of a stimulus cannot be assumed—its value must be observed. Thus, the basic task is to determine what controllable and demonstrably effective reinforcing events are available to a teacher.

Perhaps the most desirable effective reinforcer for humans is success, i.e., performing correctly and knowing that one has performed correctly. For success to be a reinforcer, however, conditions must be very precisely arranged—hence the rationale for programmed instruction. Daily experience with children suggests that success per se is not always an effective reinforcer; children frequently need to develop subsidiary behaviors before they can achieve a meaningful success. For example, the success marked by the correct making of change in a monetary transaction may be sufficiently reinforcing to strengthen a child's change-making behavior. But the many subsidiary skills involved in this complex act must first be developed before this sort of real life success can be achieved.

Where success is not a reinforcing event, other reinforcers (even contrived ones) may be necessary. Social reinforcers such as praise, attention, and recognition may be arranged positively to influence behavior. Such social events are often considered as "natural reinforcers" because they pervade the course of much human interaction and unquestionably influence behavior; these social events generally acquire reinforcing properties early in the lives of most children. Occasionally, material reinforcers such as candy, toys, or even money may be required in order initially to establish behavior. Once behavior has been established by material reinforcers, however, it may be maintained by a transfer to more natural reinforcers.

One extremely utilitarian method for the selection of reinforcers is based upon the *Premack principle* (Premack, 1959), or the notion that a child's high-probability behavior may be used contingently to reinforce and increase his low-probability behavior. In effect, this means that a child selects his own reinforcers. To illustrate, suppose that within a classroom setting a child has the freedom to choose one activity from ten available ones. Assume that his first choice is painting with water colors and his last choice is alphabet drill. Suppose further that over time the child is observed to paint with water colors whenever he has a choice. By definition, water color painting would constitute a high-probability behavior. Alphabet drill would be classified as a low-probability behavior. A teacher operating on the Premack principle might utilize water color painting as a reinforcing event *contingent* upon the execution of a prescribed amount of alphabet drill activity. In effect, the high-probability behavior of the child would be used to increase the frequency and adequacy of the child's alphabet drill behavior. (This assumes the latter to be a functional objective.) To apply the Premack principle, the teacher must carefully observe the child to determine his high-probability behaviors. Once high-probability behaviors are identified, they may be used contingently to reinforce a child's low-probability behaviors. The latter may be academic (e.g., spelling) or social (e.g., sharing playground equipment with others). For the record, productive use of this principle has been documented (Homme et al., 1963). Appropriate control over the behavior of nursery school children previously unresponsive to verbal directives or teacher requests was achieved by the systematic application of this practical reinforcement principle.

A generalized token or point-credit system based upon the Premack principle is frequently used in behavioral analysis classrooms. Such a system involves the arrangement of "credit," in terms of tokens or points earned, for the performance of certain behaviors at specified levels of quality. Thus the awarding of points or tokens is contingent upon the emission of responses consistent with instructional objectives. Points may be accumulated by a child to be traded in for items such as free time or other privileges. Free time enables a child to do whatever he wishes (engage in high-probability behavior) within the limits of the classroom. A system such as this is therefore conducive to the arrangement of highly effective reinforcing events. Research data illustrative of this system will be discussed shortly.

A reminder is in order. Since behavioral analysis subsumes an empirical concept of reinforcement, it is essential that the effects of arranged consequences be meticulously observed. This requires the continuous measurement of response rate over time so that consequent events may be verified as reinforcers. For example, if free-time tokens had no effect upon the frequency of a child's correct response performance over time (as compared to his frequency prior to the introduction of tokens), then another type of reinforcement would be sought. In any case, the selection of reinforcers is usually facilitated by the careful observation of individual children. Data from the study of children's incentive object preferences can also be helpful in the initial selection of reinforcers. In one study, for example, kindergarten, second-, and fourth-grade children alike placed highest value upon bubble gum and a rat fink charm; intermediate value was given varieties of candy and manipulables such as a balloon (Haaf et al., 1970).

5 **Behavior Shaping**   From an operant conditioning point of view, the technique of producing new behavior—establishing new types of responses—is called *behavior shaping.* To shape behavior, response variations which resemble a desired behavior are reinforced selectively while less relevant (or inappropriate) variations are not reinforced (extinguished). Thus, new and more complex forms of behavior may be developed by reinforcing gradual changes in the response being made as it comes closer to the desired operant response. The underlying principle is that of *reinforcing successive approximations*, i.e., reinforcing resemblances of the final desired response where such resemblances are in the direction of that ultimate goal. Once a closer approximation has been acquired, the lesser old approximations are no longer reinforced.

A classic example of the shaping process is provided by a child learning to write cursively. No child is likely to spontaneously write a perfect letter on the first attempt, even with a model letter to copy.[8] What will result is an approximation of the ideal. But if the child's response produces a letter in the direction of the ideal, it should be reinforced. In short, to maintain cursive writing responses so that improvement may be made, the reinforcement of progressive approximations of the model letter is essential. Both the informational and motivational functions of reinforcement would be lost if reinforcement were withheld until the child had formed a perfect letter. In fact, such a perfect performance in the absence of reinforcement would be unlikely.

Behavior shaping procedures can also be illustrated by childrens' language development. The spontaneous and correct pronunciation of most new words by a young child learning to talk is unlikely. A child's first attempts are more typically approximations of the desired response. The writer's own child, for example, first pronounced the word *rhododendron* as *rowdenon.* This was a good approximation. Gradually, however, with the assistance of selective reinforcement (and a correct language model) the correct pronunciation was achieved. There are ample data to illustrate the application of shaping procedures to language development (e.g., Staats, 1968), but the principle purportedly applies to all classes of operant behavior.

Behavior shaping has been classified as an "art," since reinforcement must be used quite selectively in order to avoid certain basic problems (Sidman, 1962). For one thing, approximations must be reinforced immediately. Neither too many nor too few reinforcements should be given for an approximation of a desired terminal response. For another, the reinforcing agent (teacher) must observe a child carefully so that successive approximations can be clearly specified. Shaping procedures can easily fail if a teacher continues to massively reinforce approximations at a level lower than would indicate progress. Obviously, behavior shaping requires a clear statement of objectives and a clear understanding of what responses constitute approximations of the desired behavior.

---

[8] This would mean that a child's operant level for writing a model letter y, for example, would be zero.

Further examples of the shaping principle applied to educational practice include (1) a teacher's praise of students' improvement (as in creative writing), even when this improvement falls short of a desired standard of competence; (2) allowing partial credit for the correct use of an arithmetic principle, even though a mechanical error has led to an incorrect answer; and (3) reinforcement for a child who has selected the correct primary colors (red, blue, and green) to make the color brown, but who may have failed to mix them in correct proportion. In the last example, if correct proportionate use of colors were the terminal behavior, it would be self-defeating to continue prolonged reinforcement of incorrect proportionate use. For shaping purposes, reinforcement would be withheld until the next higher level of paint-mixing response had been achieved.

Once behaviors have been appropriately shaped the task is to maintain the relevant response in the learner's repertoire so that they are available when necessary. In many cases, maintenance at a low rate is sufficient; in others, rate increases are desired. For example, once a child has learned to respond correctly to the question, Where do you live?, it would probably be enough to maintain his response at sufficient strength so that the child would emit it when necessary. With behavior such as that desired during show-and-tell time, however, a teacher might be interested in more than an indication of whether a child is capable of show-and-tell behavior—she might wish to increase the child's rate so that he participates voluntarily and frequently during each period set aside for that purpose. (It is after behavior has been established, incidently, that the arrangement of intermittent reinforcement schedules to maintain or increase response frequency is critical.)

Shaping is not always the crucial problem in a classroom based upon behavior analysis principles. In some instances, a child may already have a desired response but fails to emit it under the desired stimulus conditions. This point can be illustrated by referring to certain aspects of the task of learning to read. For example, a child may bring to the school situation a wealthy vocabulary, most of which he pronounces correctly. Thus, the problem is not shaping his verbal responses. The problem is conditioning the child to emit verbal responses which correspond to verbal symbols (letters, words, and sentences) presented visually.

This problem defines a core instructional endeavor for any educational approach based upon learning principles: *systematic discrimination training.* Basically, discrimination training involves reinforcing a response in the presence of a stimulus (e.g., reinforcing a child for saying *boat* in the presence of the word *boat*) and not reinforcing a response emitted when the appropriate stimulus is absent (e.g., withholding reinforcement if a child says *boat* in the presence of the word *bat*). In this way correct stimuli will come to control a correct response with a high degree of probability. When this criterion is reached, a stimulus qualifies as *discriminative.* Within the broad areas of language, academic, and social behavior, *discrimination repertoires* are gradually established. These consist of high-probability responses that will be emitted when discriminative stimuli are presented (e.g., teachers' instructions, workbook exercises, creative art materials, and reading primers).

In discrimination training, *stimulus fading techniques* are frequently employed. To illustrate, consider a child who consistently errs in discriminating between the letters *b* and *d*. Assume that a teacher wishes to program an extraneous cue to facilitate the acquisition of correct discrimination responses. In this example, the child's correct discrimination responses can be defined in terms of supplying a correct oral response (*b* or *d*) when each letter symbol is presented visually. An extraneous cue in this case may take the form of different colors to dramatize the half-circle at the base of each letter (the direction of this half-circle, left or right, represents the critical invariant feature for *b*-ness or *d*-ness). Suppose the *b*'s halfcircle was traced in red, the *d*'s in blue. A letter discrimination strategy could then be devised by the teacher in which a color stimulus is an additional prompt. Assume for the moment that with color cues in evidence, the child makes a correct and reliable verbal response to each letter. The next instructional task is to wean the child from this extraneous cue. This requires a fading technique. In our example, color can gradually (and literally) be faded through prepared successive stimulus presentations during which correct responses continue to be reinforced. The success of the fading technique will be measured in terms of the child's correct rate subsequent to complete fading.

In summary, five principles comprise the nucleus of a behavioral analysis approach to teaching: (1) final performance specification, (2) entering behavior assessment, (3) design of a favorable situation in which behavior may occur, (4) selection of reinforcements, and (5) behavior shaping. Considerable teaching skill is required for the successful implementation of these principles, which are independent of subject matter content. Hence, sophisticated teacher training procedures are called for and will be constructed upon the five basic principles just discussed.

The Behavior Analysis Follow Through Model

Several model programs for young children based upon behavior analysis principles have been developed. Examples include a preschool-primary program at the University of Washington's Experimental Education Unit in Seattle, the Juniper Gardens project (Risley, 1969), and an operant conditioning program for the development of school readiness (Sapon, 1968). Instructional sequences for the Primary Education Project (Resnick, 1967) have been derived from the behavioral analysis of learning tasks; and DISTAR also has a strong behavior modification orientation. Here, the University of Kansas Project Follow Through model is presented further to delineate childhood education from a behavior analysis viewpoint.

According to the program literature, a behavior analysis model classroom combines familiar educational techniques in a "unique way" to provide a new learning opportunity for children (Bushell, 1973). Aspects of team teaching, individualized teaching, nongradedness, programmed in-

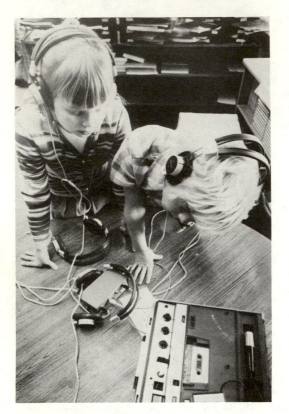

Within classrooms built according to behavioral analysis principles, the use of programmed materials such as language tapes can promote self-directed learning among children.

Photo by Peter Rinearson.

struction and, especially, a token reinforcement procedure result in a system of education that "accelerates the learning and achievement of the children, and unites professional educators, paraprofessionals, and parents in the teaching process" (Bushell, 1973, p. 164). The reader may ask, What learnings are accelerated? The answer is that reading, arithmetic, handwriting, and spelling are introduced at the kindergarten level. An accelerated mastery of these skills is emphasized throughout the entire K–3 sequence. Social skills are also stressed: self-confidence, independence in decision making, and cooperation with peers and adults. Mastery of these academic and social skills is thought to enable children to compete effectively in the public schools.

It should be noted that the five principles of behavior analysis elucidated in the foregoing section provide a procedural backbone for the behavior analysis model. Instructional objectives are precisely defined in advance to provide direction to learning. Entry behavior is assessed by a special "behavior inventory" and various diagnostic tests. These assessments enable the teacher to place a child at a spot in the instructional sequence appropriate to his initial skill level. Diagnostic tests also are embedded in materials at higher levels of achievement to provide checkpoints for mastery before children move through a given sequence. This requires that curriculum materials meet certain criteria. Generally, behavior analysis classrooms utilize commercially prepared materials that describe the behavior of which a child will be capable at the end of an instructional sequence; require frequent active responding by the child; specify clear criteria for accurate responses; provide for individual rates of progress; and enable a teacher to measure achievement gains on a periodical basis (Chow and Elmore, 1973). Examples of widely used materials include:

Sullivan Programmed Reading (McGraw-Hill)
Behavior Analysis Phonics Primer (University of Kansas)
SRA Reading Laboratory (Science Research Associates)
Handwriting with Write and See (Lyons and Carnahan)
Behavior Analysis Handwriting Primer (University of Kansas)
Spelling and Writing Patterns (Follette)

Systematic daily instruction is usually provided for children in small group settings in which both the teacher's attention and the child's rate of learning can be individualized. For a typical lesson four to six children will be seated around a table with their workbooks and worksheets. The teacher's role is to direct the children's work and provide reinforcement for progress according to the established token exchange system. Behavioral evidence of following instructions, completing tasks, and attending is the cue for immediate and frequent reinforcement. Tokens (plastic chips) are given with praise about the child's work: "That is very neat handwriting, Mark," or, "Shelley, your arithmetic work is very good this morning." Further evaluation of progress is determined by a wide range of achievement measures, weekly individual progress reports, and the ubiquitous curriculum-embedded tests.

Data-based instructional procedures are more visible in behavior analysis classrooms than in most other approaches to early childhood education. Specific lesson plans for given days are always determined by the children's documented progress. A daily schedule has three phases: planning, formal instruction, and exchange periods ("back-ups"). The latter are specified periods in which children may exchange their earned tokens for special, desired activities.[9] Early in the program, periods of formal instruction (learning periods) and special activity periods (exchange periods) are alternated frequently—10–15 minutes and 20–25 minutes, respectively, as an instance. Earning periods are gradually increased in duration as children become more skillful. By the second or third grade, it is not unusual to

---

[9] A special document has been prepared by Professor Donald Bushell, Jr., that describes, in both English and Spanish, how to establish and operate a practical token economy system: *A Token Manual for Behavior Analysis*, University of Kansas, Support and Development Center for Follow Through, Lawrence, Ks. Readers interested in further information about the use, effectiveness, and problems of token reinforcement systems should consult Kazdin (1972) and O'Leary and Drabman (1971).

find that 20 minutes of contingent special activity will support a full morning's academic work. Throughout the entire K–3 sequence, special activities—whether free time, diet supplements, arts and crafts work, story time, music, or science projects—have a specified cost. Recess activity, for example, might cost fifteen tokens, a story ten. Periodic changes are made in the content and prices of special activities in order to maintain children's interest and enthusiasm. Variety in type of reinforcements and earnings based upon successive approximations to desired goal behaviors are the key principles.

Another hallmark of the behavior analysis model is its small adult-child ratio (Bushell, 1970). Typically, a classroom of 25–30 children will be managed by a team of four adults: one lead teacher and three assistants (a full-time teaching aide and two parent aides). The lead teacher normally is in charge of overall planning and direction and the reading component of the program. Aides are trained to carry out the remaining learning activities: small group mathematics instruction and individualized handwriting and spelling work. Elaborate procedures for the enlistment and training of aides have been developed. Particularly notable is a system in which revolving groups of parents participate in the classroom. In this way, all parents have an opportunity to see firsthand the operation of the classroom and become skilled in the application of behavior analysis procedures. It is thought that such a procedure better sustains the home-school relationship and provides consistency in the management of children's behavior from one setting to the other.

Commentary   The behavior analysis model is undergoing continuous evaluation both from within and from external agencies such as the Stanford Research Institute. Preliminary results indicate a strong record of achievement for this model in terms of its stated goals for children's academic achievement. It is not yet possible, of course, to evaluate the long-term effects of education based upon systematic behavior analysis. Myriad research reports that document short-range achievement gains for young children can be found in the literature, and a sampling of such reports appears in the next section.

Meanwhile, the reader is encouraged to examine the behavior analysis model again in relation to the Parker and Day criteria for conceptual analysis introduced in Chapter 1. Although there is room for disagreement on this point, the behavior analysis model seems clearly based on a theory of development in that many behaviorists virtually equate development with learning (D. Baer, 1970). It may be more accurate to say that the model personifies a psychology of learning in action, one firmly supported by a vast collection of meticulously gathered research data. Program objectives are clearly operationalized for precise assessment. They cut across both academic and social areas of learning, although the principal focus is academic content. Great care is exercised in the arrangement and sequencing of materials. This, plus the directive role of the teacher, results in a format that is highly structured but flexible enough for much individualization of instruction. Parent participation is actively sought. And motivation is sustained by extrinsic means—possibly the most frequently criticized aspect of the model. A conscious attempt is made to promote self-satisfying learning, but the rationale for motivational strategy is built essentially upon direct, immediate, tangible reinforcement of desired behavior. It is argued that such reinforcement clarifies the relationship between behavior and its consequences and that incentives for learning neither detract from nor distort the learning process. In sum, motivation is not something that just happens—*it is taught* (Bushell, 1970). Although confirming data have not been presented, critics of this approach harbor a fear that children may become too dependent upon external sources of motivation at the expense of genuine autonomy.

Finally, with its detailed guidelines, procedures for training staff, recommended curriculum materials, specified instructional methods, and provisions for continued evaluation, the behavior analysis model must be rated high in the dimension of exportability. Three phases of development define the exportation dimension: the first phase involves substantial support for organization and training by staff from the University of Kansas; the second phase is when local leadership is developed, with a gradual transfer of training and support responsibilities to resident staff and parent coordinators; the third phase generally begins by the third or fourth year of operation, after which the program sponsor and University of Kansas staff provide only a periodic consulting service. Thus, by the time the first wave of children has reached or completed the third grade in the K–3 sequence, local persons are maintaining and extending model services. Internal evaluation continues and is supplemented by achievement data with the intent that each project be "clearly accountable to the community which it serves" (Bushell, 1973, p. 172).

BEHAVIOR ANALYSIS RESEARCH

Most approaches to early childhood education deal with groups of children immersed in a combination of content and methodological variables. Periodic measures are then taken of the total program effects, and results are reported in terms of group averages (summative evaluation). In contrast, a behavior analysis approach to research typically involves the singular manipulation of clearly specified variables in order that the effects of such manipulation on an *individual child* may be assessed. *Continuous measurement* (response counting) over time is preferred to a policy of periodic measurement (e.g., end-of-program tests). It is believed that only through the singular manipulation of stimulus events and continuous logging of performance can the optimum learning conditions for any child be identified. Once these optimum conditions are identified, they can be implemented to assist the child toward a maximum rate of educational progress. In brief, it is argued that since behavior resides in the single case, it is in the single case that behavior can best be analyzed (D. Baer, 1971). This segment of the chapter first deals with behavior analysis research. Subsequently, some examples of this approach involving young children are presented.

General Procedures for Behavior Analysis Research

Research procedures pertinent to the behavioral analysis point of view are variously described as the experimental analysis of behavior (Skinner, 1966), the functional analysis of behavior (Haring and Lovitt, 1967), or analytic behavioral application (D. Baer, Wolf, and Risley, 1968). The first approach represents the parent strategy as developed by Skinner under intensely controlled laboratory conditions. As suggested earlier, the focal point of this approach is the rate of repeated occurrences of an operant response over time. This technique stands in contrast to that whereby finite samples of behavior are obtained at one point in time (as in psychological tests) and where such samples are used to infer some general human characteristic (such as intelligence, anxiety, achievement, or creativity). Response rate is preferred as the basic datum. This is because rate is considered the best single indication of the probability that a given bit of behavior will occur at a given time (Skinner, 1966).[10] All pertinent variables (e.g., stimuli antecedent and subsequent to a response and the timing of the presentation of either) that affect the probability of a response or chain of responses in functional (observable and describable) ways must be considered. Subjects for analysis (whether human or infrahuman) are studied individually to determine what manipulations made through real time) affect relative changes in response rate over time. Changes in response rate (probability) are linked precisely to specific manipulations.[11] In this way, progressive sequences of behavioral development can be observed and charted. Only measurement through time enables one to derive this kind of probability statement and to describe the variables that influence response probability.

Since *response frequency* has the quality of an empirical event (directly observable), it has the advantage of replacing many ambiguous terms such as *interest*, *hyperactivity*, and *shyness*. For example, a child *interested* in art may talk about art and indulge in art activities *frequently*; and a *shy* child may initiate social contacts with other children *infrequently* (Ferster and Perrott, 1968).

Standard research applications of the experimental analysis of behavior generally include the *reversal* technique. An example will illustrate. Consider a psychologist whose task is to increase a nursery school child's rate of cooperative social behavior (defined in terms of sharing playground equipment). This child will first be observed over several weeks

---

[10] It is claimed that the best indication of the probability that a response will occur in the future under given conditions is the frequency with which it has occurred in the past under those conditions.

[11] To be admissable as evidence, a relationship between stimulus events and response rate must hold for all subjects in a given experiment, not for just a few or for the "averages."

for evidence of such behavior (baseline measurement). In this case, suppose that no cooperative social responses are observed, despite the existence of conditions generally favorable for such behavior. Then the childs' baseline rate is zero. The psychologist may then introduce an experimental variable, teacher attention (as defined by a smile and words of praise for the child), to be administered contingently, i.e., only when a cooperative social response (or an approximation thereof) is emitted by the child. During this period of selective reinforcement the teacher will also withhold her attention from the child whenever he makes responses incompatible with cooperative social behavior. During this period the teacher may also be requested to provide ample attention to children who exhibit cooperative behavior, making sure that the uncooperative child witnesses her attentions. Gradually, the uncooperative child may be observed to increase his cooperative behavior to the point where cooperative responses occur at a stable rate under appropriate conditions. Behavior has changed. But the question of whether or not change is truly a function of the teacher's procedure may be raised. To answer this, the experimental variable (teacher attention) must be discontinued to determine if the effected change is dependent upon it. If so, a decrease in rate of cooperative social behavior would be observed. If such a decrease is observed (a reversal), the experimental variable can again be introduced to see if a recovery in rate occurs. The observance of a recovery will substantiate a function relationship between teacher attention and cooperative behavior for this child.[12]

In summary, the reversal technique is a basic procedural design consisting of at least four elements: (1) baseline measurement; (2) introduction of experimental variable (e.g., contingent reinforcement); (3) reversal (withdrawal or modification of experimental variable); and (4) reinstatement (reintroduction of experimental variable). Behavior is measured continuously and directly throughout the entire procedure.[13]

While the reversal technique is common to the experimental analysis of behavior, it is neither always suitable nor necessary in applied settings. Yet both strategies (or variations thereof) involve the issue of *reliable* change, and all experimental variables must be specified for their correct execution. Generally, the attempt is made to relate procedures to operant conditioning principles; most analyses are concerned with a demonstration

---

[12] Since many behavioral modifications are valuable, it is neither desirable nor ethical to reverse a behavior in order to satisfy a methodological requirement. In the example above, a teacher may wish rather to maintain the child's cooperative behavior, in which case it may come under extra-experimental conditions (e.g., positive social reinforcement from peers) and no longer be dependent solely upon teacher attention.

[13] Nothing has been said here about the use of a *multiple baseline* design, i.e., a procedure by which response changes in more than one operant class may be analyzed at one time. Multiple baseline technique is perhaps the most functional for behavioral analysis research workers. See D. Baer, Wolf, and Risley (1968) and Sidman (1962) for further comment on this technique.

of the durability or generality of behavior over time. Perhaps the principal difference between the experimental analysis of behavior (as conducted in the psychologists' laboratory) and applied behavior analysis is the degree to which control can be exercised over the many variables which influence behavior. Further, applied behavior analysis has, in practice, been concerned more with specifying variables that are "effective" for the modification of important behaviors (such as social and verbal responses) in their *naturally occurring contexts* (including the classroom).

A Sampling of Behavior Analysis Research on Young Children

A large research literature documents the application of behavior analysis research to young children. Some of the more dramatic and impressive applications have involved exceptional children, including those in conventional diagnostic categories such as mental retardation, brain injury, autism, and assorted behavior disorders and learning disabilities (Ullman and Krasner, 1965). Further, principles of operant conditioning have been applied successfully to the process of toilet training (Madsen, 1966), the extinction of temper tantrums (Williams, 1959), the improvement of children's regressive patterns of motor behavior and motor skills (Harris et al., 1964) (Johnston et al., 1966), the reduction of operant crying behavior in young children (Hart, et al., 1964), and the management of hyperactive children (Patterson, 1966). In fact, from a context of operant conditioning and social learning principles, some of the most productive and practical techniques for classroom management and behavioral development, maintenance, and change have been created (Clarizio and Yelon, 1967; Krumboltz and Krumboltz, 1972).

Academic Behaviors   A variety of behavior modification studies concerned with young children's academic behavior is portrayed in Table 3.1. Most of the studies are based on the reversal technique earlier discussed and incorporate the principle of successive approximations. The reinforcement contingencies are without exception established in relation to the desired outcomes indicated in the "Observed Effects" column. Finally, the reader will note that these studies deal largely with normal preschool and primary-grade children. (Hundreds of additional studies that deal with older subjects are also reported in the literature.)

Without exception, the studies included in Table 3.1 show some impact in the direction desired by the experimenters. Not all studies conducted with young children demonstrate startling results, however, and those that fail to reveal impressive outcomes often do not find their way into the literature. It should also be noted that the effects of reinforcement procedures are not often uniform among all children. Different children may be affected differentially by the same modification procedure; occasionally, a child is not influenced at all by systematic reinforcement tactics and may even avoid a given token pay approach (Betancourt and Zeiler, 1971). In such cases, the task is to continue the environmental manipu-

TABLE 3.1 Representative Studies of the Influence of Behavior Modification Technology upon Young Children's Academic Behavior

Investigators	Subjects	Experimental Conditions	Observed Effects
Allen et al. (1967)	Male nursery school child	Contingent social reinforcement (praise and approval)	Increased persistence in constructive learning activity
Bushell, Wrobel, and Michaelis (1968)	Preschoolers	Token contingencies	Increased rate of study behaviors: independent task involvement, co-operative study, attending to instruction
Chadwick and Day (1971)	Selected elementary school underachievers	Contingent material and social reinforcement	Substantial increase in work time, rate of output per hour, and ac-curacy in academic performance
Doss et al. (1971)	Low achieving inner-city elementary children	Individually prescribed point rein-forcement system	Increased programmed reading re-sponse rate, including accuracy
Edlund (1972)	Primary grade children	Immediate material reinforcement for correct responses on Stanford-Binet Scale	Significantly higher IQ scores as compared to matched, nonrein-forced classmates
Felixbrod and O'Leary (1973)	Second graders	Contingent reinforcement for chil-dren's self-determined standards for academic performance	Higher productivity than no-rein-forcement peers and those re-inforced according to externally imposed academic standards
Goetz and Baer (1973)	Preschool girls	Contingent social reinforcement	Increased form diversity in children's block-building behavior
Goetz and Salmonson (1972)	Preschool girls	Contingent general and descriptive reinforcement	Increased form diversity in children's easel painting

113

TABLE 3.1 (cont.)

Investigators	Subjects	Experimental Conditions	Observed Effects
Hall et al. (1968)	First and third graders	Contingent teacher attention	Increased study response rate, including appropriate attention to classmates and classroom participation
Hamblin and Hamblin (1972)	Inner-city preschoolers	Peer tutoring and token reinforcement	Significant improvement in rate of learning to read as compared to an adult tutoring procedure
Holt (1971)	First graders	Fixed-ratio reinforcement scheduling in conjunction with programmed instruction	Marked percentage increases in rate of reading and mathematics tasks completed
Hopkins, Schutte, and Garton (1971)	First and second graders	Contingent access to playroom for free-time activity	Progressive increase in work rates and quality of printing and writing behavior
Kazdin (1973)	First, third, and fourth graders	Token system reinforcement	Reduction in nonstudy behaviors and generally increased task orientation
Knight, Hasazi, and McNeil (1971)	Preschoolers	Systematic presentation strategies and immediate feedback by mothers to children concerning correct and incorrect letter and word recognition	Increased reading skills
Lates, Egner, and McKenzie (1971)	Primary grade children with learning handicaps	Individualized social and material reinforcements and continuous progress charts	Increased academic and social responsivity

Miller and Schneider (1970)	Head Start children	Token system reinforcement	Progressive improvement in handwriting skills (general classroom decorum improved as unintended positive side effect)
Richard, Taylor and Libb (1973)	Elementary school children, remedial classroom	Reinforcement based upon Premack principle	Increased performance in programmed reading and mathematics activity
Salzberg et al. (1971)	Kindergarten children	Intermittent feedback and contingent access to play activities	Increased accuracy of children's printing responses.
Schutte and Hopkins (1970)	Kindergarten girls	Contingent teacher attention	Significant increase in children's instruction-following behavior
Wasik (1970)	"Culturally deprived" second graders	Contingent free choice of activity	Increased productivity in individual and group work periods
Zimmerman and Pike (1972)	Mexican-American second graders	Modeling and contingent praise	Increased question-asking skills

lation until an effective procedure can be found. Individual differences in "conditionability" surely exist, as indicated in the study of criminal pathology, for example. But it would seem to be the rare child who is not influenced in some way by judiciously applied modification procedures. The collective evidence overwhelmingly supports the validity of behavior modification principles. Even the most adamant critics of behavior analysis no longer argue that behavior cannot be modified by conditioning procedures. These critics now concern themselves with the issue of what behaviors *should* be modified and by whom and for what purpose (Semb, 1972). This issue is addressed in the latter portion of this chapter.

Social Behaviors   If studies of the impact of systematic reinforcement and cueing strategies upon children's academic behavior are considered impressive, similarly designed and executed studies of social behavior are perhaps even more so. Again, a wide range of behaviors has been investigated with resultant robust data. One classification of social behavior studies useful for teachers is based on whether given behaviors are desirable or undesirable (disruptive). Desirable behavior can be thought of as that which is broadly compatible with children's educational progress and personal-social welfare; disruptive behavior can be interpreted as behavior incompatible with these general goals.

With this distinction in mind, it is instructive to draw upon the following sampling of behavior modification studies. Again, the experimental conditions generally include a systematic procedure for social and/or material reinforcement which is often combined with verbal directions of some kind. Such conditions have been associated with desirable changes in cooperative play behavior (Hart et al., 1968), peer interaction by a socially isolated child (Allen et al., 1964; Kirby and Toler, 1970), popularity among peers (Alden, Pettigrew, and Skiba, 1970) and racial integration among first-grade children (Hauserman, Walen, and Behling, 1973).

Similarly, many studies have been designed to *decrease* behavior that disrupts a learning environment or that is potentially dangerous for a child and/or his peers. A high rate of classroom aggression is a case in point. Usually quite effective in decreasing a child's rate of aggressive responses in the classroom are reinforcement procedures which supply positive reinforcement for nonaggressive behavior rather than creating the more traditional punishment condition observed so widely in the public schools (Pinkston et al., 1973). Occasionally, children come to control their aggressive classmates' aggression through selective social attention (Solomon and Wahler, 1973). The effective use of group reinforcements for reducing disruptive behavior among Head Start children has also been reported (Herman and Tramontana, 1971). Frequently, such reinforcements are augmented by clear teacher directions to which compliance has a predictable, consistent, and positive consequence (A. Baer, Rowbury, and Baer, 1973). Increasingly, studies of this type are being carried out in regular classrooms with unselected children and teachers who are naive about the application of behavior modification principles. It is not unusual for teachers to express initial skepticism about the efficacy of planned, selective reinforcement while they are being observed to act as inadvertent reinforcers of the very behavior they find disruptive—attending primarily to aggressive behavior and ignoring task-appropriate behavior, for example. It is unusual to find a teacher who remains skeptical and unaware of his or her own reinforcement practices after having benefited from training and actual participation in behavior analysis research (Brown and Elliot, 1965; Hall, D. Lund, and D. Jackson, 1968).

In fact, one of the most extensive studies of changing children's problem behavior in the classroom has been conducted on the firing line with a regular teacher (Becker et al., 1967). In this study, a significant reduction in deviant behavior (leaving one's seat to run about the classroom, taking other children's property, blurting out, screaming, and whistling in class) was associated with the firm application of general conduct rules in combination with differential social reinforcement. The investigators are quick to say, however, that such reinforcement, though potent, is no panacea for solving behavior problems. Neither is the mere dispensation of rules nor a simple procedure of ignoring deviant behavior. These conditions should be combined with at least one other: the reinforcement of behavior is incompatible with deviant behavior (as cooperative social interaction is incompatible with physical aggresson toward others). Of further importance is the researchers' discovery that social reinforcement administered to an appropriately behaving child (e.g., a child working constructively, either independently or in cooperation with others) in proximity to a child behaving deviantly (e.g., distracting others) is very effective. A teacher who implements this strategy would not attend directly to a misbehaving child; the possibility of reinforcing deviancy is therefore reduced. In addition, a deviant child who observes an appropriately behaving child being positively reinforced is likely to change his behavior to approximate more closely that of the model child.

As a final example of behavior analysis research, consider a situation in which a teacher was faced with the task of regaining control of an entire class of children who have high rates of disruptive behavior (O'Leary and Becker, 1967). To reduce this disproportionate ratio of deviant to acceptable behavior a contingency token system was conceived. Initially, points earned by children for specified acceptable behavior were immediately negotiable for a variety of back-up reinforcers. Savings periods were then gradually increased to the point where children were required to accumulate points for four days before "purchasing privileges" were granted. A pattern of traditional social rewards and group contingencies was also integrated into the procedure. Deviant behavior decreased from an average of 76 to 10 percent of all observed behavior during the experimental period. The frustration and time-consuming features of discipline problems were reduced, and the teacher gained freedom to attend to academic skill development. This result, in turn, was associated with reduced failure rates among the children. A subsequent attempt at replicating the effects of these procedures in a different classroom has also been successful (O'Leary et al., 1969).

To summarize, many behavior modification studies involving young children have dealt with the influence of reinforcement and cueing procedures on preacademic, academic, and social behavior. Social reinforcement by adults can be a very powerful influence on young children's behavior. Thorough discussions of its contingent use in preschool and remedial settings are available and may be consulted for further detail (e.g., D. Baer and Wolf, 1968). Other types of reinforcers, such as token or point systems, interlaced with material back-up reinforcers also seem to have reliable effects. Although operant conditioning procedures have been particularly effective in modifying the behavior of deviant children and in the treatment of learning disabilities, they have been applied broadly to "normal" children. Most of the research to date indicates functional relationships between principles of operant conditioning and the acquisition of language, reading, and social responses. Gilbert (1962) may be consulted for an accounting of mathematics learning and operant principles.

Trends in Behavior Analysis Research In addition to the research activities discussed above, several well established trends in early childhood behavior analysis can be identified. One is the development of programs for training parents and nonprofessionals in the use of behavior modification principles (Christopherson et al., 1972; Cohen et al., 1971; Gardner, 1972; Hanley and Perelman, 1971; Herbert and Baer, 1972; and Wetzel, 1970). Another is the study of children's self-reinforcement and contingency selection behavior, including procedures for self-monitoring (Glynn, 1970; Liebert, Spiegler, and Hall, 1970; Thomas, 1971).

More recently emerging trends can also be observed. One concerns the organization of learning environments so that administrative arrangements can be examined for any possible reinforcing properties. An example is the study of behavioral outcomes of simultaneous participation by children in the same activity versus a situation in which the children are given an opportunity to choose among a variety of activities (Doke and Risley, 1972). Another is the study of "zone" versus "man-to-man" staffing procedures which concerns the manner in which adults supervise children individually and in groups and the effect of such procedures on children's group participation behavior (LeLaurin and Risley, 1972). A second emerging trend is the study of peer tutoring, including the use of classroom pupils as behavioral engineers (see, for example, Semb, 1972, part 4). Readers interested in a useful set of criteria for assessing these and other behavior analysis studies should consult Hanley (1970). Finally, a trend in methodology seems to be developing as this book is written—a move from a nearly exclusive use of *response rate* as the definitive behavioral criterion to a renewed consideration of the intensity, duration, and situational appropriateness of given responses (Meacham, 1973). The technology of behavior modification is firmly established, but little attention has been given to problems such as why reinforcement works better with some children than with others and why any possible unintended effects of systematic conditioning occur.

CRITIQUE

Concepts of precision teaching developed from the work of Skinner and his followers represent an ambitious attempt to improve education by developing new models of instruction. This attempt is clearly based on the idea that practices prevalent in schools today are rarely attuned to the genuine problems of individualizing instruction. Nor have efficient curricular sequencing and contingent reinforcement systems been achieved on a wide scale. From a behavioral analysis perspective, constant experimentation is required to achieve these objectives. As we have seen, the ultimate goal in behavioral analysis is the precise specification of variables that may be manipulated to "optimize learning." Admirable as this goal may be, the educational practices derived from this perspective are not free from criticism. Nor can these practices be disassociated from certain crucial issues. The following discussion, although not exhaustive, constitutes a review of some major criticisms and issues associated with behavioral analysis.

Issues Related to a Scientific Concept of Behavior

A basic assumption upon which behavior analysis procedures rest is that fundamental laws govern the behavior of organisms. Scientific analyses are performed largely to identify these laws, including those which govern the behavior of children in educational settings. Behavior analysis is therefore patterned upon a scientific conception of the child. A scientific conception of the child has not been readily accepted by many early childhood educators, nor by society generally for that matter. Skinner (1956) suggests that this resistance may be due to the vanity of man. He believes that this vanity is exemplified by man's tendency to view himself in self-deterministic, free-will terms and as being blessed with inherent qualities to help him conquer adverse circumstances in the pursuit of excellence. To acknowledge a scientific concept of behavior—that humans are controlled by certain fundamental laws—is to surrender this and other facets of a democratic philosophy of human nature. Appealing as a democratic view of human nature may be, Skinner believes that human behavior is controlled in many ways by environmental events. Experimental analyses of behavior are simply attempts to ferret out the ways in which behavior is controlled. There should be no reason, as Skinner argues, why knowledge of the laws of human behavior cannot be used to achieve better control of both our environment and ourselves. Control, then, becomes inevitable unless one depends entirely upon chance conditions to produce social improvement.

The Problem of Control   One immediate implication of the scientific conception of human behavior concerns control in the form of education. If laws can be applied to control behavior in the classroom, cannot such control be misused? To those fearful that the power to control may be misused, Skinner (1956) offers three defenses against abuse: (1) fully expose the techniques of control so that sub rosa manipulations are neutralized; (2) restrict the use of physical force, coercion, or fear-inducing tactics; and (3) develop more refined skills among adults *and* children for purposes of better environment control, including education. Similarly, the alleged exploitation by teachers of children so often charged by critics of behavior modification need not be an issue, according to Hively (1971). He argues that a teacher should make clear and justify to parents (and the general public) what, how, and why behaviors are being reinforced via incentive systems that are amenable to open evaluation. The word is *accountability.* Hively (1971) also maintains that, gloomy critics notwithstanding, the expression of creativity and critical analysis skills need not be excluded from a precise specification of desired behaviors and certainly not from rich reinforcement.

Proponents of open education (see Chapter 7) often argue that these defenses miss the point. For them the issue is any child's right to decide when, where, how, and under what conditions he will learn something. No such choice seems available when exacting objectives are determined in advance by an authority who also decides how the child shall be shaped. On the other hand, can an advanced technological society which depends, among other things, upon mass education for its advancement, afford to provide children the luxury of determining exclusively what, when, and where they will learn? Ausubel (1959), for example, has argued against the psychological soundness of curricula designed primarily according to children's professed desires. Ausubel believes that the rationale for curricula built upon the spontaneous desires of children is often based, at least in part, upon a faulty analogy derived from the nutritional finding that nutrition is adequately maintained when infants are allowed to select their own diets. He also maintains that children's spontaneously expressed interests do not necessarily reflect all of their important needs. Ausubel further argues that breadth in a curriculum, an essential feature if young children are expected to expand existing interests and develop new ones, is unlikely if educational activities are delimited simply to meet the transitory and frequently impulsive desires of the young.

In the final analysis, persons who champion instruction based solely on the child's inferred needs and interests usually seem to assume a moral imperative:

> The argument is that the child, like everyone else in a democracy, has a right to select his own goals and, within limits, pursue them as he sees fit. Psychology is irrelevant to this argument, since if it is ethically right that school programs spring from the interests and

motives of the student, then whether such a policy works well is irrelevant. The policy is followed because it is morally correct, not because it is effective. . . . a counterargument is that the good of society and the long-term good of the child should take precedence over the hypothetical immediate rights of the child (Anderson and Faust, 1973, p. 420).

The Issue of Uniqueness   A second issue concerns the charge that a scientific conception of behavior fails to account for the individuality or uniqueness of children. In fact, those who take a scientific view of behavior do not deny genetic or constitutional factors as strong sources of individual differences among children. Rather, it is conceded that these sources simply are not subject to manipulation by behavior techniques. Reinforcement techniques can be used to alter the environment in which behavior occurs; it is precisely this sort of environmental change that characterizes behavioral analysis. A point to be made here is that a child's behavior—whether "normal" or "deviant"—is viewed as a product of environmental conditions (unless, of course, organic pathology is clearly indicated). If a child has a learning problem, this problem generally is considered an outgrowth of faulty environmental conditions, not as something inherent in the child for which teacher or parental responsibility can be denied. Put into practice, this notion represents a very constructive attitude. Certainly it is a positive departure from the more usual tendency for children's problems to be viewed as personal weakness or deficiency. Moreover, if a "problem" represents a lack of motivation to perform, rather than a lack of performance *capabilities*, the optimum use of available stimulation (reinforcement contingencies included) according to behavior analysis principles is more constructive than either devising a "remedial program" or abdicating responsibility for the child's growth (Rosenfeld and Gunnell, 1973).

A third related objection sometimes raised in connection with operant conditioning is that it is inappropriate to apply to human beings the behavioral modification techniques developed under laboratory conditions with animals. This objection is frequently based on the erroneous view that behavior analysts consider human behavior to be basically equivalent to the behavior of infrahuman species. While it is true that operant conditioning principles were originally developed through the laboratory study of animals, no serious student of behavior analysis subscribes to the view that principles so developed can be simplistically applied to complex human behavior. However, it is also true that applied behavior analysis is frequently complicated by limitations in the control of variables or conditions necessary to establish definitive functional relationships (Gewirtz, 1969). It is incumbent upon behavioral scientists to communicate these limitations clearly.

Broader Psychological Issues   Broader issues in behavior analysis are associated more generally with S-R (stimulus-response) psychology as a whole. For example, positions about childhood learning and development built upon S-R concepts have long been viewed as mechanistic. This criticism is important to the extent that "mechanistic" implies that (1) children are simply passive reactors to the environment and (2) behavioral analysis evinces an apparent lack of concern for cognitive and affective processes which may mediate environmental stimuli and overt responses. Concerning the first point, there is widespread disagreement among psychologists generally. For example, in contrast to the behavioral analysis view that the child learns by reacting to or being shaped by his environment is the cognitive-developmental view that the child actively constructs his own experience (see Chapter 5). The basic issue here is the nature of childhood—an issue that has captured the attention of scholars for centuries.[14] Within psychological theory this issue has been translated to the question of whether operant conditioning actually contributes to our conceptualization of human growth. According to Langer (1969), for example, an answer depends upon the degree to which animal behavior and human behavior are comparable. It seems clear from the research that general principles of reinforcement applied across species yield similar results, but this finding need not be taken to indicate a simplistic view of the nature of man.

The second point above, dealing with psychological processes, equally illustrates disagreement among psychologists in matters related to child development theory and research. For those who take a strict behavioral analysis point of view, only overt (observable) behavior can be studied in a truly scientific way. Such behavior is presumed to be the content of psychological functioning. This position again stands in contrast to cognitive-developmental psychology, wherein overt behavior is taken to infer covert (unobservable) mental processes, which are then utilized to explain development. Thus, while supporters of behavior analysis will discuss behavior in terms of response rate, an empirical criterion, cognitive developmentalists usually resort to hypothetical statements about qualitative thought processes which are not directly observable. This issue of the true stuff of psychology, circa 1970, is made salient by the following strong words:

> No wise man has yet discovered a way to deal with minds, thoughts and feelings except when these are defined as nothing more than various behaviors in various situations. To pretend or claim to work with mental processes or internal events is, at this time, dishonest. (Ramp and Hopkins, 1971, p. ix).

Science and Education   It is probable that the issues described above are of less immediate and practical concern to teachers than are their

---

[14] See Hitt (1969) for a recent articulation of the principal differences between behaviorism and existential psychology and the implications of these differences.

own reservations about the "coldly scientific" context in which behavioral analysis procedures may be executed. Perhaps the observation of teachers who apply such procedures in the classroom has led to such reservations. Casual observation may conceivably result in a confusion between systematic contingency management and a teacher's feelings about children. Consider, for example, a child whose excessive dependency behavior (seeking help for every task he attempts) is being maintained by social reinforcement (teacher attention). If a decision is made to decrease dependency striving and increase independence striving, a good part of the strategy would necessitate removing the social reinforcement for dependency behavior. Nonreinforcement (planned ignoring) of this behavior might easily be misconstrued by a naive observer as uncaring teacher behavior. This observer might believe that to reinforce a child positively regardless of the quality of the child's behavior (noncontingent reinforcement) or to help a child rationalize (find excuses for) inappropriate behavior is better for the child's mental hygiene. Such techniques are often taken to indicate a "nurturant" teacher attitude. According to the behavioral analysis viewpoint, high rates of inappropriate or low-quality behavior could result if these techniques were widely applied. The problem is clearly arriving at a teaching style that reflects a general attitude of acceptance and benevolence toward children and a clear, ethically appropriate approach to the management of contingencies for improving children's behavior. Related to this problem is a conjectural matter. Does a precision teaching model constructed from behavior analysis principles attract personnel already predisposed toward "cool and calculating" techniques of social interaction? No data relevant to this question are available. However, there is no reason for a cold, emotionally antiseptic atmosphere to pervade this or any other approach to early childhood education. Certainly, it would be unfortunate for teachers and parents to equate systematic teaching with an emotional vacuum.

Another way to think about the issue is to acknowledge that scientific technique and the objective attitude necessary to sustain it has contributed excessively to depersonalization and dehumanization in the schools. That is, the scientific method—personified by behavior analysis in psychology and education necessarily leads the teacher away from the inner, subjective experience of being human. As we all know, these feelings are difficult, if not impossible, to communicate in measurable ways. Does a view of the scientific method as the best route to valid knowledge mitigate against humanism? Within the schools, the supreme value does appear to be accorded to "hard data," usually in the form of achievement test results, as *the* criterion to determine worth. Quantified data, whether appearing in statistical or letter-grade form, can appear so abstract that they are easily removed from their source. This makes it difficult for many teachers (and parents) to identify such data for what they are: symbols of experience. This abstractness can also result in potential consumers of research being unaffected or even alienated by "cold, synthetic, empirical" data presented by unknown empiricists.

A systematic and humane application of behavior analysis principles will include careful attention to and respect for children's individuality and their total physical, cognitive, and socioemotional development. These children in a behavioral analysis classroom are discussing with their teacher the joys of a creative dramatics activity. Photo courtesy of Media Services, University of Washington Experimental Education Unit.

A possible solution to this problem is to enlist more practitioners in action research programs, i.e., research to solve local classroom and school problems. This is precisely what many behavior analysts now advocate. Teaching and research thus become complementary activities, if not synonomous concepts. Like the scientist, a teacher becomes an expert observer, recorder, and manipulator of events. Antecedent-consequent relationships are described. But the setting is a likely classroom with all the joys and frustrations thereof. Teachers trained in the methods of behavior analysis seem to consider themselves more effective as a result. They also see more clearly the results of their actions on children. This is reinforcement. Education and science, then, are viewed as highly compatible endeavors (Axelrod, 1971).

Behavior Causation   Finally, behavior analysis is often criticized as having a simplistic view of behavioral causation. For a teacher to consider behavior at any point in time in terms of a child's "reinforcement history," for example, is of limited value. No practical means for discovering a child's reinforcement history are available to teachers. One can only assume that high rates of free operant behavior are the result of past reinforcement. Further, the deliberate avoidance of statements of causality in matters of educational diagnosis may disturb some observers. For example, consider the classic problem of underachievement, that is, a child who does not perform satisfactorily in terms of what is expected from him or from what his past experience would predict. On the assumption that underachievement is a valid phenomenon, many educators and psychologists seek first to discover the causes of the "problem." Interviews, tests, and case study procedures have traditionally been employed in the attempt to isolate the cause. Only by eliminating the cause of the problem will the problem be solved, according to this strategy.

In contrast, behavior analysts maintain that, apart from controlled experimentation, causation cannot be determined. Post hoc assumptions are avoided because they are untestable. In the case of the underachiever, the problem for behavioral analysis would not be to find the assumed cause (e.g., faulty parent relations) post hoc, but to modify the child's behavior increase, for example, his rate of persistent and constructive academic task responses. The focus is upon behavioral change instead of the etiology of behavior. As Clarizio and Yelon (1967) indicate, teachers are probably best advised to deal with behavior directly rather than with its causes for several reasons. Perhaps the most important one is that teachers rarely are trained to query the causes of behavior. Such causes frequently are considered obscure and perplexing even by experienced mental hygienists. Further, even if a probable cause is discovered, its treatment may be beyond the limits of a teacher's skill and ethical intervention.

Specific Issues Concerning Reinforcement

Additional issues, most of which pertain more directly to the psychological outcomes and limitations of reinforcement, should be examined. For example, concern is often expressed about the narrowness of behavior change effected by operant techniques. While response frequency increases may be obtained in a singular response class (e.g., attending to teacher instructions or initiating social contacts with other children), there is no guarantee that change will occur in other related response classes. This poses the issue of *allied* or *collateral change*. Few data relevant to this issue are available, although there is some evidence that allied changes can occur (Buell et al., 1968; Kennedy and Thompson, 1967). Much more research is needed in this area. At this writing it appears that reinforcement principles affect the way in which an individual selects and delimits his responses in the presence of specific cues rather than the way in which he extends his repertoire rapidly across varied situations.

Reinforcement as an Oversimplification of the Learning Process Still another issue worthy of note concerns the danger that the effects of reinforcement on learning may be oversimplified. Social learning theorists such as Bandura (1962, 1967, 1969) maintain that the ordering of reinforcement cannot claim to be the end-all of complex behavior development. The work of Bandura and his colleagues indicates that modeling influences—independent of or in conjunction with direct reinforcing consequences—result in a wide variety of behaviors including aggressiveness, fear development and modification, and nurturance. Imitation learning must be considered as a significant impetus to response acquisition. In fact, the contiguous sensory stimulation involved in imitation learning has been reported as a sufficient condition for acquisition of most forms of matching responses (Bandura, 1962). Bandura does not, however, exclude the role of *practice*, which is particularly important for the development of motor skills and where mere exposure to a model is insufficient. Neither does he deny the power of reinforcement in shaping the attentional responses of a learner. The point is that when deliberately arranged reinforcement contingencies are not apparent, children acquire many responses by modeling their teachers or peers. It is apparent, however, that the development of broad classes of imitation responses are influenced measurably by reinforcement variables.

A related notion is that many desirable behaviors may not be acquired efficiently by children through exclusive reliance upon the method of reinforcing successive approximations (Bandura, 1962). Consider, for example, how long it would probably take to teach a child to perform a complex act like tying his own shoe in the absence of verbal cues and a model to imitate. With this in mind one might argue that the stimulus events to which a child responds are as important, if not more so, than a reinforcement which may follow a response. Several studies indicate that children's discrimination learning frequently occurs quite suddenly, in contrast to the incremental and gradual process implied by the successive approximations method (Hill, 1965; Rieber, 1966; Suppes and Ginsberg, 1963).

Other reservations about simplistic application of reinforcement systems have been expressed (Horowitz, 1967; Kagan, 1969; Kuypers, D., W. Becker, and K. D. O'Leary, 1968; Maehr, 1968). For example, a token system applied mechanically without attention to supplementary procedures and principles may be self-defeating or only marginally effective. Kuypers et al. (1968) report such a finding in reference to a behavior modification program for third and fourth graders. A successful token system apparently requires skill in both the integration of differential social reinforcement and behavior shaping. The former is particularly important, since the goal of a token system frequently is to increase the effectiveness of social reinforcers for children initially unresponsive to such "natural" reinforcement. A systematic pairing of token reinforcements and ample social reinforcement must occur, especially when delays exist between responding and token reinforcement. Teachers must be trained in the principles of behavior shaping and social reinforcement scheduling if they desire to utilize token systems successfully. Excessive reliance upon token economy systems can be dysfunctional where skilled social reinforcement works equally well (Forness and MacMillan, 1972).

In other words, a full awareness of the advantages and obstacles of token systems is requisite to any implementation (Kazdin and Bootzin, 1972).

Mediating Factors in Reinforcement Although the importance of social reinforcement is strongly emphasized in the operant conditioning literature, this type of reinforcement is not the last word in behavior modification. In fact, its influence is mediated by many variables (Horowitz, 1967; Stevenson, 1965; Zigler and Kanzer, 1962). For example, younger children are apparently more strongly influenced by social reinforcement than are older children. Girls seem generally more responsive to social reinforcement than boys. The extent to which a child perceives a dispenser of social reinforcement as a person with high status is still another mediating variable. Further variables include social class status of the child, the nature of the affective relationship between the child and a reinforcing adult, and the degree to which a child may have been previously deprived or satiated with social reinforcement in a given situation. In some cases, the nature of the task (simple versus complex, motor versus intellectual) may make a difference, as may the extent to which a child is anxious about his relationships with others or is strongly dependent upon adult approval. And certain classes of behavior may be influenced more strongly by social reinforcement than others. For example, Parton and Ross (1965) report that social reinforcement does not uniformly facilitate the development of motor behavior in random samples of children. Together these findings help define a need for the careful observation of individual children if appropriate reinforcers are to be selected and used effectively. For some children social reinforcement has no apparent value. Variables other than reinforcement may be much more critical in the development of complex behaviors.

The general issue involved in much of the foregoing discussion is the limitation of reinforcement. According to Kagan (1969), reinforcement enlists a child's attention, furnishes excitement (when reinforcement is pleasant), and operates as an incentive to reproduce previously reinforced behavior. Although these functions are generally considered positive, Kagan maintains that two basic problems are inherent in the use of reinforcement. One is that a child is often tempted to predict the pattern of rewards or the schedule of reinforcement in operation during a learning activity. Once a child can predict the pattern and understands the relationship between his behavior and the reinforcing consequences (thus satisfying his curiosity), he may stop playing the game. This may be particularly true for older children. Kagan's second caution is more theoretical but noteworthy:

It is important to appreciate that the term reinforcement has no independent definition and this fact alone should make us suspect of its integrity. A reinforcement is anything that will alter the probability of an action; it is a reinforcement. If it does not, it is not a reinforcement. If breaking balloons makes a child stay a little longer at the piano, then balloon breaking is a reinforcer. This definition is a little like defining dawn at the time when people begin to arouse themselves from their sleep. In a 24 hour winter night in Stavanger, Norway, dawn exists in a pitch black sky. A functional definition therefore, has obvious flaws (Kagan, 1969, pp. 136–137).[15]

Intrinsic versus Extrinsic Reinforcement   Other critics such as Maehr (1968) are skeptical even about the motivational function of reinforcement, particularly when reinforcement occurs in the absence of challenging learning materials. Programmed materials, for example can be as unstimulating as an inadequate teacher. Certain qualities of learning materials, such as degree of novelty and degree of personal meaning to a learner, could obviate the need for a meticulously planned schedule of external reinforcement. Thus, the issue of *intrinsic* versus *extrinsic* motivation is raised again.

Traditionally, intrinsic motivation has been considered in terms of "learning for learning's sake" or "learning characterized by the positive affect that accompanies a job well done." The latter interpretation, in particular, pervades an enormous amount of research about *achievement motivation* (Crandall, 1963). Educators typically assign the highest value to intrinsic motivation; motivation prompted by tangible rewards which are extrinsic to a learning task takes a poor second. As we have seen, a good deal of emphasis within behavior analysis is placed upon extrinsic reinforcement; tokens, negotiable for candy or other goodies when proof of academic performance is offered by a child, exemplify extrinsic reinforcement.

This behavioral emphasis clearly prompts an uneasiness among many educators. For example, some teachers express a fear that if children are conditioned to receive (and expect) extrinsic reinforcements, they will refuse to learn in the absence of such incentives. Or, in the extreme, it is feared that children may learn greed and avarice within a system of extrinsic reinforcements (O'Leary, Poulos, and Devine, 1972). Other teachers argue that the use of extrinsic reinforcements is tantamount to bribery. Still others focus on the grounds that extrinsic reinforcers are distracting to children and hence interfere with learning.

These objections deserve an airing. One feature of extrinsic reinforcement systems pertinent to all of the above objections, is often unheeded: tangible reinforcers routinely are used in behavior analysis programs only when "natural reinforcers" such as praise and accomplishment do not sustain motivation. In fact, one main objective in such

---

[15] Reprinted with permission from *Young Children*, Vol. XXIV, No. 3, January 1969. Copyright © 1969, National Association for the Education of Young Children, 1834 Connecticut Ave., N.W., Washington, D.C. 20009. The reader is encouraged to examine Kagan's logic. He appears to object to the tautological nature of an empirical concept of reinforcement. See also Burgess and Akers (1966), whose ordering of definitions and propositions regarding operant behavior is an attempt to counter the charge that reinforcement principles are tautological.

programs involves conditioning children to be more sensitive or responsive to natural reinforcement (see Kuypers et al., 1968). Furthermore, after initial learnings are well established, reinforcement schedules are "leaned out" in a conditioning strategy. In this way, continuous extrinsic reinforcement is no longer necessary. A possible material reinforcement overkill also can be avoided if free time is used as the central reinforcing consequence (Osborn, 1969). Teachers have used free time as a reward for years; in behavior analysis its use has merely been systematized to accelerate academic progress.

The bribery issue is a knotty one because of the connotations of the term *bribery* itself. Literally, bribery involves a reward or promise of favors with the intent to corrupt the conduct or pervert the judgment of another person. It is questionable that the use of tangible reinforcers in school programs constitute bribery unless one views improved self-care, responsible academic work, skills in group participation, and the like, as corruptive. It is also necessary to make a distinction between the procedural aspects in using reinforcers and the social desirability of the behaviors being changed (O'Leary, Poulos, and Devine, 1972). It is true that tangible reinforcers can be and are used by many teachers and parents to influence children's behavior, usually when a child is resistant and uncooperative (such as in performing household chores, going to bed on time, doing homework, or even practicing piano lessons). If one defines *bribery* simply as something that influences a particular line of conduct, then concrete reinforcers, as much of education itself, can be considered bribery. In the broadest perspective, one can ask whether or not everyone behaves in anticipation of some sort of consequence—a phenomenon not far removed from bribery. In this connection, one is reminded of Max Weber's classic discussion (1930) of capitalism and the Protestant Ethic. Weber states that according to this ethic, an accumulation of material goods through hard work, self-sacrifice, and thrift serves as an indirect indication of the probability of one's being "saved." This is perhaps the ultimate reinforcement contingency. The point is that consequences do follow behavior; applying behavior principles to education is most simply an attempt to make the consequences positive rather than negative, effective and efficient rather than ineffective and inefficient.

A final issue about tangible reinforcement is the potentially distracting effect of such reinforcers to children engaged in learning activities. Many studies have found that the performance of children rewarded with material goods is often inferior to that of children whose reinforcement comes from more natural sources (Spence, 1970). This result is particularly true for middle-class children and less true for disadvantaged children, who often respond more positively to material rewards. The distraction hypothesis can be used to explain the lesser performance of material reward groups of learners. Equally plausible is that material reinforcers quickly lose their incentive value, especially when children are already accustomed to material advantages. The truth is unknown and the issue of distractibility remains unresolved. It is possible that children are distracted initially, but soon adapt to token economy systems (O'Leary, Poulos, and Devine, 1972). If so, organized programs of longer duration (more than several days) should not be affected adversely by concrete reinforcement procedures.

SUMMARY

As applied to early childhood education, behavioral analysis may be appropriately considered as a (1) method for studying school environments and (2) set of principles for behavior modification. The success of this approach is dependent upon a systematic arrangement of cues and reinforcement contingencies. By virtue of these arrangements children are conditioned to establish and maintain desired rates of academic and social behavior.

In a behavioral analysis approach, every attempt is made to maximize the effects of positive reinforcement on learning. The importance of reinforcement in the learning process has been widely recognized and is not confined to behavior analysis. However, the behavior analysis view is that only through the contingent use of reinforcement can desired behavior be shaped predictably. A critical teaching skill required is the prudent timing of reinforcements. Equally important, however, is skill in educational programming, that is, the efficient sequencing of learning activities so as to maximize the probability of a learner's successful academic progress.

Aside from precise contingent reinforcement, perhaps a behavioral analysis approach is most distinguished by the type of data collected by a teacher and the methods used for collecting such data. Response frequency (increase and decrease) is the primary object of study. Formative evaluation occurs by definition of behavior analysis methodology. In contrast, practically all other strategies in education rely upon testing procedures to measure end-of-instruction competence (summative evaluation). Within a behavioral analysis strategy, response rate measures are taken by means of precise observation and/or recording measures controlled by the child, who thereby records his own progress. The use of programmed materials to which children actively respond facilitate continuous response measurement. Programmed materials are therefore frequently preferred to standard materials although careful arrangements of any learning materials may be suitable. Most broadly, the practical objectives of programs built upon behavior analysis principles are twofold: (1) to increase the range and frequency of appropriate academic and social responses and (2) to decrease the range and frequency of task-inappropriate or undesirable response. Ultimately, a behavior analysis approach would make a child so proficient in self-management and basic academic skills that he could pursue his own learning productively and independently. If, in this regard, the criteria of sound programming, continuous response measurement, and contingent reinforcement are met, then the ideal of individualized instruction for each child can be realized.

While behavioral analysis principles are firmly based in academic psychology, new procedures and techniques are continually being de-

veloped. A continual reassessment of standard procedures and the development of new ones often produces a lag between laboratory and educational practice. As new procedures are applied to education, research into
the complexities of contingency management and programming is required.
However, the available data about childrens' early school learning and the
modification of behavior problems strongly suggest that a behavioral
analysis framework is a fruitful alternative to traditional methods for those
who value precision teaching.

REFERENCES

Alden, S., L. Pettigrew, and E. Skiba. The effects of individual-contingent group
reinforcement on popularity. *Child Development*, 1970, *41*, 1191–1196.

Allen, K. E., et al. Control of hyperactivity by social reinforcement of attending
behavior. *Journal of Educational Psychology*, 1967, *58*, 231–237.

Allen, K. E., et al. Effects of social reinforcement on isolate behavior of a nursery
school child. *Child Development*, 1964, *35*, 511–518.

Anderson, R., and G. Faust. *Educational psychology.* New York: Dodd, Mead, 1973.

Andrews, J. The results of a pilot program to train teachers in the classroom
application of behavior modification techniques. *Journal of School Psychology,*
1970, *8*, 37–42.

Ausubel, D. Viewpoints from related disciplines: human growth and development.
Teachers College Record, 1959, *60*, 245–254.

Axelrod, S. Education and science: compatible endeavors. In E. Ramp and B.
Hopkins (eds.), *A new direction for education: behavior analysis, 1971.* Lawrence, Ks.: University of Kansas, Department of Human Development, 1971,
336–346.

Azrin, N., and W. Holz. Punishment. In W. Honig (ed.), *Operant behavior.* Englewood Cliffs, N.J.: Prentice-Hall, 1966, 380–447.

Baer, A., T. Rowbury, and D. Baer. The development of instructional control over
classroom activities of deviant preschool children. *Journal of Applied Behavior
Analysis*, 1973, *6*, 289–298.

Baer, D. An age irrelevant concept of development. *Merrill-Palmer Quarterly,*
1970, *16*, 238–245.

Baer, D. Behavior modification: you shouldn't. In E. Ramp and B. Hopkins (eds.),
A new direction for education: behavior analysis, 1971. Lawrence, Ks.: University of Kansas, Department of Human Development, 1971, 358–367.

Baer, D., and M. Wolf. The reinforcement contingency in preschool and remedial
education. In R. Hess and R. Bear (eds.), *Early education.* Chicago: Aldine,
1968, 119–129.

Baer, D., M. Wolf, and T. Risley. Some current dimensions of applied behavior
analysis. *Journal of Applied Behavior Analysis*, 1968, *1*, 91–97.

Bandura, A. Social learning through imitation. *Nebraska symposium on motivation,
1962.* Lincoln, Nebr.: University of Nebraska Press, 1962, 211–269.

Bandura, A. The role of modeling processes in personality development. In W.
Hartup and N. Smothergill (eds.), *The young child.* Washington, D.C.: National
Association for the Education of Young Children, 1967, 42–57.

Bandura, A. Social learning theory of identificatory processes. In D. Goslin (ed.),
Handbook of socialization theory and research. Skokie, Ill.: Rand McNally, 1969,
213–262.

Becker, W. Behavior analysis and education, 1972. In G. Semb (ed.), *Behavior analysis and education, 1972*. Lawrence, Ks.: University of Kansas, Department of Human Development, 1972, 11–25.

Becker, W., et al. The contingent use of teacher attention and praise in reducing classroom behavior problems. *Journal of Special Education*, 1967, *1*, 287–307.

Betancourt, F., and M. Zeiler. The choices and preferences of nursery school children. *Journal of Applied Behavior Analysis*, 1971, *4*, 299–304.

Bijou, S. An empirical concept of reinforcement and a functional analysis of child behavior. *Journal of Genetic Psychology*, 1964, *104*, 215–223.

Bijou, S., and P. Sturges. Positive reinforcers for experimental studies with children. *Child Development*, 1969, *30*, 151–170.

Birnbrauer, J. Generalization of punishment effects—a case study. *Journal of Applied Behavioral Analysis*, 1968, *1*, 201–212.

Brown, P., and R. Elliot. Control of aggression in a nursery school class. *Journal of Experimental Child Psychology*, 1965, *2*, 103–107.

Bucher, B., and O. Lovaas. Use of aversive stimulation in behavior modification. In M. Jones (ed.), *Miami symposium on the prediction of behavior: aversive stimulation*. Coral Gables, Fla.: University of Miami Press, 1967, 35–51.

Buell, J., et al. Collateral social development accompanying reinforcement of outdoor play in a preschool child. *Journal of Applied Behavior Analysis*, 1968, *1*, 167–174.

Burgess, R., and R. Akers. Are operant principles tautological? *Psychological Record*, 1966, *16*, 305–312.

Bushell, D., Jr. *A token manual for behavior analysis*. Lawrence, Ks.: University of Kansas Support and Development Center for Follow Through, undated.

Bushell, D., Jr. *The behavior analysis classroom*. Lawrence, Ks.: University of Kansas, Department of Human Development, Follow Through Project, 1970.

Bushell, D., Jr. The behavior analysis classroom. In B. Spodek (ed.), *Early childhood education*. Englewood Cliffs, N.J.: Prentice-Hall, 1973, 163–175.

Bushell, D., Jr., P. Wrobel, and M. Michaelis. Applying "group" contingencies to the classroom study behavior of preschool children. *Journal of Applied Behavioral Analysis*, 1968, *1*, 55–62.

Chadwick, B., and R. Day. Systematic reinforcement: academic performance of underachieving students. *Journal of Applied Behavior Analysis*, 1971, *4*, 311–319.

Chow, S., and P. Elmore. *Early childhood information unit: resource manual and program descriptions*. San Francisco: Far West Laboratory for Educational Research and Development, 1973.

Christopherson, E., et al. The home point system: token reinforcement procedures for application by parents of children with behavior problems. *Journal of Applied Behavior Analysis*, 1972, *5*, 485–497.

Clarizio, H., and S. Yelon. Learning theory approaches to classroom management: rationale and intervention techniques. *Journal of Special Education*, 1967, *1*, 267–274.

Cohen, S., et al. The support of school behaviors by home-based reinforcement via parent-child contingency contracts. In E. Ramp and B. Hopkins (eds.), *A new direction for education: behavior analysis, 1971*. Lawrence, Ks.: University of Kansas, Department of Human Development, 1971, 282–308.

Crandall, V. Achievement. In H. Stevenson (ed.), *Child psychology*. Chicago: University of Chicago Press, 1963, 416–459.

Doke, L., and T. Risley. The organization of day care environments: required vs. optional activities. *Journal of Applied Behavior Analysis*, 1972, *5*, 405–420.

Doss, H., et al. Effect of contingent reinforcement on reading performance with primary special education children. Paper read at the meeting of the American Educational Research Association, New York, February, 1971.

Edlund, C. The effect on the behavior, as reflected in the IQ scores, when referred after each correct response. *Journal of Applied Behavior Analysis*, 1972, *5*, 317–319.

Felixbrod, J., and K. O'Leary. Effects of reinforcement on children's academic behavior as a function of self-determined and externally imposed contingencies. *Journal of Applied Behavior Analysis*, 1973, *6*, 241–250.

Ferster, C., and M. Perrott. *Behavior principles*. Englewood Cliffs, N.J.: Prentice-Hall, 1968.

Ferster, C., and B. F. Skinner. *Schedules of reinforcement*. Englewood Cliffs, N.J.: Prentice-Hall, 1957.

Forness, S., and D. MacMillan. Reinforcement overkill: implications for education of the retarded. *Journal of Special Education*, 1972, *6*, 221–230.

Gardner, J. Teaching behavior modification to nonprofessionals. *Journal of Applied Behavior Analysis*, 1972, *5*, 517–521.

Gewirtz, J. Mechanisms of social learning: some roles of stimulation and behavior in early human development. In D. Goslin (ed.), *Handbook of socialization theory and research*. Skokie, Ill.: Rand McNally, 1969, 157–212.

Gilbert, T. Mathematics: the technology of education. *Journal of Mathematics*, 1962, *1*, 7–73.

Glynn, E. Classroom application of self-determined reinforcement. *Journal of Applied Behavior Analysis*, 1970, *3*, 123–132.

Goetz, E., and D. Baer. Social control of form diversity and the emergence of new forms in children's blockbuilding. *Journal of Applied Behavior Analysis*, 1973, *6*, 209–217.

Goetz, E., and M. Salmonson. The effect of general and descriptive reinforcement on "creativity" in easel painting. In G. Semb (ed.), *Behavior analysis and education, 1972*. Lawrence, Ks.: University of Kansas, Department of Human Development, 1972, 53–61.

Haaf, R., et al. A developmental study of children's incentive-object preferences. *Developmental Psychology*, 1970, *3*, 275.

Hall, R. V., et al. Effects of teacher attention on study behavior. *Journal of Applied Behavior Analysis*, 1968, *1*, 1–12.

Hall, R. V., D. Lund, and D. Jackson. Instructing beginning teachers in reinforcement procedures which improve classroom control. *Journal of Applied Behavior Analysis*, 1968, *1*, 315–322.

Hamblin, J., and R. Hamblin. On teaching disadvantaged preschoolers to read: a successful experiment. *American Educational Research Journal*, 1972, *9*, 209–216.

Hanley, E. Review of research involving applied behavior analysis in the classroom. *Review of Educational Research*, 1970, *40*, 597–626.

Hanley, E., and P. Perelman. Research resulting from a Model Cities program designed to train paraprofessionals to aid teachers in elementary school classrooms. In E. Ramp and B. Hopkins (eds.), *A new direction in education: behavior analysis, 1971*. Lawrence, Ks.: University of Kansas, Department of Human Development, 1971, 158–190.

Haring, N., and T. Lovitt. Operant methodology and education technology in special education. In N. Haring and R. Schiefelbusch (eds.), *Methods of Special Education*. New York: McGraw-Hill, 1967.

Harris, F., et al. Effects of positive social reinforcement on regressed crawling of a nursery school child. *Journal of Educational Psychology*, 1964, *55*, 35–41.

Hart, B., et al. Effect of contingent and non-contingent social reinforcement on the cooperative play of a preschool child. *Journal of Applied Behavior Analysis*, 1968, *1*, 73–78.

Hart, B., et al. Effects of social reinforcement on operant crying. *Journal of Experimental Child Psychology*, 1964, 1, 145–153.

Hauserman, N., S. Walen, and M. Behling. Reinforced racial integration in the first grade: a study of generalization. *Journal of Applied Behavior*, 1973, *6*, 193–200.

Herbert, E., and D. Baer. Training parents as behavior modifiers: self-recording of contingent attention. *Journal of Applied Behavior Analysis*, 1972, *5*, 139–149.

Herman, S., and J. Tramontana. Instructions and group versus individual reinforcement in modifying disruptive group behavior. *Journal of Applied Behavior Analysis*, 1971, *4*, 113–119.

Hill, S. The performance of young children on three discrimination learning tasks. *Child Development*, 1965, *36*, 425–436.

Hitt, W. Two models of man. *American Psychologist*, 1969, *24*, 651–658.

Hively, W. What next (in behavior analysis)? In E. Ramp and B. Hopkins (eds.), *A new direction for education: behavior analysis, 1971.* Lawrence, Ks.: University of Kansas, Department of Human Development, 1971, 311–322.

Holt, G. Effect of reinforcement contingencies in increasing programmed reading and mathematics behaviors in first grade children. *Journal of Experimental Child Psychology*, 1971, *12*, 362–369.

Homme, L., et al. Use of the Premack principle in controlling the behavior of nursery school children. *Journal of the Experimental Analysis of Behavior*, 1963, *6*, 544.

Hopkins, B., R. Schutte, and K. Garton. The effects of access to a playroom on the rate and quality of printing and writing of first and second grade students. *Journal of Applied Behavior Analysis*, 1971, *4*, 77–87.

Horowitz, F. Social reinforcement effects of child behavior. In W. Hartup and N. Smothergill (eds.), *The young child.* Washington, D.C.: National Association for the Education of Young Children, 1967, 27–41.

Johnston, M., et al. An application of reinforcement principles to development of motor skills of a young child. *Child Development*, 1966, *37*, 379–387.

Kagan, J. An essay for teachers. *Young Children*, 1969, *24*, 132–142.

Katz, L. Condition with caution: think thrice before conditioning. Urbana, Ill.: ERIC Clearinghouse on Early Childhood Education, 1971.

Kazdin, A. The token economy: an annotated bibliography. Washington, D.C.: American Psychological Association, 1972.

Kazdin, A. Role of instructions and reinforcement in behavior changes and token reinforcement. *Journal of Educational Psychology*, 1973, *64*, 63–71.

Kazdin, A., and R. Bootzin. The token economy: an evaluative review. *Journal of Applied Behavior Analysis*, 1972, *5*, 343–372.

Kennedy, D., and I. Thompson. Use of reinforcement techniques with a first grade boy. *Personnel and Guidance Journal*, 1967, *46*, 366–370.

Kirby, F., and H. Toler, Jr. Modification of preschool isolate behavior: a case study. *Journal of Applied Behavior Analysis*, 1970, *3*, 309–314.

Knight, M., S. Hasazi, and M. McNeil. A home based program for the development of reading skills for preschoolers. In E. Ramp and B. Hopkins (eds.), *A new direction for education: behavior analysis, 1971.* Lawrence, Ks.: University of Kansas, Department of Human Development, 1971, 223–234.

Krumboltz, J., and H. Krumboltz. *Changing children's behavior.* Englewood Cliffs, N.J.: Prentice-Hall, 1972.

Kuypers, D., W. Becker, and K. O'Leary. How to make a token system fail. *Exceptional Children*, 1968, *35*, 101–108.

Langer, J. *Theories of development.* New York: Holt, Rinehart and Winston, 1969.

Lates, B., A. Egner, and H. McKenzie. Behavior analysis of the academic and social behavior of first grade children, or what happens when educators turn on. In E. Ramp and B. Hopkins (eds.), *A new direction for education: behavior analysis, 1971.* Lawrence, Ks.: University of Kansas, Department of Human Development, 1971, 191–222.

LeLaurin, K., and T. Risley. The organization of day care environments: "zone" versus "man-to-man" staff assignments. *Journal of Applied Behavior Analysis,* 1972, *5*, 225–232.

Liebert, R., M. Spiegler, and M. Hall. Effects of the value of contingent self-administered and noncontingent externally imposed reward on children's behavioral productivity. *Psychonomic Science*, 1970, *18*, 245–246.

Lindsley, O. Public address on precision teaching. Tacoma, Wash. November, 1968.

Lindsley, O. Public address on behavior therapy. University of Washington, Seattle, May, 1969.

Lovitt, T. Operant conditioning techniques for children with learning disabilities. *Journal of Special Education*, 1968, *2*, 283–289.

Madsen, C., Jr. Positive reinforcement in the toilet training of a normal child: a case report. In L. Ullman and L. Krasner (eds.), *Case studies in behavior modification.* New York: Holt, Rinehart and Winston, 1966, 305–307.

Madsen, C., Jr., W. Becker, and D. Thomas. Rules, praise, and ignoring: elements of elementary classroom control. *Journal of Applied Behavior Analysis*, 1968, *1*, 139–150.

Maehr, M. Some limitations of the application of reinforcement theory to education. *School and Society*, 1968, *96*, 108–110.

Maier, N. Frustration theory: restatement and extension. *Psychological Review*, 1956, *63*, 370–388.

Maltzman, I. On the training of originality. *Psychological Review*, 1960, *67*, 229–242.

McGeoch, J. *The psychology of human learning.* New York: McKay, 1942.

McMahon, M. Positivism and the public schools. *Phi Delta Kappan*, 1970, *51*, 515–517.

Meacham, M. Personal correspondence, University of Washington, Seattle, November 1973.

Meacham, M., and A. Wiesen. *Changing classroom behavior.* Scranton, Pa.: International Textbook, 1969.

Michael, J., and L. Meyerson. A behavioral approach to counseling and guidance. *Harvard Educational Review*, 1962, *32*, 382–402.

Miller, L., and R. Schneider. The use of a token system in Project Head Start. *Journal of Applied Behavior Analysis*, 1970, *3*, 213–220.

O'Leary, K., and W. Becker. Behavior modification of an adjustment class: a token reinforcement program. *Exceptional Children*, 1967, *33*, 637–642.

O'Leary, K., and R. Drabman. Token reinforcement programs in the classroom: a review. *Psychological Bulletin*, 1971, *75*, 379–398.

O'Leary, K., R. Poulos, and V. Devine. Tangible reinforcers: bonuses or bribes? *Journal of Consulting and Clinical Psychology*, 1972, *38*, 1–8.

O'Leary, K., et al. A token reinforcement program in a public school: a replication and systematic analysis. *Journal of Applied Behavior Analysis*, 1969, *2*, 3–14.

Osborn, J. Free time as a reinforcer in the management of classroom behavior. *Journal of Applied Behavior Analysis*, 1969, *2*, 113–118.

Parton, D., and A. Ross. Social reinforcement of children's motor behavior: a review. *Psychological Bulletin*, 1965, *64*, 65–73.

Patterson, G. An application of conditioning techniques to the control of a hyperactive child. In L. Ullman and L. Krasner (eds.), *Case studies in behavior modification*. New York: Holt, Rinehart and Winston, 1966, 370–375.

Pinkston, E., et al. Independent control of a preschool child's aggression and peer interaction by contingent teacher attention. *Journal of Applied Behavior Analysis*, 1973, *6*, 115–124.

Premack, D. Toward empirical behavior laws: I. Positive reinforcement. *Psychological Review*, 1959, *66*, 219–233.

Premack, D. Reinforcement theory. In D. Levine (ed.), *Nebraska symposium on motivation, 1965*. Lincoln, Neb.: University of Nebraska Press, 1965, 123–180.

Ramp. E., and B. Hopkins (eds.). *A new direction for education: behavior analysis, 1971*. Lawrence, Ks.: University of Kansas, Department of Human Development, 1971.

Reese, E. *The analysis of human operant behavior*. Dubuque, Iowa: William C. Brown Company, 1966.

Resnick, L. *Design of an early learning curriculum*. Pittsburgh, Pa.: University of Pittsburgh, Learning Research and Development Center, 1967.

Richard, H., G. Taylor, and J. Libb. Contingency management and rate of classroom productivity. *Perceptual and Motor Skills*, 1973, *36*, 1267–1273.

Rieber, M. The role of stimulus comparison in children's discrimination learning. *Journal of Experimental Psychology*, 1966, *72*, 263–270.

Risley, T. *Juniper Gardens nursery school project*. Lawrence, Ks., University of Kansas, Department of Human Development, 1969.

Rosenfeld, H., and P. Gunnell. Effects of peer characteristics on preschool performance of low income children. *Merrill-Palmer Quarterly*, 1973, *19*, 81–94.

Salzberg, B., et al. The effect of intermittent feedback and intermittent contingent access to play on printing of kindergarten children. *Journal of Applied Behavior Analysis*, 1971, *4*, 163–171.

Sapon, S. Contingency management and programmed instruction in the preschool. *Audiovisual Instruction*, 1968, *13*, 980–982.

Schutte, R., and B. Hopkins. The effects of teacher attention on following instructions in a kindergarten class. *Journal of Applied Behavior Analysis*, 1970, *3*, 117–122.

Semb, G. (ed.). *Behavior analysis and education, 1972*. Lawrence, Ks.: University of Kansas, Department of Human Development, 1972.

Sidman, M. Operant techniques. In A. Backrack (ed.), *Experimental foundations of clinical psychology*. New York: Basic Books, 1962.

Skinner, B. F. *The behavior of organisms: an experimental analysis*. Englewood Cliffs, N.J.: Prentice-Hall, 1938.

Skinner, B. F. The science of learning and the art of teaching. *Harvard Educational Review*, 1954, *24*, 86–97.

Skinner, B. F. Freedom and the control of man. *American Scholar*, 1956, *25*, 47–65.

Skinner, B. F. What is the experimental analysis of behavior? *Journal of the Experimental Analysis of Behavior*, 1966, *9*, 1–12.

Skinner, B. F. *The technology of teaching*. Englewood Cliffs, N.J.: Prentice-Hall, 1968.

Solomon, R. Punishment. *American Psychologist*, 1964, *19*, 239–253.

Solomon, R., and R. Wahler. Peer reinforcement control of classroom problem behavior. *Journal of Applied Behavior Analysis*, 1973, *6*, 49–56.

Spence, J. The distracting effects of material reinforcers in the discrimination learning of lower- and middle-class children. *Child Development*, 1970, *41*, 103–111.

Staats, A. Learning, language, and cognition. New York: Holt, Rinehart and Winston, 1968.

Stevenson, H. Social reinforcement of children's behavior. In L. Lipsitt and C. Spiker (eds.), *Advances in child development and behavior.* Vol. 2. New York: Academic Press, Inc., 1965, 97–126.

Stumphauzer, J., and B. Bishop. Saturday morning television cartoons: a simple apparatus for reinforcement of behavior in children. *Developmental Psychology*, 1969, *1*, 763–764.

Suppes, P., and R. Ginsberg. A fundamental property of all-or-none models: binomial distribution of responses prior to conditioning with application to concept formation in children. *Psychological Review*, 1963, *70*, 139–161.

Tate, B., and G. Baroff. Aversive control of self-injurious behavior in a psychotic boy. *Behavior Research and Therapy*, 1966, *4*, 281–287.

Thomas, D. Preliminary findings on self-monitoring for modifying teaching behaviors. In E. Ramp and B. Hopkins (eds.), *A new direction for education: behavior analysis, 1971.* Lawrence, Ks.: University of Kansas, Department of Human Development, 1971, 102–114.

Thorndike, E. L. *The psychology of learning.* New York: Teachers College, 1913.

Ullman, L., and L. Krasner. *Case studies in behavior modification.* New York: Holt, Rinehart and Winston, 1965.

Wasik, B. The application of Premack's generalization on reinforcement to the management of classroom behavior. *Journal of Experimental Child Psychology*, 1970, *10*, 33–43.

Weber, M. *The Protestant ethic and the spirit of capitalism.* London: G. Allen, 1930.

Werry, J., and H. Quay. Observing the classroom behavior of elementary school children. *Exceptional Children*, 1969, *35*, 461–467.

Wetzel, R. Behavior modification techniques and the training of teachers' aides. *Psychology in the Schools*, 1970, *7*, 325–329.

Williams, C. The elimination of tantrum behavior by extinction procedures. *Journal of Abnormal and Social Psychology*, 1959, *59*, 269.

Zigler, E., and P. Kanzer. The effectiveness of two classes of verbal reinforcers on the performance of lower- and middle-class children. *Journal of Personality*, 1962, *30*, 157–163.

Zimmerman, B., and E. Pike. Effects of modeling and reinforcement on the acquisition and generalization of question-asking behavior. *Child Development*, 1972, *43*, 829–907.

Photograph courtesy of Southwest Educational Development Laboratory, Austin, Texas.

chapter

the romance
with language

INTRODUCTION

If any aspect of child development can be singled out as the principal reference point for educational programming during the past decade, it is language. This emphasis was largely due to the assumption of interdependence (if not equivalence) between language and cognitive skills made by many intervention program builders. Some, as will be seen, subscribed also to the controversial hypothesis that logical thinking skills may be honed by activities for refining children's language production. In any case, the target of early and widespread concern for language development was the so-called disadvantaged child (see Chapter 1). Descriptive studies of language behavior during the preschool years have generally revealed that marked social class differences in language usage exist by age 4 and in some cases earlier (McCandless and Evans, 1973). The most often reported differences are deviations in grammar and pronunciation from the standard English form, and stylistic differences which seem to interfere with learning and the expression of conceptual thought within the classroom. Some educators have viewed these language differences as "deficits" to be overcome by systematic language training; other educators have felt that a greater opportunity should be provided for language development through general verbal stimulation and modeling by adults. In short, many early programs of the 1960s quickly and sharply focused upon language phenomena. Just as quickly arose the double-barreled question of exactly what and how to "teach for" language development. The answers to this question varied with the individual program builders' philosophies, theoretical orientations, and interpretations of research data. As programs evolved, answers also were modified.

In this chapter, selected programs with a strong language component are examined. Both variety and major points of conflict in current thinking about language education are illustrated, although this task is undertaken with some reservations. It is risky to review language education apart from a full and careful discussion of children's native language development, at least as such development is currently understood. Space limitations restrict the scope of the present discussion to representative approaches to language training and accompanying issues and problems. Consequently, the reader is referred elsewhere for background material (see, for example, Cazden, 1972; Dale, 1972; Goss, 1973; McNeill, 1970; and Palermo, 1971). The main body of this chapter, then, is developed only with an initial recognition of five points of reference.

The first point concerns the definition of language development. Most broadly, such development refers to a progressive increase in the quantity, range, and complexity of both receptive (understanding) and expressive (producing) language. Thus, while a year-old infant's repertoire is generally limited to a few words understood and spoken with meaning, this same child by age 6 will be comprehending and speaking complex sentences with a vocabulary of thousands of words. In fact, it is generally agreed that by school age, children have acquired most of their basic knowledge about the structural (grammatical) features of their own language and how to employ them for communication. The full range of pronunciation skills is normally mastered by age 8, while vocabulary continues to grow throughout the life span. This means that language develops rapidly during the early years and presumably should be most affected by variations in the language environment during this time. It is notable, however, that the course of children's language development is generally the same regardless of race or culture; it is questionable whether "preschool education"—certainly in the limited traditional sense of the term—can be viewed as a significant factor in the language development of many children.

Despite the remarkable commonality among children in their general language development, differences do exist. This brings us to the second point, namely, that at successive points in the developmental sequence increased individual language differences can be observed. These differences occur in grammatical systems, dialects, vocabulary size, modes of expression, and a host of other language attributes. In some cases— dialect, for example—factors such as ethnicity and geographic region contribute to language differences. Certainly organic pathology—cleft palate, for example—can be a source of deviation from the normal course of development. Richness and variety in early learning experiences in which language communications are salient also are involved. But irrespective of idiosyncratic and sociocultural variations, most authorities believe that all languages and dialects are inherently equal in terms of structure and complexity and that systematic deviations from any one formal, standard language form do not indicate inherent intellectual differences (Cazden et al., 1971). Exceptions to this belief exist, however, and are noted in the following pages.

Third, it must be recognized that there is presently much disagreement among scholars about the basic processes of language development, the factors which most strongly influence the rate and quality of development, and, accordingly, the most valid procedures for formal (and even informal) language education. For example, the relative roles of genetic forces, imitation learning, reinforcement, and procedures for correcting children's "improper" use of language are hotly contested among students of language development. Some attention to these points of disagreement is given toward the end of the present chapter.

The fourth point concerns the comparatively weak "state of the art" for assessing children's language development, particularly their *competence* in decoding and encoding language content. This weakness in assessment has led to problems in the evaluation of language programs. In fact, authorities argue among themselves about what criteria are most useful to seek as worthy language objectives, to say little about the search for valid and reliable criterion measures. These two issues are also highlighted throughout this chapter, although interested readers should consult Cazden (1971) for a fuller treatment.

Lest the romance with young children's language be viewed as a new one, the fifth and final point should be made: language objectives have long been considered important by early childhood educators. Montessori (see Chapter 6), for example, pressed for language enrichment in the preschool. General support for communication skills–building activities has also characterized conventional nursery school and kindergarten practice throughout the years. But current early education programs have become much more differentiated in terms of specific language objectives and instructional tactics. As suggested earlier, this is due largely to the increased attention given to language by cognitive psychologists and the presence in preschool programs (e.g., Head Start) of many children who appear in need of support for improved language development (Cazden, 1971).

Given these five points, the move to tightly structured programs for language development which shocked early childhood education establishmentarians during the sixties may now be discussed. Alternatives to structured language programming and the advent of bilingual programs are also examined. This chapter concludes with a summary and overview of some major issues in early childhood language education.

A SPECTRUM OF LANGUAGE PROGRAMS

The Leap to High Structure

Among the most marked departures from the child development–socialization model in early childhood education is the Distar Instructional System (Science Research Associates, 1972). This system is defined by a set of direct instructional techniques and coordinated, sequenced learning tasks in language, arithmetic, and reading. While suitable for use with any group of children beginning as early as age 4, the program out of which Distar has evolved actually was designed for children with severe educational handicaps manifest mostly in language production (Bereiter and Englemann, 1966). It was observed early that a good many children with such handicaps enter school already a year or more behind their more educationally advantaged age-mates. Under normal school conditions, this gap in educational progress widens with successive years of formal schooling (see the cumulative deficit hypothesis, Chapter 1). It was argued that intensive procedures to inculcate basic academic skills were needed in the early grades; only through the application of such procedures would such children's retarded rate of educational progress be accelerated. This acceleration called for, among other things, a reordering of priorities for early education so that the maximum use of time could be made for specific intellectual-academic training. It was also assumed that, since language is the lifeblood of academic development, certain language skills must be mastered. Further, these skills, deemed requisite to prevent school failure, must be refined in a compressed time period. Otherwise, the children would remain ill equipped to deal with the language of the classroom—standard English—and suffer increasingly serious conceptual inadequacies. In brief, the original premise for the program that has become Distar defined *cultural deprivation as language deprivation.*

In this section, the major features of Distar language training are described to accentuate the uniqueness of this program in relation to mainstream early childhood education. A brief review of recent evaluation research about the Distar program follows. A conceptual analysis of Distar, in summary form, concludes this section.

Distar Language Like the reading and arithmetic components of Distar, the language component consists of three levels that correspond roughly to preschool, kindergarten, and the primary grades, respectively. Accordingly, the instructional objectives are arranged in a hierarchy of successive complexity and inclusiveness. The foundation for all advanced instruction, however, is a child's mastery of certain essential objectives. Some examples of minimum language objectives (level I) will illustrate (Englemann, Osborn, and Englemann, 1972):

The ability to use both affirmative and *not* statements in response to questions (e.g., "What is this?" "This is a glass. This is not a cup.")

The ability to use both affirmative and *not* statements in response to a command (e.g., "Tell me about this pencil." "This pencil is purple. This pencil is not orange.")

The ability to handle certain polar opposites. (e.g., "If it is not _____, it must be _____.") (Concept pairs include big-little, up-down, long-short, fat-skinny).

The ability to use basic prepositions correctly for purposes of describing object arrangments: on, in, under, over, between, (e.g., "Where is the paper?" "The paper is under the pencil.").

The ability to name positive and negative exemplars of at least four concept classes (e.g., tools, vehicles, pieces of furniture, wild animals, farm animals). (For example, "Tell me something that is a vehicle." "A truck is a vehicle." "Tell me something that is not a vehicle." "A cat is not a vehicle.") A child should also be able to deal correctly with such class concepts in relation to familiar nouns. (e.g., "Is a pencil a piece of furniture?" "No, a pencil is not a piece of furniture. A pencil is something to write with.").

The ability to perform simple *if-then* deductions. (e.g., A child is presented with a diagram containing both big and little circles; all the big circles are blue, but the little circles are of various other colors. "If the circle is big, what do you know about it?" "It's blue.").

The ability to use *not* in deductions. (e.g., "If the circle is little, what else do you know about it? "It is not blue.").

The ability to use *or* in simple deductions. (e.g., "If the circle is little, then it is not blue. What else do you know about it?" "It's red, yellow, or green.").

According to the Distar language program authors (Englemann, Osborn, and Engelmann, 1972), most teachers assume that children enter school capable of performing these skills. Though many preschool children whose home language environment is rich may develop and practice them, many others do not. Either way, specific steps are programmed within Distar to ensure these skills' mastery as a firm basis for complex language learnings in the formal classroom.

General Management Procedures   A Distar program has administrative and instructional procedures to accommodate about thirty children for three hours a day, five days a week, for up to three years of total schooling. Many variations are possible. At least three teachers are required, each of whom is responsible for a subject—language, arithmetic, or reading. Children are divided into three or four groups of seven or eight members each. Assessed achievement level usually serves as the criterion for determining group membership. Thus, children of comparable learning rates and developmental status are grouped together. Each teacher deals successively with all three groups in her subject matter specialty. Academic activities are conducted for periods of about thirty minutes and interspersed with nonacademic activities such as music. Juice and cracker time and social play are provided for younger children. Hence, only one-

Distar lessons are programmed for intensive small group work based upon pattern drill exercises. These four-year-old children are in the early stages of language and reading activity. Photo by Peter Rinearson.

half (ninety minutes) of a three-hour "school day" is spent in intensive small group work. The recommended time allotments may require slight modification in a given situation, particularly in the initial stages of the program. Modifications, however, are limited strictly to amount of time spent in instruction and do *not* include a reduction of the pace of instruction. Of the constellation of instructional variables which defines the Distar system, brisk pacing is among the most sacred.

Language Curriculum   The Distar language component is composed of an integrated set of basic concepts, sentence forms, and presentation strategies. For its implementation, the functions of language as a "teaching instrument" must be understood. From this core understanding spring both the beginning and advanced phases of language training. To begin, the criteria and parameters for satisfactory language communication between teacher and child are established. It is first necessary that a child understand language is a symbolic substitution for physical reality. For example, he must learn that the expression, "Three oranges are in the brown sack," has a concrete referent which may be observed or created. A second requirement involves the feedback condition of learning, namely, that through language the child is provided with an independent check on the accuracy of his observations. For this reason, statements of fact represent the key element of Distar language. Facts are either correct or incorrect, so that feedback from teacher to child is clear. For example, a teacher may clap her hands and remark that "This is an example of clapping." The idea of clapping can be monitored according to a true-false categorization.

Distar includes a model for presentation strategies in the beginning language program, the components of which are the *identity statement* and the *second-order* statement, which modifies and expands the identity statement. These two statement forms are used to teach the basic concepts of the program. The identity statement is based upon a standard format and provides for the accurate symbolic representation of an object: "This is a (n) _____." (For example, "This is a bicycle," "This is an apple.") Plurals (for instance, "These are bicycles,) and identity negation statements ("This is not a bicycle," "These are not apples.") also fit into this format.

This second-order statement form permits the further expansion and specification of concept attributes: "This (n) _____ is _____." (For example, "This bicycle is blue," "This apple is green.") Plurals and negations are similarly handled ("These bicycles are blue," "These apples are not green"). Further variations are presented once the basic forms are mastered, for example, variations which allow for differential subject-predicate placement. Central to the model are *polar concepts* (such as hard-soft and long-short) and *nonpolar* concepts which (1) pertain only to certain members of an identity class (such as, "This cup is white" where the attribute color is nonpolar and other members of the class concept "cup" may differ in color) or (2) represent a property shared by all members of a concept class (such as, "This cup is a drinking utensil").

Throughout the language program an emphasis is placed upon the derivation of rules to guide the child's observations, analyses, inferences, and generalizations. Teaching all concepts in the same fashion provides a consistency and opportunity for practice which makes this sort of rule derivation feasible. Common objects in the environment are labeled and classified. Emphasis is placed on the basis for object classification, namely, the sensory attributes of objects and their placement in a hierarchy of successive abstractions. Language instruction is also focused upon the child's ability to formulate logically meaningful questions about the basic properties of concepts (concrete, functional, and abstract) and relationships among concepts.

The basic language teaching strategy in Distar is *pattern drill*. Teacher-pupil interchanges in the form of verbal presentation-demonstration followed by question-answer strategies conform to the statement models discussed above. A definitive sequence beginning with simple identity statements (singular) is programmed. Eventually the tricky concept of "opposites" is introduced through second-order statements which highlight polar attributes. Polar discriminations of key concepts such as *long* (short), *big* (small), *fat* (thin), *tall* (short), *fast* (slow), *dark* (light), and *straight* (crooked)—all of which rely upon the sense of vision—are introduced and standard questions asked for them. Other basic concepts involving different sensory modalities are also included. Examples are *heavy* (light) and *soft* (hard), the discrimination of which is based upon proprioceptive and tactile sensory modalities, respectively. Singular polar discriminations are followed by multiple discriminations, polar deductions ("If this is loud, it is not soft"), nonpolar concepts such as color, and preposition-linked concepts (next to, on, over, under). Other program content includes class concepts which can be broken into subclasses. In this way, the rule of deduction implicit in second-order statements is reinforced. These class concepts include animals, plants, buildings, furniture, vehicles, containers, tools, appliances, food, and clothing. The form and content of the beginning language program stimulate the development of verbal inquiry skills and provide the conceptual basis for elementary hypothesis making and testing. These goals are supposedly reached through strictly patterned vocabulary and discrimination-training activities. This phase of the language program is then succeeded by an advance phase in which these skills are further refined.

Further concept formation tasks require a learner to categorize stimuli on the basis of a property or properties shared in common by the stimuli. For example, consider the objects *wrench, file, pliers, scissors,* and *screwdriver.* Not only do these items share concrete properties such as metal, but they have a common function, namely, to serve as hand-held instruments for performing certain specified tasks. The verbal abstraction *tool* is used to categorize the items according to function. Activities in the advanced language program are designed to clarify the various bases for categorization. Unlike in most approaches to early concept development, concrete objects are not used extensively. Symbolic models, however, play an important role. Visual aids for concept illustration are provided in Distar's teacher presentation books.

Systematic procedures are employed to teach that an object can have more than one criterial attribute at a time, for example, a box can be both big and open. Learners are led from these simple statements to more complex forms such as, "This box is not big and not open." Teachers' cueing procedures to encourage question asking by the children are also programmed. The predominant pattern, however, is comprised of a specific order of question-answer exchanges between a teacher and the children as the following example indicates:

> *Teacher* presents a tall plastic bottle full of colored liquid: Is this bottle tall?
> *Children*: Yes!
> *Teacher*: Is this bottle full?
> *Children*: Yes!
> *Teacher*: Is this bottle tall and full?
> *Children*: Yes!
> *Teacher*: Say the whole thing!
> *Children*: This bottle is tall and full!

In the advanced stages of the program, verb expansions are introduced, first for the intransitive and then the transitive forms. Sense verbs (sound, smell, taste, and feel) are included as is the expansion of polar concepts (e.g., an expansion of the polar opposite big-small to big, bigger, biggest–small, smaller, smallest). This emphasis upon gradations is similar to that in Montessori sensorial material (see Chapter 6). But, unlike in Montessori education, direct sensory experiences are rare in Distar. Other more advanced tasks in Distar I involve the use of *comparatives* and *superlatives, locations* (e.g., theater, post office, shoe repair shop), *before-after sequences, if-then deductions*, and the differentiation of *some, all*, and *none*.

Distar language II and III build upon these activities and include work with questioning strategies, following instructions, synonyms, analogies (e.g., "Noisy is to quiet as hot is to _____"), and fundamental information regarding types of measurement, occupations, and the calendar. Eventually, high-priority skills for communication are developed: information analysis and processing, sentence structure analysis and processing, and writing skills (including punctuation mechanics and other rules for written expression—see Distar language III). Take-home exercises and a storybook (Distar I) also are sequenced throughout the curriculum package to reinforce and provide practice in daily lesson material.

Again, the reader is reminded that Distar language training is arranged concurrently with parallel activities in reading and arithmetic which also reinforce language concepts. These activities are designed expressly to promote clear thinking and especially deductive reasoning. Throughout all program components, pattern drill is the principal method of instruction.

Aside from its application in increasing numbers of K–3 public school programs in America, Distar forms the basis of one Project Follow Through model (see Chapter 1). This model has been implemented in some twenty different geographic locations, reaching over 10,000 children by 1973. In addition to the formal academic components of Distar, the Follow Through model utilizes materials published by Instructional Media of America, Inc.: *Language Concepts in Song* and *Language Concepts in Drawing*. Parental involvement is strongly endorsed as well. In fact, two levels of parental participation are still being tested. One involves actually training parents to serve as classroom teacher aides. The second is an organized program for teaching parents to be more effective home teachers with their children. Workbooks, weekly discussion sessions, a parent manual for behavioral management (based upon reinforcement principles—see Chapter 3), and "take homes" are included in this phase of the program. The latter, in particular, provide a concrete basis for parent-child collaboration in home-based learning.

Evaluation Research   Research data on the early experimental version of Distar are reported in the original edition of this volume (Evans, 1971b). Of more current interest are data about Distar impact as the program is now practiced. Becker and Englemann (1973), for instance, report that poor children who begin Distar in kindergarten progressively exceed

These four-year-old children prepare to leave their Distar classroom after a full morning of language, arithmetic, and beginning reading activities. Photo by Peter Rinearson.

average grade-level achievement norms, especially in reading decoding skills. By the end of the third grade, an advantage of as much as a full year in normative achievement has been documented for these Distar children.[1] By the same report, poor children who do not begin Distar until first grade generally do not show as rapid a rate of acceleration, yet still perform better than under conventional school circumstances. Gains in measured intelligence (Slosson Intelligence Test) are less spectacular, but increments over time have been observed—again to the special advantage of kindergarten Distar beginners. Nonpoor children, usually higher

---

[1] Most of the achievement data for Distar evaluation have come from using the Wide Range Achievement Test (WRAT).

than their poor peers in educational achievement at school entry, appear to profit equally from Distar, if not even more rapidly and thoroughly in measurable gains over time. Becker (1972) also has reported that achievement gains through kindergarten and early primary grades are closely related to the number of lessons taught during that period and that recent Distar system improvements are accompanied by still stronger achievement gains by children.

Collectively, these early results from Distar Follow Through evaluative research can be taken as support for the value of an early start in formal language-reading instruction *if* achievement patterns are to be strengthened among children whose prognosis is early school failure. Still other data indicate that Distar children, as compared to children in "ordinary" reading programs, can achieve a grade equivalent of 2.6 on standardized reading tests in nine fewer months of comparable instructional time (Shanner, Tallmadge, and Wright, 1972). This would be an impressive saving in a cost-effectiveness analysis of early childhood education.

Perhaps the single best collection of Distar case study reports has been compiled by Larsen (1971). These data summaries cover the period during which preliminary versions of the program were tested and revised in a wide variety of settings, including Head Start classrooms and regular kindergarten-primary programs in both rural and urban school districts. Two-year longitudinal results from the published version (levels I and II only) are also included. The surest generalization permitted by these data is that Distar seems effective in accomplishing its expressed purposes. Program success does vary from one time and place to the next; perhaps Distar is subject to subtle difficulties in external validity (see Chapter 1). But with grade-level achievement as the criterion, the measured academic growth of children for whom the program is designed usually surpasses that of comparable children in traditional curricula. Children, if taught specific skills systematically, usually learn those skills.

Few will deny that Distar children generally do better on Distar tasks than do non-Distar children. If one values the objectives of this structured program, then the content sequence and instructional methodologies of Distar seem to provide an effective way to achieve them. Questions about the more generalized effects of Distar training have not yet been answered unequivocally. Contrary to predictions, after one year's Distar experience one large sample of children were no different from a comparable sample of Head Start children in measured intelligence (Wechsler Preschool and Primary Scale of Intelligence), imitative language, or self-image; both groups, however, made significant gains in IQ (Evans, 1971a). Kindergarten and first-grade data from a similar sample of Distar children indicate a generalized training effect on measured intelligence, selected subtests from the Illinois Test of Psycholinguistic Abilities, and even divergent-semantic production (Ryckman, 1972, 1973). These data are important because they run counter to a common criticism of Distar: that the program emphasizes rote memory skills at the expense of mental operations that are associated with children's creativity.

Miller's report (1972) of a three-year follow-up study on Distar children is equally noteworthy. However, in this case, Distar children, especially boys, generally compared less favorably on a variety of cognitive and behavior rating measures with children from three other programs (conventional Head Start, Montessori, and DARCEE—a language-achievement motivation curriculum). This finding was obtained despite the Distar children's immediately positive response to training in the early stages of intervention. It must be noted that the Distar children in this longitudinal comparative study received only prekindergarten Distar instruction and then moved into different types of K–3 programs. Similarly, other reports (see Evans, 1971b) suggest that brief and early exposure to Distar may result in immediate gains; but unless the program is continued, its impact diminishes over time. This again illustrates the familiar "wash-out" phenomenon first discussed in Chapter 2. No extant program appears totally immune in this regard.

Further data from Distar Follow Through experience fit the general pattern of the importance of extended training. Long-term success with "hard-to-teach" children reportedly is increased if several related conditions are met: consistent instruction over time; administrative support for the total program; willingness of teachers to be trained (retrained, if necessary) and monitored through observation; and staff commitment to Distar education ("You gotta believe!") can make a difference (Osborn, 1973).

Conceptual Analysis   A cursory analysis of Distar according to the Parker and Day (1972) criteria explained in Chapter 1 is a suitable way to summarize this section. First, Distar is not built specifically from a theoretical frame of reference for child development. Rather, it incorporates a number of concepts from *learning psychology* which have an empirical foundation. Among these concepts are active involvement, a random- (versus fixed-) order recitation strategy, immediate feedback to the learner (especially knowledge of results and social reinforcement), a graduated sequence of learning based on task analysis, transfer of learning, and the contiguity principle (see Chapter 6). Distar *objectives*, highly explicit and operationalized in behavioral (observable) terms, are largely academic, with a strong emphasis upon content mastery. Positive affective outcomes are viewed as by-products of academic success.

In *implementation* Distar is a prime example of direct instruction in early childhood education. Activities are structured—initiated and directed by the teacher. All objectives, activities, and interaction strategies are carefully defined for the teacher; the teacher's primary responsibility is to present the curriculum according to specifications, perform basic diagnostic operations, reinforce children for correct responses, and maintain the desired instructional pace. Rate of verbal interaction is very high for teacher and child and very low among children themselves.

Distar's *criterion-reference testing* procedure also merits mention. This form of assessment attempts to evaluate instruction that is intended to create a specific level of skill proficiency among children. In other words, if instruction is administered for the purpose of promoting among all children the achievement of particular goals, it follows that assessment procedures should provide evidence of the validity of instructional procedures. Either a child has attained the objective or he has not. If he has, mastery has occurred. If he has not, procedures must be redesigned. Children are not ranked or compared to each other. The point of reference is the criterion established by a given instructional objective. In short, absolute standards prevail and testing procedures are arranged in reference to these standards—not to how well or poorly children compare to one another. The philosophy and practice of criterion-reference testing is exemplified by the in-program tests that Distar children must master before proceeding to more advanced material.

Distar, then, accentuates the teacher as technician. Precise schedules of social and material reinforcement (see Chapter 3) are utilized to sustain *motivation*. A strong effort is made to promote *parent participation* and *education*. And, finally, the Distar package is highly *exportable*. In fact, the authors (Engelmann, Osborn, and Engelmann, 1972) continue to strive for a "teacher-proof" curriculum. As this book is written, Distar continues to undergo revision, especially in the creation of learning contents which will appeal more to children's natural interests.

Final Comment As the reader may suspect, criticisms of Distar and its philosophical and pedagogical components range from mild to bitter (see, for example, Crittenden, 1970; Friedlander, 1968; Moskovitz, 1968). Since these criticisms apply to any structured, academically oriented, behavioristic approach to childhood education, it is instructive to identify two issues here: the behavioristic–cognitive developmental conflict and the question of open versus predeterministic education for children.

First, many developmental psychologists aligned with cognitive psychology are likely to reject the entire rationale upon which Distar is based. Kohlberg (1968), for example, sees specific training (direct, contrived instruction) as an extremely limiting (if not failing) strategy, especially in the cultivation of basic logical thought structures (response organizations). For this purpose, there can be no substitute for a mass accumulation of general age-linked experience. From this viewpoint, logical and physical knowledge is gradually derived from a basis of sensory-motor activities. Complex conceptual operations are structured and integrated in a progressive fashion, not by means of verbal material presented in a didactic form at levels which may represent too large a gap between present and past experience. Instead of viewing thinking as correct rule application, cognitive developmentalists focus upon the process of structuring knowledge through action. Immediate, short-term gains achieved through pattern drill are considered subsidiary to the establishment of general, irreversible mental structures (Kamii and Derman, 1969; Kohlberg, 1968). This set of arguments is not without empirical support, as will be emphasized in Chapter 5. However, the issue is fundamental cognitive operations, not the acquisition of specific discrimination and labeling skills, rote arithmetic knowledge, and the like.

The Distar creators have also evoked a timeless philosophical issue: freeing the child's creative potential by refraining from structured conditions or circumscribing the child's experience in pursuit of prescriptive, predetermined outcomes. The concern that children when forced or pushed (unduly pressured) may develop negative attitudes is hardly illegitimate. Not to be overlooked, however, are the facts that Distar is (1) addressed primarily to a population of children with observed difficulties and (2) derived from a priority system affected mainly by time limitations. In other words, given X problems and Y time, what might be done to most effectively reach Z? In this case, Z is a higher probability of school success. This goal perhaps illuminates the near-compulsion with which our society regards academic achievement. Clearly, it suggests that Distar is essentially *adaptive*, that is, conceived to facilitate the child's adaptation to the existing elementary school system (unlike Montessori, for example, whose stated objectives go far beyond—see Chapter 6). However, Distar remains a medium which can be construed by its critics as restrictive for teacher-child and child-child interactions, one that may rigidify children's learning styles prematurely. Longitudinal research is necessary for any validation of such criticisms.

A Tutorial Approach

Another dramatic alternative to the general, "total enrichment" approach to language in traditional early childhood education programs is the tutorial approach of Blank and Solomon (1968, 1969). Blank and Solomon also have assumed that disadvantaged children need consistent guidance to develop a firm basis for thinking. This means that children initially should be provided with (1) tasks that can be accomplished successfully, (2) ample practice so that newly developed skills can be reinforced frequently, and (3) specific help to develop language tools pertinent to formal classroom settings. Like Distar, this approach seeks to facilitate abstract thinking, especially among young "deprived" children. Unlike Distar, which is based upon small-group instruction, Blank and Solomon prefer a tutorial arrangement: individual teacher-child lessons for short periods of time (fifteen to twenty minutes) during a school day. Because this approach has not been commercialized, it is perhaps less widely known than are some language programs. However, this in no way diminishes its exemplary status.

A first goal of language training, according to Blank and Solomon, is for a child to realize that much information about the world is *not* immediately evident, but can be derived from past experience. This requires that a child become skilled in questioning and probing the implications of language communications. While vocabulary is important, a greater emphasis is placed upon the use of language to structure and guide thinking. In their words, vocabulary training alone cannot "lubricate" the entire language system. For example, simply teaching a child words like *apple*, *orange*, *grapefruit*, *corn*, *pea*, and *cabbage* provides no guarantee that these objects will be classified into their appropriate categories (fruit, vegetable) and further classified as members of the concept category *food*, after which objects that are food but neither fruit nor vegetable will be classified. In brief, the position is taken that language training must require children to make greater use of language "inside the head" to infer, estimate, deduce, and classify.

To stress the more abstract functions of language, Blank and Solomon have chosen concepts such as number, speed, direction, temperature, and emotions for their program content. Only ordinary and inexpensive objects readily obtainable in a usual nursery school environment are needed for teaching purposes: paper, crayons, blocks, toy cars, simple books. The heart of the tutorial method is a set of major techniques, reproduced with permission as follows from an earlier report of tutorial program impact on children's intellectual behavior (Blank and Solomon, 1968). These techniques collectively reflect their creators' perception of what deficiencies in thinking may characterize a typical disadvantaged child.

Language Tutorial Techniques

a) Selective attention.—The young child has few guidelines to assist him in discriminating selectively from the plethora of stimuli which surround him. He tends to be drawn to stimuli which may not be of great cognitive importance but which have potent perceptual qualities (e.g., blast of a horn, a whirling disk). The aim of this technique was to teach the child to recognize essential elements by requiring him to compare objects and make choices among them (e.g., if given a group of different-colored blocks, he was asked to take "two red blocks and one green block"). In this example, the higher-level concept of number helps the child restrain his impulse to respond primitively to the sensory impact of color alone.

b) Categories of exclusion.—When the adult gives specific instructions (e.g., "get a crayon"), the child does not need to reflect upon the characteristics of a particular category; he merely responds to direct commands. When the adult gives no direction, the child works aimlessly. When the child can work within the confines of exclusion, however, it means that he has understood the teacher's frame of reference and can independently make appropriate responses. To develop this skill, the child may be asked to make decisions within the confines set by the teacher. For example, the child may be asked to draw something, and he may draw a circle. To encourage the development of exclusion, he would then be asked to draw something "other than a circle."

c) Imagery of future events.—The young child can easily describe existing objects and situations. Difficulty arises when he must perceive the meaning of this information relevant to a particular context (see John, 1963). To increase this capacity, the child was required to think through the results of realistically possible but not present courses of action. The child might be first asked to locate a doll that was on the table. After the child completed this correctly, the doll would remain on the table, and the child might be asked, "Where would the doll be if it fell from the table?"

d) Relevant inner verbalization.—We have found that many deprived children will use language to direct their problem-solving only when asked to; they will not spontaneously use language when these external requirements are not imposed. Thus it is not a matter of not having the words but rather a matter of not voluntarily using these words without specific demands. This technique attempts to train the children to develop inner verbalization by retaining words as substitutes for objects. In this method, the child must use language silently and then express it upon request. He might be asked to look at a picture, say the name to himself, and then after the picture has been removed tell the name to the teacher.

e) Separation of the word from its referent.—Young children tend to respond to language automatically without fully recognizing that the word exists independently of the object or action represented. If this separation is not achieved, the child will not generalize the meaning of words beyond the particular contexts in which he hears them. To encourage the ability to reflect upon meaning, the child might be given a command which he must repeat aloud *before* acting out the command—for example, "Jump up two times," "Walk to the door and open it."

f) Models for cause-and-effect reasonings.—Our research (Blank and Bridger, 1966, 1967) has indicated that the perceptual powers of deprived children are intact; they need help, however, in organizing their observations so as to comprehend their significance. To achieve this comprehension, the child can be led to observe common but not frequently noted phenomena (e.g., "What is the weather outside today?" "Can we go out and play today?"). He can then be asked to draw upon his previous experience to determine the reasons underlying these observations (e.g., "Why can't we go out and play?" "Where is the rain coming from?").

g) Ability to categorize.—The place of categorization in thinking has been well documented, and its importance was recognized in this project. To aid the children in this sphere, elementary categories such as food, clothing, transportation, and job functions were taught. Thus, after feeding a doll an imaginary apple, the child was asked to name some other fruits that the doll might eat. Then, utilizing the process of exclusion (*b* above), the child might be asked to name some foods that were *not* fruits.

h) Awareness of possessing language.—Frequently young children are only passive recipients of instruction. This deficiency means that they are unaware that they can independently invoke language to help order their world. This weakness can be overcome by techniques such as asking the child to give commands to the teacher. The teacher might say to the child, "What shall I do with these pencils?" "Now *you* ask *me* to draw something," "Now tell me what the doll should do this afternoon."

i) Sustained sequential thinking.—Just as musical notes attain their full meaning only when heard within a melody, words attain their full potential only when imbedded in context. This is true even at the elementary level of a simple sentence, and it becomes increasingly important as chains of events extending into time and space must be understood. To be able to see objects, events, and words as located within their appropriate framework, the child has to be taught to maintain concentration and to determine all the possibilities of a course of action. For example, in discussing ways in which material can be altered, the discussion might begin with vegetable dyes (their function, their appearance, etc.). The issue can then be raised as to what can happen to these dyes under various conditions (diluting them with water, leaving them in concentrated form, etc.). In each case, the child is required to apply the necessary change (e.g., add the water) so that he can directly and immediately experience the phenomenon discussed.[2]

An inspection of the techniques in Table 4.1 reveals a strong bias toward language use in problem solving, not only in labeling and word definition. To execute these techniques, teachers are advised not to use gestures or other nonverbal cues; a strict reliance upon verbal communication is stressed. Children can be led to produce a variety of independent responses in situations created by the teacher so long as certain goals are achieved: extending the immediate present to the future by making predictions, supplying alternative courses of action which might be pursued in a given situation, providing explanations of phenomena that have been observed, inferring conditions about the past, and so on. A considerable amount of flexibility is made possible for teachers who wish to experiment, capitalize upon children's interests of the moment, and exercise creativity in the use of common materials. The tutorial "lessons" can be integrated into virtually any type of early education program. As such, they can serve as guidelines for language-specific intervention, rather than a fully organized and comprehensive language education program. One need not accept Blank and Solomon's assumptions about the needs of disadvantaged children to utilize the techniques; the approach seems suitable for most any early education setting where quasi-structured teacher-child communications are desired and where a "games" approach to language training is preferred.

Evaluation Research In an early evaluation of the tutorial program's impact on children, twenty-two disadvantaged nursery children were assigned to four groups, tutored and untutored, matched as well as possible on age, sex, and measured intelligence. The children in one experimental group each received a daily tutorial lesson, five days per week, for four months; a second group of experimental children were similarly tutored but only for three days per week. This allowed for some assessment of variation in amount of tutoring. A third group received fifteen to

---

[2] From M. Blank and F. Solomon, A tutorial language program to develop abstract thinking in socially disadvantaged preschool children. *Child Development*, 1968, *39*, 383–384. Reproduced by permission of the Society for Research in Child Development.

Individualized tutorial sessions to accentuate the use of language in thinking can be executed within the context of regular classroom activities. This child is pausing to reflect upon a cause-effect reasoning problem. Photo courtesy of Media Services, Experimental Education Unit, University of Washington, Seattle.

twenty minutes of individual contact daily, but no systematic tutoring was enacted. This third group represents an attempt to control for the "Hawthorne effect" as a hazard to the external validity of a program (see Chapter 1). The fourth group received neither tutoring nor special individual attention and thus served as a control group against which to contrast the other conditions or treatments. Using IQ gain as the criterion (Stanford-Binet scale), Blank and Solomon found that both tutored groups were significantly stronger (with the first group most superior) in their intellectual performance at the end of the program; the third and fourth groups gained little, though some gain can be expected simply from the benefit of practice in taking a formal test of intelligence.

Unfortunately, no follow-up data on these children have been reported from which a statement about the longer-term effects of this form of tutoring can be made. It is likely that a sustained program of special training would be necessary to continue such gains, particularly if practice in the Blank and Solomon thinking activities is a criterion for continued development. It is also likely that other measures of language skill would be more appropriate than the Stanford-Binet for evaluating this and similar tutoring programs. Given these ideas and that the original sample of children was quite small (roughly five per group), the original Blank and

Solomon study (1968) may be best considered as a promising pilot study in need of replication.

During the past several years, additional reports have emanated from the tutorial camp of Blank, at least one of which deserves mention for its heuristic value (Blank, Koltuv, and Wood, 1972). This more recent study is based upon a threefold concern: the influence of individual versus group contact in fostering disadvantaged children's cognitive development, the comparative ease with which cognitive changes can be effected in kindergarten-age (rather than younger) children, and the feasibility of training paraprofessionals for specific educational functions in the preprimary setting. Accordingly, kindergarten children from low socioeconomic backgrounds and whose developmental status was below average were matched and assigned to one of three programs: a structured tutorial approach along the lines indicated above, a "traditional" tutorial program concerned with broad stimulation for general personality adjustment, and a control group (regular kindergarten with no tutorial supplement). Again, intelligence test scores served as the criterion for treatment comparisons— this time the Wechsler Intelligence Scale for Children. Data were taken at the end of a four-and-a-half-month intervention period and again one year later.

Gain score analysis revealed a moderate advantage for children in the structured tutorial program; some children showed phenomenal gains (over 20 points). Some problems with the structured approach were noted, however. Clinical observations suggested to Blank, Koltuv, and Wood that these children developed a resistance to the tightly organized learning situation. Various degrees of passivity, dependence, withdrawal, and fearfulness (unintended outcomes) were observed as well. These researchers note that none of these children had experienced previous schooling, however, and were unlikely to have had much previous contact with supportive adults. If so, it is possible that older children (five years and up) are less appropriate subjects for structured tutoring than are, say, three-year-olds for two reasons: (1) a greater peer (rather than adult) orientation and (2) a more obvious consciousness about making mistakes among children at the kindergarten level and beyond. This suggests that school-inexperienced, disadvantaged children may first need a warm, supportive environment in order to learn ways of relating with adults who occupy instructional roles. Only then may such children profit from intensive ameliorative experiences for cognitive development.

This line of thought bears directly on the issue of timing (when to introduce given instructional procedures) first raised in Chapter 1. If many disadvantaged children (or children in general, for that matter) are anxious and failure-conscious when they first enter school, a policy of confronting them with structured cognitive demands may be counterproductive. Quite different methods of instruction may be required for children of different ages, even within the nursery-kindergarten-primary grade sequence. It all seems quite uncertain at this point, but Blank's research on the subject suggests tentatively that small-group tutorial procedures may be more suitable for most five-year-olds, while the one-to-one tutorial procedure is more suitable for three-year-olds. Method, of course, cannot be easily separated from content; nor should these interactive variables be considered apart from the characteristics of the context in which instruction takes place (including the personnel responsible for instruction). Blank, Koltuv, and Wood (1972) discovered, for example, that paraprofessionals who are bright and enthusiastic about early childhood education can be trained to implement structured procedures. Many such persons neither prefer nor feel comfortable with the use of such methods. Both training procedures and the philosophy of child growth and education become important considerations in the practical setting. For a further and more comprehensive discussion of preschool education from the perspective of Marion Blank, the book, *Teaching Learning in the Preschool* (Blank, 1974) can be recommended.

Although space limitations prevent a further elaboration of tutorial language programs, the reader is invited to consult other sources of data. Elardo (1971) for example, reports one of the few studies that demonstrate any effectiveness of specific language training on children's subsequent comprehension and use of various syntactic structures (passive, negative, possessive, and negative-passive). A favorable evaluation of the McNeil ABC Learning Activities program (a sequenced language-readiness program that emphasizes negation, labeling, categorizing, rhyming, numbers, relational concepts, etc.) has also been reported (Frager and Stern, 1970). The selection and eventual use of these and other tutorial programs should be preceded by a careful study of their objectives, instructional tactics, field-test research data, and general suitability for the local situation.

A Systematic, Conceptual Model–Derived Program

Teachers generally have been receptive to an integration of oral language into the regular academic curriculum for young children. But as language stimulation needs intensify within the field of early childhood education, teachers have discovered that something more than reading to children or show-and-tell activities are involved. In other words, the desire among educators to embellish early education systematically with oral language activities was accompanied by a stark realization that as late as 1960, few usable, field-tested materials were available for classroom use by teachers not trained as speech therapists. This section of the chapter concerns a pioneer effort to serve the language development needs of both normal and exceptional children in the regular classroom setting. The result of this effort was a comprehensive program for language stimulation known as the Peabody Language Development Kit (PLDK), because the basic work was done at George Peabody College for Teachers in Nashville, Tennessee (Dunn and Smith, 1965).

The origins of PLDK reside in the early clinical speech experience of Smith (1962), who was impressed by the futility of attempting individual language therapy for large numbers of needy children. The problem for Smith was twofold: insufficient numbers of trained personnel and generally inadequate resources for therapeutic services in most school districts. What was needed, Smith reasoned, was a broader approach suitable for accommodating the full range of young children's basic language development requirements. He began by developing procedures for working with children in small groups, going beyond the standard speech improvement approach prescribed for language specialists in the 1950s. Lesson plans to facilitate better receptive language skill development and an increase in the sheer quantity of expressive language among children were ventured on a probationary basis. The encouraging early returns from this intuitive approach led to a further exploration of lesson development from heuristic theoretical foundations. One theoretical component that proved efficacious was a model for conceptualizing psycholinguistic process variables according to the linguistic theory of Osgood (1957). This model is perhaps best known by its representative diagnostic instrument, the Illinois Test of Psycholinguistic Abilities (ITPA). A second theoretical component for PLDK is the structural model of human intellect extrapolated from psychometric study by Guilford (1959). This model figures heavily in activities for children's creative use of language. Further cues for lesson building are taken from verbal learning theory and research (McGeoch and Irion, 1952) and behavior modification principles. The resultant theoretical model of processes stimulated by PLDK appears in Figure 4.1.

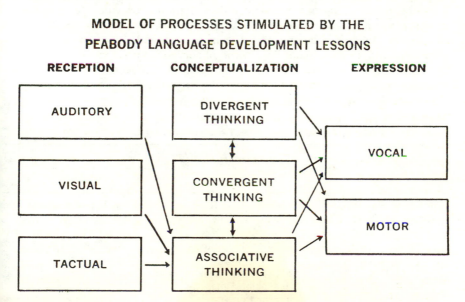

MODEL OF PROCESSES STIMULATED BY THE PEABODY LANGUAGE DEVELOPMENT LESSONS

FIGURE 4.1   Model of processes stimulated by the Peabody Language Development Lessons.

Much experimentation, field testing, and formative evaluation from teacher reports of PLDK classroom use occurred during the sixties, during which four levels of language activity programming were refined and eventually published for commercial distribution. As suggested by the model in Figure 4.1, each program level seeks to stimulate receptive, associative, and expressive language development. For these purposes, 180 individual lessons comprise each level: levels P, 1, 2, and 3, for children whose linguistic-intellectual development status is normatively equivalent to ages 3 to 5, 4½ to 6½, 6 to 8, and 7½ to 9½ years, respectively. Lessons at each level are further divided into activity areas to provide for both variety and overlearning (practice beyond the point of initial proficiency). Table 4.1 contains a sample schedule of daily activities from PLDK level 2.

It should be noted that Dunn and Smith prefer language development activities to be conducted in a gamelike atmosphere as a "daily interlude" from regular classroom work. A rich inventory of resource materials— picture cards, story posters, puppets, manikins, plastic fruits and vegetables, magnetic geometric shapes, sound recordings—is coordinated with individual lessons. Teachers are also provided with general suggestions for managing the learning environment and specific directions for the sequenced activities of individual lessons.

In addition to the careful arrangement of program content, Dunn and Smith have accepted the responsibility of providing motivation for language learning. The intermittent scheduling of social and material reinforcement is central to their approach; plastic poker chips are provided for a token economy system (see Chapter 3). Most lessons contain an activity in which free movement among children is encouraged. Program materials were validated, in part, according to the observed interest value they hold for children. And the PLDK is organized so that a teacher may pace the activities quickly if children's responsivity begins to lag. Children's spon-

TABLE 4.1   Sample Schedule of Daily Activities:
Level 2, Peabody Language Development Kit

		Type of Activity	
DAY NO.	ACTIVITY 1	ACTIVITY 2	ACTIVITY 3
1	Brainstorming Time	Classification Time	Speech Development Time
2	Vocabulary-Building Time	Reasoning Time	Patterning Time
3	Describing Time	Rhyming Time	Following Directions Time
4	Storytime	Relationships Time	Dramatization Time
5	Information Time	Pantomiming Time	Memory Time
6	Conversation Time	Speech Development Time	Activity Time
7	Vocabulary-Building Time	Reasoning Time	Guessing Time
8	Imagination Time	Information Time	Following Directions Time
9	Looking Time	Relationships Time	Touching Time
10	Listening Time	Speed-Up Time	Sentence-Building Time

taneous and imaginative use of language is a priority, with many responses rather than just one "right answer" to language game questions being a preferred criterion for successful program implementation.

PLDK Research   Two dimensions of research activity are associated with PLDK. One, of course, concerns the research necessary to arrive at a final product capable of practical application by classroom teachers, consistent with the philosophy of its creators, and true to the theoretical foundations upon which it is based. Thus, the clarity of presentation strategies, sequencing, the assessment of children's responses to individual lessons, teacher satisfaction with the range of activities, and the like were all subjected to close and continual scrutiny over the half-dozen years of the program's formulation and revision. The second dimension of research has concerned the impact of PLDK on the oral language and intellectual development of children, especially those whose language is somewhat delayed and/or who come from educationally disadvantaged backgrounds. Both of these research dimensions along with germane personal reflections by the PLDK authors are published in the manual for each program level. The essence of these formative stage investigations is aptly communicated by the following quote from the level 3 manual (1967). In interpreting this quote, it is important to note that much of the efficacy research has been based upon the classical experimental–control group method of comparison (see Chapter 1), usually with pre- and post-test measures such as the Illinois Test of Psycholinguistic Abilities, Stanford-Binet Intelligence Scale, Metropolitan Achievement Test, and the Minnesota Tests of Creative Thinking:

> The research to date with the PLDK can be viewed as heartening first steps. The lessons do appear to be effective in stimulating oral language development with disadvantaged and low achieving children in the primary grades, and with cultural-familial retarded children in special classes. The evidence is less clear on the usefulness of the lessons in training intellect, and in enhancing school achievement—with some notable successes in both cases. Recurringly, the studies suggest that boys benefit more from the program than girls, even though girls still remain generally superior to the boys. It would appear that the lessons can be taught equally well by regular and special teachers, by itinerant language developmentalists, and by educated and intelligent community workers. No measurable advantage [has been] found for dividing classes in two which results in having to teach the lessons twice per day. While it is not suggested that these variables are insignificant in all situations, the evidence does suggest that the PLDK series can be taught successfully by a variety of types of instructional personnel, with different sizes of groups. It remains for future research to advance knowledge about the effectiveness of the series for other types of children under other conditions (Dunn and Smith, 1967, p. xxi).[3]

---

[3] Reproduced by permission of **American Guidance Services, Inc.**

As a representative example of more recent research, another two-year research project can be cited (Guess, Smith, and Ensminger, 1971). A pair of former psychiatric aides were trained by the researchers to serve as language developmentalists for two groups of severely retarded institutionalized children. These children were matched with a control group (no systematic language training) on measured intelligence, language development status, and rating of social maturity. The language intervention children met for one hour daily over the two-year period, at the end of which the experimental and control groups were compared on several criteria. A statistically significant advantage in language abilities (as measured by the ITPA) was disclosed to support the idea of intensive training to facilitate development. IQ differences were also observed, with a tendency for the experimental children to excel, even though the difference was not significant.

Actually, three contributions of this study can be noted. First, it demonstrated that nonspecialists can be trained successfully to implement PLDK. Second, the study provided evidence that children with severe language deficiencies can be helped in substantive ways by this kind of language experience. And third, an analysis of repeated measures over the duration of the study revealed that experimental children tend to "pull away" from their control peers only after the program has been in effect about nine months. In other words, for PLDK and similar programs, a concern for immediate impact may be deferred to one for longer-range acceleration which apparently occurs as new language skills are consolidated.

Finally, a comment on research about the newest addition to the kits, level P (preschool), should be made. An experimental version of this level was field tested with generally favorable results in terms of oral language and verbal intelligence. The power of level P to stimulate grammatical-syntactical aspects of language was not realized to the extent desired. A similar pattern has been revealed by research on level I with disadvantaged first-grade children. In this study (Dunn and Mueller, undated), the greatest specific gains were recorded for children's ability to express ideas in spoken words and to reason with analogies. The final version of level P contains a heavier concentration of syntax exercises reinforced by a series of songs to make certain syntactical rules automatic. The data pool for level P is still smaller than that for its more advanced counterparts, and little can be said at this writing about the success of efforts to strengthen the experimental version.[4] It is likely that level P as well as the other levels of PLDK will continue to effect their most marked changes in vocabulary and general comprehension—the aspects of children's language development most amenable to training.

---

[4] Readers interested in special education are advised that ITPA subtest scores have been significantly increased among severely subnormal children who were provided with daily instruction involving level P (Shiach, 1973).

Hand puppets and animal cards for vocabulary building are among the variety of complementary materials for use in the execution of daily lessons from the Peabody Language Development Kits. Photo courtesy of American Guidance Services, Inc.

Summary Comment The PLDK is a scripted, highly presequenced language development program for children ages 3 to 9½ years. Its content is essentially cognitive, with a strong emphasis upon mathematical reasoning, social and psychological reasoning, general vocabulary, and syntax. Dominant instructional methods include teacher-child dialogue and pattern repetition, augmented by a token reinforcement system. The theoretical base of the PLDK is clear and is more strongly supported by empirical research than most. This is perhaps due in part to the fact that PLDK has both a longer history of formative evaluation and has been used more widely in the public schools than have many of the new language development programs. Critics object largely to the difficulty faced by a practitioner who wishes to alter lesson sequences to meet situational needs. It is true that sequential deviations are strongly discouraged, but lessons do not have to appear in relation to necessary constellations of other activities and it is much less response specific than other structured programs (e.g., Distar). On balance, the PLDK has much to recommend it as a source of varied language activities whose prosecution is relatively simple and straightforward.

The Tucson Model of Language Teaching

Another alternative approach to language development and education is the Tucson Early Education Model (TEEM), a systematization of children's "natural language learning" (Hughes, Wetzel, and Henderson, 1969). Educational program development from this approach rests upon two basic assumptions (Lavatelli, 1971). First is the assumption that children's normal biological capacity for language can better be activated by an environment rich in language stimulation and opportunities for language expression; this does *not* include direct training by pattern drill. Second is the recognition that a language-impoverished environment may contribute to certain language production deficiencies. It is assumed that a child's basic language capacity is not adversely affected by impoverishment; the position taken is that language production difficulties with an environmental source can be overcome by exposure to appropriate syntactic structures.

Several conditions are necessary if such exposure is to occur. One condition is that language communications be directed toward children to which children can respond in turn. Another condition is that teachers selectively model a variety of basic sentence structures in appropriate circumstances in order to raise children's language practice to increasingly higher levels. It is for this reason that TEEM is often described as a "language lift" model for early education. Children must hear, process, and then derive language rules or generalizations. Passive listening will not do. Conversations must be two-way, with teachers making a conscious effort to develop an increased linguistic awareness among their pupils and to provide them with opportunities for the satisfying practice of new syntactical discoveries (Lavatelli, 1971). Teachers' skilled use of questioning techniques with children is important as well.

The success of a language-lift approach to early education, then, demands two basic competencies of a teacher: a consciousness of oneself as a modeler of language and a firm knowledge of the synactic structure of the language being modeled. Carroll's analysis of grammar (1964) provides the basic framework for modeling. Certain basic constructions have been selected as reference points for the systematic modeling process, most of which reflect the heavy influence of transformational rules for sentence expansion, reduction, transportation, and negation (see Lavatelli, 1971). These rules are then applied in language communications which develop, mostly spontaneously, within the context of children's sensory perception experiences (e.g., feeling, smelling, hearing) and time awareness experience (e.g., reconstructing past events, time factors involved in cooking activities and walking and bus trips).

Although much simplified, the foregoing paragraphs describe the essence of the Tucson Early Education Model (TEEM). This method differs from many popular language education programs in several ways. Most importantly, the child's own spontaneous language (including vocabulary, syntax, and dialect) is used as a starting point to develop literacy skills. Hence language "lessons" are not preordained on the basis of specific objectives, sequence, and timing. Neither is language education conceived as something apart from intellectual, social, and aesthetic learnings. The key to progress is individualized instruction. As such, the Tucson method is similar in basic design to the Bank Street model (Chapter 2); but the former puts a greater emphasis on insights from the study of develop-mental psycholinguistics for conceptualizing language education.

Some Representative Activities A more concrete description of repre-sentative activities can better illustrate TEEM. First, as indicated above, general curriculum experiences such as cooking, walking trips, and bus trips are organized to develop sensory perception and provoke verbaliza-tion among children. Verbatim records of children's spontaneous remarks and stories (including errors) are recorded, analyzed, and used as cues to program subsequent strategies intended to lead children to higher levels of language sophistication.

Heavy use is made of an expansion feedback technique whereby a teacher attends to the grammatical structure of a child's verbalizations and responds with a full grammatically correct version of the child's idea. For example, during a cooking experience a child, Louis, may remark, "Water hot." This telegraphic response and other remarks about the experience may then be recorded on Louis' individual language card. Later, cards are read back to Louis (and other children) verbatim prefaced by phrases such as, "Louis said," or "Louis exclaimed." Immediately after the verbatim remark is read, a teacher will model the correct structure for Louis (depending, of course, upon specific circumstances). In this example it might be, "I saw the water get hot, too!" or, "The water got hotter!" Once correct structure has been modeled, a teacher will usually proceed by way of questioning techniques to elicit correct usage from the child and to reinforce positively the child's attempts.

Additional techniques are employed to provoke verbalization of recall among children who have shared planned experiences. Reminiscing with children about past activities is done to highlight certain forms of speech (e.g., past tense) and adjectival phrases. Systematic remembering practice may also involve skills such as sequencing (the recall of events in chrono-logical order) and categorizing (e.g., attributes such as size, shape, and color). Comparing and associating skills also receive systematic attention. Together, these skills are considered to be important background com-petencies for learning to read, making predictions, and thinking dis-criminatively. Verbatim records in these and other areas serve as a cumulative indication of progress in language and conceptual development.

Second, many specific activities are developed from intellectual kits. These kits contain common items that collectively comprise certain con-cept classes (e.g., jewelry, seeds, buttons, clothing). File cards are developed for each kit to (1) develop specific, individualized objectives for children from the more general goals areas (language competence, societal arts and skills, etc.) and (2) record the many instructional possibilities that can be realized as desired. A sample file card on the topic of "hinges" appears below:

Hinges

Dictionary Definitions

A jointed or flexible device on which a door, lid, or other swinging part turns.
A determining factor.
Turning point.
A bodily joint that permits motion in one plane.

Possibilities for Materials

hasp	spring clothespin	hair clamps
butt hinge	pillbox	bow tie
strap hinge	scissors	wallet
T or H hinge	tweezers	glass frames
pliers	nutcracker	match folder
		new and used hinges

Instructional Possibilities

Exploration: Manipulation of hinges in an interest center.
Elaboration: Structured activity: Let children discuss, build on, and extend their knowledge (Example: "Yes, that is a clothespin. Where have you ever seen anything like this before? How was it used? If you had one, how could you use it?")
Suggest looking for things in the room or on the body which work the same way.
If the term *hinge* has not come up, introduce and use it in identifying hinges in the environment.
Identify book hinges and introduce one way to make books with hinged covers.
Use books to record information or make drawings of hinges.
Make comparisons with things that hinges are like and not like.
Discuss differences in sizes and shapes.
Discuss differences in materials.
Discuss differences in weight.
Discuss differences in length.
Discuss differences in form.

The potent influence of imitation learning is channeled methodically, especially with respect to social skills and language acquisition. Information-seeking responses such as question asking and "thinking out loud" are modeled verbally by teacher demonstration and in the course of verbal teacher-child interchange. *Gratification through learning* is still another process variable instrumental to TEEM. To provide children with gratifying experiences, frequent social recognition is dispensed; materials are selected for their intrinsic value to children; and failure and frustration are eliminated. Activities are also sorted on the basis of how well they facilitate the *generalization* of *learned skills* across classroom content areas and from the formal classroom to the child's natural environment. Finally, the *orchestration process* ensures that the four major objectives do not result in independent or isolated activities. Wherever possible, singular contexts are provided for the development of skills corresponding to the four principle objectives of TEEM. The following quotation will illustrate:

> When skills are acquired in real and meaningful settings, it is possible to develop more than one skill simultaneously. A teacher organizing a small group of children in the activity of ice cream making, for example, will be teaching new words, the processes of proper order and sequence of events, new concepts, and new technical and social skills. In addition, the manner of her interaction with children plus the eating of the product will significantly influence the child's attitude towards the activity and the learning experience. (Hughes, Wetzel, and Henderson, 1969, p. 5).

The organizational components of TEEM evoke a cavalcade of guidelines: The *room arrangement* includes a variety of interest centers to meet individual differences in childrens' preferences and developmental levels. Seating strategies support independent study and small-group instruction. A teacher-pupil ratio of roughly 1–5 triggers higher rates of *interaction* than are found in traditional classrooms.

Other Components of TEEM   Central, then, to TEEM is the idea of developing language competence, a "major technical skill" believed essential for children to adapt successfully to their culture. But three other major components comprise the Tucson approach. These are intellectual skills, motivation, and societal arts and skills. The *intellectual base* skills, most of which involve the complex higher mental processes, include strategies for organizing sensory data, encouraging reproductive thought, planning for specific goal attainment, and providing skills for modeling the significant behavior of others. The last skill involves both discriminatory and evaluative power. Attitudes and values which dispose children toward productive social involvement define TEEM's *motivational base.* Also included in this category are persistence and success expectancies. The traditional academic skills (reading, writing, and arithmetic) and skills for democratic living comprise the final category of *societal arts and skills.*

As TEEM's objectives are classified so are its principal ingredients. These include process-oriented and organizational components. Of the process variables, the *individualization of teaching* is foremost. Both self-

The individualization of language education activities is a fundamental principle of the Tucson Early Education Model. Photo by Peter Rinearson.

selected and structured activities are coordinated as closely as possible with the cultural background, attitudes, and values of the children. This *local adaption strategy* is an attempt to reduce the typical discontinuities engendered when children not in the middle class encounter a stereotyped middle-class curriculum.

Finally, the *change agent* is an indispensable feature of TEEM. Most simply, a change agent serves as a technical consultant, who is responsible for introducing innovative practices and assisting teachers to apply them. In the early stages of application, a 1–5 ratio of change agents to teachers is recommended. Change agents receive continuous training at the Arizona Center for Early Childhood Education. These agents, together with teachers and teacher aides, are encouraged to exercise originality and ingenuity within the range provided by TEEM for innovation. As functional practices are developed, they may be shared by other cooperating TEEM classrooms.

In summary, TEEM represents a systematic plan for the acceleration of language learning and the control of language for intellectual and social purposes. Teachers and aides work together in order to provide a language-rich learning environment which emphasizes activities to encourage children to develop higher rates and refinements of expressive language. Individual and group language training activities are created from data obtained from the recorded verbalizations of children and a structural analysis of the English language.

Evaluation Research   Given TEEM's process orientation to education one might expect to find a lesser emphasis upon teacher questioning tactics designed to promote strict knowledge acquisition or content mastery. Conversely, a teacher's interrogative statements in a process curriculum should involve proportionately more emphasis upon intellectual skills. Precisely such a finding has been reported from a study which compared TEEM teacher-child interactions to those in "regular" first-grade classrooms (Zimmerman and Bergan, 1971). Further evidence that teachers can be trained better to develop process-oriented questioning strategies also has been provided by this study. Whether this form of questioning has a direct effect upon children's developing language competence is hard to say; but TEEM children apparently are provided with a greater than "usual" opportunity to express their thoughts and perceptions. Certainly, they are less restricted to a traditional recitation mode of classroom response.

Other evidence, less obviously related to language objectives, includes social-affective behaviors. Strong evidence has been found that children in TEEM Head Start can maintain a task-orientation better than those in local comparison classes and display less inappropriate personal-social behavior, when their teacher is absent from the classroom (Goldupp, 1972). Still further classroom comparisons provide tentative support for TEEM's success in accomplishing certain important objectives (Rentfro, During, Conrad, and Goldupp, 1972). For example, a greater incidence of child-initiated learning sequences with fewer teacher-directed learning sequences was observed in TEEM Head Start classrooms. A reverse pattern in the ratio of these patterns occurred in the Head Start comparison groups. The TEEM children were also generally favored in measured cognitive gains. Specifically, these included a superiority in word knowledge and visual memory skill, verbal memory, conceptual grouping, number questions, and reasoning by analogy. No differences were noted for verbal fluency or graphic drawing, however, between TEEM and Head Start children.

The comparative aspects of such measurement can easily be overplayed. It is perhaps more important that children have been observed to make substantial progress in most of the goal domains that define the TEEM approach, Certainly there is no strong evidence to indicate that children's educational development, in the broadest sense, is hampered by this less structured approach. Admittedly, however, data about specific academic skill development still are needed in order to evaluate the language-lift model. Parents and teachers who champion an essentialist (basic skills) philosophy of education often are apprehensive about TEEM or any other low-structure curriculum model. Standardized achievement test data from TEEM's children (Metropolitan Achievement Tests) reportedly are "mixed" and unavailable to the general consumer (Chow and Elmore, 1972). Advocates usually argue that such test data are inadequate for measuring TEEM's outcomes or objectives. Consequently, the central evaluation effort among TEEM personnel is concentrated on the development of new and more suitable criterion measures.

At this writing, the effort to satisfactorily evaluate this process-oriented approach is still underway. A new instrument—the TEEM Implementation Inventory—has been developed for experimental use as a guide to teacher self-appraisal and to summative evaluation (Henderson, 1973). A framework for creating behavioral objectives in TEEM's four educational domains also is being refined. This framework will enable teachers and children to make decisions about specific objectives within individual classrooms. It also will include a mechanism by which children's growth can be monitored over time through the charting of observational data. Goal categories for the *motivation* domain for instance, include *approach behavior*, *self-goal-setting*, *task persistence*, and *self-evaluation*. Not coincidentally, these are priority goals in most philosophies of open education (see Chapter 7). Still another instrument, the "activity preference task," is designed to measure interest in various school activities. The extent to which valid TEEM program implementation has occurred in a given classroom is also measured via a special observational device. Taken together, these steps toward better and more meaningful process evaluation indicate a healthy progress toward the assessment of TEEM's merit.

Bilingual Education

Bilingualism—the ability to comprehend and express two languages—has increasingly been emphasized as a major goal of schooling in virtually all communities where strong ethnic-based linguistic diversity prevails. This is a most significant shift away from thinking about educational goals in terms of the traditional "melting pot" philosophy in American education. It further indicates a turnabout in basic attitude toward bilingualism as a liability for children in American schools. Consequently, a fast-growing literature concerned with the theory and practice of bilingual education has appeared. Selected aspects of this literature are summarized in the present section to communicate the meaning, rationale, and major issues of bilingual education for young children.[5]

The Meaning of Bilingual Education   Bilingual education can be defined as the concurrent use of two languages as instructional media for children in any part or all of a given school curriculum into which a study of the history and culture of a child's native tongue is integrated (Andersson and Boyer, 1969; Gaardner, 1967). Most broadly, the aim of bilingual education is to provide children with a sound opportunity to become fully literate and articulate in two languages and to impart a sensitivity to the cultures in which these languages evolved. Interestingly, the history of formal attempts at bilingual education in America can be traced to the early nineteenth century. Such education was extremely limited in scope and availability until the early 1960s when a genesis of "new look" bilingual education appeared in the form of a special program for children of Cuban immigrants in Dade County, Florida. The early success of this vanguard program for the primary grades quickly stimulated efforts elsewhere in the country, principally the American southwest. Other dynamics, especially the political-social activism of various ethnic minorities, further paved the way to the bilingual education gold rush. This sudden and dramatic movement was capped early in 1968 by landmark federal legislation, the Bilingual Education Act. Since that time, special educational provisions have been made for thousands of children whose native language is not English. For the most part, the recipients of these provisions have been Spanish-speaking children (Mexican-Americans in the southwest; Puerto Ricans and Cubans on the eastern seaboard) and American Indian children (dispersed throughout the United States). However encouraging these efforts, bilingual education services still do not meet the apparent need of all America's non-English-speaking children. As late as 1972, for instance, slightly less than 3 percent of Mexican-American pupils in the southwest were enrolled in bilingual programs (Wright, 1973).

The Rationale for Bilingual Education   Many arguments favorable to an opportunity for bilingual education have been generated (Andersson and Boyer, 1969; Gaardner, 1967; John and Horner, 1971). The most frequently offered make three related points. First, it is argued that bilingual education is a more human and enriching school experience for non-English-speaking children. This is essentially a philosophical position with psychological overtones about mental health and broader cultural horizons.

A second argument is based on the premise that it is pedagogically sound to conduct children's learning of basic or primary subjects, especially reading and writing, in their mother tongue. This point often is stretched to include the contention that instruction conducted solely in English for children whose native language is not English can result in

---

[5] See Bernbaum (1971) for a concise overview of definitional problems, research, testing problems, preschool programs, and practical guidelines for educators regarding bilingualism.

educational retardation to the extent of their "deficiencies" with English. This hypothesis is based partially on data concerning the alleged poor timing and procedures whereby a non-English-speaking child is introduced to the second language. A "linguistic interference" phenomenon is thought to be involved, but there is much disagreement about both the causes and effects on learning of such interference. More will be said about this later.

A third argument is that bilingual education can provide a better framework for children's positive self-image development and basic identification with their cultural-linguistic heritage. This idea has strong logical appeal, even if few hard data exist to support it.

The centrality of the above three arguments is clear. However, additional rationales for bilingual education can be disclosed. A frequent claim is that English-speaking children can profit from learning in a school environment marked by cultural and linguistic diversity and reduced socialized ethnocentrism. Another argument concerns the potential long-range impact of education for bilingual competence on an individual's career opportunities in which a criterion for successful employment is a proficiency with two (or more) languages. The argument that cultural-linguistic diversity represents a valuable natural resource to be conserved, not extinguished, has also appeared. Collectively, these arguments have sustained a more-than-token commitment to the concept of bilingual education by many American educators. How has this commitment been translated into school action?

The Status of Bilingual Education   An answer to the above question is most difficult; a great many activities take place under the cloak of bilingual education. However, some insight into the realities of bilingual education can be gleaned from recent analyses of school practice. Kjolseth (1973), for example, has provided data to suggest that most American programs (over 80 percent)—goal statements notwithstanding—are based upon the *assimilation* model of bilingual education, which promotes an ethnic language shift from mother tongue to majority culture language. Ordinarily, this shift in preferential language use is accomplished by the end of the primary grades; thereafter, English is the principal, if not exclusive, language of instruction and little formal work is done with the children's native language. In contrast, a minority of programs, according to Kjolseth, is based upon the *pluralistic* model, whose application includes a continued maintenance of the given native language. The pluralistic model ostensibly is developed from more comprehensive data about local communities—linguistic varieties and citizen's attitudes toward bilingualism, for example. Teachers are home grown and integral members of the cultural-linguistic community. A sacrosanct balance is maintained between languages of instruction (both intralanguage and dialect variations). Parental involvement is given high priority so that continuous input about program components can be solicited. In fact, the bilingual program is designed to serve as a continuous force in facilitating civic development and organization within the ethnic communities concerned.

One is tempted to infer that the preferred model for bilingual education would reflect pluralistic model attributes. Eventually, this model may come to dominate classroom practice, but the common lack of financial support, bona fide instructional personnel, and comprehensive evaluation data about curriculum methods and materials would seem to oppose progress in this direction (Fishman and Lovaas, 1970). Even if these obstacles are overcome, many questions and issues are contained within this relatively unexplored area of early childhood education. For example, no one knows what will be the broader, long-range social consequences of bilingual education.

A second thematic variation in bilingual education can be mentioned in passing. As implied above, both the assimilation and the pluralistic models teach English as a second language and have an organized curriculum for instructing children in English, as well as in their native tongue. A strong but less prevalent viewpoint concerns teaching English as a foreign language (akin to the original Bereiter-Engelmann rationale for compensating standard English deprivation). The emphasis, accordingly, is upon the structural-sequential aspects of English; less time is allowed for the use of "situational" English or the spontaneous social uses of the nonnative language. There is some question whether the "English as a foreign language" approach is legitimate bilingual education, but it nonetheless illustrates an important point of difference in thinking among the "experts."

An Example of Bilingual Education Programming   The Bilingual Early Childhood Program (Nedler, 1973) may serve to illustrate educators' growing commitment to the welfare of non-English-speaking children. This program has as its major objective the design of a comprehensive and "developmentally appropriate" learning system for Spanish-speaking children, ages 3–6. Its thrust is toward new methods to teach English as a second language and simultaneously to cultivate further native language development. Begun in 1966, the project early faced the reality of serious lacks in suitable bilingual teaching methods and materials. Project personnel reasoned that a first step in program development should result in a learning environment wherein children could acquire basic attributes of intelligent behavior, social competencies included. The resultant three-level curriculum includes eight different types of learning activities, each of which is further broken down into terminal objectives and specific daily lessons. These levels can be summarized as follows:

Level I (three-year-olds)	Level II (four-year-olds)	Level III (five-year-olds)
Visual	Visual	Visual
Auditory	Auditory	Auditory
Motor	Motor	Motor
Ideas and concepts	Ideas and concepts	Ideas and concepts
	Syntax of English	Syntax of English
	Building vocabulary	Building vocabulary
		Prewriting
		Exploring and discovering

Several core principles on which decisions for selecting program content are based reflect an eclecticism in program philosophy and psychology. For example, variety in content, teaching methods, use of media, and instructional settings (small group, large group, independent work) is given. Both Spanish and English are used, with the sequence and ratio in amount of one language use to the other geared according to program level. New learnings, for instance, generally are introduced in Spanish and later taken up in English. Most level I teaching occurs in Spanish, although by level III English dominates the instructional process. A series of instructional units—puzzles, transparencies, filmstrips, audio recordings, games, and graphics—is infused with curriculum-based mastery tests to provide for continuous monitoring of progress. The concept of task analysis provides the basis for determining specific lesson sequence within each instructional unit. Concrete, familiar subjects always precede the introduction of more abstract and unfamiliar content. Table 4.2 contains an example of behavioral objectives by program level in one general activity area, "ideas and concepts."

The Spanish utilized for instruction accommodates colloquialisms as much as possible without excessive deviation from the standard form. Simple grammatical structures prevail at level I; thereafter increases in linguistic complexity are arranged across both the grammatical and semantic properties of language. Some English words are introduced at level I, but the real surge in English language instruction begins at level II with introductory syntax and vocabulary-building activities. Specific language modeling is integrated into the teaching process by the supervising teacher and an assistant teacher who work together in team fashion. In addition to the normal planning, teaching, and classroom maintenance tasks, team duties extend to home visits with parents. Both pre- and in-service teacher-training procedures have been devised for dissemination in manual form. School districts interested in the implementation of this program have at their disposal a delivery system comprised of training directives, staff development products, and model workshop activities executed by personnel at the Southwest Educational Development Laboratory in Austin, Texas.

Evaluation procedures for the Bilingual Early Childhood Program have been particularly strong in the formative sense: a six-stage evaluation process has evolved beginning with content analysis and followed by conceptual design activity, product design, a pilot test, a large-scale field test, and product dissemination. Throughout the formative evaluation process have been applied criteria such as teacher feedback, on-site observation, and measured student achievement and interest. Data based upon 169 classrooms in 31 different communities (Texas and Colorado) indicate that roughly 75 percent of the participating children achieve criterion mastery of program content goals. Additional "substantial gains" in Spanish and English comprehension are reported, together with increased cognitive skills as measured by the Raven Progressive Matrices. Teachers have generally indicated their support for both the program

The Bilingual Early Education Program involves a strong emphasis upon children's native heritage. These children have become remarkably skilled in a native dance activity. Photo courtesy of Southwest Educational Development Laboratory, Austin, Texas.

objectives and staff development procedures in serving the needs of their bicultural pupils. Such results are heartening, especially for educators concerned about bilingual programs with more than face validity. Perhaps it is unnecessary to remind potential program users that no curriculum, however carefully developed, is a universal panacea for a given community's educational problems. However, the judicious selection and experimental application of carefully formulated programs has the potential for contributing much to progress in such relatively unknown areas as bilingual education.

A Salient Issue in Bilingual Education   Bilingual education, with all its excitement and promise, raises many educational issues. Differences in opinion about English as a second or a foreign language and the choice of assimilation or pluralistic model have already been mentioned. The recruitment, selection, and training of teachers for bilingual education programs pose profound challenges. So does the task of developing worthy curriculum materials. The evaluation of experimental bilingual programs is still largely formative. Few conclusions can be made from summative evaluation data about such programs, although preliminary evidence sug-

TABLE 4.2—Sample Objectives from a Bilingual Early Education Program (Nedler, 1973)

Ideas and Concepts

LEVEL I	LEVEL II	LEVEL III
Introduction to school	Introduction to school	School
Body awareness	Family	School safety
Clothing	Animals	Community helpers
Food	Vehicles	Body awareness
House	Clothing	Body senses
Appliances	Musical instruments	Clothing
Animals	Food	Food
Vehicles	Community helpers	Health
Musical Instruments	Tools	Toys
Toys	Body awareness	Family
Family	Buildings	Classroom environment
Community helpers	Money	Community environment
Buildings	Toys	Materials
Self-awareness	Furniture	Plants
Natural environment	Zoo animals	Animals
Community environment	Birds, fish, insects	Transportation
	Self-awareness	Self-awareness
(Spanish)	*(Spanish)*	*(Spanish)*
Understand simple concepts related to unit topic	Understand concepts related to unit topic	Understand and explain complex concepts related to unit topic
Recognize, name, and describe objects and pictures	Name and describe objects and pictures	Participate in concrete experiences related to unit topic
Participate in concrete experience related to unit topic	Participate in concrete experiences related to unit topic	Describe and compare experiences and events
Describe experiences and events	Describe and compare experiences and events	Demonstrate understanding of models and maps
Respond to questions about similarities and differences of objects within a category	Describe similarities and differences of objects and pictures within a category	Understand and describe concepts related to knowledge of self, culture, and natural world
Recognize simple functions of objects	Describe functions of objects	
Acquire basic knowledge of self and culture	Describe concepts related to knowledge of self and culture	
Select instances of a concept	Sort, compare, and contrast concepts related to three categories.	

(English)

Understand concepts related to unit topic
Name and describe objects and pictures
Describe and compare experiences and events
Describe similarities and differences of objects and pictures within a category
Describe functions of objects
Describe concepts related to knowledge of self and culture

(English)

Understand simple concepts related to unit topic
Recognize and name objects and pictures
Describe experiences and events
Respond to questions about similarities and differences of objects within a category
Recognize simple functions of objects
Select instances of a concept
Sort, compare, and contrast concepts related to two categories

TYPES OF MEDIA

Filmstrips
Photographs
Pictures
Posters

gests that planned bilingual early education programs can be quite effective in increasing the language and communication skills of young children (Nedler and Sebera, 1971).

One issue, in particular, can serve to illustrate the ferment within the bilingual education movement. We can begin by stating this issue in question form. Does teaching a child in his second, usually much weaker, language impede his general cognitive development and, especially, his native language competence? Opinion and speculation about the answer far outweigh any relevant data that can be mustered. There is one extensive and thoroughgoing study, however, which demands our attention: the St. Lambert experiment. (Lambert and Tucker, 1972). In this experiment, two groups of English-Canadian children received their kindergarten–first grade schooling exclusively in the French language. During second, third and fourth grade, French was continued as the main language of instruction, except for two half-hour periods of English language arts per day. Throughout this five-year longitudinal study, the experimental children's progress in native and second language skills was compared to that among carefully matched groups of English- and French-speaking children (control groups) who experienced "normal" K–4 schooling (English-Canadian and French-Canadian academic programs, respectively). These children's general intellectual development (measured intelligence), mathematics achievement, self-concept, attitude toward French peoples, and program effects upon parents and teachers were also assessed.

The comparative data are striking. Experimental children demonstrated no symptoms of hampered native language development, intelligence test performance, or educational achievement based on English language competencies. They were, in fact, as substantially above the normative average on standardized achievement test criteria as were their English-Canadian controls (roughly the eightieth percentile in mathematics, for example). Experimental children also compared favorably with their French-Canadian controls in French comprehension, vocabulary, and "nativelike" command of the language when reading in French. Their oral proficiency in French, though generally lower than their French-Canadian peers, was admirable under the circumstances. Attitude measurements indicated a more liberal, acceptant outlook among the experimental children toward both Canadian and European French. And the experimental subjects persistently described themselves in positive self-concept terms at all grade levels. Parents of the experimental children and many control parents expressed enthusiasm and a strong preference for continuing the experiment and providing a regular home-school language switch opportunity for successive groups of children. Interestingly, teachers *not* involved in the experiment tended to react to it either supportively or skeptically (if not in favor of outright dismissal of the evidence). It should be noted that the experimental teachers were highly skilled and in strong agreement with the goals of the French language program.

These data attest to the fact that children can learn and develop thinking skills in a second language with no apparent adverse effects. Certainly, they call into question the validity of the earlier mentioned linguistic interference hypothesis. Why, then, do so many American children whose first language is not English fail to make minimally satisfactory educational progress in the early years of schooling? If English-Canadian children can excel in a French language–dominated school program, why cannot American Indian and Chicano children excel in an English language–dominated school program? A cogent question indeed. Many children whose first language is not English do, of course, make educational progress in monolingual (English) schools. Many, unfortunately, do not. The problem of early school failure undoubtedly involves more than the fact of language difference. Methods used, attitudes expressed, and teachers' use of expectations for children must be considered. Perhaps additional insights into this phenomenon can be culled from a study of the cultural context in which schooling occurs. One authority has observed a difference in context between the St. Lambert experiment and that which is typical in the American southwest (see Cazden, 1972, p. 178). Canadian children from the dominant language were taught a nondominant language. American Indians or Spanish-speaking children are in a situation reversed. Attitudes cultivated in the home, parent support, and general motivation of the child may all be affected by this difference. These factors may not tell the full story, but the effects of any educational experiment— bilingual or otherwise—cannot be divorced from the sociocultural context in which they are observed (this relates to external validity, discussed in Chapter 1). In fact, Lambert and Tucker caution against a generalization of their model for the solution of bilingual education problems in any given community. Rather, a more general guiding philosophy is proposed:

In any community where there is a serious widespread desire or need for a bilingual or multilingual citizenry, priority for early schooling should be given to the language or languages least likely to be developed otherwise, that is, the languages most likely to be neglected. When applied to bilingual settings, this principle calls for the establishment of two elementary school streams, one conducted in language A and one in language B, with two groups of teachers who either are or who function as though they were monolinguals in one of the languages. If A is the more prestigious language, then native speakers of A would start their schooling in language B, and after functional bilingualism is attained, continue their schooling in both languages. Depending on the sociocultural setting, various options are open to the linguistic minority group: 1) prekindergarten or very early schooling, with half-day instruction in language B and half-day in A; 2) schooling in language B only until reading and writing skills are certified, then introducing instruction via A; or 3) a completely bilingual program based on two monolingually organized educational structures which allow children to move back and forth from one language of instruction to the other. Rather than teaching language A and B as languages, emphasis would be shifted from a linguistic focus to one where languages are thought of primarily as vehicles for developing competence in academic subject matters, including various forms of creative work." (Lambert and Tucker, 1972, pp. 216–217).

Some Further Comments about Language Education

As this chapter has progressed, the reader may have realized the difficulty in separating language from other program components (e.g., education for general cognitive development, affective growth, and perceptual motor skills). This is true even when one is writing selectively about curriculum models. The intent of this chapter, however, has been to concentrate upon the variety in approaches to this language component which has resulted from different theoretical persuasions. Many additional language curriculum components could be reviewed. The ingenious *Matrix Games* (Gotkin, 1968), for example, comprise a language curriculum built according to the principles of programmed instruction. These games deserve a careful perusal by any student of language education. The language component of *The New Nursery School* (Nimnicht, McAfee, and Meier, 1969) represents another interesting language experience approach. In this program, language-lift principles are reinforced in creative ways, including the use of aids from educational technology. One such aid is the *Language Master*, a device for the recording and graphic reproduction of children's expressive language that children can use by themselves. Still another prominent language curriculum, structured according to high-frequency syntactic patterns in a multidialectical framework, has been developed at the University of Hawaii with highly encouraging results (Adkins, Crowell, and Loveless, 1970).

With so many intriguing alternatives for language education, a student may well wonder which approach is best or most generally effective for children. The answer, of course, depends upon many factors, including the needs of individual children, the social context of instruction, and the philosophy or value commitments of individual teachers. Even the empirical evidence from reasonably well-controlled comparative studies can be inconclusive in some respects. In two such field studies, highly structured and unstructured types of language training were compared (Dickie, 1968). The four-year-old children in these studies made generally equivalent gains in both types of programs with the structured approach resulting in only a slight advantage in labeling skills.

Fortunately, beneficial evaluations of preschool and early school language programs are becoming increasingly available as guides to program selection. Bartlett (1972), for example, has performed an astute analysis of twenty-one different programs, some of which have been mentioned in this chapter (e.g., Distar, PLDK). Bartlett's analysis has three important dimensions: goals, interactional patterns, and degree of pre-organization. Further insights about which language objectives warrant a high priority in young children's language education have been gleaned from the empirical literature. Moore (1971), for instance, has made a strong case for a sharper focus in language programming upon children's referential use of language (including practice with elaborated syntax), superordinate class names, and naming common objects and actions. These foci are believed to be especially important within a compensatory or special education program.

SOME PERSISTING ISSUES

Somewhat concealed by the salutary thrust toward early language education are some fundamental issues about children's language development (McCandless and Evans, 1973). The deeper one's probing into the complexities of human language, the more evident it becomes that basic questions far outnumber answers about this aspect of development. Many issues can be identified, but only three are examined here for illustrative purposes: the nativist-environmentalist dilemma, the issue of the language-thought relationship, and the interpretation of language differences among children from varying cultural backgrounds.

The Nativist–Environmentalist Dilemma

Psychologists have long puzzled about the relationship of nature to nurture in development. Applied to language development, the dilemma concerns the extent to which biological or environmental factors govern the process of acquiring language competence—or, perhaps more accurately, the nature of the interaction between nature and nurture which results in such competence. This dilemma is often termed the *rationalist-empiricist debate* (McNeill, 1970). The rationalist takes the position that language depends upon an inherent ability to interpret sentences; the concept of a sentence is presumably built into the genetic system. He usually subscribes to the notion of a species-unique language acquisition device, which is the controlling mechanism for development until about the point of mature brain growth. A normal and universal sequence of language development is assumed; environmental factors are important primarily to activate the innate processes of acquisition. Any rationalist approach to language training, however, is best conceived as facilitative in terms of what the child hears, not what he is drilled to perform. Language-lift approaches, such as TEEM, are most logically aligned with the rationalist position.

In contrast, the empiricist places much greater faith in the power of systematic reinforcement contingencies and strategies to elicit the imitation of specific syntactical forms from children. In fact, language learning is viewed no differently from the learning of any other behaviors: all behavior is said to be governed by certain basic learning principles over which an environmentalist may exert control. The role of reinforcement in language acquisition is particularly a subject of debate. Rationalists argue, and often with good evidence, that external reinforcement contributes little to language development apart from bringing specific labeling responses (vocabulary selection) under stimulus control, promoting general fluency, and influencing the topics that a child may choose to discuss with others (Ervin-Tripp, 1966). Yet we see that reinforcement is basic to many programs, Distar and PLDK to name only two.

From the research findings to date, one cannot reject the potential of judicious reinforcement as a factor in modifying expressive language (speech production) or maintaining children's motivation to perform under certain classroom conditions. The impact of reinforcement upon language competence per se remains largely at the level of conjecture. Studies concerned with the relationship of reinforcement to generative grammar phenomena are beginning to appear with greater frequency (see, e.g., the *Journal of Applied Behavior Analysis*). Interested readers will want to investigate this literature. The issue, of course, is more than moot. It has profound implications for the design and execution of strategies to refine, if not modify drastically, the quality of a child's language communication ability. The continuum of alternatives ranges from only general language stimulation to systematic modeling procedures to modeling in conjunction with feedback to highly patterned drill techniques combined with social and/or material reinforcement. Among studies worthy of attention are those by Ammon and Ammon (1971); Guthrie and Baldwin (1970); Hutinger and Bruce (1971); Nelson, Carskaddon, and Bonvillian (1973); and Rental and Kennedy (1972). The "teaching devices" present in normal mother-child interactions which comprise a language-learning environment are reviewed by Moerk (1972).

The Language–Thought Relationship

Another persisting issue is grounded in the rationale which underlies most carefully structured academically oriented programs and requires language proficiency among the children involved. This rationale can be reviewed briefly. First is the premise that academic success requires a functional repertoire of basic concepts and language skills. To be functional, language must be used to receive and transmit data which form the substance of classroom activity. Language must also serve an "inner speech" function, i.e., generate an internal guidance system for one's behavior. And, most importantly, language must become the medium through which verbal reasoning is manifest. Reasoning ability (a complex process of concept manipulation) is necessary for normal academic progress, but some— perhaps many—children cannot adequately use language to express reasoned thoughts. The remedial task is obvious: refine these children's linguistic processes so that their reasoning ability can be stimulated under accelerative circumstances.

The emphasis in many language programs upon the structural features of language to achieve this objective is reminiscent of the *linguistic relativity* hypothesis that thought is fashioned by the particular language through which it is processed. The idea, in other words, is that language shapes ideas and serves to guide one's mental behavior. The pattern and direction of thought are therefore a function of linguistic structure, making language much more than a means of social communication.

Research into the relation between thought and language has not provided incontrovertible support for the linguistic relativity hypothesis. Consequently, discrepant theoretical positions engulf the basic idea (Ervin-Tripp, 1966). For example, distinctions between language and thought are found in the work of such authorities as Church (1961), Furth (1964), Lenneberg (1967), Piaget (1961), and Vygotsky (1962). All of these authors may be used as references to argue variously against the practice of refining thought through language drill. To illustrate, Church (1961) has rejected an S-R associationistic-reinforcement view of language development to argue that children must gradually formulate their personal "constructions of reality" from the various sensory data they encounter. For Church, language categories do not determine children's thought processes. Rather, thought processes and language categories interact and accommodate to one another. On the other hand, support for a strategy of improving abstract thought through systematic language-thought training is provided by Blank and Solomon, whose work has been discussed under the topic of tutorial approaches. It will be recalled that Blank and Solomon have worked to improve children's internal symbolic system so that it is functional in organizing and classifying stimuli. Their resultant—albeit implicit—version of the linguistic relativity hypothesis and Church's opposing view can therefore be related to the rationalist-empiricist debate as well.

Because the problems encountered in language-thought research with children are so complex, the associated theoretical conflict is unlikely to be resolved. The dilemma involved, of course, concerns the search for truth about language development and thinking. Educators unaware of the range of reasoned arguments involved in the dilemma could conceivably deceive themselves about what they are or not contributing to children's development and education. For further information about this and related controversies about language and cognition, see Cazden (1972, chapter 9).

Interpreting Language Differences

This writer has consistently been impressed with two remarkable facts about children's language development. One is the similarity in the sequential aspects of language acquisition (especially syntax) which characterizes children the world over. A second is the wide latitude of individual differences in children's verbal knowledge and language usage at any given point in this developmental sequence. These differences, clearly related to variables such as social background and ethnicity, extend also to complex variations in dialect from the standard English form (or any other strictly formal language). Many children from rural New England, Appalachia, and parts of the southern United States, for example, often speak in grammar which differs markedly from standard, formal English. And, as indicated in the section on bilingual education, many American children learn to speak another language before English. When they learn English, many of the rules of their native language may also be incorporated into their second language production. Such behavior, for example, has been observed among children of American Indian heritage and those who live in communities close to Spanish-speaking Mexico.

Important issues regarding linguistic variations from standard English include how these differences are interpreted by educators and the extent to which these differences may impede children's normal school progress. In Chapter 1, it was written that such variations have often been used in the past by teachers as evidence of social or intellectual inferiority, language retardation, or a primitive linguistic system. The result was pervasive ethnocentric thinking about children, especially those from nonwhite, nonmiddle-class backgrounds. It is true that one basic manifestation of mental retardation is language disability. But we are concerned here with normal children who happen not to have learned their English in conformity with the standard, formal version.

Gradually, and fortunately for children, this attitude has given way to the view that no language system is superior in structure to any other, nor in itself contributes to greater or lesser intellectual prowess among its speakers. All languages seem equally complex in their linguistic features, although variations can be noted in the number of words languages contain or their capacity to accommodate shades of meaning. The French, for example, have encountered great difficulty in finding appropriate semantic equivalents for many technical terms coined in English. Our point here, however, is twofold: first, the professional literature about linguistic equivalence notwithstanding, variations by children from standard English form are still interpreted by many practitioners as indicative of language or intellectual deficiencies. Second, and in recognition of differences (not deficiencies), standard English proficiency still remains crucial for success in American schools, if not American life generally. Many children do enter school apparently ill equipped to deal with the properties of standard English. How, then, are educators to deal with this matter?

Protagonists of bilingual education, of course, already have proposed and acted upon one possible, if only partial, solution to the problem. Initial results are promising. This says nothing, however, about dialect differences. A second look at many language programs discussed in this chapter reveals no freedom for variation from standard English as far as formal instruction and language skill development are concerned. By implication, these programs seem designed to eradicate dialectical variations, at least within the classroom. The personal-social effects of this strategy, while largely undocumented, could be adverse. At the other extreme, one might consider early education designed exclusively within the parameters of a child's native dialect. This, too, presents many problems, since so many different dialectical variations exist in America (and even among children from the same geographical region). Moreover, no one knows if education by dialect would necessarily be more effective, although bidialectical education, like bilingual education, may be. As stated elsewhere (McCandless and Evans, 1973), this author prefers a third approach: helping all children to use formal English when desirable or necessary for their own welfare. This implies a strategy for assisting children to discriminate both when and where the use of their native dialect or standard English is preferable.

Regardless, the psychological issues that surround dialect phenomena and intellectual-academic performance should not be glibly cast aside. Interested readers will find an intriguing literature on this topic. For a beginning, the following references are recommended: Baratz (1969); Cazden, Bryant, and Tillman (1972); Foreit and Donaldson (1971); Garvey and McFarlane (1970); Gottesman (1972); Hall, Turner, and Russell (1973); Houston (1970); Marwit, Marwit, and Boswell (1972); Quay (1972); Stern and Gupta (1970); and Williams, Whitehead, and Miller (1972). And still other issues in language education can be identified. One, much too complex for a suitable treatment here, concerns the relationship of language acquisition and reading (e.g., Chomsky, 1972). Another issue, of course, is the matter of *structure*, the degree to which a language program is preplanned and sequenced according to time factors and content hierarchies. Since this issue cuts across virtually all aspects of early childhood education, it is discussed in some detail in the final chapter of this book. Further comment about desirable, if not absolutely essential, conditions for language education in early childhood is provided by Cazden et al. (1971).

SUMMARY

Chapter 4 has been concerned with a general reprioritizing of goals and objectives for language education in early childhood that has occurred over the past several years. This repriority process has been brought about in part by improved studies of the role of language in early learning, an increased awareness of how early language experience may equip children unequally for the standard English language tasks of the school, and a growing sensitivity to preserving language differences which provide cultural or subcultural identity. Several remarkably different approaches to the general task of language education in early childhood have emerged, many of which represent fundamentally different assumptions and values about how language develops, how language is involved in children's thinking, and how language training should proceed. One of the most controversial of these approaches involves highly structured language pattern drill. Known as Distar, this program has been generally observed to succeed in achieving its objectives. Criticisms of the approach usually center on possible (and largely undocumented) unintended effects of tightly constrained learning activity. Most basically, Distar exemplifies the cluster of philosophical and psychological issues associated with the "natural growth" versus "cultural training" approaches to education discussed in chapter 1.

A second departure from the more traditional language enrichment approach in early education is the tutorial method. An example of tutorial content and methodology has been presented, together with some early empirical indications concerning efficacy. The choice of such a tutorial program will depend upon many factors, including a careful assessment of local needs and resources. In addition, there is some evidence that structured tutoring should be used cautiously in relation to variables such as the age and previous experience of the children involved.

Another approach to language education, derived from formal conceptualizations of human psycholinguistic processes and intelligence, is known as the Peabody Language Development Kit. This program is composed of four progressively complex levels of language experience for children from preschool age to about ten. Judicious use of PLDK generally has resulted in positive gains by children, especially in vocabulary development. Judicious use basically means skilled, flexible, and consistent implementation of the program over time with children whose needs are best served by a preplanned approach which has specific language objectives.

Attuned most closely to informal educational approaches for young children is the language-lift technique to facilitate natural language acquisition. This technique differs from the more structured approaches in that the content for instruction depends primarily upon language cues which emanate spontaneously from individual children. Teachers' skill in modeling certain grammatical structures selectively for children and teachers' firm knowledge of the characteristics of the language of instruction are essential ingredients for a successful application of this method. Unfortunately, the evaluative research about the effectiveness of the language-lift technique is less extensive and specific than the normal evaluation conducted within the context of more direct, structured approaches to language education. Comments about the efficacy of language-lift practices must therefore remain at a relatively tentative and general level.

The meaning and rationale for still another dimension of early language education—bilingual education—have also been reviewed in this chapter. Several directions in bilingual education can be observed, including both the assimilation and pluralistic models. One program of bilingual education designed expressly for kindergarten children has been presented in some detail as an example of work in this area. The effects of second language learning upon native language competence and general cognitive development have also been discussed. Data from the provocative St. Lambert experiment were cited in relation to the linguistic interference hypothesis associated with this issue.

Some other persistent issues in research about children's language development have been discussed in the final section of this chapter: the nativist-environmentalist dilemma, the language-thought relationship, and the issue of interpreting language differences among children. Such issues merit the full attention of educators concerned with the role of language experience in overall development and how schools may facilitate or impede this development.

REFERENCES

Adkins, D., D. Crowell, and P. Loveless. Iterative research in curriculum development: a preschool language module. *Educational Perspectives*, 1970, *9*, 19–24.

Ammon, P., and M. Ammon. Effects of training black preschool children in vocabulary versus sentence construction. *Journal of Educational Psychology*, 1971, *62*, 421–426.

Andersson, T., and M. Boyer. *Bilingual schooling in the United States.* Austin, Tex.: Southwest Educational Development Laboratory, 1969.

Baratz, J. A bi-dialectical task for determining language proficiency in economically disadvantaged Negro children. *Child Development*, 1969, *40*, 889–901.

Bartlett, E. Selecting preschool language programs. In C. Cazden (ed.), *Language in early childhood education*. Washington, D.C.: National Association for the Education of Young Children, 1972, 37–71.

Becker, W. Some effects of direct instruction methods in teaching disadvantaged children in Project Follow Through. *Proceedings of the International Symposium on Behavior Therapy*, Minneapolis, October, 1972.

Becker, W., and S. Engelmann. *Summary analysis of four year data on achievement and teaching progress with 7000 children in 20 projects.* Eugene, Ore.: University of Oregon, Follow Through Technical Report 73–1, 1973.

Bereiter, C., and S. Engelmann. *Teaching the culturally disadvantaged child in the preschool.* Englewood Cliffs, N.J.: Prentice-Hall, 1966.

Bernbaum, M. *Early childhood programs for non-English speaking children.* Urbana, Ill.: ERIC Clearinghouse on Early Childhood Education, 1971.

Blank, M. *Teaching learning in the preschool.* Columbus, Ohio: Charles E. Merrill, 1974.

Blank, M., and W. Bridger. Deficiencies in verbal labeling in retarded readers. *American Journal of Orthopsychiatry*, 1966, *36*, 840–847.

Blank, M., and W. Bridger. Perceptual abilities and conceptual deficiencies in retarded readers. In J. Zubin (ed.), *Psychopathology of mental development.* New York: Grune & Stratton, 1967, 401–402.

Blank, M., and F. Solomon. A tutorial language program to develop abstract thinking in socially disadvantaged preschool children. *Child Development*, 1968, *39*, 379–390.

Blank, M., and F. Solomon. How shall the disadvantaged child be taught? *Child Development*, 1969, *40*, 47–61.

Blank, M., M. Koltuv, and M. Wood. Individual teaching for disadvantaged kindergarten children: a comparison of two methods. *Journal of Special Education*, 1972, *6*, 207–219.

Carroll, J. *Language and thought.* Englewood Cliffs, N.J.: Prentice-Hall, 1964.

Cazden, C. Evaluation of learning in preschool education: early language development. In B. S. Bloom, J. T. Hastings, and G. F. Madaus (eds.), *Handbook on formative and summative evaluation of student learning.* New York: McGraw-Hill, 1971, 345–398.

Cazden, C. *Child language and education.* New York: Holt, Rinehart and Winston, Inc., 1972.

Cazden, C., B. Bryant, and M. Tillman. Making it and going home: the attitudes of black people toward language education. In C. Cazden (ed.), *Language in early childhood education*. Washington, D.C.: National Association for the Education of Young Children, 1972, 73–81.

Cazden, C., J. Baratz, W. Labov, and F. Palmer, Language development in day care programs. In E. Grotberg (ed.), *Day care: resources for decision.* Washington, D.C.: OEO Office of Planning Research and Evaluation, 1971, 153–172.

Chomsky, C. Stages in language development and reading exposure. *Harvard Educational Review*, 1972, *42*, 1–33.

Chow, S., and P. Elmore. *Early childhood information unit: resource manual and program descriptions.* San Francisco: Far West Laboratory for Educational Research and Development, 1973.

Church, J. *Language and the discovery of reality.* New York: Random House, Inc., 1961.

Crittenden, B. A critique of the Bereiter-Engelmann preschool program. *School Review*, 1970, *78*, 145–167.

Dale, P. *Language development: structure and function.* Hinsdale, Ill.: The Dryden Press, 1972.

Dickie, J. Effectiveness of structured and unstructured (traditional) methods of language training. In M. A. Brottman (ed.), Language remediation for the disadvantaged preschool child. *Monographs of the Society for Research in Child Development*, 1968, *33*, Serial No. 124, 62–79.

Dunn, L., and M. Mueller. Differential effects of the ITPA profile of the experimental version of Level I of the Peabody Language Development Kits with disadvantaged first-grade children. Nashville: Institute on Mental Retardation and Intellectual Development, undated.

Dunn, L., and J. Smith. *Peabody language development kits, level 1.* Circle Pines, Minn.: American Guidance Service, Inc., 1965.

Dunn, L., and J. Smith. *Peabody language development kits, level 2.* Circle Pines, Minn.: American Guidance Service, Inc., 1966.

Dunn, L., and J. Smith. *Peabody language development kits, level 3.* Circle Pines, Minn.: American Guidance Service, Inc., 1967.

Dunn, L., J. Smith, and K. Horton. *Peabody language development kits, level 4.* Circle Pines, Minn.: American Guidance Service, 1968.

Elardo, R. The experimental facilitation of children's comprehension and production of four syntactic structures. *Child Development*, 1971, *42*, 2101–2104.

Engelmann, S., J. Osborn, and T. Engelmann. *Distar Language Program.* Chicago: Science Research Associates, 1972.

Ervin-Tripp, S. *Language development.* In L. Hoffman and M. Hoffman (eds.), *Review of child development research.* Vol. 21. New York: Russell Sage, 1966, 55–105.

Evans, E. *Assessment of the Satellite preschool program: a progress report.* Mimeograph report, University of Washington Department of Education, Seattle, 1971.(a).

Evans, E. *Contemporary influences in early childhood education.* New York: Holt, Rinehart and Winston, 1971(b).

Fishman, J. A., and J. Lovaas. Bilingual education in sociolinguistic perspective. *TESOL Quarterly*, 1970, *4*, 215.

Foreit, K., and P. Donaldson. Dialect, race, and language proficiency: another dead heat on the merry-go-round. *Child Development*, 1971, *42*, 1572–1574.

Frager, S., and C. Stern. Learning by teaching. *Reading Teacher*, 1970, *23*, 403–407.

Friedlander, B. The Berieter-Engelmann approach. *Educational Forum*, 1968, *32*, 359–362.

Furth, H. Research with the deaf: implications for language and cognition. *Psychological Bulletin*, 1964, *62*, 145–164.

Gaardner, B. Organization of the bilingual school. *Journal of Social Issues*, 1967, *23*, 110–121.

Garvey, C., and P. McFarlane. A measure of standard English proficiency of inner-city children, *American Educational Research Journal*, 1970, *7*, 29–40.

Goldupp, O. An investigation of independent child behavior in the open classroom: the classroom attitude observation schedule. Tucson, Ariz.: Arizona Center for Educational Research and Development, 1972.

Goss, A. E. Speech and language. In B. B. Wolman (ed.), *Handbook of general psychology*. Englewood Cliffs, N.J.: Prentice-Hall, 1973, 568–629.

Gotkin, L. *Matrix games*. Englewood Cliffs, N.J.: Prentice-Hall, 1968.

Gottesman, R. Auditory discrimination ability in Negro dialect-speaking children. *Journal of Learning Disabilities*, 1972, *5*, 94–101.

Guess, D., J. Smith, and E. Ensminger. The role of nonprofessional persons in teaching language skills to mentally retarded children. *Exceptional Children*, 1971, February, 447–453.

Guilford, J. P. Three faces of intellect. *American Psychologists*, 1959, *14*, 469–479.

Gumperz, J. J., and E. Hernández-Chavez. Bilingualism, bidialecticism, and classroom interaction. In C. B. Cazden, V. P. John, and D. Hymes (eds.), *Functions of language in the classroom*. New York: Teachers College, 1972, 84–108.

Guthrie, J., and T. Baldwin. Effects of discrimination, grammatical rules, and application of rules on the acquisition of grammatical concepts. *Journal of Educational Psychology*, 1970, *61*, 358–364.

Hall, V., R. Turner, and W. Russell. Ability of children from four cultures and two grade levels to imitate and comprehend crucial aspects of standard English: a test of the different language explanations. *Journal of Educational Psychology*, 1973, *64*, 147–158.

Henderson, R. W. Accountability and decision-making in open education. *Childhood Education*, 1973, April, 368–372.

Houston, S. A reexamination of some assumptions about the language of the disadvantaged child. *Child Development*, 1970, *41*, 947–963.

Hughes, M., R. Wetzel, and R. Henderson. *The Tucson early education model*. Tucson, Ariz.: University of Arizona, 1969.

Hutinger, P., and T. Bruce. The effects of adult verbal modeling and feedback on the oral language of Head Start children. *American Educational Research Journal*, 1971, *8*, 611–622.

John, V. The intellectual development of slum children: some preliminary findings. *American Journal of Orthopsychiatry*, 1963, *33*, 813–822.

John, V., and V. Horner. *Early childhood bilingual education*. New York: Modern Language Association of America, 1971.

Kamii, C., and L. Derman. The Engelmann approach to teaching logical thinking: findings from the administration of some Piagetian tasks. Ypsilanti, Mich.: Ypsilanti Public Schools, 1969.

Kjolseth, R. Bilingual education programs in the United States: for assimulation or pluralism? In P. R. Turner (ed.), *Bilingualism in the Southwest*. Tucson, Ariz.: University of Arizona Press, 1973, 3–27.

Kohlberg, L. Early education: a cognitive-developmental view. *Child Development*, 1968, *39*, 1013–1062.

Lambert, W. E., and G. R. Tucker. *Bilingual education of children: the St. Lambert experiment*. Rowley, Mass.: Newbury House, 1972.

Larsen, V. *Summaries of case studies on the effectiveness of the Distar instructional system*. Chicago: Science Research Associates, 1971.

Lavatelli, C. A systematized approach to the Tucson method of language teaching. In C. Lavatelli (ed.), *Language training in early childhood education*. Urbana, Ill.: University of Illinois Press, 1971, 101–118.

Lenneberg, E. *Biological foundations of language*. New York: Wiley, 1967.

Levinson, E. The modification of intelligence by training in the verbalization of word definitions and simple concepts. *Child Development*, 1971, *42*, 1361–1380.

Marwit, S., K. Marwit, and J. Boswell. Negro children's use of non-standard grammar. *Journal of Educational Psychology*, 1972, *63*, 218–224.

McCandless, B., and E. Evans. *Children and youth: psychosocial development*. Hinsdale, Ill.: The Dryden Press, 1973.

McGeoch, J., and A. Irion. *The psychology of human learning*. New York: McKay, 1952.

McNeill, D. *The acquisition of language*. New York: Harper & Row, 1970.

Miller, L. Experimental variations of Head Start curricula. Louisville, Ky.: University of Louisville, Department of Psychology, 1972.

Moerk, E. Principles of interaction in language learning. *Merrill-Palmer Quarterly*, 1972, *18*, 229–257.

Moore, D. Language research and preschool language training. In C. Lavatelli (ed.), *Language training in early childhood education*. Urbana, Ill.: University of Illinois Press, 1971, 3–48.

Moskovitz, S. Some assumptions underlying the Bereiter approach. *Young Children*, 1968, *24*, 24–31.

Nedler, S. *A bilingual early childhood program*. Austin, Tex.: Southwest Educational Development Laboratory, 1973.

Nedler, S., and P. Sebera. Intervention strategies for Spanish-speaking preschool children. *Child Development*, 1971, *42*, 259–267.

Nelson, K., G. Carskaddon, and J. Bonvillian. Syntax acquisition: impact of experimental variation in adult verbal interaction with the child, *Child Development*, 1973, *44*, 497–504.

Nimnicht, G., O. McAfee, and J. Meier. *The new nursery school*. New York: General Learning Corporation, Early Learning Division, 1969.

Osborn, J. *Proceedings of conference on the Distar instructional system*. University of Washington, Seattle, May, 1973.

Osgood, C. Motivational dynamics of language behavior. In the *Nebraska symposium on motivation, 1957*, Lincoln, Neb.: University of Nebraska Press, 1957.

Palermo, D. Language acquisition. In H. Reese and L. Lipsett (eds.), *Experimental child psychology*. New York: Academic Press, Inc., 1971, 425–478.

Parker, R., and M. Day. Comparisons of preschool curricula. In R. Parker (ed.), *The preschool in action*. Boston: Allyn and Bacon, 1972, 466–508.

Piaget, J. The genetic approach to the psychology of thought. *Journal of Educational Psychology*, 1961, *52*, 275–281.

Quay, L. Negro dialect and Binet performance in severely disadvantaged black four-year-olds. *Child Development*, 1972, *43*, 245–250.

Rentel, V., and J. Kennedy. Effects of pattern drill on the phonology/syntax, and reading achievement of rural Appalachian children. *American Educational Research Journal*, 1972, *9*, 87–100.

Rentfrow, R., K. During, E. Conrad, and O. Goldupp. *Intensive evaluation of Head Start implementation in the Tucson early education model*. Tucson, Ariz.: Arizona Center for Educational Research and Development, 1972.

Ryckman, D. Independent evaluation of the kindergarten phase of the CAMPI Satellite preschools. Mimeograph report. University of Washington, Department of Education, Seattle, 1972.

Ryckman, D. Independent evaluation of the CAMPI Satellite preschools. Mimeograph report. University of Washington, Department of Education, Seattle, 1973.

Science Research Associates, Inc. *DISTAR*. Chicago: Science Research Associates, Inc., 1972.

Shanner, W., G. Tallmadge, and C. Wright. *Distar reading cost-effectiveness study.* Chicago: Science Research Associates, Inc., 1972.

Shiach, G. The effectiveness of a Peabody Language Development Kit with severely subnormal children. *British Journal of Educational Psychology*, 1973, *43*, 294–297.

Smith, J. Effects of a group language development program upon the psycholinguistic abilities of educable mental retardates. *Peabody College Research Monograph Series in Special Education*, No. 1. Nashville, Tenn.: George Peabody College for Teachers, 1962.

Stern, C., and W. Gupta. Echoic responding of disadvantaged preschool children as a function of type of speech modeled. *Journal of School Psychology*, 1970, *8*, 24–27.

Vygotsky, L. *Language and thought: the problem and the approach.* Cambridge, Mass.: MIT Press, 1962.

Williams, F., J. Whitehead, and L. Miller. Relations between language attitudes and teacher expectancy. *American Educational Research Journal*, 1972, *9*, 263–278.

Wright, L. The bilingual education movement at the crossroads. *Phi Delta Kappan*, 1973, *55*, 183–186.

Zimmerman, B., and J. Bergan. Intellectual operations in teacher question-asking behavior. *Merrill-Palmer Quarterly*, 1971, *17*, 19–26.

Photograph by Peter Rinearson.

5

the piagetian mystique

INTRODUCTION

Much of the contemporary attention to children's cognitive development has been closely associated with the stimulating ideas of Jean Piaget, a Swiss epistemologist. Piaget began his ingenious study of child development with the careful observation of his own three children. From this beginning his investigations were gradually extended to other children and have resulted in the publication of vast numbers of papers, monographs, and books.

Piaget's conceptual system for the description and classification of children's cognitive development has been formulated independently of American psychology. As adequate translations of this system from the French language have slowly been made available, Piagetian concepts have become available on a broad scale to American psychologists and educators. There is no doubt that these concepts have made an indelible impression on the psychological and educational literature in this country.

While impressive, the collective works of Jean Piaget represent an extremely dense conceptual network. An examination of this network is arduous and subject to error. In part this is due to certain ambiguities and semantic difficulties which pervade the theory. And because the theory is not yet complete, subtle revisions occur frequently and also create difficulties for the consumer. Regardless, in this chapter the writer will attempt to encapsulate the major features of Piagetian theory, provide a sampling of Piaget-based research, and illustrate some ways in which this theory and research have influenced curriculum development and instructional strategies for early childhood education.

THE SYSTEM

Of fundamental concern to Piaget and his colleagues at Geneva has been the identification of the processes underlying and governing qualitative changes in thinking throughout the child's development. Piaget and his colleagues begin by defining *mature intelligent behavior* as the ability to reason and think critically in objective, abstract, and hypothetical terms.[1] This formal reasoning ability, as conceived by Piaget, is superordinate; that is, it rests at the top of a hierarchy of subordinate elements which are its developmental predecessors. These progressively complex predecessors are said to emerge in a distinct sequence. Certain groupings of them define qualitatively distinct states of intellectual growth, beginning in infancy with sensory-motor coordinations and ending with the aforementioned formal reasoning ability.

Among the factors which influence this progression are neurological maturation in concert with physical and social experience. A fourth factor is *equilibration*, a process by which a developing child seeks greater cognitive balance or stability at successively higher levels as new learnings are reconciled with the old. This adaptive reconciliation is further defined by an interaction of two processes or mechanisms of thought evolution: *assimilation* and *accommodation*.

When, at any given point in time, new data are integrated in a coordinated way within one's existing conceptual repertoire, one has *assimilated*. For example, consider a young child whose structure of meaning for the class concept *bird* is limited to what birds do, namely, fly. If he then perceives and thinks about a flying bat as a bird, he has assimilated the new experience according to his present comprehension level. The complementary process of accommodations may be engaged, however, when the child immediately finds that the object is not a bird, but a mammal (disequilibrium). His conceptual understanding of *bird* must be refined to handle this apparent incongruity; he accommodates his reference system to fit external reality more accurately. A myriad of such interactions is necessary for a child to come gradually to terms with physical reality. Perception and orderly cognitive functioning based upon logical operations are thus intimately related. Perceptual development, according to Piaget, is governed by the principle of *successive liberation*; that is, with age a child becomes less and less a pawn of the dominant properties of the stimulus field as he explores this field perceptually. In turn, the content and processes of *thinking* are less perceptually bound with age.

---

[1] Implied is an intimate relationship, at maturity, between thought processes and the properties of formal logic (Hunt, 1961).

The raw data from which Piaget has developed his evolutionary view of logical thought structures have come from the observation of children in their natural environments and the creative application of Piaget's *méthode clinique*. The latter technique involves primarily (1) systematic observation of a child's interactions with his environment and (2) a patterned inquiry by interview into the reasons a child is able or prefers to give for an event he has observed, either in daily life or in an experimental setting. (Obviously the second element is possible only after a child's language development enables him to respond to questions.) For example, a balloon may be blown up in the presence of a child and then released to zoom about the room. Subsequently an investigator would probe the child for any explanations he might advance for this phenomenon. Or two plasticine balls of equal size and weight may be shown to a child and one ball may then be rolled into a pancake. The line of questioning might involve asking the child whether (and why) the weight or substance of the transformed ball is *less than*, *equal to*, or *greater than* that of the untransformed one. Customarily, children of various ages are confronted with identical problems and questions. Children's responses are then classified on the basis of the age-related logic inherent (or lacking) in them. The Genevan school has not, however, limited its inquiry to concepts of physical causality, space, and number. Age-based trends in moral judgment and play have also been identified (Piaget, 1932, 1951). Throughout these avenues of study Piaget has scrutinized the active role children take in making sense out of their world. The resultant theory is essentially a commentary on the inductive learning processes of children.

The Sequence of Development

The sequence through which a child's cognitive structures evolve begins with a state of egocentrism and ideally culminates in a state of perspectivism (Langer, 1969). *Egocentrism*, in Piaget's terms, refers most generally to the inability of a child to distinguish his viewpoint from that of others and to differentiate himself from his actions. In other words, egocentrism is defined as a lack of discrimination between the subjective and the objective. Piaget's definition of childhood egocentricity thus differs from the common use of this term. An egocentric adult is so described not because he is unable to consider the other fellow's view, but because he does not wish to. Piaget's child is egocentric because he cannot behave otherwise. Out of this relative cognitive immaturity are developed greater objectivity and the ability to think reflectively. The order in which this evolution proceeds is the hallmark of Piagetian theory and has two features: invariance and cumulative development. By *invariance* is meant that the sequence of development has a fixed, defined order; to reach point Z in development a child must have started at A and proceeded through B, C, D, E, and so on. Further, this order is said to be the same for all children (a genetic conception of thought development), although individual differences in rate are possible and likely.

The notion of *cumulative development* is closely related to invariance.

This means that the quality of a child's cognitive behavior at any time is dependent upon the quality of the sensory-motor and symbolic experience relevant to a particular cognition that has come before. It is therefore assumed that cognitive structures develop and become more finely attuned (complex) by underlying processes which reflect the interaction of genetic and experiential forces. Cognitive structures (organized components of intelligent behavior) which define behavior at one point in development (stage) are incorporated into those of a later period (stage); thus these stages are hierarchically arranged and, by definition, qualitatively distinct. The qualitatively distinct periods identified by Piaget are the *sensory-motor stage* (birth to two years), the *stage of preoperational thought* (two to seven years), *concrete-operational stage* (seven to eleven years), and the *period of formal operations* (eleven years and over).[2]

Sensory-Motor Period   It is during the first two years of life that sensory-motor coordinations (looking at things heard, grasping at things seen and heard, manipulating things seen) form the action basis for subsequent symbolic thought. Gradually, reflective behavior gives way to goal-seeking sensory-motor enactments and budding concepts of time, space, and causality. Piaget has found it necessary to subdivide this initial period into six substages, the last of which marks the transition to symbolic thought. We may note here that the symbolic content of logical thought requires the differentiation of a signifier—a verbal symbol, for example—and the object or event which the signifier represents. Illustrative would be a child learning the difference between the word *apple* and its actual concrete referent. For Piaget, however, thinking operations do not emerge as a direct function of language. Neither does language figure strongly in an explanation of thinking operations and their development.

The developmental importance of the sensory-motor period can hardly be overstressed. Among the most significant learnings reported by Piaget during this stage is the concept of the object, or *object permanence.* That is, through environmental interactions the infant discovers that objects do not "disappear" when they are out of sight; objects maintain their existence even though they are not in the infant's presence.[3] All subsequent logical thought development hinges upon this discovery. Closely related during the sensory-motor stage is the development of the ability to perceive certain aspects of the environment as substantively invariant; that is, while objects or people may appear in different contexts, their identity does not change. For example, father is father whether dressed in work clothes, pajamas, or bathing suit; milk is the same whether in a bottle, cup, or dish. A third significant development during the sensory-motor stage is learning that certain actions have certain effects on the

---

[2] These age brackets are approximations and should not be interpreted restrictively.

[3] Flavell and Hill (1969) maintain that the charting of the evolution of object permanence may be Piaget's single most important contribution.

environment—rudiments of the concept of causality. Overall, there is a gradual differentiation of self from nonself (determining what is "me" and what is "not me"), a trend which leads the infant from a totally self-centered existence to one successively more object-centered (Tuddenham, 1966). New means to achieve apparently desired outcomes (intentionality of purpose) may be observed, such means being the product of mental combinations not possible during the first one-and-a-half years of life. Imitation of observed behavior also becomes more and more complex and occurs even in the absence of contiguous models (*deferred imitation*). This imitation further reflects the increased memory skills of the child.

Preoperational Stage   Accelerated language development and concomitant advances in conceptual meaning occur early in the second stage, the preoperational period, thus freeing the child from the limitations of interaction based solely upon motor activity. While symbolic mental activity persists from this point onward, the preoperational child is still faced with limitations in thinking which can be overcome only through maturation and experience. For example, the child's conceptual behavior is dominated by his perceptions. His understanding (and misunderstanding) is based largely upon what he sees in the immediate present. As Flavell (1963a) has put it, the child's judgments are based upon his perception of "before the eye reality." To illustrate, suppose a child is shown two rows of kitchen matches, containing five matches each, with the matches of one row spaced at larger intervals than the other. In this situation, it is common for a preoperational child to behave as though the more widely dispersed row actually contains more matches ("This row has more because it is longer!"). Such a phenomenon is usually observed even when the two rows are equally distributed and then one is altered spatially while the child looks on. It is as if the child is unaware or cannot comprehend that the quantity of objects remains unchanged despite changes in contextual appearance. In other words, the child fails to *conserve* number in the face of irrelevant transformations. Similar failures are noted in regard to object properties such as weight, length, and volume. In these cases it is not object identity that the child fails to conserve, rather basic properties of objects.

A second feature of early preoperational development is the child's attendance to only one object property or experience at a time, that is, a categorization of objects and experiences on the basis of single characteristics. For example, a cooking pan is either tall or wide—it does not possess height and width simultaneously. Or a banana may be big or yellow, it may be green or small, but a group of bananas will not be conceived along the multiple dimensions of big, yellow bananas or small, green bananas. Multiple classification is thus seen to be beyond the child's power of combinatory thought. Similarly, the child experiences great difficulty in establishing superordinate conceptual categorizations, as in problems that require the achievement of higher-order abstractions. For example, a preoperational child may correctly agree that a squash is a vegetable; but he will also indicate that if all the squash in the world were to be eaten there would be no more vegetables. In this case the subordinate class *squash* is seemingly equivalent to its superordinate class, *vegetable*. In short, the child does not apprehend the multiple classes subsumed under the larger concept. Problems such as these exemplify the difficulty preoperational children have in assigning more than one attribute to an object. An anecdote from this writer's own recent experience is illustrative. A four-year-old was asked if he had a mommy and a daddy, to which he replied affirmatively. Negative replies were obtained, however, to other questions such as, "Is your mommy a wife?" and "Is your daddy a son?"

Still another characteristic of preoperational thought is what Piaget terms *transductive reasoning*—reasoning·from the specific to the specific or from the particular to the particular. This often takes the form of determining cause-effect relations simply on the basis that one event follows another in time or through some remote functional properties which may associate objects and events or that since one event (*Y*) is caused by another (*Z*) the relationship is reciprocal (*Y* causes *Z*). An example of such reasoning was apparent in an interchange one Sunday afternoon between the writer and his daughter, then three years old.

Jennifer: "Daddy, what day is it today?"

Daddy: "It's Sunday."

Jennifer: "No—it can't be Sunday. We didn't go to Sunday school today!"

Other aspects of the period—all of which reflect precausal thinking— are *animism* (the tendency to attribute life or consciousness to inanimate objects, particularly where movement may be observed such as in a cloud moving or a mountain stream rushing over a bed of pebbles); *artificialism* (the tendency to conceive of all objects in the world as the product of human creation and made for our own purposes), and *realism* (the tendency to view psychological phenomena such as dreams and pretenses as concrete, real occurrences). These latter three tendencies are said to be functions of general egocentrism. There exists no other view or experience for the child but his own. Events psychological and real are not well discriminated; wishful thinking and pretense are frequently confused with objective reality.

While the preoperational period encompasses roughly five years, the latter two or three years in this stage (ages 4 or 5 to 7) are marked by an acceleration in symbolic functioning (Flavell, 1963b). Although absolute perceptions and subjectivity in judgment still prevail, certain important abilities gradually make their appearance in the child's thought. First, cognitive structures are elaborated by a grouping of objects in terms of elementary relationships. For example, concepts such as milk, milkman, cow, dairy, and farm may be integrated on the basis of functional relationships. Similarly, toward the end of the preoperational period, objects may be grouped into classes according to common properties. For example, potatoes and meat may be subsumed under the class concept *food*, men and women under the class concept *people*.[4] Classification rules used by a child during this period are rarely verbalized. Piaget takes this to indicate unawareness of the formal criteria for classification. Thus a child's perceptually bound thinking, while often correct, is called *intuitive*. Children continue to utilize single-dimension classification strategies. That is, when confronted with a group of paper animals and plants (each group further characterized by two different sizes, large and small), the child is likely to classify by class membership or size, not both. Finally, the onset of quantitative thinking means that the child can handle relationships founded upon numerical order. This involves a transition from counting actual objects to the use of numbers as symbolic referents. For example, a child may count two apples on his left, two on his right, and add them to produce four apples. Eventually, the abstraction $2 + 2 = 4$ is generalized, that is, no longer limited to or dependent upon four specific objects.

Concrete Operations   Around the age of 6 or 7, intuitive thought is incorporated into the next higher structured component in cognitive development: *concrete operations* (so called because logical operations—mental acts of reasoning—are performed on real or concrete objects and events). The distinguishing characteristic of this stage is the increasing extent to which objectivity and logic are applied in thinking. Deductive reasoning is now possible, although the starting point for thought is always the concrete and real.

One major operation emerging during this third stage of development is based upon the logical rule of *transitivity*, that is, the passage from one state or point to another along a conceptual continuum. This operation is critical for the continued development of number concepts. Transitivity is a logical operation that underlies, for example, the arrangement of objects (or referents) in a series of "less than" or "greater than." Serial ordering, or *seriation*, can therefore be performed and represented symbolically as in transitivity of length of weight. For example, if $X > Y$ and $Y > Z$, then $X > Z$. A representational instance of this relation would be if Tom is heavier than Dick and Dick is heavier than Harry, then who is heavier, Tom or Harry? *Concrete* transitivity involves making inferences about the relations among actual objects, whereas both of these examples indicate *formal* transitivity. That is, in each preceding example a relational inference must be drawn from the verbally stated hypothetical premise. The concrete-operational forerunner to a functional comprehension of formal transitivity is the seriation of observable object properties (J. Murray and Youniss, 1968).

A second important concrete-operational ability is *class inclusion*, which makes it possible (1) to think about the parts and the whole inde-

---

[4] An interesting corollary here is the placement of classification items on conventional intelligence tests. For example, it is not until around age 7 that a majority of children correctly respond with higher-order abstractions to questions such as, "In what way are a peach and a pear alike."

pendently in part-whole relationships and (2) to perform multiple classification. Technically, the operation involved is *combinativity*, in which two classes can be combined into one comprehensive and superordinate class. Suppose a child is presented with a box of twenty-five wooden pencils (twenty-one yellow and four black). We then ask him to indicate whether there are more yellow pencils or more wooden pencils. The concrete-operational child will ordinarily answer correctly. In contrast, his younger, preoperational, counterpart will likely *center* on the dominant stimulus (color) and answer "yellow pencils." In short, the younger child experiences difficulty in dealing simultaneously with the parts and the whole. Symbolically, this example translates into a relation understood in the concrete-operational stage: If $X = Y + Z$, then $X - Y = Z$. Multiple classification is also illustrated in the pencil example: a pencil can be both yellow and wooden. Moreover, a pencil can be grouped with a metal ballpoint pen and other equivalent items into the abstract class *writing instruments.*

A third logical thought operation is *reversibility.* This term has a dual meaning. First, reversibility means that for every action there exists another action which cancels it (for example, the arithmetical operations of addition and multiplication can be reversed by subtraction and division, respectively). Second, reversibility enables the child to return to the original starting point of a thought sequence in problem solving; a thought process itself can be reversed. For example, subclasses of plants can be combined into a superordinate class and reseparated into subclasses. Thus, correct answers can be given to questions such as, "If all the plants in the world were to die, would there be any flowers left?"[5]

According to theory, reversibility is a prerequisite for *conservation acquisition.* A conserving child recognizes that certain properties of objects remain unchanged, despite certain changes in the objects themselves (for example, two 12-inch pizza pies remain equivalent in, say, weight and mass, even if one is cut into four pieces and the other into eight). Conservation acquisition is thought to occur in a fixed sequence of successively more complex levels: mass, weight, then volume. Conservation is therefore not an all-or-nothing matter.

The final example of concrete-operational thinking offered here involves the principle of *associativity.* This means that the same point or objective can be reached by different routes. Symbolically, associativity can be represented as $(W \cdot X) \cdot (Y \cdot Z) = (W \cdot X \cdot Y) \cdot Z = W \cdot (X \cdot Y) \cdot Z$, and so forth, or $(5 + 1) + (3 + 6) = (5 + 1 + 3) + 6 = 5 + (1 + 3) + 6$, and so on. In other words, the child is able to recognize that the same parts may be combined in different ways and that an identical solution to a problem may be reached through two (or more) different means. A concrete example of associativity might be a child mixing paints where

---

[5] Two forms of reversibility are distinguished: reversibility of relations (reciprocity) and reversibility of classes (inversion). These two forms presumably merge into one operation during the final stage of development (formal operations).

Through water play children may find out about the volumetric capacities of various containers. This kind of informal learning relates to the important acquisition of conservation, a milestone in the development of concrete operational thought. Photo courtesy of J. Myron Atkin.

(red + black + yellow) = brown. As long as additive quantities are held constant the *order* in which the ingredients are mixed makes no difference in the final outcome.

In summary, a concrete-operational child is capable of logical seriation, class inclusion, the recognition of equivalence (for example, that objects of varying size and color can be of equal weight and height does not necessarily denote increased weight), the exercise of reversibility in thought (for example, tracing a transformational sequence back to its point of origin to account for change in appearance), conservation, and associativity. Another way to view this stage is that the child gradually comes to master *classes, relations*, and *quantities* (Elkind, 1967a). Piaget stresses that although this period is governed by these principles of thought, the child is not consciously aware of them. It is the next, and final, stage of development that "explainer thinking" emerges.

Formal Operations Operations prior to age 10 or 11 are oriented toward concrete phenomena in the immediate present; in the final stage, they encompass the potential or hypothetical and the nonpresent. Operational thought systems become integrated to form structures from which hypotheses can be generated and logical conclusions deduced purely on a symbolic level (sans concrete props). The ability to perform *combinatorial analysis* (combine in thought several rules, operations, or variables to solve problems) becomes apparent, as does the ability to formulate and execute symbolic plans of action. Logical form can be examined apart from the content of a situation or statement, and potential relations among objects can be imagined. To illustrate, consider a child's ability to deal effectively with syllogisms involving a major premise, a minor premise, and a conclusion:

Every virtue is laudable.
Kindness is a virtue.
Therefore, kindness is laudable.

In the formal operational stage, the child is capable of reasoning (and explaining) that where a conclusion necessarily follows the premises and the premises are true, the conclusion must also be true. The child also becomes capable of detecting logical incongruities in hypothetical contexts. For example, consider what is wrong with the following: The five-year-old shell of a three-tailed turtle who lived for over a hundred years was found on a mountain top. Before the stage of formal operations, a child would likely respond by saying, "Turtles don't live on mountain tops," "Turtles have only one tail." In contrast, the formal operational child would be capable of ferreting out the logical contradiction and answering accordingly.

Piaget suggests that the adolescent's proclivity for criticizing and theorizing arises from new cognitive power; that is, he can now envision alternatives to the way things are done (child-rearing, education, government) and advance hypotheses for their improvement. This newly acquired power in turn feeds the idealism of youth. The combination of idealism with neatly packaged solutions to complex problems without due consideration for the practical limitations of such solutions represents the last "high water mark in egocentrism" (Elkind, 1967a; Flavell, 1963a). Finally, during this period the child becomes capable of evaluating the quality (logic) of his own thought (termed *second-order*, or *reflective*, *thinking*).

Some Further Comments

Piaget's system of thought development is infinitely more complex and detailed than the preceding summary may indicate. Hopefully, however, the reader is by now sufficiently equipped to appreciate the general dimensions of Piaget's system. Aside from Piaget's own writing, many secondary sources are available for a more advanced study of the theory (Baldwin, 1967; Flavell, 1963a; Furth, 1969; Ginsburg and Opper, 1969; Hunt, 1961; Maier, 1965).

Two more notions of Piagetian theory require some elaboration before we proceed to a sampling of research. One concerns a problem of normative-descriptive approaches generally. The second concerns Piaget's normative (age-related) description of development. Development so described can rarely be associated with anything more specific than a child's "natural environment." Thus, statements concerning children's abilities are technically a description of what children do at various ages, not what they may be capable of doing. In many cases, the natural environment may not be a very efficient nor effective one for programming experiences which would maximize developmental potential. One might expect some variation in developmental rate to be associated with qualitative variations in environmental experience. Further, one might argue that some, if not a great many, normative-descriptive data represent behavior that would be quite different if children were taught otherwise. This point is basic to much of the forthcoming "training research."

Another problem with normative-descriptive approaches, particularly when they are based on stages, is the implication that development is governed by a predetermined unfolding process. A predeterministic concept of development can easily lead to the view that educational intervention is of minor value in the developmental process (Sullivan, 1968). Further, a generalized emphasis upon age-based behavior may lead one to operate according to central tendencies in development and to overlook the wide range of individual differences in development, and their sources. Again, these thoughts are pertinent to the ensuing discussion of educational implications.

The language-thought issue previously encountered in Chapter 4 is also embedded in Piaget's theory, and some attention to this issue may contribute further to the reader's perspective. According to one source, Piaget is "perhaps the only exponent of logical intelligence who does not see language as an intrinsically necessary element of operational thinking" (Furth, 1969, p. 109). Piaget also rejects the proposition that language is a sufficient condition for the development of thinking operations, although he acknowledges that language may be necessary for the operations of formal logic. It is true, of course, that Piaget has studied children's verbal behavior extensively. This study does not attend specifically to language acquisition, however, except to demonstrate that the developmental characteristics of logical thought are not joined in definite ways with successive advances in linguistic ability (Furth, 1969). In other words, the specific relationship of operational structure to linguistic structure is vague. But, if anything, language for Piaget is structured by logic, instead of the reverse. Thus, in the Piagetian framework, the formation of operational structures is neither dependent upon nor necessarily assisted by the social transmission of spoken language.[6]

---

[6] For evidence, Piaget cites his own work; support comes from independent research such as Furth's study (1969) of deaf children. Furth has shown that "mature intelligence" develops in the absence of early linguistic experience and a verbal symbol system. Also pertinent is a conclusion from conservation-training studies that while verbal training for nonconservers can promote attention to task-relevant features, it does not in itself result in the acquisition of operations involved in conservation ability (Sinclair-De-Zwart, 1969). In contrast, Bruner (1964) argues in favor of a functional relationship between a child's achievement of symbolic representation (representation of past events on a symbolic level) and the development of conservation skills. The entire issue is far from settled.

An example of verbal thinking may help to clarify the Piagetian point of view. Suppose a five-year-old from Wichita, Kansas, were asked: "Are there more Wichitans or more Kansans?" According to Piagetian theory, the child would answer, "More Wichitans!" In a couple of years, however, the correct answer would be routine. As Furth (1969) explains,

> In connection with this Piaget-type problem of class inclusion we may ask what language contributes as an integral part of the problem situation. Since the question was framed in linguistic symbols, linguistic competence is of course a prerequisite in this situation. Moreover, the child's general knowledge or lack of knowledge of embedded class system is expressed by the verbal reply. But is the verbal reply or any linguistic skill in general an intrinsic part of this knowledge of classes? To this question Piaget replies with an unequivocal no. He finds no theoretical reason for bringing in language nor is he able to interpret any known evidence to the effect that language in itself is a decisive contributory factor in developing the first operations (p. 119).[7]

Since Piaget has not proposed an explicit theory of language acquisition, it is difficult to evaluate the language-thought relationships that he outlines—much less develop specific implications for teaching language. On the whole, those interested in facilitating cognitive development through language training find little encouragement from Piagetian theory, at least in terms of the initial development of thinking operations. This is another point basic to the training research to be discussed shortly. Certain modifications of Piaget's position seem necessary if language training is to play an important role in the development of logical intelligence.

RESEARCH

Introductory Comment

Piagetian theory has been exceptionally heuristic; vast numbers of studies inspired by Piagetian theory have poured into professional journals in the past decade. All research workers, to one degree or another, have attended to the validity of Piaget's system, although some believe that a process of verifying the observations from which Piaget built his theory has preempted systematic tests of the theory (Skager and Broadbent, 1968). The issue of validity is, of course, central to any extrapolation from the system for purposes of instruction and curriculum development.

Many of the early studies replicated Piaget's original experiments with different and larger numbers of children (for example, Elkind, 1961, 1964). For the most part experimenters have attempted to avoid the

---

[7] Hans G. Furth, *Piaget and Knowledge: Theoretical Foundations*, © 1969, Prentice-Hall, Inc.

pitfalls inherent in Piaget's *méthode clinique* in order to quell the criticisms by "hard-core empiricists." Perhaps because of the intriguing and ingenious tasks suited to the study of concrete-operational thought and the central role of conservation in cognition, children aged five to ten have been studied most frequently.[8]

This age bracket also includes the normative period during which children make the transition from preoperational (intuitive) to logical thought. Transition mechanisms seem to have aroused the curiosity of many psychologists, perhaps because they are among the least clearly articulated aspects of the theory.

As we shall see, Piaget-based studies taken together highlight two important research variables. First, the responses of children to Piaget-type tasks vary substantially according to the amount and relevance of information provided them and the kinds of questions asked them. Since these tasks are, in effect, devices for the measurement of behavior, it should be kept in mind that the inferences made from behavior so measured are only as valid as the measurement techniques themselves. Thus, the entire theory, like others, is a function of the methods used to obtain data. In Piaget's case, the data are assumed to be cognitively based responses. Second, many of the studies related to theoretical validation highlight issues such as the relationships between perception and logical thinking and between language and thought. These issues are rooted in theoretical conflicts between the Geneva school and those who approach cognitive development from a modified perspective (for example, Bruner et al., 1966).

The following brief review is intended only to highlight features of Piagetian theory useful for the later interpretation of educational implications drawn from the theory. No attempt is made to examine Piaget's original research, as his work appears in widely available publications (see Inhelder and Piaget, 1958; Piaget, 1932, 1951, 1952).

Replication and General Validation Studies

Basic issues in the replication research have included the sequences of logical operation appearance, the age at which children perform tasks on the basis of logical thought (concrete or formal), and the degree to which operations are generalized or interdependent (Ammon, 1969). While studies are not easily categorized, the broad trends in cognitive development championed by Piaget are generally supported by data from a wide variety of sources. Examples include the trend from precausal to causal

---

[8] Studies concerned with conservation far outweigh those which have dealt with classification and seriation. Very little evidence pertinent to formal operations has accumulated. It has been reasoned that this gap in the research may be due to (1) the notion that a complete elaboration of the theory at the formal operational level is comparatively recent and (2) the possibility that many aspiring researchers have been frightened away by the complex propositions of symbolic logic involved at this level (Skager and Broadbent, 1968).

thinking (Safier, 1964), age trends in the mastery of concrete operational thinking (Dudek, Lester, and Goldberg, 1969; Smedslund, 1964), and qualitative shifts in children's thinking during the general age periods specified by Piaget (Davol et al., 1967). More specifically, F. Murray (1968) has confirmed the relationship of age of conservation acquisition, and the order in which Piaget believes conservations are acquired (the orderly sequence of mass, weight, then volume conservation) has been successfully replicated (Uzgiris, 1964).

Further support for Piaget's idea of sequential progression in thought has come from the study of distance conservation and spatial coordinates (Shantz and Smock, 1966). Such evidence has been taken to confirm the more general concept of invariant sequence, which for most cognitive developmentalists is a basic power center of Piaget's theoretical system.

Many "validation" studies have dealt with the specific ages at which children's concepts are functional. From his original work, for example, Piaget has concluded that children normally acquire the concept of probability around age 7 or 8. American researchers, have reported reliable and appropriate probabilistic behavior for children at ages 3 and 4 (Davies, 1965; Goldberg, 1966), but this discrepancy may be explained by the fact that Piaget places the ability to *verbalize* the concept at the later age, an ability preceded by a correct intuitive use of the concept. Neither the Davies nor the Goldberg studies required correct verbalizations. Rather, nonverbal assessments were used. Age descriptions discrepant with Piagetian theory also appear in the earlier work of Braine (1959). Concepts of transitivity and position order were located roughly two years earlier than Piaget's theory would have us believe. Braine's methods were also essentially nonverbal—a procedure taken by Smedslund (1963) as a distortion of Piaget's criterion for genuine transitivity. With "improved" tests Smedslund replicated Piaget's original contention regarding the emergence of concrete transitivity.

Recent cross-cultural studies, largely concerned with conservation acquisition, have provided further support for the broad Piagetian developmental sequence (Bentler, 1972; Dasen, 1972; Goldschmid, 1973). Again, however, differences in *rate* of development have consistently been observed in relation to such variables as general culture membership, socioeconomic status, early education, and racial-ethnic status. For instance, up to two years' difference in rate of developmental progress among culturally different children of the same chronological age has been documented (Guadia, 1972; Wasik and Wasik, 1971). In general, the culturally based rate difference seems to favor children from more technologically advanced societies; within the same culture, city children have demonstrated slightly more advanced development than their rural counterparts (Dasen, 1972). These data suggest a rather strong environmental impact on Piaget's child, although precisely how much and what kinds of stimulation are implicated are unknown.

While many researchers have confirmed some basic Piagetian ideas about sequential, invariant development, others report exceptions—to both ordinal development and the existence of unitary thinking at a given developmental period. Brainerd (1973), for example, has reported an order of concrete operational skills development contrary to Piaget's sequence. Berzonsky's critical investigations (1970, 1971a, 1971b) of Piagetian theory and methodology are more than mildly provocative, and discrepancies in Piaget's infant psychology have been disclosed (Miller, Cohen, and Hill, 1970). The point is that research data about many specifics of Piaget's theory are not uniformly supportive. Nor are they likely to be in the near future: too many ambiguities and methodological problems complicate the Piagetian research literature. Methodologically speaking, it has been suggested that a careful "prestudy" of children is necessary before certain theoretically derived questions can be properly tested. Griffiths, Shantz, and Sigel (1967), for example, have examined the relational concept repertoires (*more, same, less*) of children aged four and five (normally transitional). Widespread confusion among children with regard to the concept *same* was discovered. Consequently, the investigators recommended that if one intends to utilize classical (verbal) conservation testing techniques with children, one should first determine his subject's ability to discern similarities and make appropriate use of *same*. Otherwise, one's results could be an artifact of questioning. In short, it would become difficult to determine whether (1) a child cannot conserve, (2) a child can conserve but is unable to decipher a question, or (3) a child can neither conserve nor decipher a question.[9]

In sum, research data provide much support for Piaget's basic ideas about sequential cognitive development; there is now little debate about the distinctiveness of Piaget's stages. Individual differences in rate can be marked and may affect even the ultimate level of development reached by children from different background circumstances (Dasen, 1972). Cautionary progress in theory development is advised to the extent that variations in tasks (including amount and kind of information provided to children, the nature of questions posed to them, and the positioning of objects for observation or manipulation by the child) produce variation in children's observed behavior. Until methodological problems are solved, there remains the possibility that certain theoretical features are artifacts of testing. The reader new to Piaget may wish to review earlier validation studies and can refer to the first edition of this book (Evans, 1971).

---

[9] Braine and Shanks (1965) agree that the cognitive competence level of a child may be underestimated by unsuitable question-asking procedures, yet some researchers maintain that very little effect can be attributed to the kind of question asked (Pratoomraj and Johnson, 1966). This counterargument is made more extreme by Youniss and Furth (1965, 1966), who contend that verbal sophistication has little bearing upon the utilization of a logical transitivity operation. The latter studies, however, involved direct instruction and are therefore not technically comparable to conventional descriptive Piagetian studies. A further item of note has come from the observation that, for a sample of disadvantaged children, an understanding of the concepts *more, less,* and *same* may be a necessary but insufficient condition for number conservation (Halasa, 1969).

Extension Research

While methodological skirmishes continue, some investigators have utilized Piagetian concepts to study issues and behavioral phenomena previously unexplored by the Geneva school. A prime example is the work of
David Elkind, a professor of psychology at the University of Rochester.
Elkind's line of attack has involved mapping the developmental terrain
of perceptual behavior as it relates to reading. Elkind began with a developmental study of decentration, the results of which were most adequately
explained by Piaget's perceptual operations (Elkind and Scott, 1962). Data
from subsequent studies revealed increased ability (with age) for children
to perceive part-whole relationships and to explore unstructured perceptual materials systematically (Elkind, Koegler, and Go, 1964; Elkind
and Weiss, 1967). Similar age effects were noted for types of concept
acquisition (Elkind, Van Doorninck, and Schwarz, 1967) and successively
more difficult conceptual orientation shifts (Elkind, 1966).[10] All results
have been interpreted neatly in terms of Piaget's theory of decentering.

   These data have provided Elkind with a springboard for studying the
complex relationship of perceptual activity to reading. He argues that
two of our most predominantly used methods of reading instruction may
be inconsistent with perceptual development, at least when the "average
six-year-old" is taught without having been given perceptual pretraining.
The "look-say" method, according to Elkind, requires responses which are
inconsistent with a child's development in *schematization.* It is not until
age 7 and later that children are normally able to coordinate part-whole
relationships (such as letter-word) so that each maintains its identity and
its interdependence. Neither does the phonics approach escape Elkind,
who sees it as utilizing the child's spontaneous ability to reverse figure
and ground (*perceptual reorganization* in the Piaget system). In other words,
a child must come to terms with two related phenomena: (1) more than
one sound is represented by one letter (letter *a* for example) and different
letters can represent the same sound (letter *s* and *c* as in *snake* and *circus,*
for example); and (2) learning the equivalences of upper- and lower-case
letters and manuscript and cursive letters. As Elkind (1967c) states,

> In all of these instances, the real problem lies in the recognition
> that the same element can represent different things and that different
> elements can represent the same thing. . . . [The problem] is then
> directly analogous to that faced by the child in reversing figure and
> ground when viewing an ambiguous figure (such as the famous Rubin-
> Vase Profile). That such an assumption is not fortuitous is shown by
> the fact that slow readers are deficient in the ability to reverse
> figure and ground in comparison with average readers of comparable
> mental ability (p. 360).

---

[10] Conceptual orientation shift behavior refers to the changes a child can
make in his classification strategy during inductive concept formation activities,
for example, the ability to shift from a classification of objects on the basis of
function (uses) to their concrete properties and vice versa.

The implication of Elkind's work is that training in perceptual re-organization and/or schematization may facilitate the reading process. At the least, assessment of perceptual behavior may be dictated for children who experience early reading difficulties.

The apparent advantages of perceptual training are shown by a recent study of inner-city second-grade Negro children (Elkind and Deblinger, 1969). The children in one group were engaged in a program of nonverbal perceptual exercises over a period of fifteen weeks. A second group of children, matched with the perceptual trainees on the basis of reading achievement and initial perceptual ability, underwent training for the same period with a conventional reading series. At the end of the training period the perceptual training group demonstrated a significantly higher level of word and word-form recognition skills than did the control group. These data are taken to supply validity for the training techniques developed by Elkind from Piagetian thought.

Behavioral Correlates

One traditional and pervasive approach to the description of behavior by psychologists has been the *correlational* approach. Various measurements are taken from the same individuals within a selected population and then correlated, usually to (1) investigate individual differences comprehensively, (2) discover broad behavioral patterns or common characteristics which may define basic, species-specific dimensions of behavior, and (3) identify characteristics or combinations of characteristics which may lead to the more efficient prediction of behavior. Thus a teacher may be assisted toward a better understanding of, say, anxiety, by recognition of (1) what other characteristics of children are associated with variations in this emotional response, (2) what responses may combine with this attribute to define more basic personality patterns, and (3) whether this constant (anxiety) is relevant in making predictions about, say, academic achievement. Occasionally, correlational studies are also used to identify empirical interrelationships among theories linked abstractly to one another.

All of these concerns have been implicit in a series of studies by Goldschmid (1967, 1968) which exemplifies the behavioral correlates approach within a Piagetian framework. Both studies utilized conservation among first- and second-grade children as the criterion of cognitive functioning. Their combined results show higher levels of conservation ability to be associated with (1) higher IQ, chronological age, and vocabulary, (2) more favorable peer and teacher ratings, (3) less maternal domination, and (4) greater objectivity in self-evaluation. Results of the 1967 study also led to the suggestion that emotional maladjustment may impede conservation acquisition. This idea has the indirect support of Neale (1966), who found a significantly greater degree of egocentrism among institutionalized emotionally disturbed children as compared to normal controls.

Correlational data such as these pose interpretation difficulties. They cannot legitimately be stretched to infer cause-effect relationships, only a "going-togetherness." Thus, the data above indicate only a positive "going-together" of characteristics generally thought desirable in our society (a phenomenon sometimes described by the phrase, those what has, gets!). Perhaps more importantly, these data provide indirect evidence for the principle that *all aspects of development interact.* As Piaget and others have maintained, the developmental process represents a complex inter-dependence of system components. However, this seemingly obvious principle may be too often overlooked by teachers and parents.

Longitudinal examinations of the relationship between Piagetian concept attainment and the academic behavior of children are rare. What little has been done to date does, however, indicate that this is a promising area for study. Kaufman and Kaufman (1972), for example, have provided validity data for a Piaget test battery used to predict kindergarten children's composite first-grade achievement. Concerning more specific predictions of spelling and arithmetic achievement, comparable power is reported for a Piagetian concept test and a conventional intelligence test (Freyberg, 1966). This, plus the factor analytic work of Stephens et al. (1972), suggests that school achievement is at least moderately related to aspects of conceptual development not tapped by standard mental tests.

This point is reinforced by another analysis of the relationships between Piagetian and conventional psychometric approaches to mental measurement (Dudek, Lester, and Goldberg, 1969). Medium high correlations (.52 to .62) between the Piagetian and standard IQ scales were obtained; both scales were equally effective for predicting children's primary grade achievement. This means that while both assessment methods measure many of the same things, each accounts for aspects of intelligent behavior not tested by the other. Multiple correlations of .70 to .80 were found between the *combined* assessments and children's school achievement.

Finally, that abilities involving seriation, correspondence, and conservation (not typically measured by conventional scales) are positively correlated with the academic behavior (arithmetic achievement) of young school children is substantiated in studies by Dodwell (1961) and Hood (1962).

With these data in mind, it can be argued that Piagetian-derived scales (with their strong emphasis upon basic reasoning processes) measure more of what is called "fluid intelligence," while standard IQ tests are more relevant to "crystallized intelligence" (Cattell, 1963; Horn, 1968). *Fluid intelligence* refers to a pattern of abilities involving central neural organizations and mental processes less bound to specific learning and acculturation experiences. In contrast, *crystallized intelligence* is thought to reflect more particularized experience, including education and other fairly orderly cultural influences. These two kinds of intelligence are not mutually exclusive, but differ in the proportion of physiological and cultural influence they reflect. This is, however, a viable distinction which may help to explain correlational data obtained from the use of Piagetian and conventional IQ scales. It may also be useful in regard to research on the effects of direct teaching on logical structure development.

More broadly, the potential value of Piaget-based scales for measuring children's developmental status is twofold. First, such scales involve the ordering of tasks by a logic from genuine developmental theory, rather than simply by a statistical pass-fail ratio characteristic of most standard intelligence tests. Second, Piagetian scales can provide measures of the degree to which a child has attained stage maturity at any point in time, with little contamination by culturally biased content and without the necessity of a comparison of the child's performance with other children's for a interpretation of the measurements. These and other matters related to a variety of efforts at scaling from the Piagetian perspective are discussed by Meyers (1972). Ultimately, educational programming cues for individual children may be gleaned better from Piaget scale use. These possibilities are only beginning to be explored, and readers who wish to study the measurement implications of Piaget's theory may consult Green, Ford, and Flamer, 1971.

General Schooling Effects

Another set of studies concerns the influence of general schooling upon operational thought development. Generally, these studies relate to Piaget's thesis that interaction with the total environment, rather than direct tuition, is the instrumental factor in the development of logical thought structures.

For example, Goodnow and Bethon (1966) compared the conservation skills (weight, volume, and surface) and combinatorial reasoning skill of unschooled Hong Kong children to schooled American children in the same age range. It was found that variation in schooling was not associated with differences in conservation skill; however, lack of schooling was associated with lowered combinatorial reasoning ability. These results were interpreted to mean that children probably acquire conservation skills in the normal course of development through their experiences with the physical environment. The greater degree of abstract or mediational thought required by combinatorial reasoning tasks is believed to be more strongly affected by academic events in the classroom, including perhaps a model (teacher) after whom the child can pattern his thinking.[11] This finding may also imply that conservation skills are not affected greatly by instruction. The broadest conclusion from this study is that schooling (or its lack) affects various thinking operations differentially.

---

[11] Another way to view this is in terms of a distinction between *arranged* and *unarranged* experience. Basic cognitive structures of concern to Piaget could be those which develop as a function of unarranged experience. Another interpretation is that Piaget explores the "spontaneous" features of development (learning) which are essentially universal for all children as opposed to the "unspontaneous" learnings represented by formal school experience and other idiosyncratic phenomena.

A second comparison of schooled and unschooled children (ages 6 and 9) was also based upon the criterion of conservation skill (Mermelstein and Shulman, 1967). These data indicate that with age, schooling is increasingly associated with verbal proficiency on conservation tasks. That is, schooled children were significantly more successful on tasks requiring a verbal explanation with respect to conservation. Virtually all of the Piagetian probing techniques are verbally grounded, and Mermelstein and Shulman found question-phrasing variations to influence certain performance items markedly.

These results again suggest that carefully designed language training (or even general language stimulation) may facilitate Piagetian task performance. If so, Piaget's position on language and thought could be compromised. Not unrelated to this issue are several studies which indicate that both type of schooling and the language of instruction are associated with differences in Piagetian concept-task proficiency (Poole, 1968; Prince, 1968). It has also been suggested that the effects of formal schooling on Piagetian-type cognitive skills may be greater in relatively complex varied urban environments than in more austere rural settings (Glasser and Resnick, 1972). This is a stark reminder of the importance of *context* in psychological study. Further studies of the effects of schooling are needed to help sort out possible contextual factors as well as the puzzling theoretical issues involved.

Training Studies

Of perhaps greatest interest to educators (and ultimately of greatest significance to Piagetian theory) are explorations into the influence of specific instruction upon cognitive growth (logical thinking). Several practical questions may clarify an educator's interest in this domain. For example, if a teacher is to embark upon a learning experience which requires that the learner master a number conservation concept which he fails to demonstrate, can the learner be "taught" to conserve? If so, what techniques would be most efficacious for this purpose? Another practical concern is the transfer value or generalizability of specific training. For example, if a learner demonstrates weight conservation in one situation, can we assume that this ability will be demonstrated in a second, more novel situation? Or does weight conservation ability relate in a necessary way to an ability to conserve volume? Do these two abilities require experiences peculiar to each, or is formal experience even a significant factor? Can training be used to accelerate the process of logical thought structure development from one stage to the next? These and other questions define an immensely popular direction of Piaget-based research.

It will be recalled that Piaget is not impressed with the role of didactic experience in cognitive development; rather, he stresses the child's active role in assimilation and accommodation of those cognitions that are manageable at a given moment. In short, force-feeding from external sources is viewed as ineffectual, if not onerous. One can argue, however, that if a child's cognitive capacity were precisely known, appropriately sized chunks of experience could be arranged effectively and economically to assist healthy development. Training research seems increasingly to be conducted with this in mind. A typical procedure: determine, through pretesting, the extent of a child's conservation ability, then proceed with an experimental conservation task-training procedure. If a reliable improvement in conservation ability could be observed after a short-term training experience (or if a change could be noted in the developmental sequence of operational thought as charted by Piaget), considerable difficulties would be posed for Piaget's theory.[12]

The initial wave of training studies was generally consistent with the inference from Piagetian theory that systematic pedagogy is of minor, if any, value in accelerating children's cognitive development (Flavell, 1963a; Smedslund, 1963a; M. Wallach, 1963). Illustrative is an early study (Smedslund, 1963b) which concluded that unless children already have some notion of invariance, training procedures result in little or no cognitive improvement up through about age 7. An implication is that educational experiences relevant to conservation, for instance, should be delayed until a child displays invariance. Or, one might more directly assess the efficacy of planned instruction by giving systematic training and practice in reversibility, a prerequisite operation for conservation. Such a strategy for the achievement of number conservation by children ages 6 to 8 has been successful, in contrast to strategies based upon rote arithmetical operations (L. Wallach and Sprott, 1964; L. Wallach, Wall, and Anderson, 1967). The second Wallach study also concluded that to conserve successfully, children must not only recognize reversibility but also avoid being misled by irrelevant cues. Significantly, Wallach's children did not transfer their number conservation achievement to a substance (liquid) conservation task.

The frequency with which transfer failures were noted in early training studies suggests that while a specific conservation skill may be "taught," it remains splintered, i.e., ungeneralizable to other contexts. This idea finds support from a study of first- and third-grade children who were trained to solve area measurement problems (Beilen and Franklin, 1962). The problem-solving skills developed during training were transferred effectively to a new set of area measurement tasks by the older children, but not by the younger ones. Presumably, the third graders had the advantage of a firm grounding in concrete operational thought, something not yet achieved by the first graders. The Beilen and Franklin results are thus consistent with the Genevan belief that until they are mastered,

---

[12] Training for conservation is by far the most frequently attempted modification strategy. Thus, children identified as "nonconservers" or "partial conservers" are treated variously so that the influence of experiential phenomena may be evaluated. Obviously, little purpose would be served by using children who already conserve.

fundamental operations will not be generalized. In other words, younger children may deal correctly with problems for which they have been specifically prepared, but they are unlikely to solve new problems successfully until they come to conserve them "naturally."[13] This generalization is supported by F. Murray (1968), who trained nonconserving five- to eight-year-olds to conserve length. Murray's check on the transfer effects of his training provoked a serious question about the value of "premature" instruction. The problem for Murray is that such instruction may simply result in verbal responses masking a conceptual deficit which has the "magnitude of nonconservation itself" (F. Murray, 1968, p. 86).

Another exploration of conservation acquisition has compared different procedures for teaching correspondence and conservation principles to nonconserving kindergarten children (Feigenbaum and Sulkin, 1964). The principal training cue was Piaget's notion that an understanding of number concepts is contingent upon number conservation ability. This ability, in turn, is purportedly based upon the principle of one-to-one correspondence. Results indicated that teaching correspondence can facilitate impressively the number conservation concept when (1) an opportunity is given to manipulate the objects involved (beads in the vase task) and (2) irrelevant visual stimuli are removed by blindfolding the learner (this teaching technique is similar to Montessori's principle of sensory isolation). A teaching strategy based exclusively upon providing reinforcement (knowledge of results) to children for their addition and subtraction responses was ineffective. This finding is consistent also with the data of L. Wallach, Wall, and Anderson (1967).

The Feigenbaum and Sulkin (1964) study seemingly validates Piaget's sequential idea and provides a commentary on the success of direct instruction. The study also considers the cogence of perceptual cues and their elimination, a factor which crops up in a variety of research contexts. If one considers this in relation to most of the validation studies discussed earlier, firm support (at least on the surface) is given to the Piagetism that younger children operate primarily on a "before-the-eye reality" basis. The problem, however, is that some researchers are unwilling to accept that children who perform on this basis are therefore *incapable* of logical thought. This again raises the issue of interrelationships among perception, expressive language, and logical thinking.

---

[13] This facet of Piagetian theory involves a puzzling set of contentions. One contention is that a given concrete operation may not be generalized in all contexts, that is, it will reflect situational specificity, particularly in the early stages of concrete-operational thought. The other broader notion is that basic cognitive operations, such as conservation, underlie *all* forms of logical thinking once a stage of operational thought has been reached. The weight of the evidence seems to indicate, however, that conservation skills are acquired in "bits." Gottfried (1969), for example, reports that for children aged six to nine, number conservation performance was superior across the board to length conservation performance. This suggests a hierarchy of difficulty not unlike that applicable to substance conservation (mass, weight, volume).

Possibly more research like Halpern's will help to clarify these inter-relationships (1965). His study of five- to seven-year-olds disclosed that errors in solving problems of inference were most frequent in situations where perceptual data directly contradicted logic. Halpern concluded that residual perception-bound thought may occur in certain situations even after the emergence of concrete-operational thought. At a minimum, this implies that teachers would do well to carefully arrange the cues which children in this age span are provided in learning episodes.

That cue arrangement is an important variable is apparent in research by Gelman (1969), who gave discrimination learning set training on length and number tasks to a group of nonconserving five-year-olds. Virtual errorless performances were observed among these children on specific number and length conservation subsequent to training; roughly a 60 percent correct nonspecific transfer conservation response (mass and liquid amount) was also obtained. Durability of training was evident two to three weeks after formal training. Gelman concluded that conservation "failure" among young children may be a function of their inattentiveness to pertinent quantitative relationships and overattentiveness to irrelevant aspects of conservation tasks.

Training Strategies: A Closer Look   As indicated earlier, the verbal rule approach to training usually involves a demonstration of some con-servation task, an opportunity for children to indicate their understanding of the perceived event, and a statement by the experimenter of a rule which "explains" the conservation phenomenon. In a liquid conservation task, for example, nonconserving children may be presented with two equal-sized beakers of water, and a third, different-sized empty beaker. It is stressed that the amount of water in both beakers is the same, and then water from the second full beaker is poured into the third beaker. Next, children are asked if the first (untouched) and third (different-sized) beaker, which now contains water, have the same amount and why (or why not). Children's responses are accepted, then either corrected by feedback in the form of a rule; or the children are provided with a variety of demonstrations and explanations of the liquid conservation phenomenon. Eventually, however, a formal rule is stated; for example, "The rule is that when we pour all of the water from one glass into an empty glass, there is the same amount to drink as before. This is because we haven't added or taken away any water. It doesn't matter if the beaker looks bigger or smaller or how high the water is; it's the same water and the amount is the same. See? We can pour the water back into the first glass and still have the same amount. It's the same water and the amount doesn't change when we pour it into another glass."

Several of the training studies heretofore discussed attest to a per-vasive search for valid teaching strategies. This search has led to several variant approaches. While not easily and neatly categorized, the most visible strategies are based upon *verbal instruction* (which often includes providing explicit verbal rules for children), *cognitive conflict*, and *task analysis.* A common research ploy is to compare two or more such strategies in terms of their yield in immediate outcomes and transfer value. It is now time to consider briefly these three approaches.

Verbal Rule Approach Significant conservation training effects using a verbal rule approach with nonconserving or transitional children have been achieved (e.g., Beilen, 1965; Figurelli and Keller, 1972; Siegler and Liebert, 1972; Smith, 1968). Taken together, however, these studies provide no evidence of transfer to general conservation tasks. In contrast, Hamel and Riksen (1973), have documented non-specific transfer to conservation of two-dimensional space, number, substance, and height with a verbal rule training strategy for quantity conservation. Other researchers, however, have been unsuccessful with the verbal rule approach to number conservation training among preschool children (e.g., Mermelstein and Meyer, 1969). Hence, the question persists whether generalized conservation ability can reliably be developed through predominantly verbal instruction.

It is possible that both differences in children's background experience and the extent to which verbal instruction is integrated with other forms of guided experience will affect training outcomes considerably. Certainly the mastery of Piagetian concepts is not absolutely contingent upon the passage of time per se. Contrary to Piaget's predictions, guided experience has resulted in the much earlier achievement of a functional concept of specific gravity by kindergarten and first-grade children (Ojemann and Pritchett, 1963). A more rapid development of nonprecausal concepts of like has been achieved through direct instruction (Looft and Charles, 1969). And when the verbal requirements of task performance were minimized and nonverbal testing methods were utilized, children as young as three years learned a seriation task (Siegel, 1972).

Cognitive Conflict Perhaps more consistent with Piagetian theory than direct instruction is a training strategy based upon the cognitive conflict hypothesis. *Cognitive conflict* (discrepancy between what is in one's current conceptual repertoire and what is observed in the environment) is thought to trigger the acquisition of new or more refined concepts. In theory, cognitive conflict disturbs equilibrium (produces disequilibrium), which the child then strives to reestablish by resolving discrepant events or acknowledging a point of view different from his own. The conflict resolution idea has been advanced explicitly by Smedslund (1961), among others, although controversy surrounds its utility as an explanation of conservation acquisition (Winer, 1968). Some support for the value of cognitive conflict experience has accumulated (Gruen, 1965; Brison, 1966). In the Gruen (1965) study it was found that cognitive conflict combined with verbal pre-training was superior to direct reinformed practice in teaching number conservation skill to children ages 4 to 6. An important question, however, is whether cognitive conflicts will necessarily motivate behavior pursuant to conceptual change among all children. Or can additional or different incentive conditions besides conflict resolution increase the effects of training?[14]

One of the few acceleration studies relevant to this question involved the training of kindergarten children on substance-conservation tasks (Brison, 1966). The children were pretested for their entering verbal concepts (*more, less, some*), conservation ability, and preferred mode of explanation (any tendency to examine causes when formulating an explanation of an observed event). Matched nonconservers were assigned to the control or experimental group. The latter received conservation training during which conflict was induced and an external incentive for correct performance (juice to drink) was provided. Brison reported significant training effects in terms of reversibility manifest in accurate substance conservation. And in contrast to many other studies, Brison observed correct transfer to substances (sand, clay) other than that used in training (liquid). Brison has suggested that his incentive condition may have enhanced the motivation of his children, at least to the point of more concentrated attention.

Brison's data are tantalizing indeed. It must be noted, however, that uniform training effects were not achieved. Roughly 30 percent of his experimental subjects failed to conserve despite training. One might argue that those who did develop conservation were either (1) "ready" to profit from instruction and/or (2) influenced positively by the incentive, while those who failed were not. Such reasoning is grossly circular, however, and begs the question. Increased attention in training research is due both to individual differences among children and social learning principles, especially reinforcement (Curcio et al., 1972; Overbeck and Schwartz, 1970; Rosenthal and Zimmerman, 1972).

Task Analysis A third variation on the training research theme is based upon *task analysis* (Gagné, 1970) or *substructure analysis* (Siegel, Roeper, and Hooper, 1966). This involves a careful analysis of complex task performance, as in conservation of substance, in terms of the successive subskills prerequisite for success. This is extremely important from a theoretical standpoint, for if pre-training for subskill development were shown to make no difference in subsequent conservation training, strong evidence for a maturation-dependent view would be available.

With these thoughts in mind, a training procedure based upon a task analysis of weight and length conservation was devised by Kingsley and Hall (1967). Five- and six-year-olds, well below Piaget's normative standard for such conservation, were trained to the criterion (successful weight and length conservation) with this approach. No more than nine 20-minute sessions were programmed for this purpose. Positive transfer to substance

---

[14] Questions such as these are particularly important in view of the assumption of most training studies, that children are equally motivated to respond to training. Precise commentary on individual differences in motivation is not apparent in the Piagetian literature.

conservation was also observed. Since Kingsley and Hall's study is one of the more dramatic instances of positive training effects, it is surprising that additional studies of its type have not appeared in the literature. However, conservation training studies which resemble the task analysis approach have been performed with similar success (Bearison, 1969; Sigel, Roeper, and Hooper, 1966). Bearison (1969) has highlighted the importance of a child's "quantitative set" to respond to conservation problems, while Sigel, Roeper, and Hooper (1966) point to the oft-overlooked necessity of pre-training procedures in operations such as multiple classification and reversibility.[15] Mostly for children over six, task analysis procedures in training for multiple classification have been successful, but not necessarily superior to alternative training strategies (Parker, Rieff, and Sperr, 1971; Parker, Sperr, and Rieff, 1972).

Comment   Most modification studies assess only the immediate or short-term effects of training. Thus a critic might ask whether the apparent changes are maintained over longer periods of time. Of the few studies addressed to this issue, those conducted by Bearison (1969) and Jacobs and Vandeventer (1969) are most impressive. In the latter study, for example, first graders were subjected to individualized and highly structured training techniques to solve double classification problems (two different stimulus dimensions, such as color and form, must be considered simultaneously in inferring logical relations). Trained children scored significantly higher than controls on both a criterion test and a transfer test immediately after training. This significant advantage was still in evidence four months later when a retention and second transfer test were administered to the two groups.

While several of the above studies indicate that specifically arranged experience can facilitate cognitive development along Piagetian lines, others do not. For example, verbal rule instruction techniques have been ineffective for number conservation development among preoperational children (Mermelstein and Meyer, 1969). Neither were three alternative teaching techniques effective for this purpose (cognitive conflict strategy, a language activation method, and a multiple classification technique). It was concluded that due to basic cognitive limitations, children aged three to six are unlikely to profit from specific planned experience. Presumably maturational intersensory processes are implicated as well as individual children's learning styles. Such contradictory data (see also Kincaid et al., 1971) remind us that a continued and careful study of Piaget's theory is needed.

To summarize, three variables apparently mediate the effectiveness of training: (1) the type or class of problem (for example, weight, conserva-

---

[15] The basic assumption of subskills training—that the concept of conservation is achieved once a child has met the prerequisites for conservation—has been challenged (Mermelstein and Meyer, 1969). This challenge is apparently based on the notion that the whole is greater than the sum of its parts.

tion, multiple classification, transitivity of length), (2) the instructional technique used (for example, inductive-discovery, deductive rule demonstration, direct reinforcement), and (3) the developmental level of the child (subskills which are brought by the child to the training session; Sigel and Hooper, 1968). To this list should probably be added (4) the child's current state of intersensory development (to the extent that this represents something in addition to subskills). Training effects at the level of intuitive and early concrete-operational thought are somewhat equivocal, particularly in regard to the transfer of training; but conservation, in particular, *can* be accelerated. Recent data also suggest that well-executed training can produce effects that are stable over time. Of course, most studies have dealt with children normatively on the verge of conservation and usually able to provide verbal justifications for their answers. Whether it is important, or even desirable, to accelerate through training concrete operations which normally will develop anyway remains a question.

Finally, a common denominator of successful training studies usually is experience with reversibility and/or identity. Less frequently explored have been techniques for classification skills instruction (sorting, matching, hierarchical integration). Modest to impressive improvement on class-inclusion tasks has been reported, however (Ahr and Youniss, 1970; Kohnstamm, 1967; Wohlwill and Katz, 1967). A promising strategy is to have children use simple materials (e.g., blocks) to cultivate class-inclusion logic without suddenly having to coordinate knowledge about a variety of different classes (e.g., things to wear, hats, animals, pets, flowers, plants, people, children). Significantly, it is often found that young children (ages 4 to 6) can successfully perform class-inclusion problems but are unable to provide verbal explanations for their behavior (Glaser and Resnick, 1972). Truly, the preschool child is an intuitive creature.

CURRICULUM IMPLICATIONS

Piagetian theory is still a theory in the making. Because important theoretical problems still obscure aspects of the Piaget system, one can argue that curricular derivations from the theory are premature. Ammon (1969), for example, states that the empirical basis of Piagetian theory has not been sufficiently established to make practical application advisable. Even Piaget has not systematically addressed the possible pedagogical applications of his theory. Nor does he seem concerned with the problems of educators except to dismiss as folly the attempts of many educators— mostly American—to accelerate stage-based cognitive development. In one published interview (Duckworth, 1973), Piaget has acknowledged that he is mystified over the widespread enthusiasm of educators for his point of view about development. In fact, he seems reluctant to do more than to offer teachers three related points of advice: provide children with actual objects to manipulate, assist children in their development of question-asking skills, and know why particular operations are difficult for children.

Yet the remarkable appeal of Piagetian theory has led to a variety of general and specific educational implications. At the general level of implication drawing, several basic teaching-learning principles are stressed: (1) active self-discovery and inductively oriented learning experiences in which a child is able to perform transformations on materials from the environment (where direct teaching is necessary, it follows rather than precedes periods of manipulation and exploration); (2) arrangement of moderately novel experiences which capitalize upon and facilitate stage-relevant thinking operations while accommodating the child's present intellectual style; (3) a variety of patterned and enriched concrete sensory experiences; (4) the symbolization of manipulative, play, and aesthetic experiences; (5) a variety of models for imitative learning; (6) a high rate of interpersonal interaction among children with ample opportunity for role playing, sharing of different viewpoints, and corrective discussions led by adults under appropriate circumstances; and (7) the use of the clinical method to study children's progress (specifically for noting the way in which a child goes en route to a problem solution).

Statements of implications focus upon the quest for ways to govern children's environmental encounters so that their intellectual potential is maximized—particularly in respect to analytical or causal thinking. This

According to Piagetian theory, cooperative learning activities that involve manipulation, experimentation, and construction with concrete materials will facilitate the discovery of logico-mathematical concepts. Photo by Peter Rinearson.

focus involves a choice which is based largely upon the way one interprets Piaget. Does one make a systematic provision of intellectual content to increase the scope and quality of intelligence (early cognitive enrichment) or does one allow natural cognitive development to ensue while assisting with socioemotional growth (Kohlberg, 1968)? Piaget's own views on this issue are not crystal clear, although several authorities have drawn upon the concept of interactionism in an effort to reduce this ambiguity (Kohlberg, 1968; Langer, 1969). An excerpt from Piaget's writings may assist this clarification:

> The goal in education is not to increase the amount of knowledge, but to create the possibilities for a child to invent and discover. When we teach too fast, we keep the child from inventing and discovering himself—Teaching means creating situations where structures can be discovered; it does not mean transmitting structures which may be assimilated at nothing other than a verbal level (Piaget, as quoted in Ripple and Rockcastle, 1964, p. 3).

Thus, at the nursery and kindergarten level, for example, the aim would not be to teach concrete operations, but to provide experience with their prerequisites so that operativity will subsequently flower (Kamii and Radin, 1967).

One feature of Piaget's system is the explicit analysis of concepts (such as conservation) and principles or operations (such as reversibility and transitivity) which parents and teachers either take for granted or deal with only indirectly during the course of education. Perhaps this explicit analysis has also directed the attention of educators identified with Piagetian theory to applications in mathematics and the physical sciences (Kimball, 1972). Of more concern here, however, are specific curricular *frameworks* tailored from the Piagetian cloth. Three such frameworks designed for the late preschool and early primary school child are summarized below. (A fourth framework deals with the much younger eighteen- to twenty-four-month-old child and is discussed briefly in Chapter 8 under the topic of infant education.)

A Packaged Piaget-Based Curriculum

One of the most crystallized applications of Piagetian thought to a curriculum for children aged 4 to 7 has been proposed by Celia Stendler Lavatelli (1970). For Lavatelli, the general objective of this curriculum is the child's development of intellectual competence through self-activity and questioning. This objective is broken down into three components. A first concerns the ability to *classify* in order that children can achieve economy in structuring their environment. A second emphasis is placed upon *number, measurement,* and *space operations,* particularly in relation to conservation. To assist children to establish relations between objects, a third major component involves *seriation operations.* Superimposed on these curriculum activities is a model for language training, the core of which is systematic modeling and eliciting of syntactic structures relevant to logical thinking. Language training occurs largely in the context of activities organized according to the three fore-mentioned areas: short structured ten- to fifteen-minute periods with small groups of five to six children. These comparatively formal activities are reinforced with other activities throughout the day, especially self-directed play. The total curriculum is packaged for commercial distribution and consists of multiple sets of realia for the three curriculum components, detailed lesson plans and teacher directions, and a book on theory. In all, over 100 different activities are incorporated into a curriculum suitable for thirty weeks of schooling (Lavatelli, 1970).

It is not possible to detail all aspects of the Lavatelli curriculum here. An illustration is desirable, however, and for this purpose activities for the development of classification structures are summarized below. Such structures have several characteristics which must be translated into separate operations and arranged according to level of complexity in ways consistent with the child's developmental sequence. This sequence of operations begins with children's identification of object properties (for example, form, color, or size of blocks) and object matching on the basis of two or more properties (for example, form, color, and size). The underlying purpose is the development of skill in extracting the common property of a class of objects and extending the class to incorporate all objects which possess that property.[16]

A second step in the process of classification structure development requires that the child apply this extractive and incorporative skill. Now, however, the child must be mindful of two or more object properties as he seeks an object to complete a set of objects. The medium for such activity is a matrix puzzle comprised of pictures. Matrix activity is initiated by having the child respond to a "puzzle" involving pictures of "two large red flowers and a small yellow flower in the top horizontal row, and two large red apples and a blank space for which the child must select a card picturing one small yellow apple from a number of choices of flowers and apples" (Lavatelli, 1970, pp. 89–90). The difficulty of these analogy-type problems is gradually increased to the point where a child must attend to three variables or attributes simultaneously. According to Piaget, the young child solves such puzzles on a perceptual rather than on a conceptual or logical basis, but a basic purpose of Lavatelli's puzzle activity is to provide opportunities for a teacher to learn something about the conceptual level a child may be operating on.

In the Lavatelli curriculum the child proceeds from multi-property

---

[16] Lavatelli also recommends that appropriate verbal activities accompany these actions so that grammatical structures are modeled in sequence. In this case the sequence would begin with simple declarative sentences followed by transformations which would include coordinate sentences containing directives for more than one action.

classification exercises to activities arranged to promote the recognition of complementary classes. Suppose a child is confronted with ten pictures of vegetables, two of which are carrots. Will he be able to separate this set into no more than *two* classes of vegetables, carrots and vegetables–not carrots? Complementary classes are defined by such a separation. The relationship is helpful for children's understanding of what is and what is not included in a given class. In other words, when carrots (or sparrows or shoes) are discussed, a complementary class is understood (vegetables–not carrots, birds–not sparrows, clothing–not shoes) and that the specified class and its complement together comprise the total class. An important feature of this is the more general concept of negation, which is also treated although very differently in the Distar curriculum.

A fourth step in Piaget-based classification activity requires that the child take whole classes apart to determine subclasses and make comparisons of *all* and *some*. Suppose a child is working with ten wax crayons, two green and eight orange. The whole class in this case is wax crayons. Subclasses would be green wax crayons and orange wax crayons. All-some relations may be pinpointed by precision questioning by the teacher in combination with crayon manipulation by the child. Understandings to be developed would include that there are more wax crayons than orange crayons; some of the wax crayons are orange and some (fewer) are green; and that all of the crayons, regardless of color, are wax. But the broader understanding, of course, would be a generalized concept of class-subclass relations. Such understanding requires time and experience with a wide variety of objects suited to this type of activity. As in the preceding classification skills, the child's transactions begin at the sensory-motor level, progress to the level of imagery (mental and pictorial), and eventuate in verbal behavior in which phenomena are dealt with in words. The latter requires memory of the critical facts in a transaction.

The fifth set of activities in the classification sequence calls for two skills on the child's part. First, he must be able to abstract the common property of an object class ("intension"). The second skill involves extending a class to incorporate all objects that possess the given property ("extension"). Both memory and the prediction of events are involved. Suppose a child is provided with a mixed collection of minitoys—cars, soldiers, dogs, and marbles—and four boxes into which he may deposit toys that are "alike in some way" (using *all* the toys). Here the common property for each class must be abstracted, remembered, and applied to each toy that he places into a specific class. As in other classification skills, the intension-extension combination develops sequentially. Younger children begin by grouping on the basis of spatial configuration instead of abstracted properties. Gradually, criterial attributes are used as the basis for grouping, although children generally do a lot of "criterion matching" during a classification activity before they achieve a consistent set to follow through an entire grouping exercise using the same criterion.

While the fifth step depends heavily on the use of prestructured materials, many opportunities for grouping objects and defining the relations between them arise during the school day. For example, in the art corner a teacher may identify common properties of objects such as paintbrushes, paints, crayons, and towels. Children may be asked first to put all the "things we make pictures with" on the table. Later would come a suggestion like, "Let's put all the art materials in separate boxes. Here are four boxes. Let's put the materials that are alike in some way, that go together in some way, in each of these boxes." More than one classification scheme is usually possible (for example, color, function or use, composition), although a child must classify all objects.

⑥   Skill in abstracting common properties is a precursor to the sixth step in classification structure development: locating objects at the intersection of two classes. Stimulus materials for this task could include pictures of a blue truck, a yellow truck, a red truck, a green truck, and an orange truck all aligned horizontally. For accompaniment, in a vertical row would be pictured a red scarf, a red ball, a red lollipop, a red pencil, a red book. The child's task would be to select from among a separate group of pictures (which include all of the aforementioned objects) the one to place in the blank space where horizontal and vertical rows intersect in matrix fashion. Thus he would have to simultaneously note the object property common to the objects in both rows and identify a picture that contained both properties. In this example, "truckness" is the property common to the horizontal row, "redness" to the vertical row. Hence, the choice of a red truck from among the separate group of pictures would meet the intersection criterion. Abstracting ability, memory, and a concept of simultaneous membership are all requisite for the child's success.

⑦   The classification activities series culminates in experience with permutation problems, that is, making all possible combinations of a given number of elements. Such arrangements in the abstract are basic to a formal study of algebra, but at the early childhood level the experience is based upon concrete manipulations. An example would include a child's discovery that a doll whose wardrobe consists of two blouses in green and white and two miniskirts in green and white actually has four combinations of outfits. The point is not that a child derive a law or formula for the combination of elements in a set. It is that he be given real objects in order to perform actions which will constitute the groundwork for the development of mental structures.

The Lavatelli sequence has not, to this writer's knowledge, been tested longitudinally to verify the long-range vertical transfer effects its devisor believes possible. It is basically consistent with Piagetian thought on the evolution of skills and logical structure, although Lavatelli has also drawn upon the work of Bruner (1964) to formulate her position. Suggested training activities in these skill areas combined with a variety of similarly oriented informal play experiences would presumably assist children to become more capable logical thinkers than they would otherwise be.

Evaluation   Systematic attempts to evaluate the Lavatelli curriculum have been rare. Of course, the curriculum is relatively new, and meaningful longitudinal evaluation programs take time. It is noteworthy that Lavatelli includes only one report of evaluation research data in the basic source book for the curriculum rationale (Lavatelli, 1970). Other data apparently have come from informal formative evaluations by teachers involved in an early field testing of the program. The one available set of data was drawn from an experimental-control group study involving kindergarten children in a midwestern suburban community. Fifty children were selected at random to comprise the experimental group; an equal number of matched control subjects were selected. The control variables were measured intelligence, socioeconomic status, sex, and chronological age. A sequenced curriculum of Piagetian activities for small groups of children was implemented on an informal basis for five months. The two groups of children were then compared in terms of performance on a series of Piagetian tasks appropriate to the age group involved. Results indicated that the experimental group excelled in tasks of seriation and conservation of length; no statistically significant group differences were observed in conservation of matter and surface. Composite performance scores, however, did favor the experimental subjects. Basically this means that children who have experience with Piaget-based activities improve their performance on Piaget tasks more rapidly than do children with conventional kindergarten experience. A similar finding has been noted in an independent study of lower-class kindergarten children (Raph and Liebermann, 1971). The longer-range implications of this short-term difference in children's intellectual development are not known. Several issues, if not bones of contention, underly this point, as well as the entire Lavatelli methodology. These issues are treated later in the chapter, after additional examples of Piaget-based early education have been presented.

The Cognitively Oriented Curriculum

A second example of early education based largely on Piagetian thought is a cognitively oriented program which evolved from several years' experience with disadvantaged preschool and early school children in Ypsilanti, Michigan (Weikart, Rogers, Adcock, and McClelland, 1971). It is perhaps best known as the Project Follow Through model formally designated as the Cognitively Oriented Curriculum. The present curriculum has been shaped by three basic decisions. First, it was decided that curriculum making should have a structured theoretical base in order to provide consistent guidelines for planning and instructional methodologies. For Weikart and his colleagues, Piagetian theory is one of the most elaborated positions, useful primarily as a conceptual tool for classroom practitioners. Second, it was decided that children should be active participants in their own learning and that multiple, varied experience is indispensable for full development. And, third, it was recognized that teachers are basically dedicated and creative; if provided leeway (and not confined by the restrictions of a narrow, scripted teaching program), teachers will enthusiastically seek to modulate a curriculum framework in relation to children's needs and the unique teaching situation. This relates directly to the establishment of a curriculum maintenance system termed the *staff model*. This system has as its objectives the sustained involvement of teachers in curriculum planning; free and constructive personal interchange by way of team teaching activities (teachers, aides, and volunteers); and assistance and support for teachers by an experienced, knowledgeable supervisor. It is argued that unless teachers have these conditions for continual self-development and a sense of meaningful participation, any curriculum is likely to stagnate or become excessively routinized.

For Weikart et al. (1971), a child's understanding of self and world springs from two basic abilities: (1) an ability to anchor oneself in space and time and (2) an ability to order and classify events and objects. This means that children must begin to construe, then organize, relationships among the things they encounter in the environment. They also must establish mental representations of themselves and their environment for the increasingly complex and abstract purposes of thinking. These complementary phenomena set the stage for goal and content selection. Within the Cognitively Oriented Curriculum, the resultant core areas, similar to Lavatelli (1970), are presented below:

(1) Grouping, or *classification*, is approached first through having the child make relational or functional discriminations. Things go together either because they are used for some activity (e.g., a spoon and a fork go together because they are both used for eating), or because they get their meaning from one another (e.g., a hammer and a nail). More complex groupings are based on descriptive discriminations, that is, on certain attributes that can be perceived, such as size, shape, or color. The most abstract means of grouping is based on gross discrimination, or conceptual labeling (e.g., vehicles, furniture, or other such general categories).

(2) Ordering, or *seriation*, is approached through having the child deal with objects in terms of their relationships in size, quantity, or quality (e.g., *big/little*, *more/less*, *rough/smooth*). The preschool goal is to enable the child eventually to deal with four sizes and four quantities and with three qualities.

(3) How the child perceives himself in space and how he perceives relationships in space, or *spatial relations*, is approached through expressions of the orientation of the child's body and the orientation of other objects in space. Through motoric experiences, and later through verbal experience with concepts of position (e.g., *in-out*), of direction (e.g., *to/from*), and of distance (e.g., *near/far*), the child is aided in his development of meaningful construction of space and spatial relationships.

(4) To understand and respond to *temporal relations*, children begin to deal with time in terms of periods having a beginning and an end; they begin to understand that events can be ordered chronologically, and that time periods can be of variable length.

Following Piaget, the Cognitively Oriented Curriculum is committed to the child's experiencing concepts on the motoric level and being involved in direct physical manipulation of the environment at all levels of representation; involvement on the verbal level is gradually added, but the motoric level is never entirely displaced. Motoric experience with concepts provides a base for later verbal experience. By using his body to experience concepts, to operate on objects, or to employ objects for operating on other objects, the child develops a feel for the concepts, and this facilitates verbal expression. For example, a child's motoric experience of rolling gives him a basis for generalizing to objects (e.g., a ball rolling), and this experience in turn provides the basis for verbally dealing with the concept of rolling.

The cognitive goals are implemented along the levels of representation delineated by Piaget; specifically, from the index level (causally relating marks or sounds to objects or using other reference-giving cues as signals of objects), to the symbol level (identifying objects from pictures differing in degree of abstractness, models, and line drawings, and using motor encoding in various representational ways), and finally to the sign level (using words alone as representations of objects).

The motoric and verbal levels of operation are similarly integrated, or "fed," into the levels of representation. For example (1) the child uses his body to operate on objects and to experience concepts, and (2) the child is brought to progressively higher levels of verbalization, starting from the point at which the teacher provides the verbal stimulus, and progressing to the point at which the child is able to verbalize spontaneously not only actions just completed but also actions completed in the more remote past (Weikart et al., 1971, pp. 7–8).[17]

With these core areas in mind the cognitively oriented teacher will determine specific, daily goals and the methods most suitable for those purposes. Activities are then sequenced in the service of children's representational abilities. Children's levels of operation are carefully observed (motor-verbal) and subsequent planning occurs on this basis. A high degree of teacher ingenuity and skill is required, including the arrangement of physical space and materials to facilitate and reinforce desired goals. The structure and materials distribution will depend upon the time of school year, but Figure 5.1 illustrates the preferred concept of differentiated teaching-learning areas within the classroom proper.

The classroom setting is also marked by a generalized sequence of activity periods, exemplified by the following daily schedule suitable largely for preschool-kindergarten:

Planning Time (about twenty minutes). Joint teacher-pupil planning occurs with an emphasis upon thinking ahead about which activities will come first, next, last, and so on. Choice alternatives are provided. Children's ability to plan ahead and control their impulses while working toward such goals are stressed.

---

[17] Reprinted with permission from *The Cognitively Oriented Curriculum*, 1971. Published by the National Association for the Education of Young Children, 1834 Connecticut Ave., N.W., Washington, D.C. 20009.

Work Time (about forty minutes). Work chosen during planning time is performed. Children's persistence at tasks, ability to integrate activities, and general concentration ability are emphasized. Both individual and small-group activities occur in the art corner, block corner (large motor area), doll corner, and quiet corner.

Group Meeting for Evaluation (about ten minutes). Children gather together to evaluate their own and others' work. The variety of activity is reviewed, children's feelings about their work are discussed, and ideas developed about how to work more constructively in the future. The desired result of this activity is progressive improvement in the child's ability to be objective about his work.

Cleanup (about fifteen minutes). During the cleanup time, incidental teaching occurs to reinforce basic concepts and the values of cleanliness and equipment care.

Juice and Group Time (about thirty minutes). Working with smaller groups of children the teacher and aides carry on informal conversation designed to promote and enact concepts of size, number, proportion, etc., in relation to the daily consumables (juice or milk, cookies, crackers).

Activity Time (about twenty minutes). The activity period involves either indoor or outdoor time during which motor activities dominate:

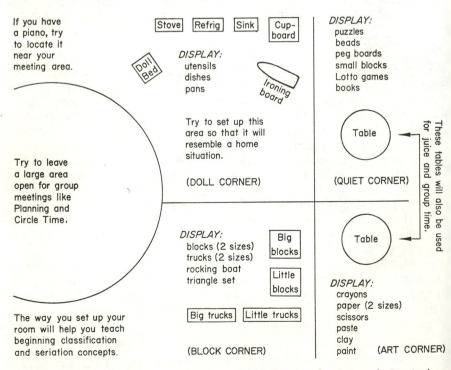

FIGURE 5.1 Sample room arrangement: the Cognitively Oriented Curriculum (Weikart et al., 1971).

games, musical activity, and varieties of general recreation occur. Again, conceptualization is stressed, especially for mathematical concepts, seriation, and spatial relations (*up, down, first, last, start, stop, fast, slow, in front of, in back of*).

Dismissal (about ten minutes). Additional teaching is given as appropriate while children prepare to leave.

Superimposed upon the general format above are field trips and opportunities for sociodramatic play (see Smilansky, 1968). A substantial home teaching program has also been integrated with the Cognitively Oriented Curriculum, with reportedly favorable results. Generally, the home teaching program has a dual aim: to provide maternal involvement in a coordinated home-school educational effort and to implement selected aspects of the curriculum on an individual mother-child basis in the home. Finally, the primary grade component of the Weikart Follow Through model is designed further to help children develop their capacity for symbol manipulation.

Evaluation   Data concerning the impact of the preschool phase of the Cognitive Oriented Curriculum have come primarily from its earlier version as a part of the Perry Preschool Project in Ypsilanti. This project dealt with the comparative and longer-term effects of several curriculum approaches upon the intellectual development of educationally deprived

Planning, reporting, and self-evaluation activities are basic to the Cognitively Oriented Curriculum. These children have just completed a science project and have recorded their experiences in writing. Photo by Peter Rinearson.

black children. Several "waves" of three- and four-year-old children were involved over a five-year period during which the Weikart curriculum became more structured along Piagetian lines. Children involved in the experimental curriculum were observed initially to excel on measures of intelligence and ratings of both academic motivation and socioemotional development (Chow and Elmore, 1972). Advantages in the latter areas have tended to persist longer than do cognitive gains among disadvantaged samples; but standardized achievement test data also have favored experimental children (compared to control children who had no pre-school and were then given the successive cognitive-oriented experiences provided by the Weikart group). This finding can be interpreted to mean that many processes underlying academic development can be encouraged by Weikart's compensatory program, although the program has not pro-duced major intellectual changes (Weikart, 1967).

More recent data on the specific effects of cognitive-oriented Follow Through experiences for primary grade children were not available as this book was written. However, generally greater across-the-board effec-tiveness has been obtained for the cognitive approach than for most other groups within the Head Start planned variation experiment (see Chapter 2). Especially impressive is the magnitude of measured IQ gains among Weikart's pupils.

But in final analysis, Weikart argues that comparing the impact of different models' *content* must be subsidiary to an examination of the *staff* components of a given curriculum. He stresses that (1) broad curricula whether focused upon tight language programming (like Distar), an open framework for cognitive development (Weikart's own model), or the more conventional unit-based child development model are equivalent insofar as they provide a wide range of experiences; and (2) a curriculum is really for a teacher's use in planning and evaluating, not for the children per se (Weikart, 1972). Since these ideas are based on a study of three *preschool* curricula (listed in number 1 above) in which no substantial outcome differences were noted, it is best to limit the notion of curriculum equivalency to that level. Differential curricula during the primary grades have been more strongly implicated in achievement differences among children. Yet Weikart's point is consistent with Piaget's notion that general and varied forms of active experience, not specific training, nourish total development.

Perhaps the most striking piece of recent news from the Weikart group in Ypsilanti concerns the present status of children who began as preschoolers during 1962–63 in the original Perry Preschool Project. Now well into their secondary level of schooling, these children, as compared to controls, have demonstrated consistently superior achievement and grade placement patterns. In fact, the range of achievement difference first attributed to the preschool program in favor of experimental children has either been maintained or, in some cases, increased over the span of ensuing years (Weikart, personal correspondence). Of even greater interest for some observers is the differential social deviancy rate of the Perry

Project children. As these children have moved into early adolescence, their deviancy rate is substantially lower, again as compared to controls. Among other things, this means that the initial costs of early intervention may well be offset, perhaps significantly, by the later savings of resources, that is, awesome amounts of time, money, and effort usually expended by society to provide remedial or rehabilitation services for young adolescents, both academically and socially.

New Directions in Piaget-Based Early Education

The final example of early education based on Piagetian theory to be discussed here—Kamii and DeVries (1974a)—is notable for two reasons. First, it is the newest Piagetian twist on cognitive-affective education for young children available for review at this writing. Second, the approach represents a nearly complete turnabout of the curriculum design (including objectives and sequenced content) earlier proposed by its senior author (Some components of Kamii's first design are discussed in the first edition of this book, Evans, 1971).

For Kamii and DeVries, educational implications must come from the epistemological meaning, rather than the literal psychological terms of Piaget's theory. This means that cues for the design of a learning environment are based not so much on studies of how a child thinks at different stages as upon a study of the nature of knowledge and how it is acquired by the child. (Knowledge, in the broad sense of structuring time and space and classifying objects hierarchically is synonomous with intelligence, according to Piaget). It is the construction of knowledge via the "indissociable" interaction between sensory experience and reason that provides the cornerstone for educational planning. And the key word is *construction.* Implied is a process—constructivism—by which a child evolves his own adaptive intelligence and knowledge. Actually, the child is said to construct three different kinds of knowledge from which representations in thought and language are built: physical, social, and logico-mathematical. Some parameters of these knowledges are sketched in the following list for illustrative purposes.

*Three Kinds of Knowledge for Piaget-Based
Early Childhood Curriculum Development*

A. The Development of Physical Knowledge: Learning about the nature of matter.
    1. Knowledge of the properties of objects which are encountered in the environment (such as weight, form, texture).
    2. Development of a repertoire of actions which can be performed appropriately on objects when unfamiliar materials are explored (such as squeezing, folding, shaking, tearing).
B. The Development of Social Knowledge: Structuralizing the effects of social action and accommodating to social convention.

1. Knowledge of social information (for example, social or occupational roles).
2. Knowledge of norms for social conduct (for example, table etiquette, cooperative play).

C. The Development of Logical Knowledge: Logico-mathematical and spatio-temporal operations.

1. Classification: The ability to group objects together through a coordination of their quantitative and qualitative aspects (colors, forms, animals, plants, and so on). Preclassification relationships are stressed for preoperational children, including grouping according to "sameness" (perceptual criteria), "similarity" (perceptual and conceptual criteria), and "going-together-ness" (conceptual criteria).

2. Seriation: The ability to compare and arrange objects along a peculiar dimension (for example, the coordination of transitive relationships with reference to length, color, temperature). Preoperational ordering activities (preseriation) would include quantity (such as *a lot* and *a little*), size (such as *large* and *small*), and quality (such as *cold* and *hot*).

3. Number: The ability to arrange objects on the basis of one-to-one correspondence (groups of cups and saucers, pencils and erasers, toy cars and trucks, and so on).

4. Space: The ability to structure topological space, out of which develops the concepts of Euclidean space (for example, *here-there*, *front-back*, *over-under*; reproduction of object placement in proximity relationships such as copying a bead-string design; spatial transformations such as disarranging a coordinated multiblock design and correctly rearranging it; and the structuring of representational space, such as copying shapes using paper and crayon).

5. Time: The ability to develop representationally temporal sequences based upon causal and means-ends relationships (for example, *before* the rain it is dry, after the rain it is wet; to buy a gum ball from a machine, the penny is inserted *first*, the handle is pulled *next*, and the gum ball is taken out *last*; *if* you drop the glass on the cement, *then* it will break).

Physical knowledge is derived by the child primarily from the regularity or consistency with which concrete objects react when manipulated or subjected to "experiments" (e.g., waterspills from an inverted cup, paper is shredded by scissor cutting). Social knowledge, since it is arbitrary and based upon consensual agreements among people, comes only from people and is learned only through feedback from people (e.g., schools close on weekends, people say thank you when extended courtesies by others, a green light means go). Piaget's conception of moral development provides a further basis for social knowledge construction: teachers are urged to provide a setting wherein children can construct moral values through autonomous choices and the give-and-take of peer relations. Modeling cooperative behavior and showing an egalitarian attitude also are musts for the concerned teacher. But significantly, logico-mathematical knowledge—constructed through the processes of reflecting abstraction and equilibrium—is not directly teachable, claim Kamii and DeVries. A teacher has mainly to provide varied opportunities and encourage children's alertness and natural curiosity. When these conditions are met, such knowledge will be constructed in a progressively coherent way and permanently remembered.

An example may illustrate how the different kinds of knowledge are involved in a learning episode. Suppose children have made an instant vanilla pudding in the kitchen area of a classroom. One child sticks his finger in the pudding bowl and licks it, whereupon the teacher suggests that it is preferable for everyone to use a plastic saucer and spoon. This suggestion constitutes social knowledge. Since the only source of such knowledge is people, Kamii and DeVries maintain that a teacher should not hesitate to provide it to children. Another child then remarks that if he puts his pudding in the refrigerator, it will freeze. Here, the teacher should encourage the child to do exactly that: test his hypothesis and obtain feedback from the object under the specified circumstance (physical knowledge). If, however, a third child has the task of bringing plastic saucers and spoons for the group's pudding, the teacher will recognize the potential of the situation for logico-mathematical knowledge and encourage children to reflect about how things can be placed into a relationship: "Are there just enough saucers and spoons?" "How do you know?" Or, "How can we be sure that each child gets the same amount of pudding?" "Do you agree, Joanie?"; and, "What does this pudding remind you of?"

Kamii and DeVries maintain that the use of such prompting questions is the best way to promote logico-mathematical knowledge construction, apart from the child's own questioning and experimenting. Teachers refrain from giving answers directly. The latter leads too often to social conformity and "school varnish"—empty verbalisms that are a product of pressure to give "right answers" without true understanding. In Kamii and DeVries' method, a concern for right answers gives way to the value of constructivism per se; wrong answers are a valued component of this process, for they too provide the medium out of which concrete and formal operational thought eventually evolve. The fundamental principle for classroom instruction, then, is to *teach according to the kinds of knowledge involved.* For Kamii and DeVries, the major fault with typical classroom teaching is that almost all knowledge is taught as if it were social knowledge—by direct, authoritative, and structured social feedback. Aside from the futility of this approach in imparting logico-mathematical knowledge, Kamii and DeVries believe that it can undermine a child's confidence in his own ability to solve problems.

This is not to say that content is unimportant. In fact, another guideline of Kamii and DeVries is to *teach for content as well as process.* Content, however, is important primarily as a source of motivation; or providing things that will interest children and generate children's ideas about what to do with given objects and information (consider, for example, the appeal and learning potential of marble play). In other words, the content chosen should include objects which children can use to produce "interesting effects" and which provide reference to aims about the three basic kinds of knowledge. Points of reference for content include situations of daily living (eating, dressing, cleaning) and activities similar to those in the general child development curriculum (see the Bank Street approach, Chapter 2). Activities for symbolizing are particularly valued: imitating objects through gross motor activities (e.g., acting as a railroad engine), using objects for make-believe (e.g., sand as gold, wooden blocks as groceries to be bought and sold), onomatopoeia, constructing three-dimensional models, and making pictures. In addition, activities drawn from Piagetian tasks are recommended—those requiring the actions of pushing, pulling, throwing, and object rolling—but *not* to the extent of teaching laboratory tasks directly. The informal curriculum differs from a general child development approach primarily in that empiricist assumptions about learning are rejected. Kamii and DeVries also claim a deeper appreciation of the nature of preoperational intelligence. For these authorities, intuitive teaching is insufficient; a teacher must be finely tuned to Piaget's theoretical wavelength.

As suggested earlier, most of a child's significant learning within the Piagetian framework requires voluntary action and active manipulation of the environment. For Kamii and DeVries, the best medium for this purpose is play. Consequently, they have attempted to capitalize upon children's "intrinsically motivated play" as the context for intentional process-derived teaching. Specifically, a set of group games classified according to the concept of *strategy* has been described for use in the classroom. A brief summary of some group games favored by Kamii and DeVries and their cognitive advantages is presented in the following list.

*Some Group Games for a Piaget-Based Preschool
or Kindergarten Classroom (Kamii and DeVries, in press, 1974b)*

Games without Strategy:

> *Imitating.* "Follow the Leader" games in which children imitate another person in representing action ideas such as running, climbing, and swimming.
> *Performing rituals.* Detailed movements are performed in precise order, as in "Mulberry Bush."
> *Collaborating.* Games that require elementary cooperation and joint coordination, such as "Wheelbarrow," in which one child walks on his hands while his ankles are held by a partner walking behind.

Games with Strategy:

> *Racing.* In simple running or skipping races, children enact ideas such as starting together at one time, and finishing as first, second, third,

etc. Physical knowledge activities are integrated with racing games, e.g., if children are running while balancing a pillow or book on their heads, they must determine how much to modify their rate of speed in order not to drop said objects. "Musical Chairs," from which children can learn number concepts as well as devising chair-getting strategies, is another example.

Hiding-Finding. In "Hide and Seek," for example, children must both decenter, i.e., view themselves from the perspective of another person, and think about alternatives for hiding and finding (spatial reasoning).

Guessing Games. Physical knowledge is further advanced by games played by keeping eyes closed, then guessing what two objects clinked together will produce a given sound. For example, a pencil clinked against a glass sounds different from that produced by clinking two pencils together. Similar games can involve guessing objects by feeling while blindfolded.

Chasing-keeping away. Games such as "Drop the Handkerchief," a familiar nursery school activity, involve ordering and spatial reasoning: knowing in what direction to move and determining the point where a chase ends.

Imitating. "Simon Says" can be used profitably to activate in children a strategy of catching other children when a mistake in the directive is made and thinking ahead to possible movements which can be modeled.

Memory Games. One variation involves an array of items first viewed by the players who then close their eyes while one or more of the items are hidden by another child. Strategies for remembering usually are developed by children—a process of sorting and structuring (classifying) the characteristics of items. The well-known game "Concentration" can serve similar purposes of strategy development.

Inventing. Games that require, for example, a consideration of unusual uses or identities for usual or conventional objects. A teacher may display a cylindrical block to children who then take turns telling what the object could be. In a given session, children might offer the following: a cigar, corn on the cob, a hot dog, a pop bottle, rolling pin, telescope, whistle. This make-believe activity emphasizes divergent thinking.

It may be inferred from the above that Kamii and DeVries endorse neither the attempt to teach specific Piagetian tasks nor to accelerate the rate of children's development. Instead, their general aim is total development; preschool education is simply a means to enrich a child's opportunities for constructivism. Long-range educational objectives center on an individual's capacity for inventiveness, discovery, critical thinking, and autonomous judgment. Shorter-term objectives are ordered along two related avenues of development. Foremost among these are the socioemotional objectives deemed necessary for any child to achieve a full range of autonomous behaviors and to express freely intrinsic motivation unhampered by anxiety: security in a democratic relationship with adults, respect for the feeling and rights of others, an initial coordination of different points of view (decentering and cooperating), and general initiative (including confidence in one's problem-solving abilities, independence in exercising curiosity, and assertiveness with conviction). The cognitive objectives, simply put, include a child's ability to construct "interesting" ideas, problems, and questions (with an accent upon divergent expression) and to place things into relationships and to notice similarities and differences.

Such objectives have a familiar ring. For Kamii and DeVries, however, the difference between this joint set of objectives and similarly virtuous objectives in other models for early education is twofold: First, Kamii and DeVries' objectives are based upon a theoretical rationale which transcends the typical goal selection by means which are arbitrary and inevitably reflect educators' personal values. And second, socioemotional and cognitive objectives are interdependent and thus more loyal to Piaget's theoretical network. Perhaps it goes without saying that this conception of education is based upon what Kamii and DeVries take to be the absolute truth about human development: what *is* also *ought* to be. Presumably this approach to the development of an early education program according to Piaget's theory has no relationship to Kamii and DeVries' personal value system except for value placed on absolute truth.

Other important aspects of the Kamii-DeVries approach include teacher training, conceptualization of staff roles and parent roles, suggestions for organizing content, and a rationale for effecting a typical preschool day. Present space restrictions prevent even a modest elaboration of these important details. Rather, this writer's intent has been to convey the philosophy manifest in the Kamii-DeVries curriculum variation of Piagetian themes. Readers are encouraged to study these details elsewhere (Kamii and DeVries, in press, 1974b). It is consistent with the general thrust of this book, however, to mention something about research and evaluation concerning the Kamii-DeVries approach.

Evaluation   First, it should be noted that the Kamii-DeVries curriculum is still undergoing development; meaningful summative evaluation data are therefore absent. Even if such data were desired, their collection would be problematical: any clear effects of this form of Piagetian teaching are dependent upon the extended passage of time, during which complex qualitative changes in thinking would be predicted. In fact, the whole question of summative evaluation may be moot. Kamii and DeVries maintain that as long as public schools continue to be a repressive force in children's total development (their assumption), it will be impossible to assess the long-range impact of cognitively oriented preschool programs. Educational discontinuity, in other words, is sure to contaminate, if not destroy, any positive long-term effects of a limited preschool experience.

Twelve years of Piagetian-based education (longitudinal study) is seen as the only relevant condition for summative evaluation. Kamii and DeVries speculate that achievement of the five socioemotional and cognitive objectives discussed above and acceleration on Piagetian tasks (a controversial aim) may be the conditions for early attainment of formal operational thinking, mature moral development, inventiveness, and a capacity to assess the proven and the unproven. These characteristics, for Kamii and DeVries, represent development of full human potential.

Having avoided illusions about summative evaluation, we must now note that formative evaluation figures heavily in the Kamii-DeVries framework, at least in principle. The curriculum has undergone development through the testing of ideas from theory and then application by a team composed of Kamii, DeVries, and a cadre of classroom teachers. This interplay, the researchers argue, has led to much creativity and important modifications of trial activities. Further ideas about formative evaluation are presently being pursued by DeVries in the Evanston, Illinois, schools. Scaled Piagetian-type tasks probably will be used with a greater emphasis on observational data (especially teacher-child and child-child interactions). As the reader might predict, standardized achievement tests have no place in a preschool or kindergarten program established along Kamii-DeVries guidelines.

In summary, the Kamii-DeVries interpretation of Piaget for early education results in a humane, relatively informal, but consciously arranged set of activities for young children which involve a lot of physical movement and object manipulation. An attempt to coordinate the socioemotional and cognitive realms of activity is made through an application of four basic principles: teaching in the context of children's play, an encouragement and acceptance of "wrong answers," instructions according to the three kinds of knowledge (physical, social, logico-mathematical), and an emphasis upon both content and process in learning. Piaget's theory is accepted as final in developmental curriculum planning and any assessment of children's educational status that may be made. With some exception, evaluation in the sense that it has been discussed in previous chapters is practically irrelevant to this approach. A full realization of the Piagetian framework for education proposed by Kamii and DeVries would in their view depend upon a major reconstruction of public school practices.

CRITIQUE

No one can deny that Piaget has contributed significantly to the study of child development. Accolades are plentiful. Representative essays consider the uniqueness of Piaget's research strategy; the many empirical questions generated by his theory; his articulated view concerning intrinsic motivation; and his epistomological system as a general source of intellectual ferment (Elkind and Flavell, 1969). Neither is Piaget's contribution to the study of children's moral judgmental behavior overlooked. Criticism also abounds, however, as was intimated in the preceding section on research.

Two dimensions of this criticism will be discussed: (1) the theory as a source for curriculum building and (2) the specific Piaget-based curricula themselves. We will first take a brief critical look at Piaget's theory and its general educational implications. We will conclude with an overview of some points of contention among Piagetian educational model builders.

General Criticisms

Various scholars have addressed themselves to contradictions or internal inconsistencies within Piaget's general system of theoretical statements. Examples include reasoned critical treatises on play (Sutton-Smith, 1966), motor development (Ausubel, 1966), and psycho-logic (McLaughlin, 1963). A major problem seems to be the nature of Piaget's hypothetical structures, which may represent a complex maze of inferences incapable of being validated by empirical study. Compound problems in research methodology and the divergent interpretations that are often made from the same data also cloud and occasionally chill the enthusiasm of students for Piagetian theory. In fact, the verbal interplay among Piaget, his disciples, and his critics often takes the form of a semantic game wherein the challengers are accused of not really knowing what Piaget means by a given term. In Piaget's defense, for example, Flavell (1963b) attributes the discrepant experimental results scattered throughout the cognitive-developmental literature to many researchers' skeptical attitude toward and shallow understanding of Piaget's theory. The pattern is familiar: those who believe Piaget conduct studies to prove the soundness of Piaget's ideas, while doubters actively seek to disprove them. In the meantime, Piaget has altered his views here and there. This pattern, combined with Piaget's turgid writing style and the difficulties inherent in translating a special psychological vocabulary from French to English, complicates the general situation.

Several other criticisms can be identified. For example, not much attention has been paid to individual differences aside from associating variation in Piagetian task performance with variations in measured intelligence and emotional stability. Piagetians have not been noticeably receptive to the possibility that the phenomena studied by them may be subject to explanations more parsimonious than those couched in the latticework of the theory (for example, Ausubel, 1965; Farnham-Diggory and Bermon, 1968). Very little systematic study has been devoted to the effect of "natural" reinforcement on children's cognitive behavior. Dissatisfaction exists with Piaget's views on thinking, language, and symbol formation (Ausubel, 1968), formal operational thinking (Bynum et al., 1972); and double classification behavior (Jahoda, 1964)—to mention three additional specific sore points. And Sigel and Hooper (1968) believe that Piaget's conviction about the hierarchical and integrative nature of thought development must be held in abeyance, since it still lacks definitive empirical support. Finally, the reader interested in serious conceptual digging may wish to apply his thinking tools to the issues provoked by the Geneva-Harvard controversy (Inhelder et al., 1966).

Neither is full agreement apparent on the educational implications of Piaget's theory. Lavatelli (1968), for example, points out that perceptual training would not be stressed in a Piagetian preschool curriculum. This notion finds support in part from the failure of perceptual training (Montessori cylinder block training) to enhance the conservation skills of kindergarten children (Ball and Campbell, 1970). Phillips (1969), however, sees perceptual-motor training techniques as basic for welding the relationship between sensory-motor constructions and intellectual performance. As we have seen, Elkind (1967) considers Piaget-derived perceptual training basic for children who are learning to read. And while Englemann (1967) believes that Piaget has provided little of use to educators (save a specification of certain skills children are not normally taught), Sigel (1969) believes that any educational innovator would be negligent not to examine in depth the relationships of Piaget's "model" to education.

Among the most thorough recent Piagetian critiques are those of Sullivan (1967, 1968). Sullivan has rated Piaget as a solid success on two counts: the potential of Piaget's stage observations for developing tools to assess intellectual capacity and the value of Piaget's probing techniques to assess learning outcomes in a developmental curriculum. For Piaget, correct answers are subsidiary to the means by which a child arrives at an answer; a child's level of understanding is the important variable. Teachers, above all, must appreciate that pat solutions given by children may be "correct" but provide no guarantee that the true basis of a problem is understood.

Sullivan's favorable impressions with regard to Piaget-derived evaluation techniques are supported elsewhere:

[There are] at least two significant advantages in using measures derived from developmental theory. First, as criteria the measures would have great generality. The skills measured ought to be consistent with the long-term goals of many different approaches to instruction. Second, theoretically based measures would be less likely to be perceived as biased toward a particular ideology about curriculum content (Skager and Broadbent, 1968, p. 6).

Skager and Broadbent (1968) are careful to point out that Piagetian theory (and thus Piagetian measures) may not be applicable to every educational program. They believe that an instructional program must be oriented toward the development of cognitive skills if Piagetian theory (and measures) are to be relevant.

Returning once again to Sullivan (1967, 1968), we find skepticism that Piaget's stage theory provides assistance in structuring and sequencing curriculum content and activities. Sullivan feels that Piaget's epistemology and developmental model are too often accepted uncritically—especially when Piagetian stages are taken as definitions of educational readiness. Sullivan finds the Piagetian concept of readiness to be both narrow and of little educational value. Recall, for instance, Piaget's conviction that a gradual accumulation of general age-related daily life experience is necessary for development. There can be no substitute for this experience; thought structures therefore cannot be taught. Furthermore, while cognitive development accrues through a child's daily activity, Piaget holds that language is of minor importance for logical thought operations. A teacher therefore is wasting her time, Piagetians maintain, if she attempts to "explain" Piagetian problems to a child. In short, if a child at a given age is unable to demonstrate mastery of an operation, it cannot be taught. Thus a teacher must wait until a child is able to demonstrate mastery, but then, of course, the operation no longer needs to be taught. Stage-dependent theory in general is characterized by this impasse, namely, that somehow time and general experience will "take care of development." Certainly this view offers little encouragement to proponents of compensatory education (see Chapter 1).

Piagetians usually counter such criticism by arguing that although operations cannot be taught, prerequisite skills can (for example, see Churchill, 1961). Further, they maintain that, if given appropriate chunks of general experience, children will develop insight in due time. If so, the major reason for school, at least in terms of cultivating cognitive structures, would be to provide better general age-related experience than a child would get in his natural environment. But this still leaves educators with the problem of defining general age-related experience in terms compatible with Piaget's.

The above Piagetian counterargument may be inconsistent with Piaget's system, for it suggests a deliberately planned curriculum of sensory and conceptual experience. Recall that for Piaget cognitive development is a matter of continuous interaction with an environment that allows a child to pick and choose, thereby regulating his own adaptational process. The child must construct his own reality and will automatically define his own sequence for learning. Direct teaching, then, apart from training for social convention, has little place in the world of Piaget's child.

A final general criticism concerns the power of Piaget's theory to prescribe a necessary atmosphere of learning (discovery-exploratory activity in a permissive tension-free environment). Sullivan (1967), for example, feels that such a prescription is based on "pure extrapolation" from the least authenticated part of the theory: equilibration. He also suggests that much of Piaget's current popularity is due to a congruity between the theory and the discovery learning fad in American education.[18] That is, Piagetian theory is not being used to provide a rationale for educational activities; the theory is simply being used to justify practices in vogue among social and educational theorists.[19]

In contrast, Duckworth (1964) believes that the necessity for a child to do his own learning, to manipulate, question, compare, and reconcile

---

[18] The reader is encouraged to consult Ausubel (1961) and Bruner (1961) for alternative views on this fad.

[19] A more general concept involved here is basic to a recent discussion of educational change (Skager and Broadbent, 1968). It is contended that decisions regarding changes in curriculum and instruction are more likely to be influenced by philosophical arguments and "professional salesmanship" than by what research workers would consider "hard empirical evidence."

discrepant events (all activities based upon the equilibration concept) is perhaps *the* commanding message from Piaget to educators. This message is by no means new, however, for it was central to the writings of John Dewey more than thirty years ago. Regardless, the notion that concrete-manipulatory activity is a necessary prerequisite to concept learning (for example, conservation of weight) has not been proven. In fact, it has been decisively challenged (F. Murray, 1969).

The Tension among Piagetian Educational Model Builders

Earlier in this chapter we reviewed three applications of Piagetian thought to early education. It is now appropriate to examine some specific points of agreement and disagreement among Piagetian adherents. As we have noted, data about the measurable outcomes of Piaget-based education are sparse. Consequently, the rifts that have developed among Piagetian educational model builders are largely on conceptual grounds. Not that some basic agreements are lacking. Kamii and DeVries (1973), for example, agree with Lavatelli (1970) on three basic points: the value of play and unstructured learning experiences (hence ample time in school for free-choice activities); the inefficiency of teaching children by telling (i.e., the vain procedure of providing to children both elaborate verbal explanations and answers to problems presented to, rather than discovered by, children themselves); and the critical role of mental activity in observing, interpreting, and reconciling environmental phenomena. Beyond this point, Kamii and DeVries and Lavatelli appear to part company. Specifically, Kamii and DeVries find Lavatelli's interpretation of Piagetian theory to be "flawed." They also charge that many crucial implications for children's education are also flawed. Kamii and DeVries feel Lavatelli's formulation suffers from (1) an incorrect conception of educational objectives, (2) a too-tight ordering of specific content to sequential development, (3) an over-emphasis upon social reinforcement, (4) an excessive concern for language-intellectual development at the expense of affective growth, and (5) a concept of the teacher as director-supervisor, instead of as initiator-guider. Kamii and DeVries maintain that Lavatelli has failed to account for the distinction between physical and logico-mathematical knowledge. They also object to any systematic attempt to teach Piagetian tasks; they believe that such tasks are best used as diagnostic tools and that a focus upon tasks-specific responses is narrow and misguided in view of the complex interrelationships among various cognitive areas. A final criticism involves an alleged inconsistency between Lavatelli's philosophy of *accepting* children's wrong answers and her procedures for *prompting* children to correct themselves when they do make errors.

So also has the Weikart group been taken to task. Kamii and DeVries (1973) are particularly critical of Weikart's "undue and exaggerated emphasis" upon children's representational ability at a cost of experience with reflective abstraction. In addition, they argue that the Weikart group has misinterpreted the meaning and overall role of classification and seriation, extrapolated incorrectly from Piaget's view of spatio-temporal knowledge, developed only a limited relationship of curriculum objectives to Piagetian theory, established vague and restricted principles of teaching, and emphasized inappropriate language stimulation procedures (the "verbal bombardment" approach). In spite of these contentions, Kamii and DeVries do find a common philosophical bond between themselves and the Weikart group, particularly in respect to two principles: the necessity for (1) children's active involvement in learning and (2) teacher participation in formative curriculum evaluation. Kamii and DeVries seem to credit the Weikart group with greater flexibility and much less "scripting" for teaching-learning activities than, say, the Lavatellian approach. It must also be noted that the Weikart group—in the spirit of any good experimental program—has made changes (e.g., Weikart and Hohman, 1973) which make irrelevant some of the above criticisms. In fact, a thoroughgoing statement of the Weikart curriculum from preschool to third grade will be published late in 1975.

As this book is written, Lavatelli's response to her Piagetian critics has not appeared in print. In her defense, however, it can be said that the Lavatelli program is not intended as an inviolable curriculum for children. Rather, it is a tool for training teachers in Piagetian concepts and a springboard for experimentation. The Weikart group seems comfortable with having modified Piaget's theory to meet their own objectives for curriculum development. Furthermore, this group acknowledges openly that a purist Piagetianism is not the sole basis for their educational program. Indeed, the Weikart curriculum is a mix of many things and can be viewed as eclectic, but with substantial Piagetian foundations. Weikart himself suggests that his application is more accurately "storefront" than "high church" Piaget (Weikart et al., 1971). Furthermore, Weikart suggests that much of the rhetorical conflict is irrelevant. In his words, "the task of education is not finally to implement a model interpreted by those who claim they understand it, but gradually to structure an educational alternative which accepts some discipline from theory but builds in the necessary correction from the real world by input from practice. As one of our curriculum people commented, "Piaget gives you the peaks, but it takes lots of work to fill in the valleys" (Weikart, 1973). In other words, Piagetian theory leaves much room for interpretation, and the issue is whether the Kamii-DeVries interpretation is the only correct one, if theirs is itself correct.

As for the Kamii-DeVries approach, this writer believes that these model builders correctly view the relationship of the child to the curriculum as requiring a *long-range* intervention program. Whether or to what extent progressive structural elaboration will be facilitated by their recommended range of general activities remains to be seen. Unclear, for example, are their procedures for inducing learning according to basic Piagetian-derived principles: arranging classroom encounters which require reasoning slightly above a child's predominant operational level or devising situations which result in partial structure contradiction (disequilibrium). Presumably, Kamii and DeVries prefer not to arrange learning experiences systematically for these purposes. But if intellectual development—specifically the acquisition of formal operational thought—is the desired goal of education, then a curriculum should be an active source of cognitive conflict.

Providing a setting for salutary cognitive conflict requires a careful and continuous assessment of individual children's "cognitive structure profile" across a broad band of physical and logical concepts (e.g., classification, time, space, causality; Strauss, 1972). Considering the *méthode clinique* necessary for such assessment, it is doubtful that many teachers could manage such a task. Moreover, any agegroup of children will have a wide range of structural development. This fact implies the necessity for a large number and variety of learning situations and formative assessments. The practical problems inherent in such a varied approach are mindboggling. Admittedly, a strong counterargument against such pessimism can be made: simply provide a smorgasbord of classroom activities and materials where any child, like water, can seek his own level. But steps are needed to (1) ensure that such a smorgasbord curriculum is multileveled and (2) guarantee that a child will create his own disequilibrium in class better than he would in the absence of formal school experience. In addition, there are indications that children at one level of structural development need systematic interactions with children at higher levels; social interactions seemingly serve as an inducement to structural elaboration (F. Murray, 1972). Most educators will prefer not to leave such matters to chance. Even with such minimal guarantees, the complete development of a legitimate Piagetian multi-level curriculum for children beyond the preschool years is a task of monumental proportions.

More broadly speaking, critics surely will maintain that Kamii and DeVries have provided us with little that is new. Theirs is a desirably humane child development curriculum which may differ from mainstream nursery school education largely at the level of rhetoric. Whether distinctly observable and reliable differences will emerge between a Kamii-DeVries classroom and, say, a Bank Street model classroom, remains to be seen. It can be argued that the basic principles advocated by Kamii and DeVries have been practiced for years by competent preschool teachers oblivious to, or ignorant of, Piagetian theory. Yet Kamii and DeVries claim that their curriculum differs from global, traditional practices in several important ways: (1) a greater emphasis upon thinking, to the point of acting on objects and considering the consequences, (2) a teacher's differential role in dealing with three kinds of knowledge (social, physical, logico-mathematical); and (3) a teacher's role as a creator of a responsive learning environment in which children's ideas are extended. These are subtle nuances to which conventionally geared preschool teachers will react with varying degrees of persuasion. Perhaps Kamii and DeVries' signal accomplishment is the studiousness with which they have built from theory a rationale for young children's general education. How this rationale will accommodate the task of academic skill building (reading, writing, and arithmetic computation) is still an open question.

SUMMARY

Jean Piaget's genetic approach to intellectual development is one of the most thoroughly articulated and influential theories in contemporary psychology. According to this theory, an individual continually strives toward progressively higher levels of cognitive integration, a process marked by confrontation with, and adaptation to, physical and social reality. This adaptation is said to be both sequential and invariant. The sequence is comprised of four interrelated developmental stages. The first of these stages, termed the period of sensorimotor intelligence, encompasses roughly the first two years after birth. During this time the infant learns to coordinate sensory inputs, attains object permanence, and achieves a gross level of intentional goal-directed activity. The second stage, that of preoperational intelligence, is an extended period of transition to higher-level cognitive functioning. During this period, the child's thought is dominated by his absolute perceptions; the unique cognitive achievement is mastery of the symbol or representational thought.

Around age 7, the third developmental stage becomes manifest in the form of concrete operational thought. Thinking during this stage is still stimulus bound, but is characterized for the first time by logical properties such as reversibility, transitivity, and associativity. Both conservation and multiple classification are achieved. In fact, the concrete operational stage can be defined as that which involves the mastery of classes, relations, and quantities. The fourth stage occurs between ages 10 and 12. A final transition in the nature of thought occurs and terminates in what Piaget has called "formal operational thinking." This final stage is characterized by the ability to think reflectively and perform hypothetico-deductive operations.

These successively complex stages, or hierarchies of logical thought structures, are utilized to describe how particular contents of intellectual behavior are produced at predictable points in the developmental cycle. Piaget's primary interest has been the quality (kind) of children's cognitive operations which culminate in action, not whether a given action is successful or correct from the standpoint of adult criteria. Piaget's views are among the most explicit concerning the distinction between cognitive process and product: he believes that as much, if not more, can be learned by the "mistakes" or incompletenesses inherent in a child's thinking as can be learned by observing what a child does correctly.

An astonishing amount of recent child development research literature has consisted of Piaget-inspired studies. Piaget's concept of stage-sequence growth has generally been supported by independent research, although many details of the theory have yet to be validated and even specified clearly. Many types of studies have been conducted, but those concerned with the effects of general schooling and specific training upon operational thinking have held the greatest interest for educators. Such research has identified a number of specific variables which educators must account for as they design a developmentally appropriate learning environment. Unfortunately, research about the long-term advantages of a Piaget-based education for young children is unavailable for inspection.

Several unresolved issues also exist in the matter of precise curriculum building from the Piagetian blueprint. However, the blueprint does provide valuable cues in its specification of educational objectives and procedures for the assessment of cognitive growth. The blueprint also calls for careful attention to active, discovery-oriented learning experiences which may provide the stuff for thinking in logical, causal terms. In general, however, a Piaget-based approach to early education does not provide much support to educators who seek either a dramatic acceleration of children's intellectual development or a proven set of "curative" experiences for children whose development may be retarded.

Despite its many imponderables, much enthusiastic support exists for Piaget-based education during the early childhood years. Enthusiasts collectively stress three dimensions of Piagetian curriculum planning: use of the cognitive-developmental sequence as a guide to decisions about program content and timing, a preference for self-directed exploratory learning, and a strong emphasis upon social interaction within the peer group to enhance both cognitive and moral development. Still, there remain many differences in interpretation among persons identified with the Piagetian perspective in early education. Some interpretations are more "purist" than others, and differences exist in the degree of translation of Piaget's theory of development to educational programming. As a group, however, Piagetians are most clearly identified with child-centered natural learning methods and a philosophy of informal education.

REFERENCES

Ahr, P., and J. Youniss. Reasons for failure on the class inclusion problem. *Child Development*, 1970, *41*, 131–143.

Ammon, P. Logical thinking in children: research based on Piaget's theory. *American Educational Research Journal*, 1969, *6*, 293–295.

Ausubel, D. Learning by discovery: rationale and mystique. *Bulletin of the National Association of Secondary School Principals*, 1961, *45*, 18–58.

Ausubel, D. Neobehaviorism and Piaget's views on thought and symbolic functioning. *Child Development*, 1965, *36*, 1029–1033.

Ausubel, D. A critique of Piaget's theory of the ontogenesis of motor behavior. *Journal of Genetic Psychology*, 1966, *109*, 119–122.

Ausubel, D. Symbolization and symbolic thought: response to Furth. *Child Development*, 1968, *39*, 997–1001.

Baldwin, A. *Theories of child development.* New York: Wiley, 1967.

Ball, T., and M. Campbell. Effect of Montessori's cylinder block training on the acquisition of conservation. *Developmental Psychology*, 1970, *2*, 156.

Bearison, D. Role of measurement operations in the acquisitions of conservation. *Developmental Psychology*, 1969, *1*, 653–660.

Beilen, H. Learning and operational convergence in logical thought development. *Journal of Experimental Child Psychology*, 1965, *2*, 317–329.

Beilen, H., and J. Franklin. Logical operations in area and length measurement: age and training effects. *Child Development*, 1962, *33*, 607–618.

Bentler, P. A cross-cultural investigation of conservation. In *Proceedings, second annual UAP conference: Piagetian theory and the helping professions.* Los Angeles: Children's Hospital, 1972, 50–58.

Berzonsky, M. Effects of probing children's phenomenistic explanations of cause and effect. *Developmental Psychology*, 1970, *3*, 407.

Berzonsky, M. Interdependence of Inhelder and Piaget's model of logical thinking. *Developmental Psychology*, 1971, *4*, 469–476. (a)

Berzonsky, M. The role of familiarity in children's explanations of physical causality. *Child Development*, 1971, *42*, 705–715. (b)

Braine, M. The ontogeny of certain logical operations: Piaget's formulation examined by nonverbal methods. *Psychological Monographs*, 1959, *73*, No. 5.

Braine, M., and B. Shanks. The development of conservation of size. *Journal of Verbal and Verbal Behavior*, 1965, *4*, 227–242.

Brainerd, C. Order of acquisition of transitivity, conservation, and class inclusion of length and weight. *Developmental Psychology*, 1973, *8*, 105–116.

Brainerd, C., and T. Allen. Experimental inductions of the conservation of "first order" quantitative invariants. *Psychological Bulletin*, 1971, *75*, 128–144.

Brison, D. Acceleration of conservation of substance. *Journal of Genetic Psychology*, 1966, *109*, 311–312.

Bruner, J. The act of discovery. *Harvard Educational Review*, 1961, *31*, 124–135.

Bruner, J. The course of cognitive growth. *American Psychologist*, 1964, *19*, 1–15.

Bruner, J., et al. *Studies in cognitive growth.* New York: Wiley, 1966.

Bynum, T., et al. Truth-functional logic in formal operational thinking: Inhelder and Piaget's evidence. *Developmental Psychology*, 1972, *7*, 129–132.

Cattell, R. Theory of fluid and crystallized intelligence: a critical experiment. *Journal of Educational Psychology*, 1963, *54*, 1–22.

Chow, S., and P. Elmore. *Resource manual and program descriptions: early childhood education.* New York: Educational Products Information Exchange, 1972.

Churchill, E. *Piaget's findings and the teacher.* London: National Froebel Foundation, 1961.

Curcio, F., et al. Compensation and susceptibility to conversation training. *Developmental Psychology*, 1972, *7*, 259–265.

Dansky, J., and I. Silverman. Effects of play on associative fluency in preschool-aged children. *Developmental Psychology*, 1973, *9*, 38–43.

Dasen, P. Cross cultural Piagetian research: a summary. *Journal of Cross-Cultural Psychology*, 1972, *3*, 23–29.

Davies, C. Development of the probability concept in children. *Child Development*, 1965, *36*, 779–788.

Davol, S., et al. Conservation of continuous quantity investigated as a scaleable development concept. *Merrill-Palmer Quarterly*, 1967, 13, 191–199.

Dodwell, P. Children's understanding of number concepts: characteristics of an individual and of a group test. *Canadian Journal of Psychology*, 1961, *15*, 29–36.

Duckworth, E. Piaget rediscovered. *Journal of Research in Science Teaching*, 1964, *2*, 172–175.

Duckworth, E. Piaget takes a teacher's look. *Learning*, 1973, *2*, 22–37.

Dudek, S., et al. Relationship of Piaget measures to standard intelligence and motor scales. *Perceptual and Motor Skills*, 1969, *28*, 351–362.

Elkind, D. Children's discovery of the conservation of mass, weight, and volume: Piaget replication study II. *Journal of Genetic Psychology*, 1961, *98*, 219–227.

Elkind, D. Discrimination, seriation, and numeration of size and dimensional differences in young children: Piaget replication study VI. *Journal of Genetic Psychology*, 1964, *104*, 275–296.

Elkind, D. Conceptual orientation shifts in children and adolescents. *Child Development*, 1966, *37*, 493–498.

Elkind, D. Egocentrism in adolescence. *Child Development*, 1967, *38*, 1025–1034. (a)

Elkind, D. Piaget's conservation problem. *Child Development*, 1967, *38*, 15–28. (b)

Elkind, D. Piaget's theory of perceptual development: its application to reading and special education. *Journal of Special Education*, 1967, *1*, 357–361. (c)

Elkind, D., and J. Deblinger. Perceptual training and reading achievement in disadvantaged children. *Child Development*, 1969, *40*, 11–20.

Elkind, D., and J. Flavell (eds.). *Studies in cognitive development.* New York: Oxford, 1969.

Elkind, D., R. Koegler, and E. Go. Studies in perceptual development: II. part-whole perception. *Child Development*, 1964, *35*, 81–90.

Elkind, D., and L. Scott. Studies in perceptual development: I. the decentering of perception. *Child Development*, 1962, *33*, 619–630.

Elkind, D., W. Van Doorninck, and C. Schwarz. Perceptual activity and concept attainment. *Child Development*. 1967, *38*, 1153–1161.

Elkind, D., and J. Weiss. Studies in perceptual development: III. perceptual exploration. *Child Development*, 1967, *38*, 553–561.

Engelmann, S. Cognitive structure related to the principle of conservation. In D. Brison and E. Sullivan (eds.), *Recent research on the acquisition of conservation of substance.* Toronto: Ontario Institute for Studies in Education, 1967, 53–72.

Evans, E. *Contemporary Influences in early childhood education.* New York: Holt, Rinehart and Winston, Inc., 1971.

Farnham-Diggory, S., and M. Bermon. Verbal compensation, cognitive synthesis, and conservation. *Merrill-Palmer Quarterly*, 1968, *14*, 215–227.

Feigenbaum, K., and H. Sulkin. Piaget's problem of conservation of discontinuous quantities: a teaching experience. *Journal of Genetic Psychology*, 1964, *105*, 91–97.

Figurelli, J., and H. Keller. The effects of training and socioeconomic class upon the acquisition of conservation concepts. *Child Development*, 1972, *43*, 293–298.

Flavell, J. *The developmental psychology of Jean Piaget.* Princeton, N.J.: Van Nostrand, 1963. (a)

Flavell, J. Piaget's contributions to the study of cognitive development. *Merrill-Palmer Quarterly*, 1963, *9*, 245–252. (b)

Flavell, J., and J. Hill. Developmental psychology. *Annual review of psychology.* Palo Alto: Annual Reviews, Inc., 1969, 1–56.

Freyberg, P. Concept development in Piagetian terms in relation to school attainment. *Journal of Educational Psychology*, 1966, *57*, 164–168.

Furth, H. *Piaget and knowledge.* Englewood Cliffs, N.J.: Prentice-Hall, 1969.

Gagné, R. The conditions of learning, 2d ed. New York: Holt, Rinehart and Winston, Inc., 1971.

Gelman, R. Conservation acquisition: a problem of learning to attend to relevant attributes. *Journal of Experimental Child Psychology*, 1969, *7*, 167–187.

Ginsburg, H., and S. Opper. *Piaget's theory of intellectual development.* Englewood Cliffs, N. J.: Prentice-Hall, 1969.

Glaser, R., and L. Resnick. Instructional psychology. *Annual Review of Psychology*, 1972, *23*, 219–276.

Goldberg, S. Probability judgments by preschool children: task conditions and performance. *Child Development*, 1966, *37*, 157–167.

Goldschmid, M. Different types of conservation and nonconservation and their relation to age, sex, I.Q., M.A., and vocabulary. *Child Development*, 1967 *38*, 1229–1246.

Goldschmid, M. Different types of conservation and nonconservation and their relation to age, sex, I.Q., M.A., and vocabulary. *Child Development*, 1968, *39*, 787–802.

Goldschmid, M. A cross-cultural investigation of conservation. *Journal of Cross-Cultural Psychology*, 1973, *4*, 75–88.

Goldschmid, M., and P. Bentler. The dimensions and measurement of conservation. *Child Development*, 1968, *39*, 787–802.

Goodnow, J., and G. Bethon. Piaget's tasks: the effects of schooling and intelligence. *Child Development*, 1966, *37*, 573–582.

Gottfried, N. The relationship between concepts of conservation of length and number. *Journal of Genetic Psychology*, 1969, *114*, 85–91.

Green, D., M. Ford, and G. Flamer (eds.). *Measurement and Piaget*. New York: McGraw-Hill, 1971.

Griffiths, J., C. Shantz, and I. Sigel. A methodological problem in conservation studies: the use of relational terms. *Child Development*, 1967, *38*, 841–848.

Gruen, G. Experiences affecting the development of number conservation in children. *Child Development*, 1965, *36*, 963–979.

Guadia, G. Race, social class, and age of achievement of conservation on Piaget's tasks. *Developmental Psychology*, 1972, *6*, 158–165.

Halasa, O. A developmental study of number conservation attainment among disadvantaged children. Paper read at the meeting of the American Educational Research Association, Los Angeles, February 1969.

Hall, V., et al. Cognitive synthesis, conservation, and task analysis. *Developmental Psychology*, 1970, *2*, 423–428.

Halpern, E. The effects of incompatibility between perception and logic in Piaget's stage of concrete operations. *Child Development*, 1965, *36*, 491–497.

Hamel, B., and B. Riksen. Identity, reversibility, verbal rule instruction, and conservation. *Developmental Psychology*, 1973, *9*, 66–72.

Hood, H. An experimental study of Piaget's theory of the development of number in children. *British Journal of Psychology*, 1962, *53*, 272–289.

Horn, J. Organization of abilities and the development of intelligence. *Psychological Review*, 1968, *75*, 242–259.

Hunt, J. McV. *Intelligence and experience*. New York: Ronald, 1961.

Hunt, J. McV. Piaget's system as a source of hypotheses concerning motivation. *Merrill-Palmer Quarterly*, 1963, *9*, 263–275.

Inhelder, B., and J. Piaget. *The growth of logical thinking from childhood to adolescence*. New York: Basic Books, 1958.

Inhelder, B., et al. On cognitive development. *American Psychologist*, 1966, *21*, 160–164.

Jacobs, P., and M. Vandeventer. The learning, transfer, and retention of double classification skills by first graders. Paper read at the meeting of the American Educational Research Association, Los Angeles, February, 1969.

Jahoda, G. Children's concepts of nationality: a critical study of Piaget's stages. *Child Development*, 1964, *35*, 1081–1092.

Kamii, C. Evaluation of learning in preschool education: socioemotional, perceptual motor, cognitive development. In B. Bloom et al. (eds.), *Handbook on formative and summative evaluation of student learning.* New York: McGraw-Hill, 1971, 281–344.

Kamii, C., and R. DeVries. Piaget-based curricula for early childhood education: three different approaches. Presymposium paper read at the meeting of the Society for Research in Child Development, Philadelphia, April, 1973.

Kamii, C., and R. DeVries. Piaget for early education. In R. Parker (ed.), *The preschool in action.* (rev. ed) Boston: Allyn and Bacon, in press, 1974. (a)

Kamii, C., and R. DeVries. *Piaget for early education.* Vols. 1–3. Englewood Cliffs, N.J.: Prentice-Hall, in press, 1974. (b)

Kamii, C., and N. Radin. A framework for a preschool curriculum based upon Piaget's theory. *Journal of Creative Behavior,* 1967, *1*, 314–324.

Kaufman, A., and N. Kaufman. Tests built from Piaget's and Gesell's tasks as predictors of first grade achievement. *Child Development,* 1972, *43*, 521–535.

Kimball, R. Piagetian theory related to science and math curriculum development. In *Proceedings, second annual UAP conference: Piagetian theory and the helping professions.* Los Angeles: Children's Hospital, 1972, 17–20.

Kincaid, C., et al. A study in training nursery children on logical operational skills. Paper presented at meeting of the American Educational Research Association, New York, February 1971.

Kingsley, R., and V. Hall. Training conservation through the use of learning sets. *Child Development,* 1967, *38*, 1111–1126.

Kohlberg, L. Early education: a cognitive-developmental view. *Child Development,* 1968, *39*, 1013–1062.

Kohnstamm, G. Teaching children to solve a Piagetian problem of class inclusion. Uitegevess, Netherlands: Mouton, 1967.

Langer, J. *Theories of development.* New York: Holt, Rinehart and Winston, Inc., 1969.

Lavatelli, C. A Piaget-derived model for compensatory preschool education. In J. Frost (ed.), *Early childhood education rediscovered.* New York: Holt, Rinehart and Winston, Inc., 1968, 530–544.

Lavatelli, C. *Piaget's theory applied to an early childhood curriculum.* Boston: American Science and Engineering, 1970.

Looft, W., and D. Charles. Modification of the life concept in children. *Developmental Psychology,* 1969, *1*, 445–446.

Maier, H. *Three theories of child development.* New York: Harper & Row, 1965.

McLaughlin, G. Psycho-logic: a possible alternative to Piaget's formulation. *British Journal of Educational Psychology,* 1963, *33*, 61–67.

Mermelstein, E., and E. Meyer. Conservation training techniques and their effects on different populations. *Child Development,* 1969, *40*, 471–490.

Mermelstein, E., and L. Shulman. Task of formal schooling and the acquisition of conservation. *Child Development,* 1967, *38*, 39–52.

Meyers, C. Can Piaget's theory provide a better psychometry? In *Proceedings, second annual UAP conference: Piagetian theory and the helping professions.* Los Angeles, Calif.: Children's Hospital, 1972, 5–10.

Miller, D., L. Cohen, and K. Hill. A methodological investigation of Piaget's theory of object concept development in the sensory–motor period. *Journal of Experimental Child Psychology,* 1970, *9*, 59–85.

Murray, F. Cognitive conflict and reversibility training in the acquisition of length conservation. *Journal of Educational Psychology,* 1968, *59*, 82–87.

Murray, F. Stimulus abstractness and the conservation of weight *Proceedings of the 77th Annual Convention, American Psychological Association,* 1969, 627–628.

Murray, F. Acquisition of conservation through social interaction. *Developmental Psychology*, 1972, *6*, 1–6.

Murray, J., and J. Youniss. Achievement of inferential transitivity and its relation to serial ordering. *Child Development*, 1968, *39*, 1259–1268.

Neale, J. Egocentrism in institutionalized and noninstitutionalized children. *Child Development*, 1966, *37*, 97–101.

Ojemann, R., and K. Pritchett. Piaget and the role of guided experiences in human development. *Perceptual-Motor Skills*, 1963, *17*, 927–940.

Overbeck, C., and M. Schwartz. Training in conservation of weight. *Journal of Experimental Child Psychology*, 1970, *9*, 253–264.

Parker, R., M. Rieff, and S. Sperr. Teaching multiple classification to young children, *Child Development*, 1971, *42*, 1179–1189.

Parker, R., S. Sperr, and M. Rieff, Multiple classification: a training approach. *Developmental Psychology*, 1972, *7*, 188–194.

Phillips, J., Jr. *The origins of intellect: Piaget's theory*. San Francisco: Freeman, 1969.

Piaget, J. *The moral judgment of the child*. New York: Harcourt, 1932.

Piaget, J. *Play, dreams, and imitation in childhood*. New York: Norton, 1951.

Piaget, J. *The origins of intelligence in children*. New York: International Universities, 1952.

Poole, H. The effect of urbanization upon scientific concept attainment among Hausa children of northern Nigeria. *British Journal of Educational Psychology*, 1968, *38*, 57–63.

Pratoomraj, S., and R. Johnson. Kinds of questions and types of conservation tasks as related to children's conservation responses. *Child Development*, 1966, *37*, 343–354.

Prince, J. The effects of Western education of science conceptualization in New Guinea. *Child Development*, 1968, *38*, 64–74.

Raph, J., and D. Lieberman. Influences of a Piaget-oriented curriculum on intellectual functioning of lower class kindergarten children. Paper read at the meeting of the American Educational Research Association, New York, March 1971.

Ripple, R., and V. Rockcastle. (eds.) *Piaget rediscovered: a report of the conference on cognitive studies and curriculum development*. Ithaca, N.Y.: Cornell University School of Education, 1964.

Rosenthal, T., and B. Zimmerman. Modeling by exemplification and instruction in training conservation. *Developmental Psychology*, 1972, *6*, 392–401.

Safier, G. A study in relationships between the life and death concepts in children. *Journal of Genetic Psychology*, 1964, *105*, 283–294.

Shantz, C., and C. Smock. Development of distance conservation and the spatial coordinate system. *Child Development*, 1966, *37*, 943–948.

Siegel, L. The sequence of development of certain number concepts in preschool children. *Developmental Psychology*, 1971, *5*, 357–361.

Siegel, L. Development of the concept of seriation. *Developmental Psychology*, 1972, *6*, 135–137.

Siegler, R., and R. Liebert. Effects of presenting relevant rules and complete feedback on the conservation of liquid quantity task. *Developmental Psychology*, 1972, *7*, 133–138.

Sigel, I. The Piagetian system and education. In D. Elkind and J. Flavell (eds.), *Studies in Cognitive Development*. New York: Oxford, 1969, 465–489.

Sigel, I., and F. Hooper. (eds.). *Logical thinking in children*. New York: Holt, Rinehart and Winston, Inc., 1968.

Sigel, I., A. Roeper, and F. Hooper. A training procedure for acquisition of Piaget's conservation of quantity: a pilot study and its replication. *British Journal of Educational Psychology*, 1966, *36*, 301–311.

Sinclair-De-Zwart, H. Developmental psycholinguistics. In D. Elkind and J. Flavell (eds.), *Studies in cognitive development.* New York: Oxford, 1969, 315–336.

Skager, R., and L. Broadbent. *Cognitive structures and educational evaluation.* Center for the Study of Evaluation of Instructional Programs. Berkeley, Calif.: University of California Press, 1968.

Smedslund, J. The acquisition of conservation of substance and weight in children, V: practice in conflict situation without reinforcement. *Scandinavian Journal of Psychology*, 1961, *2*, 156–160.

Smedslund, J. Development of concrete transitivity of length in children. *Child Development*, 1963, *34*, 389–405. (a)

Smedslund, J. The effect of observation on children's representation of the spatial orientation of a water surface. *Journal of Genetic Psychology*, 1963, *102*, 195–201. (b)

Smedslund, J. Concrete reasoning: a study of intellectual development. *Monographs of the Society for Research in Child Development*, 1964, *29*, Serial No. 93, 3–39.

Smilansky, S. *The effects of sociodramatic play on disadvantaged preschool children.* New York: Wiley, 1968.

Smith, J. The effects of training procedure upon the acquisition of conservation of weight. *Child Development*, 1968, *39*, 515–526.

Stephens, B., et al. Factorial structure of selected psychoeducational measures and Piagetian reasoning assessment. *Developmental Psychology*, 1972, *6*, 343–348.

Strauss, S. Learning theories of Gagné and Piaget: implications for curriculum development. *Teachers College Record*, 1972, *74*, 81–102.

Sullivan, E. *Piaget and the school curriculum: a critical appraisal.* Toronto: Ontario Institute for Studies in Education, 1967.

Sullivan, E. Piagetian theory in the educational milieu: a critical appraisal. Unpublished manuscript, Ontario Institute for Studies in Education, 1968.

Sutton-Smith, B. Piaget on play: a critique. *Psychological Review*, 1966, *73*, 104–110.

Tuddenham, R. Jean Piaget and the world of the child. *American Psychologist*, 1966, *21*, 207–217.

Uzgiris, I. Situational generality of conservation. *Child Development*, 1964, *35*, 831–841.

Uzgiris, I., and J. McV. Hunt. *Ordinal scale of infant development.* Urbana, Ill.: University of Illinois, Department of Psychology, 1966.

Wallach, L., and R. Sprott. Inducing number conservation in children. *Child Development*, 1964, *35*, 1057–1071.

Wallach, L., A. Wall, and L. Anderson. Number conservation: the roles of reversibility, addition-subtraction, and misleading perceptual cues. *Child Development*, 1967, *38*, 427–442.

Wallach, M. Research on children's thinking. In H. Stevenson (ed.), *Child Psychology*. Chicago: University of Chicago Press, 1963, 236–276.

Wasik, B., and J. Wasik. Performance of culturally deprived children on the concept assessment kit: conservation. *Child Development*, 1971, *42*, 1586–1590.

Weikart, D. Preschool programs: preliminary findings. *Journal of Special Education*. 1967, *1*, 163–181.

Weikart, D. Relationship of curriculum, teaching, and learning in preschool education. In J. Stanley (ed.), *Preschool programs for the disadvantaged.* Baltimore: The Johns Hopkins Press, 1972, 22–66.

Weikart, D. Personal correspondence. October, 1973.

Weikart, D., and C. Hohman. Classification in the High/Scope Cognitive Curriculum. Paper presented at the bi-annual meeting of the society for Research in Child Development, Philadelphia, March 1973.

Weikart, D., L. Rogers, C. Adcock, and D. McClelland. *The cognitively oriented curriculum: a framework for preschool teachers.* Washington, D.C.: National Association for the Education of Young Children, 1971.

Winer, G. Induced set and acquisition of number conservation. *Child Development*, 1968, *39*, 195–205.

Wohlwill, J., and M. Katz. Factors in children's responses on class-inclusion problems. Paper read at the meeting of the Society for Research in Child Development, New York, April 1967.

Youniss, J., and H. Furth. The influence of transitivity on learning in hearing and deaf children. *Child Development*, 1965, *36*, 533–538.

Youniss, J., and H. Furth. Prediction of causal events as a function of transitivity and perceptual congruency in hearing and deaf children. *Child Development*, 1966, *37*, 73–82.

Photograph courtesy of J. Myron Atkin.

6

the montessori
method

The growing federal commitment to early childhood education has been paralleled by a dramatic rebirth of interest in the Montessori Method. Perhaps the first truly systematic attempt to educate children under six years of age, the Method was widely acclaimed in Europe shortly after its inception around the turn of the century. Initial enthusiasm in America for the Montessori Method was short-lived. Not only did Montessori education receive a cool reception among distinguished members of the professional educational establishment (e.g., Kilpatrick, 1914) but the onset of World War I apparently did much to prevent the concept of Montessorian education from gaining widespread acceptance in America. A sufficient number of early devotees were successful, however, in establishing a handful of Montessori schools in America (Martin, 1965), and since 1958 the number of schools has increased markedly.

Paradoxically, Montessorian education in America has been the province of highly privileged children instead of the underprivileged children for whom the method was initially designed. Probably the greatest single reason for this is that Montessori schols are private operations and require a tuition that low-income families cannot afford.[1] To this writer's

---

[1] By 1965, the national average cost per child for a year of Montessori education was five hundred dollars (Miller, 1965). The annual cost is higher by several hundred dollars in many of the more exclusive schools.

knowledge bonafide Montessori schools have never been affiliated with nor supported by public school systems in America, although many Montessorian concepts have been incorporated into public school practice.

Several factors have combined to rekindle the sparks of Montessorian education in America. One factor has been the search for appropriate methods to educate disadvantaged children (Fisher, 1971). Another has been an increasing awareness of the congenial relationship between Montessorian principles and Piagetian theory (Hunt, 1964; Elkind, 1966). A third has been the appeal of discovery learning, the stylistic features of which have been articulated by influential psychologists such as Jerome Bruner (1961). A highly popular book, *Learning How To Learn* (Rambusch, 1962), also has done much to alert the public to the Montessori Method. Conventional nursery and kindergarten practices historically have been influenced to some degree by the Montessori Method as well. In spite of this interplay, it is often surprising to observe just how little American teachers and college students know about Montessorian education. Because of these factors and relevancy of Montessorian principles to many current issues in early childhood education, this chapter is devoted to the Method. It begins with an introduction to Montessori the person. This introduction is followed by a description of the essential Method for children ages 2½ or 3 to 6, a sampling of Montessori-based research, and a general critique based upon both historical and contemporary analyses.

The Person

Maria Montessori (1870–1952) became interested in learning problems through her contact with mentally retarded and disturbed children while she was working toward a medical degree at the University of Rome. Her search for more adequate techniques of instruction for these children led her to study the earlier work of O. Eduoard Seguin (1812–1880), a French psychiatrist whose pioneer efforts to treat the problems of the mentally ill were exemplary. Seguin developed a set of ingenious didactic materials to facilitate learning of basic discrimination skills by retarded children. Montessori, duly impressed, drew heavily upon the principles underlying the Seguin materials and became totally proficient in their application.

After becoming the first woman in Italy to earn a medical degree, Montessori served as a faculty member at the University of Rome and simultaneously did postgraduate work in psychiatry. In 1898 she accepted an appointment as directress of Rome's Orthophrenic School, a tax-supported institution for "subnormal" or retarded children. Her phenomenal success with these children, attributed largely to her materials and methods, gained Montessori great visibility. This success also prompted her to question the effectiveness of regular public school educational practices for normal children. She reasoned that if retarded children could progress to an academic level comparable to that of normal children in conventional educational settings, then much more could be done for normal children in a properly designed educational environment.

An opportunity to test this thesis came in 1907, when Dr. Montessori accepted responsibility for the education of slum children in Rome, a population of children which had created considerable concern among officials of the Italian government. Involved were the now famous *casa dei bambini* (houses of children) in which were brought to life the ideas about the learning environment Montessori thought essential for the self-realization of children's potentials. It was through the medium of such houses that the Montessori Method matured and attracted worldwide attention. Firmly convinced that the most critical period in a child's development was the first six years of life, Montessori devoted the remainder of her life to the service of young children. Accordingly, her efforts were coordinated to capitalize on the spontaneity and "natural energy" of children during these early years.

THE METHOD

The Prepared Environment

An fundamental component of the Montessori Method is the *prepared environment*, an organized and coordinated set of materials and equipment which will promote significant learnings in the child. The arrangement of the prepared environment is predicated upon the child's need to order and attach meaning to his world. Among other things this means that the environment is scaled both physically and conceptually to children, not adults. For example, child-sized furniture and utensils are viewed as prerequisites for meaningful learning.

The original Montessori house consisted of a set of rooms (a central room for intellectual work in which the children spent two hours a day; shelters for individual play or sleep; a club room for games and music; a dining room; a dressing room) and a garden. Today's Montessori schools are rarely so elaborate. Most, however, still subscribe to the objective involved, namely, the development of children's skills for the care of self and property. Foremost among procedures designed to achieve this objective are the exercises of practical life. These exercises in the care and management of self and property are instrumental for motor education, one of the three primary components of the Montessori Method. (The other two components, sensory education and education for language, will be treated subsequently.)

Motor Education For Montessori, freedom of movement is the key to motor education. Such education is effected by developing various self-management skills in children. Imperative is the provision of *order* to motility; all motor activities are goal-oriented and functional for the child in managing his environment. Basic motor acts such as walking, sitting, and carrying objects are given precise attention. Various exercises in opening and shutting drawers, pouring water from pitcher to basin, folding and packing linens, cutting with scissors, buttoning, and lacing are considered fundamental and preparatory for the development of practical life skills. Occupational skills such as sweeping, washing, brushing, and caring for plants and animals are also emphasized. Integrated into such motor education are responsibility training (based upon the concept that plants and animals are dependent upon the children for their survival) and training to develop patience (the children must wait to observe natural growth).

While play-like activities pervade a Montessorian classroom, Montessori did not consider fantasy play to have a place in children's education; all activities have a purpose and are geared toward the building of self-discipline and a work orientation. For example, gymnastic exercises and rhythmic movement exercises are provided not just for exercises or to promote social interaction. Rather, they are provided systematically to facilitate the child's developing sense of equilibrium; Montessori reasoned that the period from three to six is critical for the development of this sense.

In sum, motor education is imparted by activities many people take for granted. They are, for the most part, activities which children perform "naturally," such as playing in water. Montessori believed such common activities to be of supreme importance in the development of the work habits necessary to accomplish more complex learnings. In effect, all learning is thought to have a sensory-motor base; the acquisition of knowledge rests upon the development and refinement of motor and perceptual skills. Freedom for the child to move and involve himself actively with concrete materials is necessary in order for him to create his own learning situations. For Montessori, practice in the coordination of the musculature with the sense organs contributes to "readiness" for later academic learning.

Most motor activities are taught initially by precise demonstration. Verbal instructions are rare. Subtle cues from the teacher (directress) substitute for explanations, for example, a touch, a hint or two—just enough to get the child started. A Montessori classroom depends heavily upon the learning that children do by observing and interacting with one another. Even in the practical life exercises a regular sequence of actions is stressed. One such activity, table scrubbing, involves a sequence of pouring water into a basin, wetting and soaping a brush, scrubbing, rinsing, drying, and cleaning up. This routine may take fifteen to twenty minutes and is one intended to assist a child to lengthen his attention span. In a sense, the practical life exercises are prototypic of all subsequent exercises in that a fixed sequence of actions is involved. There exists only one right way to deal with the materials in the prepared environment.

Sensory Education   Once a child has mastered the practical life exercises, he is considered ready to sample the main course of the Montessori pre-academic menu: sensorial exercises. Education of the senses is made possible through involvement with elaborate didactic materials. These varied materials are designed to promote sensory discrimination skills and concepts of form, size, color, weight, temperature, and texture. It is

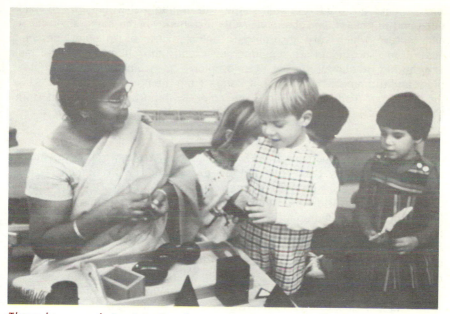

These boys are being introduced to sensory materials by their teacher. Photo courtesy of Aline Wolf.

significant that the sensory materials are coordinated so that a child's activities are not at all haphazard. It is the teacher's job to ensure that the proper sequence of activities is followed and that appropriate materials are studied simultaneously.

Most of the sensorial materials are designed to foster the child's techniques of observation and decision-making abilities. An example is the popular *cylinder block*. This apparatus consists of a block of wood into which are bored sockets of graded size. Cylinders sized to correspond to the sockets may be placed into the block. The cylinders are identical in form and color and vary in one dimension only—size. The experience of placing the cylinders in correct order into their respective sockets helps the child to sharpen his discrimination of different-sized objects. As such, the target behavior is the child's visual sense. This exercise has another significant feature. Each cylinder has a small knob at its top which the child must grasp with the three fingers he will subsequently use to hold a pencil. Hence the exercise is designed to provide practice in sensory-motor coordinations and establish control over the small finger muscles necessary for cursive writing.

Other materials important to the education of the child's visual sense are the *pink tower* (blocks of the same color, shape, and texture but different size; the child's task being to construct a tower with the largest block as its base and build upward with successively smaller blocks), the *brown stair* (blocks of the same length but different width and height;

these blocks are graded in stair fashion to highlight the concepts of thickness and thinness), and the *color tablets* (tablets of the same size, shape, and texture which vary according to color; exercises in color matching and chromatic grading are provided; eventually the child tackles the task of ordering graduated shades of one color, e.g., from darkest to lightest blue; and ultimately the pairing of colors from memory is achieved). While the ability to discriminate form and color is important in its own right, Montessori saw it fundamental to the growth of a child's aesthetic appreciation.

The child's *tactile* sense is educated by materials which dramatize texture and form. Touchboards with surfaces ranging from rough to smooth are introduced and then followed by experiences with feeling various cloth such as wool, silk, velvet, linen, satin, and cotton. Delicacy of fondling is stressed after the children have washed their hands thoroughly. Form tracing is encouraged by another set of materials, namely, wooden tablets upon which are nested plane geometric inserts. Form identity is sought through tracing outlines of squares, circles, triangles, and other shapes. This tracing experience again anticipates the motor movements involved in writing. Eventually the child is required to match the geometric figures with their respective *outline drawings*, a strategy intended to bridge the gap between concrete reality and abstract representation. Geometric solids are also provided and the names of all forms are taught.

Other exercises oriented to the child's sense of feeling include the *thermic bottles*, which involves matching and grading by temperature. This "thermic sense" is reinforced by having the children dip their hands into water of varying temperatures.

Aural sense education is initiated by introducing cylindrically shaped sound boxes in which are housed objects of various kinds. Consistent with the principle of graduation, these cylinders are graduated according to sound intensity. The sound cylinder exercises are analogous to those discussed earlier regarding color. Specifically, children engage themselves in the process of (1) matching cylinder pairs of equal intensity and (2) sequencing the sound cylinders in gradations of softness to loudness. Montessori's original strategy involved blindfolding the children while they worked with auditory materials, so that each child was free to concentrate his full attention on sounds. Similar matching and grading exercises are performed on musical bells, resonant metal tubes, and wooden bars. As the reader probably suspects, these exercises are all viewed as essential preparation for musical skill cultivation.

Montessori's appreciation for things delicate and subtle is reflected in a unique activity related to aural sense education, namely, the *lesson of silence*. This lesson first seeks to establish immobility among the children so as to permit auditory training in a quiet atmosphere. It ends with the directress (or another child) whispering each child's name. The child whose name is called must make his way, blindfolded and as quietly as possible, to his caller. The immediate purpose of such an activity is to familiarize

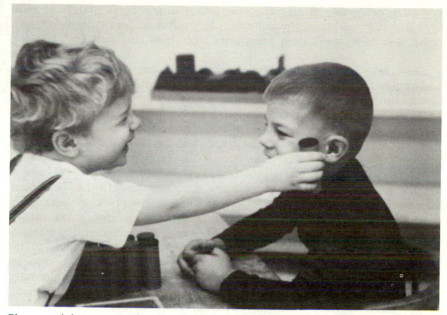

The sound boxes provide a medium for auditory discrimination training. These boys are taking turns to match and grade the boxes according to intensity of sound from loudest to softest. Photo courtesy of Aline Wolf.

children with silence and sharpen their sound perceptions. Montessori also intended this exercise to help children to savor and prefer an unraucous environment. The longer-range objective of this and similar lessons is much more philosophical: the development of self-inhibitory powers and cooperativeness within one's social community. Such self-control and cooperation were seen by Montessori as imperative if social groups were to achieve a common purpose.

Up to this point we have considered examples of *visual, tactile*, and *auditory sense* education. Other senses educated via didactic materials are the *baric* sense, the *olfactory* sense, and the sense of *taste*. The baric sense refers directly to the ability to discern weight. Thus, kinesthesia is involved. Basic tablets of the same size but different weight may be manipulated with the initial objective being to distinguish heavy and light. Smelling activities such as matching spices and identifying foodstuffs by type and quality while blindfolded are arranged to cultivate the olfactory sense. Similar procedures are employed for tasting exercises—for example, matching sweet, sour, salty, and bitter substances.

To summarize, three objectives are sought through sensory education procedures: the ability to recognize and match identities; the ability to recognize contrasts and extremes in a series of objects; and the ability to discriminate among items quite similar in shape, color, texture, weight, and other properties. Systematic discrimination and classification of sensory attributes are especially important in view of Montessori's hypothesis about orderly thinking as a prerequisite for true creativity.

Language Education   Of the preparatory sensory material exercises, auditory training is most closely related to language development in a Montessori classroom. The sounds of articulate language are thought to require powerful discrimination skills. It should be noted that language education occurs in conjunction with, not subsequent to, sensory education. At no time, however, does language training *precede* discrimination learning.

An inviolable principle in Montessori language education is the use of precise pronunciation by the children's principal model—the directress. Equally important is the three-period sequence applied to vocabulary development. The first period, *naming*, is initiated by the directress, usually during a demonstration period. For example, a child manipulating the blocks of the brown stair will be shown (by pointing) which ones are thick. ("This is thick") or thin ("This is thin"). In the second period, the *recognition* phase, the child is required to respond to identity statements which take the form of a request. The teacher says, for example, "Give me the thick" or "Give me the thin." Eventually, the child enters the third period, the *pronunciation* phase, and is able to respond appropriately to such questions as, "What is this?"

Children are expected to achieve a high degree of accuracy in their use of words to describe their environment. For example, when only one dimension is varied in sensory materials such as the color tablets, objects are identified as dark and light. If the target dimension is length, the correct identification is in terms of long and short. If the defining criterion is height, the descriptions tall and short apply, and so on. An interesting example of the concern for precise language apparently shown in authentic Montessori classrooms is provided in the original handbook (Montessori, 1914). After the directress had ruled a blackboard with extremely fine lines a child explained spontaneously, "What small lines." "They are not small," reminded a second child, "they are thin!" The example serves also to illustrate a basic objective of language education: a crystallization of basic ideas through the use of exacting terminology.

Academic Learning   The experiences described are preparatory or, in current terms, pre-academic. Normally, the child who has reached this point in the Montessori program is four years of age and ready to commence activities of the "essential culture": writing, reading, and arithmetic. Such activities are thought to represent a natural extension of all that has gone before. The child has presumably mastered his fundamentals and possesses an appropriate sense of responsibility, cooperation, and initiative. His movements in space are satisfactorily coordinated, and he is predisposed to make ordered observations in his environment.

Writing and Reading   Readers will recall that prior activities, such as form tracing, represented indirect preparation for writing. Hand movement exercises which constitute more direct training are now pursued. Direct training procedures initiated at this time are based upon Montessori's analysis of the writing act. Exercises which enable the child to manage the instruments of writing are critical. Again, a prescribed sequence of activities is applied. The sequence is initiated when the child traces geometric figures on paper with colored pencils. A series of ten double-outline figures are used. Next, the double-outline tracings are filled in by the child using line markers and taking great care to stay within the traced form. Subsequently, prepared designs of varied shapes and sizes are introduced to give the child more practice. The child then graduates to the next series of exercises, which involves the famous *sandpaper letters.*

Montessorian alphabetical lessons utilize a series of smooth-surfaced cards to which are attached (1) the letters of the alphabet cut from sandpaper and (2) combinations of letters grouped on the basis of form analogy (*1, b, f,* for example). Vowels typically appear on red cards, consonants on blue ones. Letters and letter groupings are traced using the index and middle fingers in movements which correspond to actual writing. During this tracing process, the teacher pronounces letter sounds (vowels are named, consonants are sounded). In this way the child simultaneously sees a letter, feels its shape, and hears its sound. Having learned the sandpaper letters and their sounds, the child is ready to construct words composed of letters from a large movable alphabet. Ordinarily, experience with large letter vowels precedes that with smaller vowels and consonants.

As words are constructed—usually small words with a personal reference—the child learns to read them. Three-letter words with a short vowel sound are early encouraged, and the child sounds out the letter sounds as he combines the letters. In effect, this represents a single-letter method of reading and word construction as opposed to the word methods found in many conventional schools. The process is generally quite gradual; most children engage in word building for some time before they realize that reading responses are now possible. Such a revelation is associated with great excitement, an excitement magnified even more when the child discovers that he is also now capable of writing entire words.[2]

Notable is the combination of didactic materials and exercises which culminates in beginning skills of writing and reading. Still more elaborate materials are introduced for advanced work in sounding out vowel-consonant combinations; learning the parts of speech, grammar, word and picture matching; and responding to command words. For the latter activity, cards printed with action words such as *jump, sit,* and *run* may be provided.

---

[2] The incorporation of reading and writing by Montessori is unique. Elliot (1967), for example, comments favorably upon the ability of this technique to facilitate reading skill acquisition, particularly during the "sensitive period" for reading thought by Montessori to occur during the late preschool period.

As each card is presented, the children execute the correct activity. Such procedures are extended to more complex directions such as, "Place the pencil on the chair," or "Close the lid on the blue box."

Arithmetic The reader will recall that inherent in many of the sensorial materials are certain concepts basic to mathematical learning: quantity, identity, and difference. Formal introduction to numbers comes with the presentation of the *red and blue rods*, a set based upon the decimal system. These sets are carefully scaled so that the smallest rod represents a model unit of measurement, i.e., the next smallest rod is twice the size of the first, the next largest is thrice the size of the first, and so on. Thus, these rods may be graded in succession from one through ten, during which time the number names and their corresponding symbols are taught in the customary sequence.

Greater levels of complexity follow the rod exercise, including exercises which teach the meaning of zero, odd and even numbers, and the decimal system. To accomplish the latter objective, Montessori designed an ingenious device known as the *golden bead material*, in which a single bead represents a unit. The quantity 10 is represented by a vertical row of ten beads, a square composed of ten vertical rows of ten beads each represents 100, and a cube comprised of ten 100-squares indicates 1000. Activities which require the child to count large quantities of beads dramatize the need for a more economical strategy than the counting of single units. Thus substitutions may be made by the child when necessary (exchanging one 10-bar for 10 units, for example), thus illustrating a basic principle of the decimal system.

The Golden Beads may also be used for games designed to teach the basic mathematical operations. However, still other didactic materials are introduced at this stage in order that the child may teach himself the teen numbers, fractions, and the processes of squaring and cubing. Basic to all these materials is the coordination of movement with symbolic activity. At this time, activities of science education may also be interposed, including exercises in botany and geography. The child has now completed his preparatory program and, according to Montessori, is ready to encounter higher levels of cultural experience. Through intense exercise the child's mind has been made healthy and capable of receiving newer and more complex materials. For this purpose, an advanced program for children ages 6–12 was designed and first published in 1917 (Montessori, 1965a).

Fundamentals of the Method

The Montessori Method is a provocative combination of philosophy, psychological concepts, and pedagogical techniques. It is fueled in principle by love for the child and respect for his natural capabilities. It is the child in whom Montessori placed her hopes for a world based upon fundamental values such as cooperation, self-control, order, responsibility, patience, and the common good. In fact, the Golden Rule is perhaps the foremost operational principle of the Montessori Method. For Montessori such kindness requires the sensitive interpretation of other's needs and a willingness to sacrifice, if necessary, one's own desires in deference to those of others.

Philosophically, Montessori was linked quite early to the Rousseau-Pestalozzi-Froebel group (Kilpatrick, 1914), although she reflects disagreements with each in her original writings. This group early emphasized the inherent goodness of children, the spontaneous nature of development, and the importance of deriving educational practices from children's natural interests. The Montessori Method is clearly predicated upon a belief in liberty of the spirit; such liberty is thought to develop best in an environment organized around sensory experiences. This Montessorian emphasis upon individual freedom of action must not be misconstrued, however, for its limit is the collective interest. Montessori clearly subscribed to policies which discourage children from acting in ways libertine or otherwise offensive to others. Out of the chaotic world of the small child must be generated order. Order, a condition requisite for security, is combined with the objective of self-discipline. This master objective literally transcends any academic or social one.

Role of the Teacher   A child-centered philosophy of behavior and education has as its natural extension the building and maintenance of positive interpersonal relations. Yet social games and dramatic play are not a part of the authentic Montessori Method. Rather, a climate of emotional support, helpfulness, and consideration is to be established by the teacher. To be successful, the teacher must relinquish a pontifical or pedantic role and serve more as a resource person, a catalyst for progress. Hence, deductive teaching is rare; inductive learning prevails. Also imperative is the abandonment of evaluative tactics, especially those based upon a comparison of a child to his peers. The teacher does, however, serve in a demonstration role. Above all, she must be a highly skilled observer, capable of determining when and under what circumstances a child is ready to successfully encounter advanced exercises. Ideally, observational data taken by the teacher enables her to collaborate with the child in the construction of his individual learning activities. In this way may be achieved what Montessorians term *functional independence.* Appropriately, scientific techniques of child study are stressed in Montessori teacher training which, incidentally, is controlled entirely by organizations such as the *Association Montessori Internationale.*

Montessori seemed convinced that poorly arranged learning materials and insensitive authoritarian teachers presented obstacles to children which produced such negative consequences as rebellion, failure, and aggression. She also condemned such teacher behaviors as verbally imposed rules (the often arbitrary "don'ts" so frequently encountered by children), moralizing, and the interruption or rushing of children's work. Experimentation on the part of the teacher is encouraged primarily in order to observe children's reactions to various materials so that poorly received ones may be discarded. It should be apparent that the Montessori directress must be a sound model for her children temperamentally, linguistically, and organizationally.

Preeminent qualities for an effective teacher are, in Montessori's view, imagination and faith in the child's ability to realize himself through purposive work activities. In theory, teacher efforts incorporate a tripartite function. The first function is essentially custodial. Meticulous order, clean apparatus in good repair, and a generally attractive environment must be maintained. This stress upon attractiveness and dignity includes the teacher's own person, as she is the most significant part of the child's environment. The second function involves the exercise of the teacher's motivating power. Prior to the achievement of full concentration, children need to be enticed, charmed, and stimulated within the context of developmentally appropriate activities. During this stage the teacher may intervene in the interests of classroom socialization. Her third and final function is served when the children begin to manifest genuine concentration. At this point, the teacher must not interfere in any way. Praise, assistance, or attention of any sort will have the effect of interrupting the child. Thus, once a captivated child initiates independent task behavior the teacher must behave as if the child no longer exists (Montessori, 1967). A teacher's normal affections for the child must be subordinated to the more advanced level of love for the spirit of men. Once she has achieved this level, the teacher will find that the children proceed to organize an orderly society unaided by adults. Disorder and negativism which develop *after* children have established concentration are considered evidence of teacher failure.

Concerning teacher preparation, Montessorians offer no substitute for direct practical experience. A first objective entails learning to distinguish between the "purely impulsive" behavior of children and their spontaneous expressions of energy which may be harnessed for educational purposes. Categories of responses identified by Montessori to indicate a lack of inner discipline include: (1) disordered voluntary movements (ill-coordinated motor movements), (2) distractibility and low levels of objective concentration, and (3) an affinity for imitating the inappropriate behavior of others (i.e., to be "seduced" into undesirable acts). General principles of human interaction and development must guide a teacher in the management of discipline problems. Yet the ultimate authority in such matters is the teacher's own judgment based upon an assessment of the particulars of a given situation. Practical life exercises for the child are thought to serve an important preventive function. The reality contacts inherent in these exercises are intended to strengthen the child's capacities for free choice, persistence, and order—all of which are basic to self-discipline. Self-discipline is equally important for the teacher, who must refrain from creating dependency relationships with her children. This points up one of the most basic differences between conventional nursery-kindergarten practices and the Montessori Method. The former stresses the creation of an emotional bond between teacher and child; a strong teacher-pupil relationship is frequently viewed as the key to the child's successful learning.

For Montessori, however, the critical relationship is between the child and his learning materials.

Principles of Learning and Instruction

A number of instructional and learning principles pervade the Montessori Method, some of which apply to the didactic materials, others to the management of the children. These include heterogeneous grouping by age; active involvement; self-selection and pacing in the use of materials; self-correctional nature of the materials; graduated sequence; sensory attribute isolation; provision of extraneous cues to facilitate subtle discriminations; practice; and the principle of contiguity.

Heterogeneous Grouping by Age In the preparatory Montessori program, around thirty children ranging in age from three to six or seven are gathered together in the same classroom. This practice is markedly different from American public school education which traditionally has been age-graded. There are several rationales for such grouping. For one thing, it is thought to provide a sound precondition for social development. Since all of the children will not be working at similar levels, they will neither need nor want the same materials at the same time. Thus, conflict among children is avoided.

Heterogeneous grouping also provides the variety in companionship thought desirable by Montessori for young children. Related is the notion that the older children may serve as models for their younger counterparts. Three points may be made in connection with this *modeling hypothesis.* First, a child of five, for example, may be a better teacher of some things to a three-year-old than an adult. Second, the act of teaching another is one of the most effective learning experiences possible. And third, the excitement conveyed by older children learning to write and read may be very contagious to the younger ones. Thus a motivational advantage may be gained.[3]

Finally, heterogeneous grouping is thought to make possible (within the parameters of the Montessori classroom) the operation of peer-based social controls which are both more natural and effective for maintaining order than are adult-imposed controls.

Active Involvement Unquestionably, Montessori was committed to action and movement as the basis for learning. Virtually all of the didactic materials are based upon Montessori's concept of the relationship between physical and mental development and require the performance of some response by the child in order that an effect be observed. Particularly notable is the accentuation of hand movements. Such a performance orien-

---

[3] Psychologists have recently initiated the study of young children's teaching styles; see Feshbach and Devor (1969), for example.

tation is not dissimilar to the Deweyian notion of "learning by doing." Few would argue with the soundness of this principle, especially as far as children are concerned.

Self-selection and Pacing   A concrete manifestation of freedom within structure in Montessori education is the child's prerogative of selecting from among designed alternatives the didactic materials which suit him at the moment. Technically, a child may spend as long as he wishes with any set of materials. Also important is the flexibility which allows the child to proceed through a sequence of materials at his self-imposed rate. In this sense, Montessori education is individualized education; unblocked time periods prevail. This feature has led Miller (1965), for example, to envision a Montessorian classroom as the original ungraded learning environment. All children must, however, engage themselves with the same materials in proper sequence at some time. Such vital issues as when and how rapidly this occurs are determined largely by the child. The reader will perhaps recognize these concepts as fundamental to contemporary techniques of programmed learning (Glaser, Reynolds, and Fullick, 1966).

Self-correctional Materials   Montessorian didactic materials are carefully designed so that errors (and successes) are for the most part self-evident. In other words, the child may correct his own mistakes by modifying his actions upon the materials. This amounts to a trial-and-success process in which the probability of error is low. Children do not depend heavily upon the teacher for evaluative feedback. Auto-educative materials are used either correctly or incorrectly. For example, the cylinder blocks fit only one way; the Golden Beads work only one way; the brown stair can be built in only one way. Hence, the child's task is to converge upon the correct combination of actions; he knows immediately how successful he has been. Teacher intervention may occur on occasion, although intervention is more likely to prevent materials from being misused than to indicate "answers" to the child. It should be noted that Montessori viewed the commission of errors as natural and important aspect of auto-educative learning. Reinforcement or reward is said to emanate primarily from the child's sense of pleasure in accomplishment.

Graduated Sequence   As we have seen, the major components of the Montessori program are carefully sequenced in graduated steps from simple to complex. Sensory-motor movements are perfected first, followed by discrimination skill and vocabulary training. All sensory discrimination tasks follow the pattern of *gross to fine*. A fixed order in a particular sense presentation is not demanded, but each sense follows the gross-to-fine pattern in presentation: contrasts, identity matching, and qualitative gradations for purposes of finer discrimination. Didactic materials are integrated so that the activities of writing and reading flow naturally from preceding sensorial tasks. Montessori strove for complete consistency in her approach to pedagogy. While one might question the necessity of all the steps children must take, there can be little argument that a coordinated matrix of stimulus elements characterizes the Method.

Isolation of Sensory Attributes   To promote concentration and sharpen discriminations Montessori arranged for children to deal with one sensory modality at a time. Thus, children are frequently blindfolded when working with auditory and tactile materials. Further, a single sensory (conceptual) dimension of a given set of materials is highlighted. For example, when color is varied for a given exercise, size, form, and texture are held constant. Likewise, while size is varied, other dimensions such as form, texture, and color are held constant.

Provision of Extraneous Cues To Facilitate Fine Discriminations   Noteworthy is Montessori's strategy for introducing cues, especially color cues, in stimuli which pose initial discrimination difficulties. These cues have the effect of drawing the child's attention to the critical or defining attribute of a stimulus and enriching its meaning. For example, in the grammar exercises each part of speech has its peculiar color. (Nouns are black, for without a verb they "lack life.")

A legitimate procedural question may be raised in reference to the strategy of extraneous cues, namely, whether children may be trained to be dependent upon artificial prompts. As an initial training strategy, however, there is evidence that the principle of cue provision is efficacious (Deese and Hulse, 1967; Meyer, 1964).

Practice   Montessorian materials lend themselves to highly repetitive use. Freedom to practice making discriminations, manipulating objects, tracing, counting, and the like is thought to facilitate a high degree of proficiency in these skills. As indicated in the psychological literature on learning, such practice is directly related to rates of retention (Rock, 1958). That is, while learning may be accomplished in one trial, the retention of what is learned may depend upon a repetition of experiences.

The Contiguity Principle   Contiguity refers to the position or occurrence of objects or events close together in place or time. Although the basic idea of association by contiguity may be traced to Aristotle, a generalized law of learning based upon contiguity has been formalized (Guthrie, 1935). This law concerns the strength of an association between a stimulus pattern and a response. Full associative strength develops, according to this view, on the first pairing of a stimulus pattern and a response. When a stimulus pattern which has been accompanied by a movement recurs, it will tend to be followed by that same movement. Thus conditioning is involved. When one considers the nature of Montessorian didactic materials, it appears that an application of Guthrie's principle anticipated its eventual formalization. By the simultaneous or contiguous association of the sensorial materials and motor responses, in this case the association of symbol and sound, learning is achieved. As Craig (1966)

The dressing frame exercises are designed to promote specific dressing skills—buttoning, snapping, buckling, lacing, zippering and tying bows—the acquisition of which requires much practice. Photo courtesy of Aline Wolf.

suggests, application of the contiguity principle provokes concern for cues which will simultaneously direct a learner's attention *and* prompt an appropriate response. Precisely this concern is reflected in the design of most Montessori materials.

To conclude, the Montessori Method reflects several important principles from learning psychology which have been validated by modern research techniques. As will be seen later in this chapter, there also exist some interesting parallels between Montessorian thought and developmental psychology. First, however, some examples from Montessori-based research must be presented.

RESEARCH ON THE METHOD

Throughout this book, a basic of the scientific method has been stressed: continued and systematic investigation into the effects of manipulations upon phenomena, be these changes in chemical substances or educational methods. And now the issue of objective evaluation must be raised for Montessorian education, theoretical or doctrinaire claims of its adherents notwithstanding. Unfortunately, comparatively few adequate evaluations of Montessori practices have been made. Certainly the professional journals of American psychology and education contain few reports of Montessori research. In contrast, there is no dearth of subjective testimonials and enthusiastic anecdotal reports, especially by protagonists of the method—for example, Rambusch (1962), Standing (1966), and contributors to *Communications* and *Children's House*, official publications of the *Association Montessori Internationale* and the American Montessori Society, respectively.

What little Montessori-based research has appeared in print represents several types of investigations. One type has involved the longitudinal measurement of changes in the behavior of one group of Montessori children whose growth is presumed to reflect the total impact of the Method. An example is Naumann's study (1967) which documents substantive reading and spelling gains for children aged three to five who spent a full year in a Montessori classroom. These data were interpreted to suggest that such gains, as measured by the Wide Range Achievement Test, are greater for slow learners than for bright children. Neither slow nor fast learners demonstrated much improvement in arithmetic skills. The absence of a non-Montessori group of children for comparative purposes (control group) makes it impossible to say how much better (or worse) a Montessori experience was for these children in terms of academic gains. It should also be noted that the subjects of this study were all volunteers and mostly children of college personnel. One might ask whether such children are more or less disposed to respond favorably to a Montessorian classroom experience or are stimulated at home to the point that any formal preschool experience would benefit them. At best such a longitudinal study indicates that young children *can* develop academic skills in an atmosphere which encourages self-teaching.

Another example of this one-group design has dealt with a heterogeneous group of mildly retarded and normal children (Naumann and Parsons, 1965). A basic purpose of this short-term project (seven weeks) was to demonstrate the efficacy of teaching an integrated group of preschoolers who vary substantially in their measured ability. (Much more typical in American education is the strategy of special classes for retardates). The researchers collected selected test and observational data which indicated that moderately retarded and normal children can learn together "effectively" in the Montessorian setting. That is, progress in the acquisition of skills such as self-care, autonomous selection and utilization of materials, courteousness, counting, and object naming was observed. Certain modifications were reported to have been made in the Montessori Method for this group of children, however, including more group-based experiences than the classical Method would provide.

A more prevalent investigative design for Montessori education (and early childhood education generally) is the standard "group comparison" design. This approach involves a comparison on selected criteria of children from a Montessori classroom with children from one or more non-Montessorian classrooms. Several recent studies of this type have been reported. For example, Banta's ongoing Sands School project (1967) is addressed to a wide range of effects attributable to Montessori experience in comparison with an ungraded primary classroom and a conventional graded kindergarten-primary experience. (Also built into this project is an evaluation of the cumulative effects of preschool education, since three of the four groups of children involved have attended preschool). Preliminary data indicate a pattern of test results (e.g., impulse control, analytic thinking, innovative behavior, and curiosity) in favor of children whose preschool and primary education was Montessorian. Banta points out, however, that children from a non-Montessorian preschool followed by an ungraded primary program scored almost as high. Lowest test performances were noted among children who had no preschool and went on to a conventional graded primary class. A fourth group, representing preschool in combination with graded primary experience, performed at a level between those of the ungraded classes and the no-preschool group. For the most part, differences between the two highest groups and the two lowest groups were significant. Although supportive of Montessori education, Banta's data perhaps speak more broadly to the apparent advantage of *continuity* from prekindergarten to ungraded primary education.[4]

The apparent influence of the Montessorian curriculum on children's cognition has been explored recently by Dreyer and Rigler (1969). Montessori children were matched on age, sex, social class, and measured intelligence with children from a traditional nursery school. Significant differences in behavior were observed—with Montessori children being less socially oriented and creative, but more task-oriented than their nursery school counterparts. An analysis of these children's creative drawings revealed less use of people and greater use of geometric forms by the Montessori children. Moreover, while Montessori children tended to describe commonplace objects by their physical characteristics, the nursery children utilized functional terms more frequently in their verbalizations. These data seemingly illustrate a function of the Montessori materials, whereby children are sensitized to particular features of the physical environment. The Dreyer and Rigler study—more than any other—appears to confirm certain long-standing criticisms of Montessori education, namely, its relative deemphasis on social and creative development. It must be remembered, however, that techniques for the measurement of such development during early childhood are far from perfect; some, including the test of creativity used by Dreyer and Rigler have been hotly disputed.[5]

Kohlberg (1968) reported the responses to a yearlong Montessori program of socially disadvantaged black children (not dissimilar in background from the deprived children in Rome for whom the method was originally conceived). Significant increases in intelligence test performance (Standford-Binet) and decreases in personal distractibility were observed for these children. A positive correlation between IQ increase and

---

[4] This finding is relevant to the concept of open education discussed in Chapter 7; the reader is advised to make a mental note of Banta's findings.

[5] Dreyer and Rigler utilized one segment of the figural portion of Torrance's *Tests of Creative Thinking* (1966). This battery, including both verbal and figural sections, has been published as a research edition.

attention increase (.65) revealed by this study led Kohlberg to suggest that perhaps the most valuable contribution of a Montessori program is its potential to promote the development of attentional responses basic to cognitive task learning. This, of course, refers to the concentration factor emphasized by Dr. Montessori.

Related to the Kohlberg data are the results of two independent longitudinal comparisons involving Afro-American and Puerto Rican children (Berger, 1969). Several groups of three- and four-year-old children were assigned to one of two treatment programs. One treatment was Montessorian and executed by certified Montessori teachers. The other was a conventional prekindergarten program prescribed by the New York City Board of Education and implemented by certified early childhood teachers. Data collected from all children at the end of one year's treatment indicated an advantage in autonomous problem solving and perceptual discrimination skills for Montessori children. As in the Naumann study (1967) mentioned earlier, this advantage was notable chiefly among children whose initial status was below average. Measures of motor impulse control, field independence, and task persistence also indicated a trend favoring Montessori children. All three of these characteristics seem to foster efficiency in structured problem-solving situations.

With respect to curiosity—exploratory responses, verbal and memory skills, and unstructured problem-solving tasks—Berger noted no reliable differences between the groups. However, where differences in these phenomena were observed among children, Berger suggests that teaching style, rather than program variables, was the key factor. Teaching style (tightly prescribed-mechanistic versus permissive-fluid) was not clearly associated with either the Montessori or conventional programs. This suggests that teaching style may vary considerably from classroom to classroom, even when all classes may be identified as Montessori, conventional, or whatever. Support for this suggestion comes from Banta (1966), who has observed a substantial range of differences among Montessori schools on several counts, including the degree to which activities are structured by Montessori teachers, the percentage of didactic activities initiated by teachers, and the actual time spent by children in the didactically correct use of materials.[6]

A few additional studies of Montessori practice also give some encouragement for the approach. Johnson (1965), for example, has reported favorable intellectual-academic and social-emotional outcomes for disadvantaged children with Montessorian experience. Greater advantages in haptic (tactile) perception have also been reported for Montessori- as compared to non-Montessori-trained children (Concannon, 1970). Greater

---

[6] Banta's study (1967) illustrates a third type of Montessori research, namely, that designed to describe through systematic observation the activities of Montessori classroom, including the behavior of children, teachers, and their interactions. Still another example is Naumann's behavioral interaction analysis technique (1966).

than normal improvements in impulse control have been linked to a Montessori preschool experience as well (McCormick and Schnobrick, 1970). Oddly enough, however, Taminen (1967) indicates that when Montessori toys were added to a Head Start program, cognitive gains among the children involved were less than those achieved by their regular Head Start counterparts. It is possible that simply placing didactic materials in the classroom, without a careful sequencing and integration with other class activities, is not the soundest policy for those who wish to capitalize upon the strengths of the Montessori Method. Still, some would argue that the didactic materials represent the essence of the method and should be able to stand collectively on their own as a means to promote pre-academic skills. If this is not the case, the teacher's role in implementing the didactic materials would appear to make more of a difference than many students of Montessori have been led to believe.

Finally, the elaborate multi-curriculum evaluation of Miller (1972) should be noted. According to this report, children who first experienced Montessori education at age 4 and then "graduated" to a Follow Through K–3 program, performed somewhat below three other preschool Follow Through combinations on the Metropolitan Readiness Test at first-grade entry. (These other programs were traditional Head Start; Distar; and DARCEE, a balanced program designed to develop language, cognitive skills, and achievement motivation). When the preschool experience was followed by a regular (non–Follow Through) K–3 experience, however, the Montessori children tended to surpass their Head Start, Distar, and DARCEE peers on the same criterion. Apparently, then, the later-readiness test performances of Montessori children is somehow mediated by the nature of the follow-up experience. The reasons for this are obscure, but some interaction between the qualitative aspects of pyramidal learning environments is presumably involved. (See Beller, 1973, pp. 575–579, for a more detailed summary of the entire Miller, 1972, evaluation study).

The variations mentioned above highlight a major difficulty of research strategies which compare one method to another. Without knowing precisely what features within a program are operating to produce change one is left with a prodigious speculative task. This is clearly the case with the Montessori Method. As Kohlberg (1968) correctly observes, Montessorian education is simultaneously a philosophy with ideological overtones, an aggregate of concepts of development, learning, and teaching, and a package of specific, concrete materials. Add to this the important component of individual teacher skill and personality. What orchestration of these dimensions is the most productive in terms of objectives sought by the method?

In summary, the research data on record tend to reinforce the idea that Montessori education may benefit the child chiefly in the development of a learning style, including manipulative skills and to some extent curiosity-inventiveness. Montessori children often demonstrate favorable progress in the development of persistence, discrimination learning sets, and attentional responses; but a Montessori preschool experience may be less effective than other more didactic approaches in promoting early academic performance. This statement must be qualified by considering the nature of the children involved. Gains attributable one way or the other to Montessori education seem to vary according to the initial status of the child. Montessorian experience may be more potentially valuable for children with specific deficits than for those whose overall developmental status is average and above.

All of this research suggests that many questions about Montessori education remain to be answered. For example, in what precise ways and for what specific children is the Montessori Method truly superior to other preschool approaches? Does a Montessori preschool experience produce lasting effects on the learning styles and motivational qualities of children? What are the effects on children of a transition from a Montessori school to a regular public school classroom? How are children placed initially in Montessori classrooms by their parents different from children placed in other types of programs? For that matter, are there reliable differences among parents who do and do not elect to place their children in a Montessori school? And, if so, do these differences in parental characteristics condition the effectiveness of Montessorian education?[7] How much variation in Montessori children's behavior is due to the teacher's skill, the didactic materials, and the presence of other children as agents of instruction? The exploration of these questions will require carefully executed research within authentic Montessori classrooms. Obviously, the label *Montessori* does not necessarily make a Montessori classroom. As Pitcher (1966) remarks, Montessori schools in America range from the ultra-orthodox to the "neo-Montessori," in which notable modifications have been made in both methodologies and materials. No one knows what is the best or most appropriate "mix," especially for children whose needs are varied.

CRITIQUE

In a critical analysis of early education programs, the Montessori method can be set apart from many other approaches in the present book. First, the Montessori method has existed for a good many years, thereby providing us with the luxury of historical perspective and an evolution of thought, critical and otherwise, over time and social conditions. Most other curriculum approaches have not yet undergone such an evolution. Second, Montessorian education developed abroad, independent of American public school development, and still thrives outside of the mainstream of American education. These and other factors are stressed in the present section,

---

[7] Only one study relevant to the question of parental differences is known to this writer. Dreyer and Rigler (1969) found no measured differences between the parents of Montessori children and non-Montessori nursery school children on various parent and social attitude scales. Both the small number of parents and the attitude scales involved limit the study's generalizability.

which began with some early reactions to the original Montessori awakening and proceeds to more recent analyses of Montessorian education—especially those concerned with the method's social and language development aspects.

Some Early Reactions to Montessorian Education

Notable among the many early responses to Montessori philosophy and pedagogy were those of Kilpatrick (1914) and Morgan (1912). These reports are representative of those published in North America, most of which dampened the initial enthusiasm for Montessori (only their criticisms will be discussed). The reader should keep in mind the social context and times in which these reports appeared.

Morgan (1912) addressed his criticism primarily to Montessorian philosophy and contentions about learning. A nearly exclusive emphasis placed upon the child's mastery of the physical environment, contended Morgan, blunted the social character of learning. The cultivation and analysis of higher thought processes and feeling, he charged, were crucial elements missing from Montessorian education. Morgan further maintained that to attempt sensory education independently of the acquisition of knowledge about self and real life phenomena was to flirt with total educational failure. Finally, he maintained that Montessori was guilty of a logical conflict in her proposals regarding liberty and discipline. For example, while espousing the "law of liberty," Montessori observed that a teacher must exercise enough authority for the child to distinguish between individual freedom and the good of others. Admittedly, this requires the drawing of a very fine line. Critics of Montessori seem never to have felt comfortable with this facet of her doctrine. Self-expression, usually considered to be the essence of freedom, finds little encouragement from the didactic materials.

While Morgan's critique was among the first to appear in the United States, Kilpatrick's essay (1914) is generally considered to be the most tarnishing exposition. Kilpatrick acknowledged the attitude he sensed to accompany Montessorian education, namely, a feeling that the chains of repressive educational practices were being broken. However, Kilpatrick felt this revolutionary ideal to be presumptious in light of the stirrings of American progressive education. In fact, the concepts and philosophy of progressive education, as articulated by Kilpatrick's colleague John Dewey, were believed to be much more consistent with contemporary theories of learning and child development. Kilpatrick questioned seriously Montessori's assumptions about the transfer of learning. He perceived the Method's success as being based upon excessive practice of highly specific skills which could not be shown to generalize to broader classes of behavior. He also criticized the restriction of children's individuality. In sum, Kilpatrick maintained that Montessori's personal contribution to education and psychology was minor, particularly in view of her heavy reliance upon concepts earlier advanced by Seguin and Pestalozzi.

Despite early criticisms, Montessorian principles and materials have influenced early education throughout America. For example, template materials similar to these authentic Montessorian geometric figures are now commonly found in all types of nursery school and kindergarten classrooms. Photo courtesy of Aline Wolf.

As one of the most respected members of the educational elite in America, Kilpatrick had a deadly impact on Montessorian education. His criticism was probably one basic reason for the relative (and persistent) isolation of Montessorians from other professional educators. Meanwhile, other developments—such as the trend toward progressivism in American education and the exciting influence of theoreticians such as Sigmund Freud (psychoanalytic concepts of child development), Edward Thorndike (learning theory applied to education), and the Gestalt psychologists—attracted the attention of American educators. Montessori is, however, credited with having stimulated innovations in equipment and materials for kindergarten practice in this country. And the fact that her child-centered orientation was firmly consistent with the tenets of progressive education probably added momentum to the forces which were pressing for change at that time.

Recent Analysis

The passage of time has provided an opportunity to place Montessori in a broader, more elaborate context. Emergent social conditions have apparently done much to provoke a revisitation of Montessori by many psychologists and educators. This "second wave" of interest is somewhat paradoxical, since Montessori schools have been operating all over the world for more than fifty years. Nevertheless, American professional journals in psychology and education have shown a noticeable increase in the number of articles pertinent to Montessorian concepts.

In one eminently influential statement, Hunt (1964) has suggested that the relative neglect of Montessori is due in part to dissonance created by a comparison of her educational psychology to the more popular conceptions of her day. For example, implicit in early twentieth-century American psychology, Hunt reasons, were the beliefs that (1) early cognitive experience is unimportant, (2) the development of intelligence is essentially fixed by genetic phenomena (hence, environmental influences are of minor importance), and (3) motivation is essentially a homeostatic process based upon drive reduction. Montessorian educational strategies were, therefore, perceived as basically irrelevant, if not rejected as inaccurate. As the discipline of psychology has matured, these beliefs have been altered (Hunt, 1964). Consequently a more favorable orientation toward Montessori is possible.

In further analysis, Hunt has argued that a significant obstacle has long impeded the process of achieving one's maximum intellectual potential. This obstacle, termed *the problem of the match*, concerns a motivational mechanism critical to the success of an individual's transactions with his environment and the pleasure he derives from them. According to this notion, success and pleasure are dependent upon the degree of incongruity one encounters in new situations. *Incongruity*, as used by Hunt, refers to the gap between one's expectations and abilities and the circumstances (tasks required) with which one must deal in a given situation. If the gap is too large, an individual may withdraw, become fearful, or become apathetic. If no gap exists, one is not motivated to respond in ways which result in learning. At some point between complete congruity and excessive incongruity a situation becomes sufficiently challenging and appealing to prompt constructive responses with concomitant positive affect. This point, called *optimum incongruity*, represents a solution of the problem of the match. Optimum incongruity provides the motivational basis for continuous cognitive growth, or for what Montessori interpreted as spontaneous energy and interest in learning.

Hunt believes that Montessorian materials provided within an atmosphere of personal freedom represent a great step toward a practical solution for the problem of the match. Further, since psychologists and educators do not currently know how to solve these match problems for children from without, it is reasonable to allow children to solve the problem for themselves through the self-selection of appropriate activities and materials. This solution assumes a careful arrangement of well-sequenced events, the acme of which may not be the Montessori method. Thus, Hunt has revealed an important psychological basis for strategies such as Montessori's. Moreover, his basic idea can be likened to Piaget's notion of equilibration.

While the favorable relationships between Montessori practice and current psychological evidence are highlighted by Hunt (1964), so also is the caution customary to the scientist. Foremost among these cautions is that Montessorian didactic materials should not be considered so sacred that innovation and scrupulous evaluation are restrained: whether all the didactic materials designed for retarded and poverty-stricken Italian children seventy years ago are relevant for American children, impoverished or otherwise, is not absolutely clear. Nor should rigidity prevail, Hunt warns, in the use of the materials. A greater variety of experiences, particularly aesthetic ones, may be necessary to provide a more balanced program. Finally, Hunt notes that Montessori's theory lacks heuristic power. In other words, the method is deficient in providing for research which would help to resolve issues raised by the method itself. Related to this caution of Hunt's is the present writer's observation that Montessori teachers and administrators seem more concerned with perfecting their pedagogical technique than with supporting a continuous inquiry into the validity of the methodological procedures involved. Research by outsiders, especially when it may involve some intrusion into the classroom, is often discouraged, if allowed at all. The careful observation of children for purposes of educational decision making is what constitutes "research" in many Montessori classrooms.

Dr. Riley Gardner (1966) of the Menninger Foundation in Topeka, Kansas, has also noted the relevance of Montessorian contributions to current priorities in early cognitive enrichment for children. Focal in his commentary on Montessori's genius are her provision of sensory-motor underpinnings for subsequent conceptual growth and the sophistication of her observational techniques.[8] Gardner likens Montessori's concept of autonomy to that basic to successful psychotherapy. Montessori was concerned with cognitive growth and psychotherapists are concerned with emotional growth, but both are dependent for their success upon self-initiated change. Such change is likely only within a context which is free of negative evaluation and encourages personal responsibility for change. This context, combined with the meaningful activity characteristic of a Montessori child's interactions with reality, is thought to positively influence the development of *cognitive style*, or the characteristic way in which a child perceives, decodes, and encodes sensory input. Riley thus generates an empirical question which may conceivably be answered with controlled research. Perhaps the most telling issue raised by Gardner's analysis is whether the Montessori Method accommodates individual differences among children. Is the same sequence of activities, for example, ideal for all children? Does the prescriptive format blunt individual dif-

---

[8] With few exceptions, notably the developmental psychology of Jean Piaget, theory building in child development has not involved extensive observation of children. Rats and monkeys have been carefully observed, emotionally disturbed adults have been carefully observed, but too infrequently have children been carefully observed.

ferences in creative expression? Is the Montessori Method in actuality a means to "individualize" conformity? In fact, the didactic materials are quick to impose on a child intellectual distinctions made in advance by adults. Whether this feature of the Method is viewed as an asset or a liability will, of course, depend upon one's personal philosophy of education.

Montessori and Piaget   Earlier in this discussion a brief reference was made to the similarity in thinking about Hunt's belief (1964) about Montessori and the problem of the match and Piaget's notion of equilibration. The bridge between these ideas clearly is the child's role as an active learner and a resolver of discrepant events. Piaget himself has not attempted any theoretical connections between his thinking and the conceptual underpinnings of the Montessori Method. Nor is there strong evidence to suggest that Piaget was even influenced by Montessorian thought as he developed his own genetic psychology. Interrelationships between Montessorian and Piagetian thinking, however, have become more striking in recent years. One of the most explicit treatments of possible interrelationships is provided by Elkind (1966), who sees some important parallels and some striking divergences between the two points of view.

Elkind begins by noting that both Piaget and Montessori have a predominantly biological orientation to human development. They also emphasize the normative aspects of behavior more than the concept of individual differences. And certainly both authorities are numbered among history's most astute observers of children. At a deeper level Montessori and Piaget share three fundamental independently developed ideas. The first shared idea ascribes a dual character to nature-nurture interaction. For mental *capacities*, nature is directive and nurture is subordinate; the reverse is true for the *content* of thought. The second idea that Piaget and Montessori share is that mental capacity determines learning. At any developmental level the child's existing mental structures set the limits for learning. To say it another way, the quantity of knowledge acquired by a child does not change the child's qualitative capacity for problem solving. Third, Elkind notes, Piaget and Montessori both seem to support a conceptual relationship between cognitive need and repetitive behavior. A child's repetitive behavior frequently signals the emergence of new cognitive abilities and the need to develop them through activity of one sort or another.

It is significant that such basic ideas about learning and development could come from such differently motivated child study approaches. Piaget, of course, has from the beginning been concerned with pure science, epistemology, and deeply theoretical matters. Montessori, in contrast, was early committed to child welfare and education as a means to better social life in general. Her focus was necessarily upon the pragmatic aspects of child development and education. It is important also to note a basic difference in the curriculum derivations of Piagetian and Montessorian thought (Elkind, 1966). Montessori's emphasis has always been upon a child's learning the discriminant attributes of objects—their sensory characteristics—as the cornerstone of all intellectual development. Piaget's critical concern is causality—learning the effects of actions upon objects and events. In fact, Piaget has recently commented upon this matter, particularly in relation to the Montessori didactic materials (Duckworth, 1973). Among other things, Piaget believes that such materials are too "closed," or excessively predetermined. Too little variation in their use, he argues, limits the contribution of Montessorian materials to genuine intellectual development. This is not to say that Montessorian materials could not be used in more divergent ways for such a purpose. Piaget further places equal, if not greater, value upon the errors that children make in their attempts to solve problems. Teachers can learn much from such errors in Piaget's view. Montessori teachers, again in contrast, place the highest value upon children's correct performance of Montessorian tasks. If children cannot perform without error, they must wait until later before trying again.

Some Further Points of Criticism

Any interpretation of similarities and differences between Montessori and Piaget should recognize that Montessori preceded Piaget on the educational scene by many years. One could argue that Montessori has exerted a much more profound influence on the education of children than has Piaget or any other contemporary figure. Travers (1968), a widely recognized authority on learning psychology, believes otherwise. The important contributions for which Montessori should be recognized are actually few in number, Travers maintains. One contribution is in the form of a pedagogical principle: if children are to create their own learning situation, then activity and freedom of movement are requisite conditions. A second contribution is Montessori's insight that motoric behavior and expression are a function of a child's idiosyncratic physical proportions. Her idea that sensory learning facilitates the later learning of more complex perceptual skills (proactive facilitation) anticipated contemporary psychological thought, as did her (and Seguin's) techniques of elementary discrimination learning. Also anticipatory were Montessori's views on the critical effect of early experiences upon mental development, and her concept of intrinsic motivation upon which the didactic materials were founded. On the other hand, Travers (1968) correctly identifies features of Montessori which are unacceptable to most psychologists today. Among these are the recapitulationism implicit in her concept of development, i.e., that children in the course of their development recapitulate the cultural evolution of man.[9] Another involves the untestable assumptions Montessori made about human nature; these assumptions were apparently a function of her highly

---

[9] Montessori was in good company at the time, for recapitulationism was basic to the theory of G. Stanley Hall (1916), who is generally viewed as the father of modern child psychology.

religious commitment. One does not, however, have to accept Montessori's philosophical assumptions in order to make constructive use of her pedagogical insights.

The motivational power of the Montessori method emerges as the distinctive feature in other analyses (e.g., Morra, 1967). Current motivational theory maintains that children do, in fact, act upon their environment to effect changes rather than simply to maintain a state of psychological equilibrium; such theory also suggests that a variety of stimuli presented across varying sensory modalities will have the effect of maintaining optimal arousal. Theoretically, optimal arousal, a precondition for effective learning, is generated by the Montessori apparatus. Thus, the aggregate of opportunities for an aroused learner to act and effect changes upon his environment may represent the most fertile component of the Method. Furthermore, the child's activity appears to be self-maintaining and essentially independent of artificial rewards.

Less enthusiastic views of Montessori, however, are dispersed liberally in the psychoeducational literature (e.g., Beyer, 1962; Edmondson, 1963; Pitcher, 1966). Generally, the writers have similar criticisms of Montessorian theory and practice. Most authors are skeptical of the many claims made by Montessorians for the dramatic success of the Methods in changing children's behavior. As a matter of fact, most "evaluative reports" of Montessori programs are anecdotal and subjective in nature. Therefore, cautious skepticism is not unwarranted. The failure of the Method to provide for "creative" problem solving is frequently mentioned. So is a lack of attention to the value of social and emotional play. In contemporary thinking, Montessorian inattention to play can be viewed as a serious weakness for two reasons: (1) motor play is thought to be an important medium for emotional development and (2) cooperative, small group play activities have long been considered important for social development. Finally, the relative lack of emphasis upon verbal interaction and language development is occasionally questioned, particularly in light of contemporary developmental psycholinguistics. The criticisms involving social and language development are perhaps most worthy of additional comment. Let us consider first the issues related to social development.

Social Development   Montessori defined *social life* as a continual process of solving social problems, during which one must behave in concert with other people and cooperate in striving toward goals desired by the social collective (Montessori, 1967). Given such a philosophy, it seems odd that the Method is often considered to be at variance with the concept of group adjustment so persuasive in American society. According to Montessori, the pathway to genuine social consciousness is first marked by an identification with one's peer group. This makes possible cohesive action. Such a phenomenon is said to be a natural occurrence when children are placed in a social embryo characterized by purposeful activities. Later the child will develop intellectual concern for customs and laws, leaderships, and organized government.

Montessori's ideas on child growth are so intertwined with her political philosophy that it is her discussion of social group development which probably marks her ideological zenith. Montessori's commitment to the achievement of harmony and mutual cooperation among people cannot be questioned. According to Montessori, this objective requires, among other things, respect for the work of others. The rationale for certain techniques applied in the classroom is clarified by this premise. For example, if an item wanted by one child is being used by another, the first child must wait until his peer has finished.

Relevant to the development of social consciousness are Montessori's views on the function of obedience. This characteristic is seen to unfold naturally in a series of three levels. On the first level, obedience is sporadic because the child lacks ability to obey an order save when it correlates with a "vital urge." In short, the child's capacity to obey is limited until about age 3. During the next three years, a consolidation of powers occurs which allows the child to absorb the wishes of another person and manifest them in behavior (conformity). Thus, the second level is reached. Montessori charged that most public school teachers are satisfied if children achieve this stage and fail to stimulate further development.

Under appropriate circumstances, the second level is succeeded by a higher form of obedience. A child who has reached this third stage says to a significant other in effect, I submit my will to you. I want to obey for I enjoy the feeling it gives me. (This is roughly parallel to the notion of psychological identification discussed so widely in the behavioral sciences literature). The power to obey and experience positive affect as a consequence purportedly is the apex in the growth of the child's *will*. Thus Montessori saw true sociality as requiring a combination of self-imposed controls, initiative, and the will to subordinate oneself in the interest of others. The validity of her pedagogy to achieve such goals of socialization remains to be established. Further, Montessori's views in respect to the development of social behavior are at a highly theoretical level.

Language Development   There can be little disagreement that Montessori did not assume verbal behavior to have much significance in early education. Clearly, the Method depends very little upon verbal interchange to accomplish learning. Equally clear, however, is Montessori's professed appreciation for the complexity and ultimate importance of language. This apparent contradiction may be resolved, in part, by noting Montessori's belief about language. First, she did not believe that language was taught to the child by others. Language occurs as a spontaneous creation (she spoke of an "absorption process" which occurs at an unconscious level in the mind), although it is subject to certain laws which hold for all children (Montessori, 1967, p. 111). A "border line" in the formation of the child's mentality was thought by Montessori to be reached at about age 2½. This was believed to mark a new period, encompassing ages 2½ to 6, during which language is organized. The perfection of syntax and vocabulary development are the child's major tasks during this stage. Consequently, the Montessorian emphasis was upon vocabulary building. Apparently, Montessori felt that syntax refinement comes naturally through the child's interaction with appropriate language models. In spirit, this is similar to the thinking behind the language-lift approaches to language education first discussed in Chapter 4. Of course, much more is known now about selective modeling and the sequence of syntactical development than was known in Montessori's time. The reader will also recall that vocabulary building is not currently viewed as the most powerful technique for language system development (see the section on tutorial approaches to language training in Chapter 4).

Montessori's view of the tremendous "explosiveness" of children's language development in natural settings seemed to reinforce her belief in the general spontaneity of human behavior. Her writings contain frequent references to phenomena presently interpreted in terms of inductive language learning and concept formation. While environmental circumstances were paid their due, Montessori invested most heavily in the idea of genetic determination. Since a capacity for language is species-unique, Montessori reasoned that genetic factors must dominate the process of language development. Among other things, this means a predictable, orderly sequence of development. As evidence, Montessori referred to the apparently fixed progression in children's language development from sounds to syllables to words to sentences. But, apart from emphasizing the importance of a model and providing a strategy for vocabulary development, Montessori offers few specifics to educators concerned with language development and education.

To conclude, Montessori's position on language development is not sufficiently comprehensive to satisfy modern criteria for a theory of language. In view of the complex relationship of language to thought and the current research literature on language acquisition, one can legitimately question the Montessori Method (at least in its original form) for its relative lack of stimulating language activities.

One final note. Montessori herself was unquestionably concerned about and took measures to improve parent education during her long tenure as the principal spokesperson for the Method. In America, however, the parent involvement and education component in many Montessori schools seems limited in comparison to most contemporary models for early childhood education. This writer has often been amazed at the lack of knowledge about Montessorian principles and procedures expressed by many parents whose children are enrolled in Montessori programs. Although there surely are occasions for parental involvement in Montessorian education, this curriculum component does not appear to be very sustained in many schools. There are, of course, notable exceptions, but at issue is the general case. Readers may wish to explore the current practices regarding Montessorian parent involvement and their associated rationale. It seems likely that the nature of a Montessorian learning environment precludes much participation by the children's parents.

SUMMARY   *conclusion*

For Montessori, a spontaneous, natural process of education is primarily a function of learners acting upon their environment—it is not something a teacher does to a child. Individual activity is the source of nourishment for all educational growth. A teacher's principal task is to prepare and order a sequence of activities which capitalizes upon children's innate motive structures. Therefore, the best of all possible educational environments allows the child to develop the powers with which he has been endowed by nature.

The Montessori program for children ages 3 to 6 consists of three broad phases: exercises for practical life, sensory education, and language activities (writing and reading). This Method strives to develop proficiency with the basic tool subjects and basic concepts of geography and science earlier than is customary in conventional American schools. Fundamental is the concept that mental development is related to physical movement or, more specifically, is dependent upon such movement. Therefore, the coordination of motor with mental activity is a guiding Montessorian principle. Montessorian "preschool" education differs from conventional nursery school practice on several grounds, including a lesser emphasis upon group activity, much less attention to fantasy play, and a stronger orientation to pre-academic and early academic skill development.

For the most part, the principles of learning reflected in Montessorian didactic materials are supported by contemporary psychological evidence. In contrast, most of the claims (and testimonials) for Montessorian education have yet to be verified independently by controlled scientific research. With published literature of the past fifty years as evidence one can, however, note that considerable emotionalism surrounds the method. Responses range from a complete acceptance on faith of the entire Montessori complex to cautious objective scrutiny to total rejection on philosophical and methodological grounds. This controversy, as we shall see, is by no means limited to Montessorian early childhood education. Controversy notwithstanding, American educators should be able to profit from many features of the Method, including its stress upon the careful observation of children and the utilization of children's behavior as the criterion for determining the validity of educational procedures.

With control of Montessori teacher training maintained by private societies, it remains to be seen how extensively Montessori education may be extended to young children in America. State departments of public instruction are unlikely to negotiate for tax-supported Montessori schools. Nevertheless, Montessorian techniques of sensory education and concepts of freedom and order have found their way into many nursery schools and kindergartens in this country. There can be little argument over Montessori's lasting influence on early childhood education. As Banta (1966) has observed, four Montessorian orientations are generally relevant for early childhood educators. One is the child-centeredness of the Method. A second is a concern for learning style development based upon freedom. A third is the contribution of structure as an assist to this freedom. And a fourth is a commitment to the child's moral development so as to promote "responsible" freedom, that is, freedom without license.

REFERENCES

Banta, T. Is there really a Montessori method? Paper read at the meeting of the Ohio Psychological Association and Ohio Psychiatric Association, Cincinnati, Ohio, February 1966.

Banta, T. *The Sands school project: first year results.* Cincinnati, Ohio: University of Cincinnati, Department of Psychology, 1967.

Beller, E. K. Research on organized programs of early education. In R. Travers (ed.), *Second handbook of research on teaching.* Skokie, Ill.: Rand McNally, 1973, 530–600.

Berger, B. An investigation of Montessori vs. conventional pre-kindergarten training with inner city children: an assessment of learning outcomes. Paper read at the meeting of the American Educational Research Association, Los Angeles, February 1969.

Beyer, E. Let's look at Montessori. *Journal of Nursery Education*, 1962, *18*, 4–9.

Blank, M., and F. Solomon. A tutorial language program to develop abstract thinking in socially disadvantaged preschool children. *Child Development*, 1968, *39*, 379–389.

Bruner, J. The act of discovery. *Harvard Educational Review*, 1961, *31*, 124–135.

Coladarci, A. The relevancy of educational psychology. *Educational Leadership*, 1956, *13*, 489–492.

Concannon, J. A review of research on haptic perception. *Journal of Educational Research*, 1970, *63*, 250–252.

Craig, R. *The psychology of learning in the classroom.* New York: Crowell-Collier-Macmillan, 1966.

Deese, J., and S. Hulse. *The psychology of learning.* (3rd ed.) New York: McGraw-Hill, 1967.

Dreyer, A., and D. Rigler. Cognitive performance in Montessori and nursery school children. *Journal of Educational Research*, 1969, *62*, 411–416.

Duckworth, E. Piaget takes a teacher's look. *Learning*, 1973, *2*, 22–27.

Edmondson, B. Let's do more than look—let's research Montessori. *Journal of Nursery Education*, 1963, *18*, 20–25.

Elliot, L. Montessori's reading principles involving sensitive period method compared to reading principles of contemporary reading specialists. *Reading Teacher*, 1967, *21*, 163–168.

Elkind, D. Piaget and Montessori. *Harvard Educational Review*, 1966, *36*, 535–545.

Feshbach, N., and G. Devor. Teaching styles in four-year-olds. *Child Development*, 1969, *40*, 183–190.

Fisher, M. Educational assumptions for constructing objectives and evaluating programs for culturally disadvantaged children. *ERIC: ED 047 047*, 1971.

Gardner, R. A psychologist looks at Montessori. *Elementary School Journal*, 1966, *67*, 72–83.

Glaser, R., J. Reynolds, and M. Fullick. Studies of the use of programmed instruction in the intact classroom. *Psychology in the Schools*, 1966, *3*, 318–333.

Guthrie, E. *The psychology of learning.* New York: Harper & Row, 1935.

Hall, G. S. *Adolescence.* 2 vols. New York: Appleton, 1916.

Hunt, J. McV. *Revisiting Montessori. Introduction to the Montessori Method.* New York: Schocken Books, 1964.

Johnson, H. The effects of Montessori educational techniques on culturally disadvantaged Head Start children. *ERIC: ED 015 009,* 1965.

Kilpatrick, W. H. *The Montessori system examined.* Boston: Houghton Mifflin, 1914.

Kohlberg, L. Montessori with the culturally disadvantaged: a cognitive-developmental interpretation and some research findings. In R. Hess and R. Bear (eds.), *Early education.* Chicago: Aldine, 1968, 105–118.

Martin, J. Montessori after 50 years. *Teachers College Record,* 1965, *67,* 552–554.

McCormick, C., and J. Schnobrick. Longitudinal corroboration of a cross-sectional study of development of preschool children with the Arrow-Dot test. *Perceptual and Motor Skills,* 1970, *30,* 269–270.

Meyer, W. *Developmental psychology.* New York: Center for Applied Research in Education, 1964.

Miller, B. Montessori: the model for preschool education? *Grade Teacher,* 1965, *82,* 36–39, 112–117.

Miller, L. Experimental variations of Head Start curricula: a comparison of current approaches. Louisville, Ky.: University of Louisville, Department of Psychology, 1972.

Montessori, M. *Dr. Montessori's own handbook.* New York: Frederick A. Stokes, 1914.

Montessori, M. *The Montessori elementary material.* Cambridge, Mass.: Robert Bentley, 1965. (a)

Montessori, M. Spontaneous activity in education. Cambridge, Mass.: Robert Bentley, 1965. (b)

Montessori, M. *The absorbent mind.* New York: Holt, Rinehart and Winston, 1967.

Morgan, S. *The Montessori method: an exposition and criticism.* Toronto: Ontario Department of Education, 1912. Bulletin No. 1.

Morra, M. The Montessori method in light of contemporary views of learning and motivation. *Psychology in the Schools,* 1967, *4,* 48–53.

Naumann, T. Behavioral interaction analysis: a new approach in child study. Ellensberg, Wash.: Central Washington State College, Department of Psychology, 1966.

Naumann, T. Academic learning of young children in a Montessori class. Paper read at the Mental Health Research Meeting, University of Washington, Seattle, November 1967.

Naumann, T., and B. Parsons. A creative learning environment for normal and handicapped pupils. *American Montessori Society Bulletin,* 1965, Spring, 31–35.

Perryman, L., et al. (eds.). *Montessori in perspective.* Washington, D.C.: National Association for the Education of Young Children, 1966.

Pitcher, E. An evaluation of the Montessori method in schools for young children. *Childhood Education,* 1966, *42,* 489–492.

Plank, E. Reflection on the revival of the Montessori Method. *Journal of Nursery Education,* 1962, *17,* 131–136.

Rambusch, N. *Learning how to learn: an American approach to Montessori.* Baltimore: Helicon Press, Inc., 1962.

Rock, I. Repetition and learning. *Scientific American,* 1958, *199,* 68–72.

Smith, T. The Montessori system in theory and practice. New York: Harper, 1912.

Standing, E. M. *The Montessori revolution in education.* New York: Schocken Books, 1966.

Taminen, A. An evaluation of a preschool training program for culturally deprived children. Final report. *ERIC: ED 019 135,* 1967.

Torrance, E. P. *Torrance tests of creative thinking.* Princeton, N.J.: Personnel Press, 1966.

Travers, R. Analysis of the characteristics of children implicit in the Montessori method. In J. Frost (ed.), *Early childhood education rediscovered.* New York: Holt, Rinehart and Winston, 1968, 96–101.

Willcott, P. Initial American reception of the Montessori method. *School Review*, 1968, *76*, 147–165.

Photograph courtesy of J. Myron Atkin.

*open
education*

Several approaches already discussed in this book—notably the Bank Street method (Chapter 2), The Tucson Early Education Model (Chapter 4), and Piagetian approaches (Chapter 5)—are varyingly consistent with a philosophical position described by the term *open education*. The open education philosophy of how children's learning and development occur cannot be separated from the values espoused by its advocates (Barth, 1972). The psychological dimension of this approach, for example, is dominated by ideas about children's motivation (innate curiosity; mechanisms of activity, exploratory behavior), the social nature of learning, individual differences in rate and style of intellectual development, and a general permissiveness toward socialization.

Despite these unifying themes and the inclusiveness of the phrase, the term *open* is subject to much leeway in interpretation. For some it refers to spatial arrangements—the *open classroom* or a school without walls. For others it means simply an open system of communication among all persons involved in the educational enterprise. For still others it means having an open mind about education in general. All of these ideas are pertinent. But according to most writers (e.g., MacDonald, 1970), the essence of open education is a concept of *transaction*. Open education is therefore defined as a form of education organized to facilitate transactions characterized by freedom of choice and highly individualized activity. In contrast, a *closed* system of education is based upon roles that must be enacted in certain predetermined ways. In theory, the objectives, content, and procedures for learning in open education arise from an array of classroom alternatives and are the collective outcome of transactions between a teacher and children working together as joint decision makers. This process of transaction is the most highly valued element in open education; intellectual education becomes more an incidental than an explicit, overriding goal—especially in terms of programming specified academic experiences. Structure emerges from, rather than dictates in advance, the learning children experience. Development of the individual child is the ultimate source of curriculum development. A playful attitude of self-expression and "messing about" with all kinds of learning materials is encouraged. Teachers stimulate but never coerce or dominate. Fact accumulation, then, gives way to a process of inquiry for inquiry's sake. And, perhaps most importantly, open education is oriented to children as persons, not as objects to be manipulated (Spodek, 1970). Trust and respect for children are basic principles of classroom interaction. In this sense, open education is consistent with humanistic psychology in America (Stephens and Evans, 1973).

Given this thumbnail sketch of its characteristics, the reader may view open education as a new name for the American progressive education of the 1930s. Modern-day open education certainly has much in common with the rhetoric of progressive education. But the concept of open education has evolved from different roots, with the most recent impetus being provided by educational practices for young children in Britain. Known as the new British infant school movement, or innovation in English primary schools, informal education in Britain has awakened a sleeping giant of educational thought in America. In this chapter the new British infant school movement is discussed first. Then examples of open education efforts in America are described. These major sections are followed by commentaries on the "free school" movement and recent developments in affective education. These last two developments can be viewed as a means to "open up" the classroom experiences of young children to include more than just intellectual-academic content.

THE BRITISH INFANT SCHOOL MOVEMENT

Increased interest among American educators in "informal education" for young children is in large part a function of innovations observed in selected British infant schools. These infant schools are generally equivalent to the kindergarten-primary grades in American school systems; they enroll children from ages 5 to seven or eight. From the infant schools, children go on to junior schools designed to accommodate children until about age 11.

A document that has done much to direct the attention of American educators to the British infant school movement is a government-sponsored study of early education in England and Wales known as the Plowden report (Plowden, 1967). This report provides (1) a survey of the status of early education in England and (2) proposals for needed educational reform. Among other things, this elaborate document includes favorable references to the informal classroom procedures followed in about one-third of the infant schools in England. These procedures are seen as resulting from a "tradition of revolution" which has influenced England over the past several decades.

This tradition of revolution has several key elements (Featherstone, 1967). One is the latitude of freedom among school personnel to determine what will go into a curriculum—a freedom which if exploited can contribute substantially to educational reform. A second element of this tradition is a gradual role shift among the governmental educational officials responsible for overseeing public instruction. This change in role from "inspector-evaluator" to "advisor," has been especially noticeable in the schools of Leicestershire County, England. It was in Leicestershire County that experimentation with informal educational procedures began in earnest. A third aspect of the infant school revolutionary tradition is the insights from contemporary developmental psychology which have shaped English educators' concepts of children's learning and motivation. Piagetian psychology is most widely acknowledged as the source of these insights. It would perhaps be more accurate to say that good practice has generally preceded, if not outdistanced, the theoretical underpinnings (Perrone, 1972).

The following comments concerning British infant school practice are based primarily upon schools which have patterned themselves on the Leicestershire County plan; these comments do not apply to *all* British infant schools. For purposes of discussion, the term *new infant school* will be used.

General Features of the Infant School Movement

One source for the descriptive assessment of evolutionary new infant school practices is provided by L. G. W. Sealey (1966). For nine years (1956–1965), Sealey served as an advisor to the Leicestershire County schools. Sealey's advisory strategy was organized around *growth points*, program components that provide evidence of change. Sealey got personally involved in the day-to-day workings of the Leicestershire County schools and became an intermediary for change. He allied himself with teachers who shared his goal. As forces for change were mobilized, mutually supported new patterns for learning were created. It should be noted that the changes in infant schools have largely been due to the initiative and creativity of teachers—not to proposals developed by "experts" outside the classroom.

The Integrated Day Among the most significant new patterns developed from a growth point is the integrated day.[1] An integrated day has

---

[1] Much of the credit for this concept has been given to an American advisor in Leicestershire County, Dr. Anthony Kallet.

no class lessons based upon prescribed time allotments. Rather, class-rooms are typically organized into various learning centers—one for general purpose activity, a second for science and mathematics, a third for visual arts, and a fourth for reading and language arts (Sealey, 1966). Some classrooms may also be equipped with programmed learning materials and other supplements. The personnel of new infant schools believe that, if aided by subtle teacher guidance, children will accept the responsibility to synthesize their own learning experiences—some of which may be fleeting and others of which may involve several weeks of related activity. Neat, tidy, and fettered teacher-centered learning activities are therefore rare. Children's productivity and teacher skill in planning and organizing the learning centers are seen as directly related, although children usually assist in such planning. Sealey maintains that the physical and curricular rearrangements in infant schools are probably less important than the freedom to experiment these rearrangements make possible. The following example of an integrated learning experience can provide the reader with a general idea of this important feature of infant school practice.

> When a class of seven-year-olds notice(s) the birds that come to the bird table outside the classroom window, they may decide, after discussion with their teacher, to make their own aviary. They will set to with a will, and paint the birds in flight, make models of them in clay or papier mâché, write stories and poems about them and look up reference books to find out more about their habits. Children are not assimilating inert ideas but are wholly involved in thinking, feeling and doing. The slow and the bright share a common experience and each takes from it what he can at his own level. There is no attempt to put reading and writing into separate compartments; both serve a wider purpose, and artificial barriers do not fragment the learning experience (Plowden, 1967, p. 199).[2]

The sort of project described above lends itself to a full deployment of interest centers, individual interests and levels of conceptual involvement, independent and cooperative planning and thinking, and task-oriented social interaction. The work flow is not interrupted by artificial time barriers and subject matter divisions. Furthermore, such a pupil-centered orientation gives a teacher as much freedom as she needs to spend more time with individual children. On the surface, such a policy has a high potential for dealing with the wide range of individual differences typical of any classroom group.

Other accounts of new infant school practices—notably those in Leicestershire County, England—are consistent with the pattern suggested above. Hawkins and Hawkins (1964), for example, have noted that children spend most of their time pursuing activities of their own choice. Integrated learning episodes take precedence over specified periods for separate subject orientations, an instructional principle inherent in the bird study

---

[2] Reproduced by permission of Her Majesty's Stationery Office.

example described above. Instead of being confronted successively with reading, art, arithmetic, and writing periods, children are free to engage in painting or ceramics, nature study or experimentation, writing stories about these experiences, and exchanging stories in order to read about the activities their peers have pursued. In a classroom of thirty children, thirty different classroom activities may be occurring simultaneously, although small clusters of children are often seen working together on "mutually absorbing" tasks. The following personal observation of Yeomans (1969) exemplifies further the panorama of new infant school activities based upon the integrated day concept:

> Forty to forty-five children, ages 5 through 7, attached to the room, but not necessarily in it, with one teacher.
>
> Focal-points, consisting of tables, chairs, bookshelves, bins, lockers, pegboards, sinks, a carpentry bench, a clay table, a stove, easels, and a sand table, all placed around the walls or in the middle of the room, or out on the terrace if the weather was good.
>
> Two girls in the "Wendy House" (a child-sized playhouse), dressed in Victorian costumes, serving "tea" to each other and to passers-by.
>
> A "green-grocer's" store (small booth and bright-colored awning) in which a 7-year-old and his 5-year-old helper are selling stage fruits, for stage money, to a line of customers being particular about the change.
>
> A small individual reading alone in a nook partitioned off from the outer bustle by screens that double as bookshelves.
>
> Two boys and a girl sawing and sandpapering wood on the carpenter's bench on the terrace.
>
> Three others painting at easels on the terrace.
>
> An animal-lover feeding the hamster; another observing the tadpoles in an aquarium.
>
> A group of six at tables in the center of the room with the teacher, working with attribute blocks and plastic and wooden shapes which, when combined correctly, make geometric patterns in either two or three dimensions.
>
> An older and a younger child at another table reading aloud to each other.
>
> A group of four making clay animals at the clay table.
>
> This does not account for all forty-five, for the others were out of the room engaged in various projects. Teaching was taking place, but

in orthodox ways. The teacher had an eye for everything and everyone, but the children typically sought her aid on problems that were occupying them. She would visit a group of children writing stories and help them with their spelling; or hear an individual read aloud; or suggest another way of pressing clay into a mould; or invite someone she thought had been doing puzzles long enough to try reading this book. Older children were helping younger ones and then turning back to their own work (Yeomans, 1969, pp. 13–14).[3]

The activities Yeomans describes would not be possible without a wide variety of multi-purpose raw materials for learning. Such materials need not be expensive or prepared in advance for specific purposes. What is important is the provision of a variety of materials suitable for the children's "natural learning environment." A teacher has the responsibility to see that such materials are used constructively. Constructive use of classroom materials can occur at different times and different levels depending upon childrens' intentions and their perceptions of the properties of the materials. There is no established formula for an integrated day; diversity in the degree of structure, groupings and content in infant school classrooms is the rule rather than the exception (Yeomans, 1969).

Vertical Groupings   A second growth point has evolved from a modification of grouping practices. In lieu of instructional groups formed homogeneously according to age, measured intelligence, or other arbitrary criteria, the policy of *vertical* or *family* grouping is preferred in many new infant schools. This means that classes are composed of children from ages 5 to 7 or 8, who intermingle for learning and recreational activities.[4] It also means that a child is likely to spend his entire infant school life with one teacher or with two teachers who share the responsibility for two classes. This "unclassification" makes it possible for a cross-section of an entire school population to be represented in each classroom. New infant school teachers have reported that such organization emphasizes individuality, rather than disguising it under the cloak of artificial age and/or ability grouping practices. Vertical grouping also eliminates the many hours required each year for a teacher to become acquainted with successive new classes. Instead, a teacher may grow increasingly aware of pupil needs and learning styles over a two- or three-year period with the same children and their parents.

Not all new infant schools practice vertical groupings; nor is there a consensus about the advantages of this organizational concept (Blackie, 1967). In final analysis the method of organization is surely less significant than the quality of infant school teaching faculties. Nevertheless, members of the Central Advisory Council for Education (England), whose

---

[3] Reproduced by permission of the National Association of Independent Schools.

[4] The reader may recall the rationale for this strategy proposed formally by Montessori (see Chapter 6).

These Inner London children are justifiably proud of their cardboard carton and papier-mâché camel. Their study of Arab lands has focused on all aspects of life styles, including dress, transportation, and literature. Photo courtesy of J. Myron Atkin.

studies culminated in the Plowden report were impressed by the "liveliness and good quality" of the activity in vertically grouped infant schools. Council members found the advantages of vertical groupings to outweigh the disadvantages, at least for purposes of infant school education.[5] Supportive evidence for this practice is largely anecdotal, and no particular advantage for double or triple age grouping has been reported in junior school practice.

Additional Components of Infant School Practice The integrated day and vertical groupings are two of the most significant new infant school growth points. Other policies have evolved, however, as several reports have indicated (Blackie, 1967; Sealey, 1966; Yeomans, 1969). The broadest

---

[5] Among possible disadvantages are children's being exposed for an extended time to the weaknesses of a given teacher; younger children being overpowered by older class members; and limited adult contact. However, all of these pitfalls can be easily avoided or remedied by alert professionals.

of these additional policies concerns a refocus of educational objectives. Specific, convergent, and factual outcomes ostensibly are assigned a substantially lower priority than a *thought process orientation*. In other words, a greater value is placed upon inductive thinking and the development of problem-solving strategies. This value has implications in the provision, selection, and use of materials (see Yeomans, 1969, for evidence of these implications). As Yeomans (1969) has put it, a child's work manner—the quality of his self-control and responsibility—is considered more relevant to educational development than is the child's absolute level of academic achievement.

Another conceptual accent in new infant school policy is an avoidance of the work-play dichotomy described as so firmly entrenched in traditional schools. The potential of children's play for the achievement of worthwhile learning objectives and the general value assigned to *play activity* is communicated by the following passage:

> Play is the central activity in all nursery schools and in many infant schools. This sometimes leads to accusations that children are wasting their time in school: they should be working. But this distinction between work and play is false, possibly throughout life, certainly the primary school. Its essence lies in past notions of what is done in school hours (work) and what is done out of school (play). We know now that play—in the sense of "messing about" either with material objects or with other children, and of creating fantasies—is vital to children's learning and therefore vital in school. Adults who criticise teachers for allowing children to play are unaware that play is the principal means of learning in early childhood. It is the way through which children reconcile their inner lives with external reality. In play, children gradually develop concepts of causal relationships, the power to discriminate, to make judgments, to analyze and synthesize, to imagine and to formulate. Children become absorbed in their play and the satisfaction of bringing it to a satisfactory conclusion fixes habits of concentration which can be transferred to other learning (Plowden, 1967, p. 193).[6]

The reader will recall that a similar idea about play is fundamental to traditional American nursery school practice (see Chapter 2). Moreover, educational practice based upon the work-play dichotomy has been identified as one of several variables associated with differences in children's creative output (Torrance, 1963). That is, a low frequency of divergent thinking responses has been noted in classrooms characterized by an "austere, no-fun" atmosphere in which school activities, apart from recess, are clearly labeled by teachers as work to be endured.

Also consistent with the pupil-centeredness of new infant school practice is another policy accent: an attitude among teachers that children

---

[6] Reproduced by permission of Her Majesty's Stationery Office.

can be trusted to do their own learning.[7] Coercive measures designed to force children's learning are avoided. So are artificial incentives. Motivational strategies which capitalize on children's exploratory responses and natural curiousity are preferred. This trust in the child's capacity for initiative and responsibility has undoubtedly been fostered by improved professional relationships between classroom teachers and their superiors. According to Blackie (1967), a major force behind the infant school revolution has been the conviction that teachers do their best work if allowed to exercise their initiative and judgment at every opportunity. In short, greater teacher productivity is likely when teachers are given liberty and responsibility by administrators rather than when teachers are closely directed, circumscribed, and obligated to follow a set program.

Another feature of new infant school practice which has impressed many American observers is the apparent lack of obsession over children's futures among teachers. Instead, the prevalent teaching value is to make the most of a child's current learning situation. In other words, the enrichment of children's lives in infant school takes precedence over a concern about what they will be able to do at the end of one, two, or three years. This is several degrees removed from most American approaches, which gauge program effectiveness in terms of long-range results. It would be a mistake to assume, however, that new infant school teachers have shed the responsibility for children's school futures. Rather, these teachers are committed to the idea that the best assurance a child has for the future is a meaningful, absorbing, and productive present. After having read about new infant schools, American observers often are surprised to find that such schools can be very academic places.

More managerial-related components of new infant school practice worthy of note include the team efforts of teachers, intended as a means to capitalize upon each other's strengths and experience as well as to divide various classroom responsibilities. The open space concept of classroom organization is fully endorsed as well. Finally, a serious effort has been made over the years to establish compatible school-parent relationships. From all reports, communications between parents and teachers, parental support of and satisfaction with school practices, and parental visitation in the schools are frequent and generally positive. Even so, infant school headmasters are invested with a striking amount of authority to move in whatever directions they deem desirable. Parental objections can be overruled with little argument. For better or worse, this authority often borders on paternalism. In view of the politicization of American education, such local autonomy would not be likely to thrive here. However, one important and oft-overlooked feature of British early education

---

[7] Observers of American educational practice, in contrast, conclude that if teachers' attitudes can be inferred from their classroom behavior, American teachers generally do not believe that children can be trusted to do their own learning. See C. Rogers (1967) for a treatment of this issue.

probably mediates this school-home relationship. Infant schools rarely exceed an enrollment of 300 children, and these schools draw upon a comparatively small community of people. A headmaster, with a typical staff of ten teachers, is in a position to know well the children and the community the school serves. Under most conditions curriculum practices can be personalized and articulated to parents better than, say, in larger American elementary schools. At issue is school size and its effect on a general sense of community among all concerned.

Commentary on Innovative Practices

According to Susan Williams (the director of Gordonbrock Infant School in London, 1967), the greatest difference between the "new" and "old" infant school approach is the new schools' use of cues from children to guide learning rather than the use of a lesson prepared in advance. This difference requires that the new infant school teacher be alert at all times for signs of "readiness" from the children. Thus while overall planning and master objectives are always subtly present, specific advance planning is played down. New teachers are advised above all to *talk with the children* to find out about their interests and past experiences. Occasionally, lessons of a more formal nature are conducted with small groupings of children who are "ready" for such an experience. Rules exist, but largely to prevent chaos. While a playlike atmosphere seems to dominate new infant school classrooms, teachers generally insist that children must either write or talk about what they have done. This can be considered as something of a system of accountability. An order to the child's learning is assumed, i.e., concrete experiences *precede* labeling or describing. Such an order, it may be recalled, is consistent with a Piagetian view of developmental learning and, as mentioned earlier, new infant school practices are generally consistent with cognitive-developmental theory. Both the Plowden report (1967) and Blackie's *Inside the Primary School* (1967) contain frequent references to Piagetian concepts for educational strategy. For many British educators, these concepts represent the best that is known about the nature of children's development. Cognitive-developmental theory also points up the need for individual approaches to learning, and it has been around this need that the entire new infant school movement has been organized.

Some Problems and Issues

What has developed in selected British infant schools may seem to be close to an educational Utopia. But, as with any educational approach, problems can be noted (Blackie, 1967; Grannis, 1973; Hawkins and Hawkins, 1964; Yeomans, 1969). Some of these problems are beyond the immediate control of teachers; others are perhaps inherent in any attempt at "open education." In the first category is the problem of overcrowded classrooms. As class enrollments increase, so does the density of demands for teachers to (1) plan, coordinate, and integrate individual learning activities and (2) assist each child frequently and constructively.[8] With such a high demand density, teachers may not conduct a sufficient number of task-oriented discussions nor provide adequate and frequent summaries of activities. Monitoring of progress, especially the diagnosing of learning difficulties, can become grossly weak. Obviously, not just any teacher is capable of coordinating a classroom of thirty to forty children in which genuine pupil-centered instruction is applied. Success in any case is highly dependent upon individual teaching skill; new infant school methods, like any other educational methods, are not foolproof. As Blackie (1967, p. 50) has remarked, "No method is better than the teacher who is using it." This remark does not mean that method is irrelevant and that all children really need is a "good" teacher. Rather, new infant school methods are thought to take good account of both subject matter and the nature of children. Therefore, these methods should be "better" in the hands of a strong teacher than would other methods in the same teacher's hands— methods that account for neither subject matter nor the course of children's development. Whether new infant school teachers are better than, say, American primary teachers is a moot question. What is impressive to this writer about the infant school movement is the dedication of school faculties to self-analysis and continued improvement.[9] It is remarkable that so many English teachers can apparently implement a style of education which Americans consider applicable only in small classes.

Considering that infant school teachers have been delegated such heavy responsibility for curriculum development and that individual teacher skill is so critical for new infant school success, the problem of monitoring the infant school enterprise can be raised. In other words, what measures have been taken to prevent anarchy or a proliferation of incompetent teaching? Observers generally have not expressed fear that practices will deteriorate without close control, possibly because several checkpoints exist for purposes of monitoring the system. These checkpoints are (1) separate organizational authorities, which in combination facilitate school and classroom inspection; (2) widespread exchange of teaching ideas; (3) formal procedures to provide for school and curriculum improvement, extensive in-service training, and teachers' control of their own work (Blackie, 1967).[10]

---

[8] Crowded classroom conditions in many infant schools are apparently a function of (1) statutory restrictions (one new teacher for every forty new children in 1964) and (2) a shortage of teachers. Class size is perhaps a lesser issue than school size, as was implied in the discussion of a sense of community among teachers, parents, and children.

[9] Hawkins and Hawkins (1964) report, for example, that new infant school teachers regularly visit each other's classrooms to evaluate practices and share new ideas. Such visitations are virtually unheard of in American schools.

[10] These organizations include Her Majesty's Inspectorate of Schools, local education authorities, and the Schools Council for Curriculum and Examinations. For details on the structure and functions of these bodies, see Blackie (1967).

A second problem, particularly notable throughout the Leicestershire experiment, was a frustrating and long period of transition from a formal to a self-directed instructional approach. This period of adjustment for both teacher and children can hardly be used as a logical argument against the policy of open education, but it does point to á hazard to be overcome. Perhaps more critical is the transition for children from the informal atmosphere of a new infant school to that of a traditionally operated junior school. Few reports have treated this transition on systematic empirical basis, and most observers express concern over the lack of school continuity in many parts of England. There is some evidence that junior school practices are becoming more "relaxed."[11] Yet junior schools in general represent a vivid contrast to the Leicestershire County infant school concept. Perhaps the most concrete evidence for junior school change is the gradual abolishment of the traditional "eleven-plus" examination, an achievement test administered for years to children as they completed their primary school education. British educators then used the results of this achievement battery to determine the direction of children's secondary school education. Children who failed this test were virtually excluded from a secondary education which would qualify them for eventual college or university entrance. The intense pressures of the eleven-plus examination apparently contributed in the past to inflexible curricula, a lack of experimentation and innovation in the schools, and to undesirable social and economic side effects among children who failed.

Evaluation in Infant School Practice   According to Sealey (1966), many infant school innovations have been introduced gradually and unsystematically. Perhaps because of this, formal research evaluations were rare during Sealey's tenure as advisor (1956–1965). Sealey reports that in lieu of psychometric assessment, four evaluative criteria fostered the growth of "creative" infant school practice:

1. Whether or not teachers and children desire to continue a new procedure.
2. The extent to which "sense of fun" is engendered by new learning experiences.
3. Whether a new learning situation involves children actively and induces persistence.
4. The degree to which a new experience or procedure helps a teacher to be more responsive to children's individual needs.

Underlying this approach is a generalized belief that appropriate means to evaluate the purported outcomes of new infant school practice are not currently available. As Barth (1969) puts it, the evaluative assump-

---

[11] Implicit in this relaxation is the assumption that what is desirable for the infant school population is equally desirable for the junior school population— an assumption which requires close examination.

tion is twofold: (1) that the best measure of a child's work is his work; and (2) that one needs to observe the cumulative effects of experience over long periods before evaluation of a child's progress is relevant. For the latter purpose, anecdotal records, *jottings*, are taken continually to log the characteristics and progress of individual children. As these jottings accumulate a teacher is believed to be able to develop a comprehensive academic and social portrait of individual children from which to glean teaching cues. Thus, pupil evaluation is less a matter of accounting a child's achievement than a matter of seeking data for planning purposes.

A de-emphasis of traditional means for pupil evaluation, especially standardized achievement testing, may be disturbing to educators who value technical evidence, e.g., empirical statements of validity and reliability. In England, however, this trend toward less formal evaluations may continue if the recommendations of the Plowden report (1967) are accepted:

> We have considered whether we can lay down standards that should be achieved by the end of the primary school but concluded that it is not possible to describe a standard of attainment that should be reached by all or most children. Any set standard would seriously limit the bright child and be impossibly high for the dull. What could be achieved in one school might be impossible in another. We have suggested . . . that, with the ending of selection examinations, teachers—and parents—will need some yardstick of the progress of their children in relation to what is achieved elsewhere. Without it teachers may be tempted to go on teaching and testing in much the same way as they did before. We therefore envisage that some use will continue to be made of objective tests within schools. Such tests can be helpful—and then norms can serve on a basis of comparison—as long as they are used with insight and discrimination and teachers do not assume that only what is measurable is valuable. (Plowden, 1967, pp. 201–202).[12]

Evaluative Research and Observational Reports

Comprehensive reports of systematic, controlled research about new infant school practice are not readily available; nor for that matter do many exist. Perhaps the best single source of general data is the Plowden report (1967). Concerning children's reading achievement, for example, the authors of this report point to a general rise in achievement among Britain's children since the late 1940s. Other data published by Britain's Department of Education and Science indicate that eleven-year-old children in 1964 were reading on an average level of 17 months higher than had their counterparts in 1948 (Sobel and Tejirian, 1973). For whatever reasons, this trend in increased reading standards seems to have leveled off during the late 1960s and early 1970s and may even be a little lower than the

---

[12] Reproduced by permission of Her Majesty's Stationery Office.

mid-sixties (Start, 1972). Despite this puzzling situation, new infant school proponents argue that informal education does not impair children's reading ability and may contribute to higher levels. Such an argument is appealing but hazardous. Since the data were taken from children in all types of junior schools, clear comparisons of those who had attended new as opposed to traditional infant schools were not made. One comparative study of matched pairs of formal and informal (new) infant school children covering a period from 1951 to 1963 is available, however (Silberman, 1970). Several tests of achievement and attitude served as criterion measures in this large study, the results of which generally favored the new infant school children. Specific areas of advantage included spoken and written English, drawing and painting, attention and memory, "neatness," "ingenuity," and breadth and depth of extra-school interests. The superiority of one educational approach over another cannot be proven with only a few data, but supporters of new infant schools maintain that any fears that parents (and teachers) may have about deteriorating standards under conditions of informal education are largely unjustified. This is particularly interesting given that the most recent surveys of children leaving infant school reveal that increasing numbers of them have made only a bare start in learning to read and require "infant methods" in reading during the junior school years (Start, 1972). In sum, the data are so mixed that it is difficult to say whether many children's reading progress is impeded by informal methods, whether a freer and relaxed approach lends itself to desirable delays in reading instruction, or whether junior school practices are somehow implicated. Another variable is the kind of reading skills measured. Within the informal approach a child's attitude about reading and how he uses his mechanical skills for personal benefit are at least as important, if not more so, than mere fluency (V. Rogers, 1971).

Of course, it is risky to generalize about broad educational approaches. The issue is whether informal (or formal) education is more or less suitable for all children, regardless of their circumstances, stage of development, and educational needs. Even when they reveal a general advantage for the "average child," gross comparisons may upon careful analysis be shown as differentially effective for some and ineffective for other children. This comment holds for any method comparison design, not just the present formal-informal question.

Aside from providing a source of general survey data about children's achievement, the Plowden report has generated a program of action research about the educational needs of preschool children in Britain which will presumably have implications for infant school practice and parent education (Halsey, 1972). The National Children's Bureau in London also has a number of related research projects under way which bear upon early school practices and accomplishments in England. In the meantime, we must content ourselves with tangential studies of new infant school phenomena and a growing body of anecdotal reports about what goes on in such schools. Examples of somewhat tangential research in-

Movement activity in this English school takes place in a large, general purpose room. Here, and almost everywhere in England, the children shed their outer garments for dance and bodily movement activity. The work in movement offers considerable opportunity for spontaneity and expressiveness on the part of the children. In many local education authorities, movement work is considered central to the informal curriculum approaches that are being explored. Photo courtesy of J. Myron Atkin.

clude the study of the relationship between anxiety and ability grouping (streaming) in progressive and traditional schools (Levy, Gooch, and Kellmer-Pringle, 1969); teacher-child interaction in new infant school settings (Resnick, 1971); and the influence of infant–junior school transitions upon reading achievement (Shields, 1969).

But the variety of casual observational data continues to dominate the thinking of practitioners interested in open, or informal, education. Although this state of affairs may be unsatisfying from many points of view, independent (albeit subjective) observational reports of new infant school operations do seem to be reliable. At least observers indicate in their reports that they are seeing and being impressed by the same general features (e.g., Chittendon, 1973).

According to most observers, the highest relative levels of achievement attained by new infant school pupils are in the arts. High degrees of inventiveness with wood, cloth, and clay; a sharp increase in the number of children who elect to pursue instrumental music; and evidence of creative body movement are reported. But the skill in reading and free writing shown by infant school children seems to produce the most awe in American observers. This is largely because no "classes" in reading and writing are held. Teaching in these skill areas generally is confined to an individual basis with many methods and materials placed at the disposal of teachers and children. The guiding principle is to enjoin and coordinate reading and writing with moment-to-moment learning activities. According to the reports of new infant school teachers, if a child does not learn readily he is rarely the object of worry or increased instructional effort. This provides a sharp contrast to the uptightness of many American teachers and parents, a tension that may increase rather than solve a child's learning "problem." This relaxed English attitude, combined with informal approaches to reading instruction, is viewed as instrumental to the extremely low incidence of nonreaders in the new infant schools.

Observers also report favorably on the "good beginnings" in mathematics and science among new infant school children.[13] Hall and Armington (1967) maintain that many of the Leicestershire infant schools are "far ahead" of their American counterparts in multi-base arithmetic. These observers believe that English classrooms present a more favorable learning climate and greater flexibility in respect to "readiness" for learning than do most American classrooms. They also report that new infant school children are neither restrained from pursuing advanced learnings nor coerced to participate in formal drill. In contrast, many kindergarten children in the United States are prevented from learning to read on the grounds that "reading is not taught until first grade." Although favorably impressed with the flexibility in new infant schools, Hall and Armington (1967) remark that the technology of some language-based activities is weak; for example, they note a lack of focus upon the development of phonetic analysis skills. They also observe that variation in quality among the Leicestershire schools makes it very difficult to derive sound generalizations about general classroom operations and their effectiveness.

Some dimensions upon which infant school teachers' behaviors vary have been explicated by Chittendon (1973) and can be summarized in three points. First, great latitude in the degree to which teachers become involved in children's learning is noted (periodic monitoring at one extreme, direct participation at the child's level at the other). Second, another area of difference is teachers' ideological views of open education (a means to effect profound or radical change in children's lives for some teachers, simply a better instructional format for others). And, third, teachers are observed to differ in their ability and/or willingness to

---

[13] Programmed materials for these two subjects are sometimes utilized in the new infant schools, but their use is more common in junior schools. The Nuffield Mathematics Materials, with conceptual roots in Piagetian psychology, are reported as widely used in new infant schools.

analyze their instructional procedures and curriculum plans. Chittendon also reports that teachers often have difficulty in stimulating their pupils to develop innovative inquiry projects, in contrast to the responsibility the children demonstrate in carrying out these projects once identified. Chittendon (1973) believes the pattern often is reversed in American classrooms.

Even though many observers are reliably impressed with the degree of responsibility shown by children in new infant schools, others (e.g., Yeomans, 1969) have not seen clear evidence of sustained work in certain areas of study, especially history and literature. Again, this would seem more a matter of teacher skill in providing an underlying structure and organization of interrelated studies than a natural tendency for children to avoid such subject matter. As A. Bessell (1973) has said, a weak teacher may not be able to manage a genuinely open classroom so that meaningful learning among children is ensured. In fact, a weak teacher may attempt to cope with the demands of such a classroom by permitting or even encouraging a lot of "useless time filling" (A. Bessell, 1973). The ultimate issue here is teacher selection and training. Since informal education has a longer history in Britain's infant schools, one assumes that suitable training procedures exist in Britain's teacher education institutions. Again, however, it is important to recall that informal education is practiced in only about 30 percent of Britain's infant schools. Undoubtedly, much of the teacher education for new infant school practice is on-the-job training.[14]

Anecdotal reports, however thoughtful and interesting, cannot substitute for systematic evaluation. For hard-core empiricists there is still a paucity of "clean" evidence to validate (or deny) the effectiveness of new infant school practices. We have inferred, however, that new infant school practices do not impede children's subsequent progress in the junior school and beyond. Furthermore, conventional research techniques, especially group testing, which focus upon product are not entirely consistent with the new infant school focus upon *process*. A rethinking of research questions and procedures appropriate to a process-orientation is needed. Perhaps this reanalysis will soon result in the identification of more specific antecedent-consequent relationships within new infant school classrooms.

Faith in the value of pedagogical change or belief in the success potential of new methods among teachers may have influenced the outcome of the infant school movement in positive ways. Yet it is the fundamental value of classrooms patterned after the Leicestershire experiment that continues to impress visitors: a reasoned reorganization of the total early school framework to facilitate the intellectual and emotional

---

[14] See Denny (1970) for comments about training new infant school teachers and Lomax (1972) for a review of British research in teacher education. Both Packard (1973) and V. Rogers (1970) can be consulted about ways to manage individualized, child-centered education in environments such as the new infant school.

emancipation of children. Many observers agree that the real strength of Leicestershire may be an avoidance of formulae, convergent systems, and pedagogical conformity. There has been no obsession to "prove" one theory or method better than another. All theories are considered and utilized as deemed appropriate to the situation; the classroom teacher remains the best judge of applicability. Thus far, personnel of the British new infant schools have demonstrated that open education apparently works, even in large classes, therefore providing an object lesson for American educators. Conditions must be right, however, and a most important condition is that teachers be allowed to exercise the same responsibility and initiative as are wanted for their pupils (Yeomans, 1969).

OPEN EDUCATION IN THE U.S.: SOME EXAMPLES

With a few major exceptions, open education in the United States occurs largely in scattered public and private schools or classrooms and laboratory programs in colleges of education. Evidence of prolonged success with such informal approaches is even more sparse. Several decisive steps toward a greater implementation of open education concepts have been taken in recent years, however. One step is symbolized by a Project Follow Through model for continuing growth presented by the Educational Development Center (EDC) in Newton, Massachusetts. This plan, perhaps more than most open education models in America, has been influenced in a number of important ways by the British new infant school movement. A second step toward more widespread open education is the Vermont Design for Education. Both of these steps are discussed in the present section with some ideas about the importance of social context for workable open education.

The EDC Continuing Growth Plan

The plan for continuing growth (Armington, 1968) is an attempt to achieve an educational environment that (1) eliminates the persistent contradiction between educational ideals and practices and (2) paves the road for children's "personal fulfillment" (Armington, 1968). A requisite to such achievement is ample encouragement and reinforcement of any school faculty for the development of its own unique identity. Experimentation and personal freedom are seen as necessary role enactments for school personnel and as a substitute for enactments constrained by prescribed curricula. The aim of this shift from "prescription" to "freedom" is improved teacher responsiveness to individual children's needs and to individual teaching styles.

Key Elements for Continuing Growth   Two key elements form the conceptual substance of the continuing growth plan: the open classroom and the advisory service. An open classroom is defined in terms of openness in communication (dialogue), classroom organization, time, and space. Most fundamentally, openness applies to *self* (teachers as well as children). Teaching methods and conditions are primary concerns; intellectual content is secondary. Growth in communication skills, intellectual curiosity, self-confidence, and responsibility are among the favored educational aims in this plan. The characteristics of a classroom necessary for the attainment of such aims include (1) a rich variety of learning materials, (2) freedom to plan one's own activities, (3) an interdisciplinary approach to "work," (4) flexibility in scheduling, (5) cooperative interchange among pupils, and (6) a supportive teacher role. The latter involves both careful observation of and active participation in classroom life.

Life in open classrooms is further sustained by the second key element mentioned above: the advisory service. The *advisory* consists of a team of advisors (not supervisors)—which performs a variety of functions to implement the open classroom philosophy and develop practices consistent with it. The concept of advising is built upon three principles. One is that changes in educational practice are only effective when teachers feel the need for and desire change. Thus, the advisory purports to enhance and capitalize upon the readiness for change exhibited in a given situation. Members of the advisory must always be accessible and immediately responsive to requests for their services. The second principle is based upon a "way of working" with teachers, which involves both a responsiveness to the demands of specific situations and an attempt to help teachers realize their full capabilities. The third principle is defined in terms of various integrated advisory functions: direct services (e.g., seminars, provision of curriculum materials, parent education); research and curriculum development services; the provision of a workshop and resource center within which consultations may ensue; and the communication of ideas, problems, and needs among classroom teachers.

It is difficult to write in more detail about the continuing growth plan. There is no curriculum in the usual sense, and certainly none that satisfies the criterion of exportability power. Curriculum suggestions are provided, however, and consist largely of *ideas in green*: one- to three-page statements about possible classroom activities. Sample topics include water play, woodwork, combining music and poetry, improvising with dance, and exploring color. Some of the more conventional pre-packaged curriculum materials for early childhood education may be recommended from time to time, but any list is intended only to be suggestive. Parent involvement occurs largely at the level of classroom observation and assistance with the preparation of learning materials. Occasionally parents will serve as resource persons in the classroom and, consistent with Follow Through guidelines, be represented on the model's policy advisory committee. Formal evaluation procedures are actively *not endorsed*. The gathering of observation data is stressed, but not for purposes of comparing classrooms or children within classrooms. Heavy emphasis, of course, is placed upon well-trained, personally secure teachers.

Evaluation   Since formal evaluation does not figure as a part of the continuing growth plan, it is nearly impossible to say how effective the plan is in meeting its objectives. In addition, only about a dozen school districts in America have even participated continuously in the plan. Accordingly, only a very general idea about the impact of the plan can be gleaned from the gross evaluation of early education models by way of the planned variation experiment. Project Follow Through data about the EDC plan are equivocal; preliminary results for the Head Start planned variation experiment indicate that the plan is "average" in its effectiveness across major outcome variables as compared to other models (see Chapter 2).

With so little meaningful data at our disposal, it may be helpful to turn to some broadly related research for clues about the impact of open education on children. In variously well-designed and executed evaluative research programs, authorities report advantages among children in open (versus traditional) schools or classrooms in independence, self-esteem, creativity, and school attitudes (Bleier et al., 1972; Minuchin et al., 1969; Perrone, 1972; Wilson, 1972). Others (Ruedi and West, 1973) report no differences in self-concept measures between children in open and traditional schools and question the suitability of such measures for comparing entire school systems. Some reports (Sobel and Tejirian, 1973) note salutary progress in school achievement among children of various social and ethnic minorities who participate in open schooling. Still other data (Burnham, 1971) call into question the idea of scholastic superiority one way or the other. Given such mixed data, those who identify with open education probably will seek and find data to justify their claims; those who prefer a more tightly organized basic skills approach to learning will do likewise. Anything but general long-term evaluation is less than relevant to EDC personnel anyway. For the moment, these personnel reportedly are gratified to have learned that a "large percentage" of teachers and parents with whom they work support their aims and methods. Additional gratification has come through the development of the EDC advisory system, which can serve as a model to concerned educators who work in school district administration.

Vermont Design for Education

The State of Vermont has developed a student-centered philosophy of education very similar to that underlying the British new infant school movement. The Vermont philosophy includes an integrated set of principles related to the motivation of behavior, human relations, and individual psychology. It also emphasizes the learning process rather than the teaching process. This distinction is a matter of degree rather than kind, although it is based on the postulate that one does not teach children. Instead, one arranges conditions conducive for children to learn. Immediately, the issue of optimal conditions arises. For the Vermont design, a humanistic teacher-student relationship is the most basic condition. The following principles have been cultivated from this premise:

1. A student must be accepted as a person.
2. The teacher's role must be that of a partner and guide in the learning process.
3. All people need success to prosper.

A second related component of the Vermont design is based on the concept of individual differences. For example:

4. Education should be based upon the individual's strong, inherent desire to learn and make sense of his environment.
5. Educators should strive to maintain the individuality and originality of the learner.
6. Emphasis should be upon a child's own way of learning—through the discovery and exploration of real experiences.
7. A child's perception of the learning process should be related to his own conception of reality.
8. A child should be allowed to work according to his own abilities.
9. Expectation of children's progress should be individualized if individualized instruction is sought.

A third philosophical constituent of the Vermont design involves the need for effective personal and social growth through educational experience:

10. One of the most important human accomplishments is the formulation of a basic set of values by which to guide daily living.
11. Schools should establish a context within which children are able to learn from one another.
12. The development of a sense of responsibility should be encouraged for every child.

As the reader can see, the Vermont design is essentially an abstract and general statement of principles consistent with the open education viewpoint. Nothing can be said definitively at this time about the design's effect on school practices, even in Vermont. But this design is a reaffirmation of humanistic commitment to child welfare in the public schools and provides an exemplar of philosophical leadership at the level of state departments of education.[15]

---

[15] An impressive document aligned generally with the open education movement has also been published by the Provincial Committee on Education in Ontario, Canada and entitled *Living and Learning* (1968). A principal strength of this document is its impressive list of 258 recommendations for change in the educational complex of Ontario.

Comment on Open Education

To what extent open education, particularly as symbolized by new infant school practice, will thrive and perpetuate itself in the United States cannot be predicted. In fact, it may be unrealistic to think that the total infant school idea will work well in this country. It is easy to forget that the infant school movement developed over an extended period in Britain and under peculiar social, economic, and pedagogical circumstances. American educators continue to receive warnings about the naivety, if not outright hazards, of attempting to export and transplant an approach to education which has evolved in a different context.

If the new infant school idea does not work well in this country, it could be due to a number of factors (Featherstone, 1967; Grannis, 1973). Certainly one cannot expect much success apart from a full understanding of the circumstances under which open education came to flourish in about one-third of Britain's schools for young children. One must also be specific in delineating the qualities that set superior infant school classes apart from mediocre ones. This, among other things, requires careful research based upon classroom observation of the extent to which open education principles are manifest in actual practice (Walberg and Thomas, 1972).

Open classrooms in American schools frequently involve groupings of different-aged children in expansive physical settings to promote freedom of movement to varied activity centers. In this school, grades one, two, and three are placed in the same wing of the school building. Retractable walls can be closed or opened at the discretion of teachers working together. Photo by Peter Rinearson.

Even if these criteria can be satisfied, there is the problem of sociological differences between England and America.

Adult-child roles, for example, seem more clearly differentiated in England, a phenomenon that may work to the advantage of British teachers in a classroom full of young children (Grannis, 1973). We noted earlier that education has become more politicized in America, a factor that works against the concepts of a strong and absolute local headmaster (principal) and an autonomous teaching faculty. So also are the goals of education at issue. American parents, possibly to a greater extent than their British counterparts, value education as a means to better group adjustment and "getting a better job" (Gallup, 1971). With such social and pragmatic values in operation, the open education emphasis upon individualized, self-seeking activity and aesthetics of various kinds will probably continue to meet resistance in many quarters of American society.

Protagonists of open education may also contribute to problems of implementation and credibility. The movement easily lends itself to a cultism or orthodoxy which can irritate even the most tolerant educator. This writer, for example, has observed that supporters of informal education often declare their approach is superior because it is by definition warm, open, flexible, and supports creativity and uniqueness; anything less than this, especially any attempt at formal education, is dismissed out of hand as cold, authoritarian, rigid, and therefore bad. One cannot deny that the control techniques used by many teachers in formal (and informal!) educational settings are sometimes (even frequently) insidious. The fact remains, however, that the type and degree of children's learning are controlled to a large extent both by the selection (or exclusion) of learning materials and the selective reinforcements inevitable in any classroom. As Barth (1972) puts it, the real problem facing informal education is a definition of the division of responsibility for learning inherent in any adult-child relationship. In part, this issue of responsibility involves the extent to which children and their teachers are accountable to each other in the open classroom. This writer has observed that clear, specific guidelines for children's task accomplishment are too often missing in informal educational settings. Constructive teacher feedback, including encouragement and special assistance when necessary, is often sorely lacking. In fact, this writer has witnessed children who may go for as much as a week or more without meaningful planning and evaluation periods, where teacher feedback about children's written work is both poor in quality and excessively delayed, and where raucous social activities occupy a disproportionate part of the school day. Such problems need not occur. It is basically a matter of organization and management, the details of which require much teacher skill as well as responsibility among the children themselves. In short, the informal classroom can easily be abused. When this occurs, its viability as a healthy alternative to schooling is seriously threatened.

Unquestionably, the specifics of dividing responsibility are essential in working to establish a successful open education environment. But this is not the full story. Two unique elements from the Leicestershire experience should again be identified (Ascheim, 1973). One is the intangible yet pervasive ethic of experimentation and change, as opposed to a preservation of the status quo. Open education appears to derive much of its sustenance from the experimental attitude. The second, more tangible, element is the advisory. In the United States, experimentalism per se possibly suffers less than attempts to move away from the mystique of expertise, that is, a dependence upon certified experts or specialists to initiate and direct change at the school faculty level. Perhaps American teachers need to work more actively toward a system of nonevaluative advising, the focal point of which are resource centers operated by and for teachers themselves. As Ascheim (1973) suggests, such centers would be stocked with basic classroom supplies and means for constructing learning materials. Also appropriate would be "scrounged junk materials" and a comprehensive catalog of commercial goods, educational toys, and the like. Such a file can help teachers keep abreast of new materials and equipments; but even better, it provides a pool of ideas from which various items may be constructed locally.

Teacher centers for self-directed, continuing education and planning educational change are appearing as this book is written. One recent estimate sets the number of such centers at over 100, mostly in large urban settings (Raskin, 1973). Some centers are funded by federal sources, but most are the result of grass-roots activity among teachers voluntarily seeking to improve and refresh themselves professionally. Successful centers seem to share the elements of teacher (versus administrator) control, open access to all who wish to participate, nonevaluative atmosphere, and voluntary attendance. Financial problems usually represent the major obstacle to spontaneous teacher centers. Occasionally, teachers concerned with innovation fail to receive support for any new procedure unless it promises to raise children's achievement test scores. The resource center trend is encouraging because of the professional commitment it represents: a quest for practical, imaginative, in-service education directly pertinent to specific classroom needs and with the locus of responsibility centered on the participating teachers themselves (Raskin, 1973).

But the need for sound empirical research about open education practices remains. Many important questions have yet to be answered. For example, when children determine how they will use their own time, how great is the problem of excessive random activity? What contingencies mitigate against the ideal of self-propelled educational development or lead children to "take advantage" of openness to pursue social rather than intellectual goals? Who is accountable if a child does not achieve the aims of informal education and what "remedial" steps will be appropriate and effective if children do fail? If there are certain curriculum universals (content areas) which all children need, can they be left to personal choice? Is there, as Barth (1969) suggests, a danger that new infant school practices will be "haphazard, disordered, and misunderstood" unless they are guided by a clear theoretical framework? To what extent does the emphasis upon intuitive teaching and evaluation conflict with educators' attempts to build a science of teaching? To what extent is informal education, with its potential strengths and weaknesses, consistent with a society's national goals? Why, as it is often claimed, does the educational establishment in England and the United States seemingly resist change in the direction of large-scale open education? What is the best way to prepare teachers and children for a successful open education experience? Are new infant school children developing greater independence and responsibility which will serve them advantageously throughout their school years and into adult life? Is the near-idyllic existence of new infant and junior school children too far divorced from the realities of life to be the best learning experience?

Perhaps these questions will be answered more satisfactorily in the next decade. Meanwhile there is much to commend in the efforts of British and American educators to provide a school community in which children may live as children—to discover, to create, to experience the pleasure and excitement of cooperative learning—in short, to make child-centered education work. And it does take plenty of hard work. Hopefully, however, a proper perspective on open, as well as any other approach to, education will be maintained. As Grannis (1973) has stated:

> Like the whole child, the open educator's pedagogical creed keeps coming out whole, rather than recognizing that different educational settings have different purposes, and that if "openness" is to have any meaning at all, it will characterize some settings and their purposes better than others (p. 552).

A Word about the Free School Movement

The extreme, if not radical, form of open education in America is generally referred to as the *free school movement*. Although there is some question about the extent and even reality of this movement, the literature about nonpublic free schools and parallel diversifications within the public education sector has grown (Barr, 1973). In theory, the basic concept of free schools is that children should be free to learn in a completely uncompulsory, unauthoritarian climate. The classic prototype for American free schools is A. S. Neill's Summerhill (1960), wherein students, instead of teachers, develop and guide their learning process to whatever extent and in whatever direction is momentarily desirable. In this sense, the free school movement in America is fired by a pedagogical ideology specifically opposed to the structure and policies of public schools including age grading, large classes, preordained curricula, testing, ability grouping, and competition for grades (Graubard, 1972). In another sense, the free school movement clearly reflects a political ideology. This is especially true in settings characterized by active demands for consumer-controlled schooling as a means to better achieve social equality. In practice, the political ideology of free schools is more apparent among ethnic minority power groups. Many of the schools established for political reasons do not fully implement a pedagogical concept of freedom and are perhaps more accurately called *alternative schools* (Graubard, 1972).

Because of the diverse rationales associated with the free school movement, it is difficult to define a free school. Variety in free schools is the rule rather than the exception. However, the number of schools purporting to be "free" has increased substantially over the past several years. One of the few surveys available at the time of this writing provides data on 346 free schools of one kind or another (Graubard, 1972). Of these schools, over half involve predominantly white children of elementary school age. Located for the most part in California, New York, Massachusetts, and Illinois, these schools' average enrollment is thirty-three students; few schools enroll more than sixty children. This suggests a genuine concern for an interpersonal intimacy usually absent in regular public schools. Summerhillian-type schools and parent-teacher cooperatives seem to dominate the free school experience for younger children. These school types are consistent with, if not focal points of, all kinds of liberationist thinking. But young children can also be found in a third type of free school, usually spawned in black communities, in which highly political activity dominates. Transcendant goals include black consciousness and pride, the push for economic power, and the forceful seeking of expanded opportunity structures. Even if one includes all the varieties of free and alternative schools, however, the "movement" has not yet touched more than a tiny percentage of American school-age children; moreover, from 20 to 50 percent of nonpublic schools reportedly do not sustain themselves for much longer than eighteen to twenty-four months (Barr, 1973).

An assessment of the impact of the free school movement upon early childhood education would be premature. Broadly speaking, the idea of freedom for children to learn according to their natural curiosity, interests, and individual styles is compatible with long-standing ideals in traditional nursery school practice and the value of alternatives manifest in planned variation (see Chapter 2). One can argue, however, that the real issue concerns how *freedom to learn* is translated in the child's world of schooling. This issue is often obscured—sometimes to the point of self-deception —by adults' many diverse interpretations of freedom (Kozol, 1972). Lack of agreement about what constitutes freedom is combined with the many practical difficulties of maintaining a free school practice. Many such schools are aborted for these reasons plus the more serious one that little of substance is taught or learned within them (Kozol, 1972). This seems particularly true for basic skills, such as reading which free a young child to become a student. Undoubtedly adding to this instructional problem of free schools is the quality (both in commitment and pedagogical skills) of personnel needed to sustain any school, however small.

In this writer's experience, free school advocates and participants reflect two different psychological orientations. The first is a genuine and strong belief about the inherent worth of pedegogical freedom for young children. This includes a faith in the validity of such education and a deep devotion to children. The second orientation seems to imply a motivation of expediency or opportunism, i.e., the free school as a means primarily to benefit adults. Children's needs are secondary—if even thought deeply about. For example, some free school activists use the movement to work out their own problems of personal-social adjustment, notably authority conflicts. Others give of themselves in only token fashion, as if their fleeting involvement somehow salved their consciences about inequities of one kind or another. Either way, the second orientation makes children pawns in political or psychological struggles. One wonders if children can possibly benefit educationally under such circumstances. At worst, some free school activists seek, however unwittingly, to create children in their own image or to indoctrinate them with certain ways of adult thinking. The irony of such a practice is evident.

These comments, like most commentaries on the poorly documented free school movement, are largely speculative. But in an honestly pluralistic society, a legitimate free school option will be available to those who prefer it to other educational alternatives, and actively and collectively supported (at least in spirit) by educators of all persuasions. If so, the free school movement firmly established by the early 1970s should not wither and die. Its impact upon the public schools can already be observed in communities where reform is manifest in the "school within a school" approach. Whether this sort of reform can (or does) maintain a purist concept of pedagogical freedom is difficult to say. Any evaluation of a free school approach must occur on moral-ethical grounds. The functions of psychology, especially the empirical validation of programs, are basically irrelevant to the free schools, since a prior and sweeping judgment has been made about what and how children ought to learn. Finally, if one extends the free school idea to its logical conclusion, a child should be free to opt for no schooling. This strikes at the heart of compulsory education with all the attendant reverberations. It is instructive periodically to assess the virtues and problems on both sides of the compulsory education principle (Johnson, 1973).

INFLUENCES IN AFFECTIVE EDUCATION

In Chapter 1, the move toward a greater balance of curriculum emphases for young children's cognitive and affective development was briefly discussed. Similarly, in the present chapter we have seen that open or informal educational approaches clearly stress the importance of children's feelings and beliefs about themselves and their schooling, hopefully positive. In fact, most early childhood educators long have maintained that a child's self-concept—one's self-knowledge and the evaluative tendencies that accompany one's beliefs about one's self—must carefully be nurtured during the early years if zestful and confident school learning is to occur. This thesis or some variation was implicit in the original early childhood education movement. But surprisingly few programmatic attempts to act upon this thesis have appeared in past years. In other words, humane teaching within a benevolent low-pressure environment is seen as a basic condition for promoting positive emotional development; yet few organized attempts to "educate" for self-growth have been made. One early exception was the human relations approach developed by Ojemann (1958), although it focuses largely upon older children. The emotional education banner has also been flourished at different times and to different degrees by many other humanists (e.g., Dinkmeyer and Dreikurs, 1963; Drews, 1966; and Prescott, 1938). Related concerns appear in the general mental health literature (e.g., Clarizio, 1969; Seidman, 1963; Torrance and Strom, 1965) and the study of children's anxiety, especially as it may affect learning behavior (e.g., Ruebush, 1963; Sarason et al., 1960).

More recently, however, the trail of affective education has been explored in greater detail. Glasser (1969), for example, has articulated some basic principles of "reality therapy" for use in educational settings, with a heavy accent upon teacher-pupil relations and responsibility training. Similar principles are advocated for school application by Ginott (1972) and Purkey (1970). Collectively, these authorities are concerned first with eliminating conditions that purportedly stunt or negate healthy beliefs children may have about themselves and other persons. Such negative factors include systems of competitive evaluation, ability grouping, retention in grade, corporal punishment; and teachers who are inauthentic and preach and moralize to the point of rejecting children outright.

More elaborate from the standpoint of curriculum procedures and content is Smith's concept (1973) of "people teaching," a model for assisting young children to develop their self-awareness and human relations skills. Five general themes, translated into many specific lessons, are included in this model: (1) aggression, violence, and conflict resolution; (2) fantasy and feeling; (3) self-esteem and kind behavior; (4) sensory awareness and body image; and (5) social interdependence. Among the people-teaching strategies utilized in this model are life-space encounters, group activities, storytelling, and puppet dramatizations. Many other guides for affective education, including materials prepared specifically for commercial distribution (the validity of which is unknown) could be listed here (e.g., Castillo, 1974). For purposes of illustration, however, a description of only one program for children's self-development is described in this final section of Chapter 7. This program has been selected for three reasons. First, it has been developed by a pair of trained psychologists from personality theory and actual clinical experience with children. Second, the program has somewhat more visibility and popularity than do many of the more commercially oriented programs. And third, the program applies to children as young as age 4.

A Human Development Program for Young Children

The *human development program* (H. Bessell and Palomares, 1967) is based upon a conviction that remedial means are not the best way to approach the many emotional problems faced by adolescents and adults; remediation, in other words, simply is not effective enough to solve these emotional difficulties. Rather, Bessell and Palomares prefer to apply preventive mental health techniques during childhood before these problems are developed. The basic task of affective education therefore is to help children develop a sound emotional outlook which will cumulatively increase their resistance to society's many pestilent features, including aversive human interaction in the schools. A first step in this process is to help the child overcome his fears about such things as his safety, his acceptance by others, his helplessness, and his lack of power.

Three specific problems contributing to children's fears have suggested a framework for emotional education: inadequate understanding of the cause-effect relationships in social interaction, insufficient understanding of the motives underlying human behavior, and low self-confidence. These problem areas in combination have provided the stimulus for the human development curriculum, which seeks the achievement of improved (1) *social interaction* skills (understanding and accepting others), (2) *self-awareness* (insight into and acceptance of one's own feelings), and (3) *mastery* (achievement of responsible competence). Also basic to this tripartite framework are the objectives of self-control and personal authenticity. Published curriculum materials and guidelines covering the range from preschool-kindergarten through grade four (five levels) currently are available for school use (H. Bessell, 1972). The materials have also been translated into both Spanish and French for use abroad.

The medium for human development education as interpreted by Bessell and Palomares is the *magic circle.* This arrangement places eight to twelve children and the teacher in a smaller (inner) circle with the remaining children seated in a larger concentric circle. The inner circle of children is the participating body. Members of the outer circle observe. Circle membership varies from day to day as the teacher initiates topics for discussion (twenty-minute periods daily) relevant to the three main process themes. Up to six weeks are devoted at one time to a theme. The clarification and analysis of children's *feelings* and *perceptions* permeates these discussions. This is preferred to a more traditional concern for the *content* of children's verbalization. Consistent attempts are made, however, to help children build a more effective vocabulary for the expression of feeling. H. Bessell (1968) believes that younger children are not yet "at war" with themselves as are most adults, and therefore they exude a spontaneity which sustains the activity of the magic circle. Bessell is also convinced that children (1) will respond favorably to opportunities for sharing in the decision-making processes, (2) can assume leadership roles (for Bessell the golden age of leadership development is the period from six to eight years), and (3) will help others, including the teacher, in constructive ways if they are allowed to. This program also is designed gradually to shift leadership responsibilities from the teacher to the children. Consequently, leadership tasks can be shared by the children. Ordinarily, this shift does not begin until the primary grades but involvement is sought at all stages of the program. Such involvement, in fact, is seen as the key to successful human relations training. Again the emergence of responsibility is suggested by an equation: *as responsibility is divided, involvement is multiplied.* In short, Bessell is convinced that if one wishes to promote responsibility among children, definite opportunities must be provided in the classroom. The human development program therefore represents a semistructured effort to capitalize upon children's social nature and their resources for cooperative personal assistance for the purpose of achieving self-responsibility.

Evaluation   The enthusiasm with which the Bessell program has reportedly been received (mostly in the western United States) is perhaps a testimonial to the need many teachers perceive for organized human development activities for young children. Anecdotal data from teachers who have utilized the program in their classrooms indicate a reduction in discipline problems, higher motivation, greater verbal expressiveness, and smoother social interaction among children. H. Bessell himself (1969) reports data from a school system in Las Cruces, New Mexico, which indicate "slightly higher" academic achievement and a reduced absentee rate among children who have experienced the program. However, at the time of this writing few carefully designed and executed studies of this program have occurred, despite ample opportunities for evaluation. To assist in this regard, H. Bessell and Palomares (1967) have designed a rating scale for teacher use in assessing behavioral changes associated with the program. Many standard observational and self-report techniques could also be used with caution for this purpose. It is also important to recognize the theoretical basis for the program, which is essentially a mix of neoanalytic and self-actualization personality theories (Adler, 1927; Horney, 1950; C. Rogers, 1942). Accordingly, any success of the program will depend in large part upon a teacher's acceptance, empathy, and group leadership skills. Possibly the principal issue facing Bessell, and other like program builders, is not the program as much as it is the training of those who may elect to use it. Particularly dangerous would be a situation in which a teacher uses such a program to attempt psychotherapy or group-encounter activities with children. These activities are insufficiently understood even by many professionally-trained therapists.

A still more basic issue associated with any human development program is whether schools even should attempt to promote affective development through organized educational experiences. Bereiter (1972), for example, argues eloquently against attempts to influence such development even informally. Explicit teachings for the development of values, moral judgment, and socioemotional content neither are nor can be performed well in schools according to his viewpoint. Only parents have the

There is little argument among educators about the values of self-understanding and the feeling component of school learning, but much controversy surrounds the specific ways in which these values are translated into classroom practice. Photo courtesy of Southwest Educational Development Laboratory, Austin, Texas.

right to pursue affective education; teachers should recognize and accept this in order to concentrate better upon basic skills training and supportive, informal custodial care. In short, too much has been expected of the schools, and they have frequently failed even in their more clearly defined responsibilities for training children for "survival skills" mastery. Little is known about the course and processes of affective development, much less about how to influence it in directions and through procedures acceptable to consumers, including parents. To inflate the importance of schooling for affective "education," then, is to invite ethical and pedagogical problems which have little chance of satisfactory solution.

Meanwhile, a persistent criticism of American education is its lack of attention to the feeling component of learning, so that too often what is learned does not help children as persons. It is argued that systematic attention to this problem and all its facets is needed at all educational levels, including the education of teachers themselves. What forms the solutions attempted will take is a matter for reasoned debate. Whether the limitations of school practice are externally or self-imposed, does the positive development of children's self-images as learners deserve to be a basic goal of education? Whatever action educators take in approaching the affective side of schooling, Bessell's observations about the implementation of his human development program are instructive. First, it appears that all children eventually will talk about themselves in highly

personalized ways when given the opportunity. Second, children's attention spans grow quite long when someone listens carefully to their discussions of thoughts and feelings. And third, teachers can be profoundly
affected by the airing of fears, desires, problems, and puzzlements of the
children in their care.

SUMMARY

Chapter 7 has focused on the principles and practices of open education
and the related matter of affective education for young children. Perhaps
the most salient influence in the open education movement has been a
constellation of practices associated with the "new" British infant schools.
This constellation of practices is firmly anchored by a genuine commitment
to informal child-centered education. Among the distinguishing organizational and instructional components of new infant school practice are the
integrated day, vertical grouping, subjective assessment procedures, and
a broadened emphasis upon the process rather than the products of children's school learning. Protagonists for the new infant schools maintain
that such components are vastly more consistent with the true nature of
children's growth than are the traditional lockstep practices still prevalent
in the United States and much of Britain. Conventional research and
evaluation procedures have not been extensively applied in the changing
infant schools; anecdotal reports from teachers and outside observers
provide efficacy data. Such reports generally convey a strong excitement
about open education and confidence, if not satisfactory evidence, about
the power of informal methods to effect desired outcomes.

There are many similarities, both philosophically and psychologically,
between new infant school practice and the American progressive education of the 1930s. A more widespread acceptance and support of such
educational foundations, and more valid applications of the progressive
idea seem to have developed in Britain. This is usually explained in terms
of important differences in social-political conditions throughout Britain
as contrasted with the United States. Nevertheless, some salutary examples of open education in this country can be cited, including the EDC
continuing growth plan and the Vermont Design for Education. How influential these and similar models of educational thought will be upon
public school practices cannot yet be determined.

The most radical form of open education, if even legitimately grouped
with informal approaches in the spirit of progressivism, is represented by
the so-called free school movement. This movement has faced many
problems, including a lack of agreement among adherents about goals and
methods and a lack of skilled teachers to implement the complex principles of open education. The future of this movement is obscure, but
many credit it with having served as a catalyst in generating alternatives
within the established public school system.

This chapter concluded with a discussion about activities designed
to influence children's affective development in positive ways. Much con-

tinues to be written in relation to this aspect of children's educational growth, but little is known about the actual impact of affectively oriented materials on children. One such human development program was described in some detail to illustrate both the major features of affective education and the various issues that surround this sort of activity.

REFERENCES

Adler, A. *Practice and theory of individual psychology.* New York: Harcourt, 1927.

Armington, D. A plan for continuing growth. In *Descriptions of Follow Through Programs* C1–C12. Washington, D.C.: U.S. Office of Education, 1968.

Ascheim, S. Pursuing change. *Learning,* 1973, *2,* 24–27.

Barr, R. Whatever happened to the free school movement? *Phi Delta Kappan,* 1973, *54,* 454–457.

Barth, R. Open education. *Theory and Philosophy of Education.* Kensington, Australia, 1969.

Barth, R. *Open education and the American school.* New York: Schocken Books, 1972.

Bereiter, C. Schools without education. *Harvard Educational Review,* 1972, *42,* 390–413.

Bessell, A. Slow down, yank. *Learning,* 1973, *1* (6), 10–11.

Bessell, H. The content is the medium: the confidence is the message. *Psychology Today,* 1968, *2,* 32–35.

Bessell, H. Personal correspondence, July 6, 1969.

Bessell, H. Human development in the elementary school classroom. In D. Solomon and J. Bergen (eds.), *New perspectives in encounter groups.* San Francisco: Jossey Bass, 1972, 349–367.

Bessell, H., and U. Palomares. *Methods in human development.* San Diego, Calif.: Human Development Training Institute, 1967.

Blackie, J. *Inside the primary school.* London: Her Majesty's Stationery Office, 1967.

Bleier, M., et al. A comparison of yielding to influence in open and traditional classrooms. *Childhood Education,* 1972, *49,* 45–50.

Burnham, B. Achievement of grade one pupils in open plan and architecturally conventional schools. *ERIC: ED 065 908,* 1971.

Castillo, G. *Left-handed teaching: lessons in affective education.* New York: Praeger, 1974.

Chittendon, E. What makes the British bandwagon roll? *Learning,* 1973, *1* (6), 6–9.

Clarizio, H. (ed.) *Mental health and the educative process.* Skokie, Ill.: Rand McNally, 1969.

Denny, M. Provision for individuality in schools for young children of 3 to 7 or 8 years. *International Review of Education,* 1970, *16,* 96–99.

Dinkmeyer, D., and R. Dreikurs. *Encouraging children to learn: the encouragement process.* Englewood Cliffs, N.J.: Prentice-Hall, 1963.

Drews, E. Self-actualization: a new focus for education. In *1966 Yearbook, Association for Supervision and Curriculum Development.* Washington, D.C.: National Education Association, 1966, 99–126.

Featherstone, J. Schools for children. *The New Republic,* August 19, 1967, 17–21.

Gallup, G. The third annual survey of the public's attitudes toward the public schools, 1971. *Phi Delta Kappan,* 1971, *53,* 33–48.

Ginott, H. *Teacher and child.* New York: Crowell-Collier-Macmillan, 1972.

Glasser, W. *Schools without failure.* New York: Harper & Row, 1969.

Grannis, J. Informal education and its social context. *Teachers College Records,* 1973, *74,* 547–557.

Graubard, A. The free school movement. *Harvard Educational Review,* 1972, *42,* 351–373.

Hall, W., and D. Armington. Leicestershire revisited. *ERIC Report,* PS 00617, 1967.

Halsey, A. (ed.). *Educational priority.* Vol. 1. *E.P.A. problems and policies.* London: Her Majesty's Stationery Office, 1972.

Hawkins, D., and F. Hawkins. Leicestershire: a personal report. *Elementary Science Study Newsletter,* 1964, June, 1–3.

Horney, K. *Neurosis and human growth.* New York: Norton, 1950.

Johnson, H. Are compulsory school attendance laws outdated? *Phi Delta Kappan,* 1973, *55,* 226–232.

Kozol, J. *Free schools.* Boston: Houghton Mifflin, 1972.

Levy, P., S. Gooch, and M. Kellmer-Pringle. A longitudinal study of the relationship between anxiety and streaming in a progressive and a traditional junior school. *British Journal of Educational Psychology,* 1969, *39,* 166–173.

Living and learning: the report of the Provincial Committee on aims and objectives of education in the schools of Ontario. Toronto, Canada: Ontario Department of Education, 1968.

Lomax, D. A review of British research in teacher education. *Review of Educational Research,* 1972, *42,* 289–326.

MacDonald, J. The open school: curriculum concepts. In B. Spodek (ed.), *Early childhood education.* Englewood Cliffs, N.J.: Prentice-Hall, 1970, 92–107.

Minuchin, P., et al. *The psychological impact of school experience.* New York: Basic Books, 1969.

Neill, A. S. *Summerhill: a radical approach to child rearing.* New York: Hart, 1960.

Ojemann, R. Basic approaches to mental health: the human relations program at the State University of Iowa. *Personnel and Guidance Journal,* 1958, *36,* 198–206.

Ojemann, R. Incorporating psychological concepts in the school curriculum. *Journal of School Psychology,* 1967, *3,* 195–204.

Packard, R. Do we have what we want today? structure in an open classroom. *Teachers College Record,* 1973, *74,* 553–557.

Perrone, V. *Open education: promise and problems.* Bloomington, Ind.: Phi Delta Kappan Educational Foundation, 1972.

Plowden, Lady Bridget. (chairperson) *Children and their primary schools: a report of the Central Advisory Council for Education in England.* Vol. 1. London: Her Majesty's Stationery Office, 1967.

Prescott, D. *Emotion and the educative process.* Washington, D.C.: American Council on Education, 1938.

Purkey, W. *Self concept and school achievement.* Englewood Cliffs, N.J.: Prentice-Hall, 1970.

Raskin, B. Teachers helping teachers. *Learning,* 1973, *2,* 29–32.

Resnick, L. Teacher behavior in an informal British infant school. Paper read at the meeting of the American Educational Research Association, New York, February, 1971.

Rogers, C. *Counseling and psychotherapy.* Boston: Houghton Mifflin, 1942.

Rogers, C. The facilitation of significant learning. In L. Siegel (ed.), *Instruction: some contemporary viewpoints.* San Francisco: Chandler Publishing Company, 1967, 37–54.

Rogers, V. English and American primary schools. *Phi Delta Kappan*, 1969, *51*, 71–75.

Rogers, V. *Teaching in the British primary school*. London: Collier-Macmillan Ltd., 1970.

Rogers, V. Primary education in England: an interview with John Coe. *Phi Delta Kappan*, 1971, *52*, 534–538.

Ruebush, B. Anxiety. In H. Stevenson (ed.), *Child Psychology*. Chicago: University of Chicago Press, 1963, 460–516.

Ruedi, J., and C. West. Pupil self concept in an "open" school and in a "traditional" school. *Psychology in the Schools*, 1973, *10*, 48–53.

Sarason, S., et al. *Anxiety in elementary school children*. New York: Wiley, 1960.

Sealey, L. Looking back on Leicestershire. *ESI Quarterly Report*, 1966, Spring-Summer, 37–41.

Seidman, J. (ed.). *Educating for mental health*. New York: Crowell, 1963.

Shields, M. Reading and transition to junior school. *Educational Research*, 1969, *11*, 143–147.

Silberman, C. *Crisis in the classroom*. New York: Random House, Inc. 1970, 260.

Smith, C. Introduction to people teaching. Presentation for the national conference of the National Association for the Education of Young Children, Seattle, November, 1973.

Sobel, H., and E. Tejirian. The case for open education. *Teachers College Record*, 1973, *74*, 559–565.

Spodek, B. Extending open education in the United States. In G. Engstrom (ed.), *Open education*. Washington, D.C.: National Association for the Education of Young Children, 1970, 64–77.

Start, K. Thirty years of reading standards in England. *Educational Researcher*, 1972, *1*, 8–9.

Stephens, J., and E. Evans. *Development and classroom learning*. New York: Holt, Rinehart and Winston, 1973.

Torrance, E. P. *Education and the creative potential*. Minneapolis: University of Minnesota Press, 1963.

Torrance, E. P., and R. Strom. (eds.). *Mental health and achievement*. New York: Wiley, 1965.

Walberg, H., and S. Thomas. Open education: a classroom validation in Great Britain and the United States. *American Educational Research Journal*, 1972, *9*, 197–208.

Wilson, F. Are pupils in the open plan school different? *Journal of Educational Research*, 1972, *66*, 115–118.

Yeomans, E. *Education for initiative and responsibility*. Boston: National Association of Independent Schools, 1969.

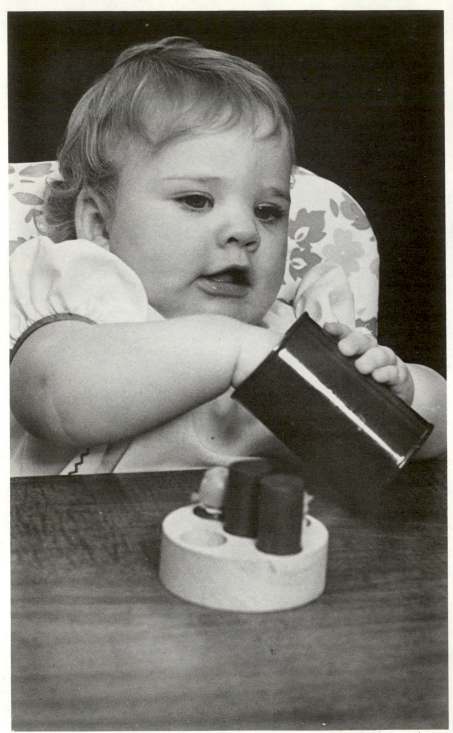

Photo by Gary Easter, courtesy of High/Scope Educational Research Foundation.

chapter

8

infants,
parents, and
television

In Chapter 1 we noted that in the 1960s early intervention movement educators developed a deeper appreciation of the importance of home factors in young children's development and education. Both nutrition and the quality of parent-child relationships were briefly discussed, as was the realization that schools depend heavily upon parental support and involvement for any potential positive impact from early education. We also learned that intervention efforts in the form of crash programs for children only a summer or even a full year before regular school entry often fail to demonstrate any lasting effect in subsequent educational development. Two ideas also related to educators' concerted effort to maximize opportunities for young children's development can now be explicated. The first involves a growing conviction that judicious intervention must occur earlier than age 4. This conviction is best illustrated by the move to infant education programs, the first topic presented in this chapter. Intimately tied to the idea of consistent educational experiences as early as infancy is the idea that parents themselves can be helped to become more competent teachers of their children. Accordingly, the second major section of this chapter is devoted to forms of parent education and parent involvement within the context of comprehensive early childhood education. The third, and final, section of this chapter concerns the pervasive role of television in the lives of children and their parents and concentrates on the trend to promote educational development through television. Throughout this chapter the emphasis is upon descriptions of representative experimental activities, associated evaluative research data, and issues associated with infant education, parent involvement, and educational television for young children.

INFANT EDUCATION

Technically speaking, the term *infant education* should be limited to programs for children below age 2. In practice, infant stimulation projects often include children ages 2 and 3. The growing interest in infant education seems partly a response to the early lack of hoped-for success within educational programs for older preschool children (see Chapter 2). Certainly, the increasing social pressures for expanded services for the infants and toddlers of working mothers, especially within the scope of developmental day care programs, has contributed to this interest. To these factors can be added a consensual belief among most students of infancy that human beings are the most malleable during this very early period of life (White, 1971). In a nutshell, the argument is that much of what mediates the impact of formal schooling at age 5 or 6 and after has developed or occurred within the home environment long before that time. For instance, early language experiences, intellectual stimulation, and general cultural atmosphere prior to age 4 are considered awesome factors in providing a base for subsequent intellectual-academic progress.

Two broad approaches to educational programs for infants are most generally in evidence. One approach involves an organized system of home teaching by trained persons who visit parents and their infants periodically to deliver an extended series of salutary services, including education. A second approach involves bringing infants together on a regular basis in group settings such as a day care center. Both approaches have relied increasingly upon parenting skills and strengthening the family unit. There are many variations on this theme, however, including a varied focus upon the infant or the parents as principal recipients of service.

While systematic stimulation activities are thought desirable for all American infants, the situation of the infant from impoverished circumstances has aroused the most concern. As early as age 3, economically disadvantaged children (especially blacks) have been observed to score lower than their more advantaged age-mates on virtually any standardized intelligence scale (e.g., Golden, Birns, Bridger, and Moss, 1971). Explanations tend to cluster around the environmental factors associated with poverty (e.g., poor nutrition and prenatal care) and ethnic or subcultural variations in parents' teaching styles and children's learning styles. The progressive importance of basic verbal abilities as determinants of age-related test performance can also be mentioned (King and Seegmiller, 1973); and, as mentioned in Chapter 1, the perplexing role of genetic influences has figured in many discussions of intellectual differentiation. A

few exceptions to the finding of measurable, social class–related intellectual differences by age 3 can be cited (e.g., F. Palmer, 1970). But the weight
of the evidence suggests that it is in the period before this age that important variables operate more strongly to affect the general course of
development (especially as mapped by measured intelligence).

This information, together with other strong hypotheses (see Schaefer,
1971), usually provides the rationale for infant education. Even so, there
are surprisingly few absolutes about infant development (White, 1971).
For this reason, it can also be argued that much more basic research
regarding developmental processes in infancy must precede the development of any prescriptive, authoritative infant education program. For the
moment, however, strong beliefs and social values have prevailed in the
move to extend education ever downward. In the following section, some
examples of social action infant programs are examined. For this writer,
such programs are best viewed as experimental or exploratory pilot projects. Programs currently being tested range from home-based teaching
projects to elaborate child care center activities, from theoretically derived to atheoretical designs, and from interventions as early as the
neonatal period to as late as age 2 or 2½. Most of the more carefully
researched programs are university-based demonstration projects or other
field-based, quasi-experimental programs funded through federal anti-
poverty legislation. Finally, it is important to note that space restrictions
limit the number of, and extent to which, infant programs can be discussed.

Some Examples of Infant Education Programs

Early Attempts   Among the first studies in the new wave of infant
education was Painter's attempt (1969) to enhance the developmental circumstances of "disadvantaged" infants. The intervention procedure consisted of a yearlong structured program of stimulation for infants ages 8
to 24 months in the areas of language, conceptual, and sensory-motor
development. Stimulation activities were carried out in these infants'
homes with a strong component of maternal involvement. End-of-year comparisons were made between the experimental infants and a group of controls (infants initially apparently equal in developmental and socioeconomic
status, but who did not experience any special training.). Standard developmental criteria were used for this comparison, including the Stanford-
Binet and assorted language-conceptual tasks. In general, the results indicated developmental advantages for the experimental group. From these
summative evaluation data, Painter concluded that (1) specific early intervention can make a positive difference in total development and (2) the
home environment provides a suitable medium for early intervention. Since
follow-up data have not yet been reported, it cannot be said that the
experimental advantages will persist or mediate future development in
positive ways. The external validity of the intervention program is also

at issue due to the strong possibility of a Hawthorne effect (see Chapter 1). However, the study has served a vanguard function, especially in terms of designing home-based intervention strategies.

Similar work has been pursued by Schaefer (1970) who did, in fact, find that once home tutoring procedures were terminated, measured gains (IQ) began to decline. Schaefer's early work consisted of "imported" home stimulation activities for infants beginning at age 15 months and extending through about age 3. With much candor, Schaefer has identified two basic errors in the design of his intervention strategy. First, he believes that home tutoring was commenced too late and discontinued too early. The second error, Schaefer speculates, is that home tutors should work less directly with infants and more directly with their parents. Like the Painter (1969) project, then, this early attempt at systematic infant stimulation has led to more hypotheses about the variables to be accounted for in the design of future infant projects. Particularly in the case of Schaefer's work, thinking about infant stimulation has been reoriented in two ways: (1) a focus upon parent-centered, rather than child-centered, education and (2) a recognition of a need for early and continued supportive experiences rather than shorter-term intervention.

A Touch of Piaget   Many, if not most, of the pioneer infant education projects are based in a reasoned eclecticism about intervention principles for relatively systematic application, either in the home or a special group setting. Palmer's work (1970) with two- and three-year-olds and the longitudinal intervention program designed by Robinson and Robinson (1971) for infants as young as two months of age are noteworthy examples. Concurrently, there have appeared attempts to devise infant education practices explicitly from developmental theory. Not surprisingly, Piagetian psychology has become a source of cues for such program development. A program established in New York State at Syracuse University Children's Center utilizes Piaget's stages of sensory-motor development (see Chapter 5). The program's purpose is to enhance the quality, rate, and generalizability of cognitive structures during the first year of life (Honig and Brill, 1970). Infants of volunteer mothers—black and of limited financial means—have been observed to perform higher than control infants on a Piagetian, but not on a conventional psychometric (Cattell scale), measure of infant intelligence. Far from being discouraging, these preliminary data have provided some clues for program revisions as well as modest support for the efficacy of a Piaget-based infant intervention model. Any attempt at an acceleration of cognitive development within a Piagetian perspective is, of course, subject to question along the lines discussed in Chapter 5.

Interested readers will find the broader family development research program at Syracuse University an especially rich source of data about infant care in general. This program is a longitudinal study of the delivery and measured impact of comprehensive family services upon low-income parents and their children (Lally, 1973). This program includes a (1) system of home visitations for the purpose of supplying cognitive, nutritional, health, and prenatal care information to disadvantaged homes. (2) day care service for infants ages 6 to 15 months, (3) full-day family style program for toddlers 15 to 48 months of age patterned after the new British infant school (see Chapter 7), and (4) series of parent workshops. Evaluative data about this program will be available periodically during the next few years. Preliminary data (Lally, 1973) attest to the strong potential of an integrated long-term delivery system for promoting positive human relations and development.

Piaget's description of sequential development has also influenced decisions about the timing and content of the Early Childhood Education Project (ECEP) in Buffalo, New York (Sigel, Secrist, and Forman, 1973). ECEP is a set of actions to "influence the anticipated course of development" of two-year-old black children from impoverished families. Major objectives include the development of competence in conceptual-symbolic and personal-self behaviors. The hub of ECEP activities is *representational competence*, or knowledge that a real object can be represented in several different modes (e.g., its concrete form, as a three-dimensional model, in photographic form, and an abstract graphic form) and still be a member of the same conceptual class. Since representational thinking, according to Piaget, begins to emerge just before age 2 (see Chapter 5), intervention to promote representational thinking skills is thought to be most effective— if not critical—for children at this stage in their development.

It follows that a foremost principle of curriculum development within ECEP is based upon *distancing behaviors*, i.e., events which create psychological distance between ostensive reality and its construction (Sigel, 1971). Distancing behaviors are central to the tutoring segment of ECEP. Individualized tutorial sessions are coordinated with a daily classroom program that serves to (1) elevate the level of children's socialized behavior and (2) promote attainment of selected cognitive objectives. The latter includes thinking in past and future terms (the nonpresent), developing alternative problem-solving strategies, recognizing the multiple properties of objects, and becoming aware of temporal and physical relationships. Children attend ECEP in half-day sessions four times weekly.

Initial evaluation methods are still undergoing refinement and have provided mixed, though promising, early results. Among the strengths of the ECEP project are the procedures for deriving curriculum experiences from developmental theory and the intense effort of its personnel to develop and validate innovative assessment tools. Sigel and his colleagues are particularly attuned to issues and problems in intervention policy, and a cautionary attitude pervades their reporting practices (Sigel, Secrist, and Forman, 1973).

A Developmental Learning Approach   In Chapter 1, the work of William Fowler was cited to exemplify the general move by developmental psychologists toward cognitive stimulation during early childhood. Fowler's efforts have recently culminated in a model group day care–education program for infants of working mothers (including single parents) and poor families in Toronto, Ontario. Fowler agrees with White (1971) that the zenith in human malleability is infancy. The resultant approach has many features in common with the comprehensive infant education programs currently being tested. For this reason, Fowler's model has been chosen for a detailed discussion.

Basic Design   To explore the significance of enrichment activities during infancy, two groups were formed by Fowler (1972). The intervention group, prepared for full-day experiences in a group setting, consisted of thirty advantaged and nine disadvantaged infants of ages 2 to 30 months. For comparative purposes, a group of stay-home infants was selected from hospital records to be paired with the intervention group on several important variables: age (matched within two months), sex, developmental status (as measured by the Bayley mental and motor scales), and level of parental education. Periodic assessments were thereafter made in relation to three clusters of objectives: perceptual-cognitive processes, socioemotional relations, and motor development–physical health. Each pair of matched infants was studied for an average of fifteen months during the three years of this study.

Curriculum   Programmatically, Fowler's demonstration project (1972) had three major components: student teacher education, parent education and guidance, and the infant care program. The three activity areas of the infant care component were standard day care routines (e.g., attending to physical needs), free play (both indoors and out), and guided learning in interactive play (mostly tutorial, with individual infants or groups of two to five infants each). Each activity area served program objectives in different ways. Rough groupings of infants were made according to developmental pattern characteristics. The first grouping included infants from ages 3 to 12 months, a developmental period characterized by relatively high dependency. The second group consisted of infants from ages 13 to 21 months, an age period during which infants are comparatively more mobile, autonomous, and socially involved. The third group, infants of 22 months and older, experienced longer periods of "minimally regulated" activity and play, but received guided learning more complex than in the first two groups.

Methods of infant care and education applied in these group settings were based upon Fowler's concept of developmental learning (see Chapter 1). The heart of such learning is the evolution of rule systems which unify cognitive, affective, and perceptual-motor behaviors in a cumulative fashion. Examples of cognitive rule systems include "principles bearing on understanding the organization and processes of the physical and social world (how it works), rules for acting on or operating in the world (problem solving and construction strategies), and rules for coding, communicating information, and acting symbolically about the world (language systems—verbal, mathematical, art)" (Fowler, 1972, p. 151). Careful attention is given to the design of opportunities for creative play; play activities extend to the guided learning component of the curriculum as well. Each child's sessions (three or more five- to fifteen-minute specialized activities daily) are tailored to individual interests and developmental levels. The flavor of such guided learning activities can be obtained from this quotation:

> Projects on learning information concepts (i.e., the names, characteristics, functions, groupings, etc., of common objects), problem solving (e.g., learning to use objects as tools or learning to get around barriers), and language syntax (e.g., how subjects and predicates can describe people performing actions) were experimented with in specialized research projects that were intrinsic to the regular program. A variety of routine sessions setting up play and guidance with sensory motor toys (e.g., form boards, stacking toys, puzzles) and teacher-initiated plans on information concepts, similarities and differences, spatial relations, object features, and sensory qualities (texture, odors, etc.) were typical of other more or less regular offerings in the program. Much of the activity was organized in terms of analytic and synthesizing operations with part-whole relations, features and functions, relational concepts (between objects, and objects and environments), and limited grouping activities. Among our primary objectives were to develop complex mental processes rooted in strong motivations, deep interest, and a sense of efficacy and self-worth as a competent child, rather than simply to impart information— though this, too, was an important aim (Fowler, 1972, p. 153).

Evaluative Research   The experimental infants' developmental progress in Fowler's demonstration project (1972) cannot be summarized simply. Variations in program exposure, age of entry into the program, sex and ethnic differences among infants, and discrepant sample size between the "advantaged" and "disadvantaged" subgroupings confound an analysis of measured developmental change. A few tentative generalizations about program impact are nonetheless apparent from the ample data collected during the course of Fowler's project. For purposes of clarity, these generalizations are grouped into the three categories below. These categories are based upon data from several measures, including the Bayley Scales of Mental and Motor Development, portions of the Stanford-Binet scale, the Bayley Infant Behavior Record, The Schaefer-Aronson Infant Behavior Inventory, and Specially Constructed Autonomy and Infant Adaptation Scales.

A. Mental Development
   1. Despite an initially higher mean IQ score (110.6 versus 100.0), gains in mental development among advantaged children surpassed those of their disadvantaged age-mates to a significant degree. Gains among the disadvantaged subsample also were substantial, however.[1]

---

[1] These data are in slight contrast to those reported by Robinson and Robinson (1971), who found that their disadvantaged infants responded most dramatically to early intervention.

2. Mental gains were somewhat greater for infants who entered the program earlier and remained longer, especially if they were males; females generally exceeded their male counterparts in total gains, even though females tended toward lower performance at initial entry into the program.

3. Day care infants showed generally more favorable gains than did stay-home infants, although the gains among girls in both groups were virtually equivalent.

B. Motor Development

1. In general, the intervention program had much less measurable impact upon motor development than upon mental growth.

2. Motor development gains among the disadvantaged infants were sufficiently greater, so that by program departure time these infants demonstrated a slight advantage in motor skills as compared to the advantaged subsample.

C. Socioemotional Development

1. Generally speaking, changes in socioemotional development were ambiguous; however, the total sample of day care infants was rated more consistently or stably over time than was the home-reared sample (possibly an artifact of rater familiarity with the infants).

2. Changes revealed by socioemotional measures were generally small, even though positive. The clearest "improvements" came in rated motivational characteristics such as curiosity-exploration or inquisitiveness. Somewhat larger gains in verbal expressiveness were noted for both advantaged and disadvantaged infants. The principal and most reliable differences between these two subsamples involved irritability and belligerence, with the disadvantaged infants doing more poorly.

3. Females were observed to change more than males on socioemotional measures, especially social responsivity, although the general level of sex differences at the time of final assessment was not widely disparate. Females whose program experience was extended beyond one year tended toward higher levels of general desirable social traits, including independence.

Commentary   Together these data show that a program of infant care can be qualitatively sufficient to promote adequate development among tiny persons from various socioeconomic backgrounds. If cognitive and socioemotional development are more subject to the influence of coordinated care than is motor development, several factors could be involved. For one thing, the former domains are probably more subject to environmentally produced variations. For another, they are probably dealt with more specifically in most infant programs—and certainly in Fowler's. More important, however, is the strong suggestion that a positive response to coordinated care is more likely if such care is begun at or before age 1 and continued longer than eight months. This possibility lends support to

Schaefer's earlier mentioned contention (1972) about the benefits of starting earlier and working longer with infants, whether at home or in day care centers.

As Fowler himself suggests, the *quality* of a day care education program possibly is more crucial than the setting in which it occurs (home or institution); but certain social advantages may accrue in group settings, particularly for infants without siblings. Fowler's reported sex differences are a bit puzzling in this regard and complicated still further by the interaction of sex with family socioeconomic status. Further research will perhaps clarify these relationships. Programs wherein autonomy, intellectual curiosity, and achievement are stressed equally for males and females may be able to affect the traditional expectations of parents for their female offspring so that the course of socialization becomes more balanced. For girls who have initially been socialized less emphatically than boys in these areas, changes could be more sudden and striking. Furthermore, females may benefit more than males from an all-female day care staff with feminist liberation leanings, whose values would inevitably influence the pattern of caregiven-infant relationships (Fowler, 1972). If so, one might press for male caregiver representation on day care staffs without risking any loss in a "socialization for competence" emphasis in the case of female infants and toddlers.[2] Ethically speaking, infants of both sexes have an equal right to same-sex and cross-sex caregiver-child interactions. Thus a day care staff should be represented by both sexes to honor this right.

The final aspect of Fowler's approach to be discussed here concerns the families of infants who have dropped out of the day care education milieu. It was observed that infants who entered but did not remain in this quality care program typically came from economically disadvantaged circumstances. Apparently, the general life situation of many low-income families is such that additional forms of support are needed if day care services are to be sustained over time. Several other problems are highlighted by the Toronto project, including transportation, satisfactory communication between parents and day care personnel, and the appropriate and consistent application of day care program methods in the home.

Some Issues in Infant Education

On balance, the preliminary results of infant education programs are sufficiently encouraging to support the continued explorations of intervention practices during infancy. Unfortunately, substantive long-term follow-up data are still scarce. Much more is advocated for infant education than we have solid empirical evidence to justify. In White's words (1973) we have at our disposal some "programs of consequence, but no proven programs." It has become increasingly clear that the programs that do achieve

---

[2] See Baumrind (1971) for a thoroughgoing treatment of sex role factors related to socialization for instrumental competence.

meaningful consequences, are designed with specific goals and a system of resources which can be delivered in an organized and consistent way. But the not-so-simple truth is that no one really knows what are the most suitable combinations of experiences and the most desirable conditions for infant stimulation. Certainly, as White (1973) suggests, one should not compound the "Head Start error" by claiming miracles from infant education.

The issues surrounding infant education are essentially those first discussed in Chapter 1 regarding early childhood education as a whole: *what, when, how, who, where*, and *why*? The last issue has been addressed generally throughout this first section of Chapter 8; and the preceding five issues have been reflected to some degree in the infant programs reviewed. Attempts to resolve the what of infant programs are perhaps more similar than different among existing programs. Most program builders view infancy as a period of "platform building" for the development of learning sets and attentional skills upon which more specific later learnings are based. Language-conceptual contents seem to be dealt with more uniformly than the more ambiguous and more crucial motivational aspects of infant learning. Indeed, a strong argument has been made that content specificity in infant programs is far less important than curriculum scope, variety, and structure (Weikart and Lambie, 1972). The clearest trend concerning the what of infant care and education is a rapid move away from the simple custodial model to the sort of developmental approach first mentioned in Chapter 1.

Even more pertinent in infant care and education is when to intervene, an issue discussed more thoroughly in the final chapter of this book. For the moment, it is enough to say that strong feelings pervade any process of decision making about when organized day care–education services are provided to infants. And it is difficult to separate the when from the where issue. For example, there has long existed a clinical concern about the possible adverse effects on infants of maternal separation and multiple mothering, especially prior to age 3. This concern has caused resistance to infant education efforts in group settings. Such resistance is partly overcome by home-based teaching and child care. The problem is that such an approach is not only very expensive in terms of resource deployment but impractical as a single type of service for working mothers. Various demonstration projects (e.g., Keister, 1970) are providing data to show that early and extended group care need not interfere with normal development during infancy and thereafter. Of course, the design of quality care and education outside the home and measures for upgrading care within the home itself must be emphasized in such programs. Clearly, parents are the key to any real success in infant education. More about this is said in the next section.

Equally complex are the how and who issues. The development of valid "instructional techniques" for use with infants seems at a more primitive level even than those for older children. Tutorial methods, which permit genuine individualization in the teaching-learning process, are currently most in favor. Certainly, play cannot be slighted as a medium for much learning, even in its most simple form of adult-infant interaction prior to the walking stage. The reader is urged carefully to study the details of methods being developed for purposes of infant education, formal or otherwise.

Methods for training professionals, paraprofessionals, and parents warrant equally careful scrutiny (see, for example, Dittman, 1973, pp. 64–92). The issue of who cares for and educates infants outside the home extends to problems of selecting and training day care workers and evaluating staff. Staff diversity in sex role models and ethnic representation, for example, looms as a challenge. Staff attitude is also important; a service orientation is much preferred to a "we know best" approach. Further and more elaborate treatments of background factors and issues inherent in infant education are provided by Dittman (1971), Grotberg (1971), and Honig (1972; 1973).

To conclude this brief section on infant education, it can be said that few adults deny the right of infants to quality physical care and emotional support. (Admittedly, some adults behave otherwise, as the growing and distressing literature on child abuse too clearly indicates.) The funda-

Extensive parent involvement is fundamental for a sound infant stimulation program. In addition to efforts at strengthening family relationships among program participants, educators often include a careful study of parent–infant interactions in various kinds of learning situations. In this way, a better understanding of the role of early experience in infant development may be achieved. Photo by Gary Easter, courtesy of High/Scope Educational Research Foundation.

mental issue is whether or to what extent systematic attempts at *educa-tion* should begin as early as infancy. If we intervene on the grounds that failure to do so will result in irreversibly negative or incomplete growth and development, we may be guilty of self-deception. Recent evidence gathered in another cultural setting has reminded us once again of children's remarkable resiliency (Kagan and Klein, 1973); these data indicate that even "absolute retardation in the time of emergence of universal cognitive competencies during infancy is not predictive of comparable deficits for memory, perceptual analysis, and inference during preadolescence" (p. 957).

Of course, most advocates of infant education are not concerned only with the intellectual domain. Socioemotional development also figures prominently in such programs as Fowler's (1972), for example. In this writer's view, much can be done to improve the general quality of parent-child relationships and human understanding in America. If infant stimulation programs successfully strengthen and make more enjoyable these relationships and understandings, their continued support and expansion is in order. Ends, however, do not by themselves justify means. Certain premises must be guaranteed. One is a consensus about priorities in the development of human resources, including the joy of being human and relating humanely to others. A second guarantee must be in the form of ethically acceptable and psychologically sound educational programs. We have only just begun.

PARENT INVOLVEMENT IN EARLY EDUCATION

Introduction

In the preceding section, we have seen how instrumental a role parents can play in any systematic approach to infant education. And sprinkled throughout earlier chapters have been references to various programs for parent involvement in preschool and primary education.[3] Since the mid-1960s, for example, certain basic requirements for parental involvement must be met by Head Start centers and Project Follow Through model sponsors; some model sponsors, in fact, have gone far beyond these guidelines to utilize parents as classroom teachers (see Chapter 3). And beginning in 1967, a system of parent-child centers was established by federal legislation to provide health, education, and social services for impoverished parents and their infants and toddlers (Pieper, 1971). These, and other developments have made parent involvement and education a *cause célèbre* in recent years. The present section is devoted to a brief discus-

---

[3] A brief clarification of terms may be useful here. *Parental involvement* refers to some degree of participation at all major stages of an early education program: planning, execution, evaluation, and modification. Decision-making responsibilities for parents are stressed. *Parent education*, often integrated into strategies for parental involvement, is concerned with methods for the development of effective parenting skills (Stevens, in press, 1975).

sion of some background factors which have combined to produce renewed support for parent involvement in early education. Various forms and levels of parent involvement in early education are discussed and an exemplary approach is explored. This section concludes with a reference to some evaluation research and major issues associated with parent involvement and parent education. Justice to the staggering proliferation of parental involvement literature cannot be done in this short section; an attempt is made only to give some highlights of this literature. Finally, the focus of this discussion is parent involvement in early education as opposed to day care programs, although much overlap exists between these two activities.

Some Background Factors at Work

As suggested in Chapters 1 and 2, ideas about and an appreciation for parent involvement in early childhood education extend back to the early years of America's child welfare movement, including family life education and the advent of parent-cooperative nursery schools. Organized parent groups concerned with questions of child-rearing, especially religious and moral training, date back even earlier (Brim, 1959). However, aside from activities attempted by variously effective parent-teacher associations, there is little traditional evidence for meaningful and productive working relationships between public schools and parents of school children. Certainly this seems to be true of most public school systems known to the writer. Teachers rarely are trained in techniques for effective parent-teacher communication, much less in the complex details of coordinating home-school curriculum activities, enlisting and rewarding parental support of school programs, and helping motivated parents to become better teachers of their own children. Many reasons for this lack can be hypothesized, ranging from naivety to confusion to outright competition with parents for the control of educational processes, if not children themselves. The point is that the situation has changed rapidly because of a chain of events associated with the 1960s early intervention movement.

Three links in this chain can be clearly identified. One link is the fairly elaborate body of research about the influence on young children of home factors, especially parental teaching styles and general attitude toward self-improvement through intellectual activity. This body of research (summarized elsewhere, e.g., Hess, Block, Costello, Knowles, and Largay, 1971; Nedler, 1973; Schaefer, 1972; Streissguth and Bee, 1972), indicates sharp contrasts in parent-child interaction patterns which seem to affect children's learning styles, attitudes about school and intellectual-academic activities, and general cognitive development. These contrasts are most vivid along social class lines and generally favor middle-class parents and children—for whatever reason. Substantial ethnic group differences in maternal teaching style have also been documented (Steward and Stewart, 1973).

A second link is the insights from early efforts at compensatory education (see Chapters 1 and 2). Programs that produce more than temporary desirable effects on children are most likely to have made some provision for parent involvement and education (see Klaus and Gray, 1968). In other words, parental involvement is one factor that early distinguished more from less potent compensatory education programs.

A third link in this chain is the sudden upsurge in direct political pressure for general community involvement in education (Hess et al., 1971). Ethnic nationalism, of course, has contributed to this increase in political pressure, as has a growing dissatisfaction with public schooling among parents from all social and ethnic components of American society. One extreme form of this citizen group involvement has been the free school movement discussed in Chapter 7. However, the great majority of American parents has stood by the public education system. Many now continue to seek more responsibility for and input into this system. The more fortunate parents are encouraged and sometimes led toward greater participation by public school authorities.

These three factors, together with an interesting series of innovative experiments in parent education (Scheinfeld, Bowles, Tuck, and Gold, 1970), have helped most professional early childhood educators to realize several important benefits of parental involvement. Most obviously, even a minimal effort to involve parents in their children's education can bridge the continuity gap which often exists between home and school. Second, properly informed and equipped parents can provide home practice opportunities for their children in many school-related activities. This can be extremely important for children whose educational progress is problematical. Third, by contributing in meaningful ways to their children's development and education, many parents may achieve an improved sense of self-worth and respect. If so, the general affectional relationships among parents and children may also improve. Of course, these and other possible advantages of parental involvement in early education must be decided in large part by systematic research. This matter will be taken up later. In the meantime, it is instructive to consider forms of parental involvement which have evolved for application in early education.

Forms of Parental Involvement

Forms of parental involvement within early childhood education circles vary according to the age of the *children* for whom principal benefits are sought (Nedler, 1973). As we have seen, home-based programs with procedures for home visitations by trained parent educators and child workers are usually reserved for parents of infants and toddlers. However, attempts to train mothers of the very young in special locations outside the home also can be cited. These include the parent-child centers funded by federal monies and various parent-oriented nursery programs, especially those designed for exceptional children (e.g., Luterman, 1971).

A wider variety of parent involvement strategies may apply to educational programs for children of age 3 and over. These strategies can be

Parent involvement has fast become a watchword in contemporary thinking about early education. These parents have met to discuss better ways and means of interracial education for their young children. Photo courtesy of Camera Craft.

conceptualized along a continuum from "minimal involvement" to virtually complete parental control of the early education program (Gordon, 1970a). Briefly, this continuum can be viewed as follows. First, "minimal involvement" usually means that parents serve as an audience for educators who pass along words of wisdom about child development, education, and the things that parents should know and understand about such matters. Minimal involvement may also extend to a system for periodic parent observation, albeit passive and acceptant, of activities in the school setting.

A second, more advanced, form of parent involvement is designed to promote participation by parents in the direct and active teaching of their children. Ordinarily this requires a decision by educators about what and how parents can do something consistent with the existing school program. By definition, then, this form of participation sets up a school program and methods as the authority parents must support or adapt to. Most commonly, language activities to promote children's verbal facility, games to enhance school attitudes, and informed procedures for the management of children's behavior (disciplinary techniques) are prescribed at this level of parental involvement.

A still more advanced form of parental involvement has parents serve in a voluntary capacity as aides or assistants to teachers in the classroom. This may involve the parent's provision of inexpensive educational materials or supplies and handling of classroom routines such as children's snack, rest, and play times. Or it may include responsibility for auxiliary teaching functions under the careful supervision of the teacher. In its most advanced form, this strategy of parent involvement has the parent share some of the teacher's major instructional responsibilities. In this case, explicit parent training in the technical aspects of instruction is called for. We have seen an example of this last approach in the Kansas behavior analysis Follow-Through model discussed in Chapter 3.

Apart from alternative or free schools, the most advanced form of parental involvement in early education requires that educators honor parental wishes, if not rights, to control the entire school system. This means that parents no longer are simply recipients of a service. Rather, they become the principal decision-making power in determining the curricula, teacher selection, and the like. Davies (1973) has referred to such citizen involvement as the "emerging third force in education."

Local circumstances would seem to dictate which of the above forms (or combination of forms) of parental involvement is most efficacious at a given time. Absolute parental control has been only rarely seen. But the widely publicized move toward the decentralization of schools in large urban communities suggests that such control may materialize in the next decade or so. Theoretically, of course, parents *are* in control of their schools through the long-standing republican system of representation, i.e., school boards composed of and elected by the citizenry. The move toward decentralization, however, seems designed to establish a less remote connection between parents and their schools. And it is notable that initial social experiments with community-controlled schooling, although rare, have demonstrated some highly desirable outcomes among parents, children, and teachers alike (e.g., Guttentag, 1972).

Minimal involvement, described elsewhere as "educational imperialism" (Levin, 1967), hopefully is fast disappearing as a preferred form of involvement. According to Gordon (1970b), the trend is in the direction of a home-school partnership which allows active participation by parents as well as giving them more than a token voice in basic decision making about the nature of their young children's schooling. In any case, certain issues must be faced, including what parents should be doing, why they should be doing it, and how best to evaluate both the process and outcomes of parental involvement (formative and summative evaluation). Some attention is given to these issues later in this section.

An Example of Parent Involvement Strategy

One of the most widely known models for parent involvement is the Florida Parent Education Program (Gordon, 1968). The Florida model makes explicit provision for self-improvement among the mothers of children ranging from infancy through the primary grades. Maternal self-development, in other words, is seen as possibly the most powerful medium to enhance child development. From the period of the child's infancy through age 2, trained parent educators make home visits to project mothers once a week. Home visits have as their basic objective the teaching of concrete, specific mother-infant activities to promote cognitive and affective growth. Weekly visits are continued for two- and three-year-olds and are supplemented by the "backyard experience." This experience brings groups of four or five project children together in the home of a given project mother usually twice a week for about two hours each session. The parent educator who regularly works with that project mother uses three sessions to conduct short individual tutoring sessions with the children. A majority of time is spent in specially designed play activities, language activity, and group games. Piagetian thought has strongly influenced the design of these activities (see Chapter 5). Project mothers serve as assistants in this educational phase of the program and are normally joined by a third adult (often a graduate student in training) who serves as a data collector.

The most advanced level of the Florida program is the Follow-Through model for K–3 education. Again, the paraprofessional parent educator is a key figure, spending a portion of the school day in actual classroom activity and another portion of the day in home visits during which mothers are taught specific ideas to complement their child's school learning. Thus, the distinguishing characteristic of the Florida model is the strong liaison role for home-school communication taken on by the parent educator. Parents are also encouraged to participate in the design of learning tasks, serve as classroom volunteers, represent project parents as active members of a policy advisory committee, and become trained as parent educators.

Criteria for successful implementation of the Florida model include (1) increased parental competency and self-esteem, (2) enhanced intellectual development and self-image among project children, and (3) enhanced capacity for institutional change among participating schools. Evaluation progress has been slow and subject to many of the difficulties associated with other models discussed earlier in this book (for example, see the TEEM model, Chapter 4). However, results from the infant stimulation phase have been consistently positive. As compared to control infants and parents, Florida project participants have demonstrated greater mental development and self-confidence in parenting ability (Gordon, 1970b). Supportive data have also been gleaned from an unusually well-implemented version of the Florida model, of which this writer has intimate knowledge (Project Home Base, Yakima, Washington). Among the findings in this second version have been increases in the extent and quality of mother-child interactions among project participants and superior pre-academic skill development among model (as compared to control) children.

Many other approaches to parent involvement can be cited. An approach with particularly well-designed procedures for continuous evaluation and coordinated home instruction, classroom instruction, and family services is the *behavior-oriented prescriptive teaching model* (Carter and Hodges, 1972). The creative use of toys as a means to enhance parent-child interaction and children's problem-solving and language skills has figured prominently in several other promising parent involvement education strategies (e.g., Levenstein, 1970; Nimnicht and Brown, 1972). Many other programs, ranging from local school district procedures through university-based experimental projects to national programs (including Head Start) are reviewed by Gordon (1970a). Attempts at developing a theory of parent education in systems terms have even begun (e.g., Buckland, 1972). Clearly, these developments illustrate a growing conviction that the best way to provide children with total and prolonged positive development is through their parents.

Some Comments About Evaluation

We have just raised the broader question of parent involvement evaluation research. And it was earlier suggested that parent involvement is often a factor in determining the impact on children of early education programs. A few specific findings concerning the Florida model have also been reported. But what of the general case? Is parent involvement actually the best way, or a generally effective way, to nurture children's development? A definitive answer to this question seems premature. However, the evidence thus far accumulated can be taken to tentatively support several generalizations (Hess et al., 1971; Nedler, 1973). First, in programs where parents gradually become *primary teachers* of their own children, positive effects on intellectual behavior usually are noted; little is yet known about the noncognitive effects of such parental teaching, but there is little reason to believe these effects would be negative. There is, of course, the possibility that if parents are even more strongly sensitized to the value of early intellectual stimulation and training in the home, they may subject their children to greater pressures for achievement. This sensitization could also affect parent-child interactions so that children would be evaluated or accepted by their parents primarily on the basis of their success in progressing toward goals imposed by parental involvement programs. But this need not happen and is unlikely to where such hazards are fully exposed and individualized programming prevails. In short, a broad perspective should be maintained in order to avoid an undue and excessively narrow parental teaching orientation.

A second generalization supported by the evidence on parental involvement is that parents who become more active as teachers of their children usually value their involvement, report an improved sense of competence and self-esteem regarding parental skills, and report improved verbal interactions with their children. These effects apparently are not mediated drastically by program type. That is, desirable outcomes are associated with both outside-the-home parent education programs and programs which involve home visits. The relative advantages and disadvantages of each approach may, of course, change with individual parent circumstances. In other words, logistics problems (e.g., transportation) may affect parents differentially and should be taken into account by program designers.

One apparent advantage, regardless of program type, is the interesting *vertical diffusion* effect (Gray and Klaus, 1970), in which the positive effects of parent education often spread to the siblings of the target child. This suggests that the parenting skills being learned through an intervention program can influence the total family interaction pattern. Vertical diffusion has been observed especially to occur among siblings younger than the preschool or early school child around whom the program for parent education is built. Vertical diffusion, like most other program effects, is partially a function of program *length*—with longer-term parent involvement programs being more effective than more expedient approaches.

The variable of program length is well illustrated by Radin (1972), whose longitudinal research is typical of the improving parent education literature. From a compensatory education preschool program with seventy-one children enrolled, three matched groups were formed. Maternal involvement experience was varied across the three groups, ranging from intense to moderate to none. Intensely involved mothers were present at home tutorial sessions and at weekly meetings in small groups with a social worker; moderately involved mothers were present during biweekly tutorial sessions, but had no social worker contact; and mothers who had no involvement were not present at tutorial sessions or social worker meetings. Group meetings for the intensely involved group included discussions of reinforcement techniques, activities for intellectual stimulation, and the dynamics of achievement motivation.

At the end of the first year, no real differences in several growth measures were found among children of the three groups (Stanford-Binet scale, Peabody Picture Vocabulary Test, and behavior ratings of curiosity, conduct and academic motivation). Only mothers in the two involved groups showed measured changes in relation to two major program objectives: increased amount of educational materials in the home and decreased authoritarianism in their attitude toward children. Follow-up data taken at the end of the second (kindergarten) year indicated substantially larger IQ gains for the children of the two maternal involvement groups as compared to the children of the no-involvement group. Apparently, then, the sustained influence of improved parent skills, rather than the lack of any immediate effect, warrants scrutiny in the evaluation of parental involvement strategies.

Some Principal Issues in Parental Involvement Programs

Many complex issues are found within the parental involvement literature. Central, of course, are the issues concerned with what should be the goals and content of parent involvement and parent education. Perhaps the most basic issue in this joint domain is whether parents should be educated and involved primarily to accept a given school model as correct and to implement it further in the home, or whether parental involvement should be more specifically designed to change the school even in fundamental ways (Gordon, 1970a). This issue touches a deep philosophical nerve, but it seems to this writer that the former judgment about program focus has prevailed. Regardless, values associated with intellectual-academic achievement have been dominant in guiding the selection of program content. We have seen examples of this in the foregoing discussion; further examples include programs to improve tactics for achievement motivation training (Kowatrakul, Robinson, and Stivers, 1971) and question-asking skills (Henderson and Garcia, 1973). Other authorities (e.g., Naylor, 1970) stress more the "universal" tasks of parenthood. Hopefully the real and pressing needs of parents will be assessed and accommodated in any approach to parent involvement. Educators can easily be mistaken if they assume that parental needs are the same, regardless of time and social context (Stevens, in press). Up to now, there has also been a relative lack of attention to parental (in contrast to maternal) role behaviors. Although this omission is understandable in view of the heavy preoccupation of psychologists and educators with maternal influences (see Nash, 1965), future parent involvement strategy hopefully will include the father more specifically. Much can also be learned from basic socialization research about patterns of parental authority (Baumrind, 1971), possible antecedents of self-esteem (Coopersmith, 1968), and parental influences on children's cognitive development (Freeberg and Payne, 1967).

The when issue in parental involvement and education seems to have been resolved by the strong trend toward programs for parents of infants to be continued through at least the children's early school years. A flurry of activity concerning even earlier education for parenthood beginning with adolescents in the high school setting has also been witnessed (Stevens, in press). Such education typically combines instruction in principles of child development and learning with some sort of student laboratory experience with preschool children in a day care or nursery program. Among the strongest advocates of such basic education for parenthood is Staats (1968). Staats feels that most parents are well intentioned in their approach to child rearing, but too often employ "haphazard and psychologically unsound procedures." The problem, he maintains, is that parents have little skill in the systematic application of learning principles to children's socialization. For this lack, parents cannot be faulted. The problem, Staats argues, is that we have nurtured in our society a faulty concept of human behavior and development: a belief that the development of basic skills and abilities for effective problem solving occurs through physiological maturation (rather than complex learning experiences) and that parents can be instrumental in such development only by providing a benevolent environment. Staats urges that parents be helped to assume much of the responsibility for developing the child's "basic behavioral repertoire," which he believes is essential to all later learning, including educational progress in the school. Staats sees parents as active trainers of children as well as benevolent caretakers. The specifics of the basic behavior repertoire are discussed in Chapter 9.

The who and where issues of education for parent involvement can also be considered in relation to sample programs already discussed.

Currently, the most favored view of the who issue is that parent educators should be parents from the community they will be serving, i.e., parents whose circumstances are similar to those with whom they will be working. This view does not discount the role of professionals—parents must initially be trained in the mechanics of any given program. But a sense of community identity and free and open communication among people are probably nowhere more critical for success than in the area of parental involvement and parental education. As suggested earlier, where this education occurs is largely a matter of specific local circumstances, including the fund of human and economic resources.

The how issue is perhaps the most problematical. Obstacles to satisfactory parental involvement and parental education seem to greatly outnumber the proven methods for these purposes. This statement applies even more strongly to the problems of involving parents *initially*. Parents and educators frequently behave as though mutually intimidated or threatened by each another. An attitude on the part of educators that "we are here to show you how to be better parents" can be disastrous (even if educators can deliver on their promise). Other problems include parents and professionals' unrealistic expectations for change, value system conflicts, apprehension about formal evaluation, community instability (as in migrant farm worker locales), and parents and professionals who lack a genuine commitment to child welfare. It is encouraging that successes are being realized despite the obstacles. Parent involvement is fast becoming a top priority in education. Interested readers are advised to seek further information about more specific principles and techniques in this area of endeavor (see Colvin and Zaffiro, 1974; Gordon, 1972; Karnes, 1969; Pickarts and Fargo, 1971).

EDUCATIONAL TELEVISION FOR YOUNG CHILDREN

In this final section of Chapter 8, attention is given to the phenomenon of educational television for young children. Because it is both a "groundbreaker" and can serve as an instructive case study in educational television programming for young children, the Children's Television Workshop (CTW) program, "Sesame Street," is discussed in some detail. Certainly, most of the issues, including evaluation, that surround children's educational television can be emphasized strongly by this example. Chapter 8 concludes with a few suggestions for improved television programming for young children.

The Advent of "Sesame Street"

"Sesame Street," an instructional program developed primarily for preschool children, was conceived with three major realities in mind (Cooney, 1970). First is the presence of a television set in approximately 97 percent of American homes. Second is the vast amount of time spent by an average preschool child in front of a television set before school entry.

It is estimated that a child's television watching hours exceed the time spent in the classroom for the first five years of formal schooling. A third factor, as we have seen repeatedly, is the growing conviction among educators that children's education should begin before kindergarten or first-grade entry. In the beginning, "Sesame Street" was underwritten by various private foundations and the federal government as an eight-million-dollar two-year experiment (Culhane, 1970). Its first year was earmarked for basic developmental research, the second for the preparation and broadcasting of 130 program hours, and an evaluation of their impact upon young viewers. Television teaching techniques were adapted from the tactics employed by commercial television to capture and sustain young children's attention. From the outset, "Sesame Street" programmers faced the issue of how to entertain without perverting or destroying the desired instructional value of the program. Subsequent to the initial experimental period, the goal areas of "Sesame Street" were expanded to include *symbolic representation skills* (e.g., letter recognition, word matching and meaning, number labeling and enumeration), *skills of cognitive organization* (e.g., mastery of relational concepts, perceptual discrimination abilities, and classification), *reasoning and problem-solving skills* (e.g., making inferences, evaluating solutions), *concepts of self* (e.g., body parts and functions, recognizing emotion), and *knowledge of social roles, groups, and institutions* (including awareness of the man-made features of the environment).

Early exploratory research efforts led to the validation of several crucial ideas still reflected in "Sesame Street" programs (Little, 1969; E. Palmer, 1969). One idea is that repetition can be effective as a principle of instruction for preschool children. A second is that young children's attention can be effectively captured by the well-known commercial "spot method." A third is that letters and numbers can be learned by children through tracing the movement in film animation (kinesthesia). These and other concepts provided the basis for program development, testing, and revision. Eventually, "Sesame Street" was beamed to millions of American homes in the autumn of 1969.

Since that time, "Sesame Street" has continued to occupy a central role in children's educational television. Evaluation efforts have been extended by the Educational Testing Service (ETS), Princeton, New Jersey. Predictably, both kudos and biting criticisms have been given to this pioneer broadcasting enterprise. Early evaluation results and a summary of criticisms now follow.

Evaluative Research about "Sesame Street"

"Sesame Street" evaluation began in 1968 before the program had been publicly broadcast. The major work was the contracted responsibility of Educational Testing Service, whose personnel developed and field-tested a battery of measures (including parent questionnaires) relevant to

"Sesame Street's" objectives and target audience (specifically children from low-income homes). Evaluation strategy early was conceived as a longitudinal design (permitting follow-up study) to include assessments of the major intended and some possible unintended outcomes (e.g., impact of "Sesame Street" on maternal aspirations for children's education).

The First-Year Evaluation For the first-year evaluation, a large ($N = 943$) and disparate sampling of three-, four-, and five-year-old children of both sexes was drawn. Included were economically disadvantaged inner-city children, suburban advantaged children, rural children, and disadvantaged Spanish-speaking children. More of the disadvantaged children were black than white and more of the children watched "Sesame Street" at home than at school. The principal measures of knowledge utilized were body parts, letters, forms, numbers, relational terms, sorting skills, classification skills, and puzzles. The dominant orientation was to children's cognitive behavior. The total sample was divided into quartiles according to the amount of "Sesame Street" viewed during the first twenty-six-week season. Quartile I, for example, consisted of children who watched Sesame Street only rarely (or never); quartile IV included children who watched an average of five or more times a week. All data analyses were based upon this quartile distinction.

First-Year Results The major finding of the first-year evaluation was a positive relationship between children's program viewing time and their test performances; children who watched "Sesame Street" the most apparently learned most. This generalization held across the total sample, regardless of a child's socioeconomic, ethnic, sex, or residential (geographic) status. Additional findings of importance can be summarized by three points. First, with rare exceptions, the skills learned best were those that had received the most program time and direct attention (e.g., letter-related skills). These skills, moreover, were shown to have some positive transfer value in that they facilitated the development of skills not directly taught (e.g., writing one's name and recognizing full words). Second, young viewers' learning of program content apparently was not dependent upon concurrent formal adult supervision. It was discovered, however, that children who logged greater amounts of viewing time also tended to have maternal company and reportedly more frequent discussions with their mothers about program content. Third, younger (three-year-old) children tended to profit more from "Sesame Street" than did older (five-year-old) children. Subsequent analyses of first-year data have also suggested that (1) gains among disadvantaged children were generally equivalent to those of more advantaged children and (2) certain children (e.g., children for whom English is a second language) may be particularly receptive to positive "Sesame Street" influences.

The Second-Year Evaluation Two separate efforts comprised the Educational Testing Service's second-year evaluation (Bogatz and Ball, 1971).

One, called the "new study" ($N = 282$) was intended to replicate the first-year evaluation and to provide data about the expanded goal areas for "Sesame Street's" second year of production. Roughly 50 percent of the children in the new study sample was successfully encouraged to watch "Sesame Street," the other half was intentionally not encouraged. The other major portion of the second-year evaluation was termed the "follow-up study" (coincidentally, $N = 283$). The follow-up study involved further assessment of a subset of the first-year sample: at-home disadvantaged children, including sixty-six Spanish-speaking youngsters. A revised essential test battery was administered on a pre-post basis as were parent and teacher questionnaires. The latter dealt with teacher impressions of general school readiness among first-year "Sesame Street" viewers who entered school in the fall of 1970. In considering the findings that follow, the reader should be mindful that roughly 30 percent of air time on "Sesame Street" was concerned with prereading and arithmetic goal areas. Slightly more than 5 percent of this time was spent on goal areas concerned with perceptual discrimination, natural environment, and self-concept. Less than 5 percent of time was spent on the remaining goal areas (geometric forms, relational terms, classification, problem solving, social units, social interactions, and the man-made environment).

The New Study Results   Results from the new study generally reinforced the major findings of the first-year evaluation. Disadvantaged preschoolers, in particular, benefit from a program emphasis upon basic knowledge and skills in "Sesame Street's" basic goal areas. Both amount of viewing and encouragement for viewing were positively related to children's test gain scores. Viewers also scored significantly higher than nonviewers on the Peabody Picture Vocabulary Test. Program impact seemed to be greatest among children whose previewing attainments were weakest and whose parents' socioeconomic status was lowest. Children's attitudinal change data were inconclusive (not surprising in light of the measurement problems involved), as were data about program impact upon parental expectations for their children, parental attitudes toward education, and general family television viewing habits. The exceptional gains noted among Spanish-speaking children during the first-year evaluation were not repeated by a similar sample in the new study, although these children did show some progress.

The Follow-Up Study   "Sesame Street" in its second year appeared to exert an influence in two major areas. Children who continued to view the program at home in the second year performed better on measures of the more complex goals than did children whose viewing was limited just to the first year. These more complex goals were essentially cognitive

---

Only a few short years ago, Sesame Street was but an imaginative idea in the minds of a handful of people. Now, the world of Sesame Street and its colorful inhabitants are known to thousands of children everywhere. Such is the power of television in modern society. Courtesy of Children's Television Workshop. (facing page) (e.g., number-numeral correspondence, addition and subtraction, letter sounds, and decoding). Second-year viewers also demonstrated significantly more positive attitudes toward school and the racial identity of others.

A second point of analysis in the follow-up study concerned the possible effects of first-year "Sesame Street" viewing by children who subsequently entered school. In the fall of 1970, rankings of children's "readiness" (on eight criteria) were performed by teachers who were unaware of their pupil's viewing history ("blind rankings"). The net result was that the most frequent viewers received the most favorable teacher rankings, which included attitude toward school and effectiveness of peer relationships. "Sesame Street proponents" use these data to counter any apprehension about school being dull by comparison to the lively sensory appeal of "Sesame Street." At least the follow-up study data collectively suggest that "Sesame Street" can promote mastery in certain background skills which mediate children's school interest and the regard in which children are held by teachers.

To summarize, the ETS evaluation projects support the idea that "Sesame Street" can have a measurable impact upon preschool children who regularly view the program. A positive side benefit is the knowledge gained by such evaluations for continued modification of educational programming for children's welfare. Parent and teacher guides to "Sesame Street" have been published and are distributed upon request by the Children's Television Workshop. A children's periodical, *Sesame Street*, is available on a subscription basis, to say nothing of the numerous books, toys, and educational toys which have been inspired by "Sesame Street" and its colorful inhabitants. The program has become truly international in character and is now transmitted into more than fifty countries, with foreign language versions also utilized.

Some Reactions to "Sesame Street" Evaluation

No doubt the ETS reports summarized above have contributed to "Sesame Street's" expanding influence. But these evaluation reports have not escaped criticism. One critique, for example, has focused upon an allegedly spurious sampling design, questionable procedures for assigning children to "treatment" (viewing) conditions, and a failure to account for measurement error in the statistical analysis of gain scores (Ingersoll, 1971). This critique also contains some alternative interpretations of the ETS results. For example, Ingersoll argues that the conclusion that children who watch "Sesame Street" the most gain the most could have an equally plausible interpretation: such gains are in large part a function of children's pretest performances. In other words, if pretest scores can be considered as a learning aptitude measure, gains are more simply a matter of "smarter children learning more"; or the greater educational value of "Sesame Street" is for children who bring to the program a more highly developed cognitive repertoire. However, Ingersoll's interpretation does not mesh well with the ETS contention that larger gains tend to occur among children with lower initial test performances.

Other critical reactions to the Educational Testing Service reports have appeared. One is in the form of an empirical study, albeit on a much smaller scale than the massive ETS projects. Sprigle (1971) set up a comparison of twenty-four matched pairs of children; one member of each pair was then treated to a full series of "Sesame Street" episodes and coordinated curriculum activities. Each counterpart became a "control," who spent equal time in activities with similar content, but with an emphasis upon social emotional development and no television. At the conclusion of this experiment, the "control" children scored higher than the "Sesame Street" group on the Metropolitan Readiness Test. Neither did the television group demonstrate any real advantage in Stanford achievement test performance over a second comparison group of first-grade classmates best described as an "unprepared" control group.

At first glance, the Sprigle (1971) study contradicts the major ETS findings. Sprigle, however, worked with five- and six-year-olds. "Sesame Street" is ostensibly aimed at four-year-olds; its greatest impact seems to be upon children of this age and younger. Sprigle's sample also is considerably smaller; no pretest data are provided; and his initial matching procedures are unclear. Finally, pitting "Sesame Street" against an organized curriculum for early childhood can constitute an unsuitable basis for comparison. Hence the issue is whether the Sprigle study provides legitimate counterevidence to the ETS reports. At least, the Sprigle data remind us that an attitude of cautious scrutiny by both professional and lay persons is desirable for evaluating any kind of new programs. And Sprigle himself argues convincingly that staff members at the Children's Television Workshop have frequently been unrealistic regarding the preparatory role of Sesame Street for poverty children's first-grade achievement. His general message is aptly conveyed by a twist on a famous eulogy to Winston Churchill; Seldom have so few done so little for so many.

Further questions about the longer-term effectiveness of intensive television programming, notably "Sesame Street," have also been raised (Stanley, 1973). Until such programming can be shown to interact with children's later schooling so that their learning is generally improved, can the time and expense involved be really justified? Similarly, can satisfactory reasons be offered for "teaching" skills via "Sesame Street" that many, if not most, children will learn satisfactorily in school, home, or general community activities? It has been observed that "Sesame Street's" viewing audience is disproportionately middle class. That is, the children who view the program least tend to be those who are most disadvantaged. This calls for serious attention to means for increasing the probability that those who may profit most from special programs in fact receive them into their homes (Ball and Bogatz, 1973a).

Further Criticisms of "Sesame Street"

The mixed empirical evidence for "Sesame Street's" influence continues to accumulate. Concurrently, a number of philosophical and conceptual salvos have been fired at "Sesame Street," as the following list of criticisms will attest (Holt, 1971; Ratliff and Ratliff, 1972; Rogers, 1972; Sprigle, 1972): the program is too far removed from structured teaching to qualify as school-relevant; it is too heavily dependent upon the high-pressure tactics of commercial television; it is based too strongly on the twin assumptions that learning is (1) a passive process and (2) unlikely to occur unless deliberate teaching is involved; children are too often forced to adopt a reactionary, rather than an initiative-taking, role; children are seen but not sufficiently heard with respectful acceptance by the adult characters on "Sesame Street"; reinforcement of short rather than sustained spans of attention is given; the program fails to reflect the realities of city street life (Sesame Street is an imaginary place); authoritarian modes of controlling children's behavior are modeled; there is a lack of individualization in adult-child contacts; there is too much haphazard rote learning; there is undue emphasis on letter-naming activities, at best a dubious prerequisite to learning to read; there is a narrow convergence on counting at the expense of the properties and uses of numbers; the program does not deal systematically with problems of attitude formation and change, yet has an implicit overkill on white middle-class values; the program fails to adapt instructional tactics to the unique needs of disadvantaged children; the pace is too rapid; and the program does not exploit the full power of nonverbal communication. As the reader can see, these criticisms reflect concerns about all three major components of "Sesame Street" programming: goals, content, and style of teaching and learning. Some critics, of course, can never be satisfied; but most of the points listed can be used constructively to assess certain aspects of any educational television program.

Expectedly, the case for "Sesame Street's" defense has been built upon three premises (Culhane, 1970; E. Palmer and Connell, 1971; Rosenthal, 1970). First, "Sesame Street" is an experiment in innovation; it is and will continue to be in a formative stage of development for some years to come. A perfect and universally acceptable product was neither expected nor attempted on the first broadcast. Second, many of the criticisms concerning academic matters have both been acted upon over the past few years and utilized in the development of "Sesame Street's" counterpart for primary grade children, "Electric Company."[4] Third, "Sesame Street" was not conceived as a substitute for a comprehensive preschool program staffed by humane competent teachers capable of high-level individualized instruction. Neither were all viewers expected to be equally captivated and influenced by all program contents. Rather, it was intended that a variety of subjects and activities be provided in a "take it or leave it" framework. Children, it is argued, learn in different ways and profit differently from varied experiences.

---

[4] The latter program began in the fall of 1971 as the first broad-scale attempt to utilize a television format for basic reading instruction. Its main target audience, however, is children in second through fourth grade who are experiencing reading difficulties. Preliminary evaluation data are largely positive and teachers generally seem to approve of the program (Ball and Bogatz, 1973b).

A Point of View about Television Program Development

Technical, conceptual, and philosophical controversies will continue to envelop "Sesame Street" and any other organized efforts to reach children through television for educational purposes. Much has been learned, and much remains to be done. Meanwhile, the constructive and scholarly commentary by Meichenbaum and Turk (1972) can serve as one guidepost for thinking about "Sesame Street" and like programs. These authorities begin by accepting that children can and do learn from television. For them, the central question is what to teach. This question can be answered in part by careful monitoring of the research on disadvantaged children's needs. Meichenbaum and Turk agree that the so-called cognitive deficit research (see Chapter 1) suggests a performance rather than a learning ability deficit. Specifically, many disadvantaged children can be described as having a shortcoming in the spontaneous use of words and problem-solving strategies, i.e., nonperformance in the absence of explicit demands. From a review of training procedures for cognitive and language development, Meichenbaum and Turk (1972) conclude that "programs that emphasize the ability to use language in order to organize thoughts, to reflect upon situations, to comprehend the meaning of events, and to structure both the environment and personal behavior in order to choose among alternatives prove most advantageous; in contrast, programs that focus mainly on enlarging vocabulary for description and communication are less advantageous" (pp. 34–35).[5] In short, it is proposed that activities designed to prompt comprehension, activity, spontaneous production of verbal mediators, and the use of such mediators to control nonverbal behavior should be focal in programs for the disadvantaged. This is strikingly similar to the viewpoints expressed in Chapter 4, especially in the section on tutorial approaches to language training.

With such a conceptual foundation, "Sesame Street" can be examined from the standpoint of its potential for overcoming the alleged deficiencies of its disadvantaged preschool viewers; recommendations for a more research-based televised instructional format can thus be advanced. For example, at the heart of many weaknesses charged to "Sesame Street" (including the criticisms about instructional tactics) is the concept of *modeling.* "Sesame Street" adults and muppets rarely model many activities potentially helpful to disadvantaged children. This audience would benefit if "Sesame Street" characters showed ways to size up and comprehend learning tasks and if the show illustrated the spontaneous production of mediators and problem-solving strategies ("thinking aloud" behaviors which express aspects of self-control), the feeling components of learning, the ways of coping with frustration-failure, and the reality of desirable parent-child interactions. The latter could involve modeling of positive reinforcement schedules and the use of successive approximations, sociodramatic play, and role enactments to bring adult and child

---

[5] Reproduced by permission.

together in mutually enjoyable and constructive activities (Meichenbaum and Turk, 1972).

These recommendations appear reasonable and sound. If they are acted upon, many other criticisms of Sesame Street might also be tempered—the bias toward "Sesame Street" children's passive learning style and lack of attention to noncognitive aspects of behavior, for example. Still, an appropriate perspective must be maintained. Educational television is limited as a single force in counteracting the effects of poverty upon children's development. Television's power should not be underestimated, but neither should one expect too much—especially in the absence of coordinated follow-up experiences involving real children and adults in a challenging supportive learning environment. Big Bird seems to be here to stay; but with his Sesame Street friends, he falls understandably short of being a panacea for childhood education (as would any other single approach to the problem).

A Final Note

One apparent spin-off of the early commitment to evaluation and product improvement by the Children's Television Workshop was the creation in 1972 of the Center for Research in Children's Television in Cambridge Massachusetts. This center, operated in conjunction by CTW and Harvard University, has two major objectives: generally to explore the effects of visual media on children and to provide research and television production training opportunities for interested persons. A similar project also is under way in England. At the University of Leeds, the Centre for Television Research has been established to conceptualize and research the role of television in children's socialization. Other admirable developments include the excellent television guidelines for early childhood education (National Instructional Television, 1969) and a much increased consciousness among basic researchers regarding the influence of filmed material on children's prosocial, as well as antisocial behavior (e.g., Friedrich and Stein, 1973). Scholarly reviews of such research have been provided by Bryan and Schwartz (1971), Liebert, Neale, and Davidson (1973), Stein (1972), and Stevenson (1972).

Some educators have made creative efforts to use television lessons systematically with other schooling services. One vanguard approach with a distinctive educational television component is the Appalachia Preschool Program based in Charleston, West Virginia (Chow and Elmore, 1972). This program is designed to reach a widely dispersed population of preschool children via coordinated home visits by trained staff, televised lessons concerned primarily with language and cognitive skill development, and a mobile classroom (a motor van equipped with portable classroom materials). Televised lessons are supplemented and reinforced by periodic home visits, which, in turn, provide the basis for mobile classroom activities. These activities involve small groups of children who live within the radius of various points along a route through rural

Appalachia. A team of curriculum specialists and field workers provides regular services to as many as 135 children per week who would otherwise be unable to participate in organized preschool programs. The Appalachia program is a unique alternative to traditional schooling in that a major portion of the educational services are brought directly into the home. Yet the social advantages of regular group activity are also sought through the medium of the mobile classroom. In addition to the cognitive emphasis, other aspects of Appalachian children's lives are enriched through songs, games, artwork, and puppet play—all of which are built into the series of television programs.

Evaluation data generally have supported a continuation of this program since its inception in 1968. Younger children (three-year-olds) have seemed especially responsive to the kinds of services provided. The Appalachia program is certainly among the most novel early childhood education programs extant and can serve as a model for the conceptualization of educational activities for children in other parts of rural America.

Finally, the role of commercial television in the education for parents needs examination. One unfulfilled potential of television, for example, is for parent education about child-rearing and development. Several studies suggest that the rate of commercial television watching tends to be higher for low-income viewers than for the general population, especially for daytime programs (Nedler, 1973). While most all parents regardless of socioeconomic standing probably can profit from child development information, low-income parents may be helped even more in developing improved teaching styles and techniques of child management. More than a few promising cues for program design in this area can be gathered from the comparatively meager educational television research to date (Nedler, 1973).

A major obstacle, however, is the apparent reluctance of commercial networks to commit themselves to the cultural, much less the specific educational, welfare of the consuming public. Certainly this seems true in the case of children's programming. It was thought by many that the early success of educational network programs ("Sesame Street," "Electric Company") and other respected programs (e.g., "Misterrogers' Neighborhood") somehow would influence the commercial networks to modify their apparent obsession with offensive cartoon fare and culturally distasteful situation comedies as the principal television diet for young children. At this writing, educational television continues to manifest leadership with new programs such as "Inside-Out," a realistic program that deals with affective behavior and development and touches on topics such as divorce, death, love and altruism. With few exceptions (such as ABC's series of after-school specials), the commercial networks have not changed their late afternoon and weekend programming for children's viewing. More widespread and powerful children's advocate groups are needed to apply pressure upon both the networks and commercial program sponsors for responsible and worthwhile children's television. A particularly noteworthy example is the Massachusetts-based organization,

Action for Children's Television. Such groups also can support organizations like Prime-Time School Television, a Chicago-based firm which attempts to bring the best of commercial television into the educational world by providing free services and materials to teachers. This organization has probably met with its greatest success in activities for older children. Hopefully, more work will soon be done with the late preschool and early school-age child.

SUMMARY

Throughout Chapter 8, the diverse nature of infant education, parent involvement in early education, and educational television programming for the presumed benefit of young children have been examined. All three areas of activity have a comparatively recent history, yet each is a significant development. Attempts at infant education have become more prevalent in part because of the conviction that earlier stimulation can more profoundly influence the course of human development. These attempts largely revolve around some version of a home-teaching program and/or an extra-home program for groups of infants with similar life circumstances and needs. Several examples of infant education were presented, the most extensive of which involves a developmental learning approach to infants whose mothers work full-time outside the home. This extensive approach illustrates many of the basic issues in infant education: logistics, goals, content, methodology, timing, staffing, and the choice of locale for program implementation.

The role of parents in early education can be conceived both in terms of *education*—the development of effective parenting skills—and *involvement*—the degree of participation in the major areas of decision making about educational programming, even to the point of participation in the instructional enterprise itself. Much has happened during the past decade to convince large numbers of educators about the indispensable functions that competent and concerned parents can perform in early childhood development and education. Accordingly, provisions for both parent education and parent involvement have increasingly been made within comprehensive early education curriculum models, usually with positive results. Several forms of parent involvement can be identified, one of which provides the basis for an exemplary parent involvement strategy discussed in this chapter. The discussion of parental roles in early education was concluded with references to the evaluation of parent education programs and to some key issues in parent involvement practices. Even though the research basis for parent education and involvement is at an early stage of development, many valuable clues for program implementation can be gleaned from it by practitioners.

The final section of Chapter 8 has dealt with the phenomenon of children's educational television. The highly visible program, "Sesame Street," was singled out to provide a concrete frame of reference within which to consider basic issues, including the evaluation of program impact on children. Preliminary data suggest that regular "Sesame Street" viewing can make a difference in children's repertoire of academic readiness skills. To separate the "Sesame Street" experience from the matrix of children's general home experience, however, is an extremely difficult task for research workers. Furthermore, many varied criticisms have been leveled at "Sesame Street" and related programs. Program modifications have occurred over time and the program has gathered strong support in spite of its detractors. Critical viewers hopefully will apply their talent and energies with equal vigor to children's commercial television over the next few years. Specifics of "Sesame Street" aside, broader and more fundamental studies are now being conducted to assess the effects of televised content upon children's personal-social behavior and development.

REFERENCES

Ball, S., and G. Bogatz. *The first year of Sesame Street: an evaluation.* Princeton, N.J.: Educational Testing Service, 1970.

Ball, S., and G. Bogatz. Research on Sesame Street: some implications for compensatory education. In J. Stanley (ed.), *Compensatory education for children, ages 2 to 8.* Baltimore: The Johns Hopkins Press, 1973, 11–24. (a)

Ball, S., and G. Bogatz. *A summary of the major findings from "Reading with television: an evaluation of the Electric Company."* Princeton, N.J.: Educational Testing Service, 1973. (b)

Baumrind, D. Current patterns of parental authority. *Developmental Psychology Monographs*, Part 2, January 1971, 1–103.

Bogatz, G., and S. Ball. *The second year of Sesame Street: a continuing evaluation.* Princeton, N.J.: Educational Testing Service, 1971.

Brim, O. *Education for child-rearing.* New York: Russell Sage, 1959.

Bryan, J. H., and T. Schwartz. Effects of film material upon children's behavior. *Psychological Bulletin*, 1971, *75*, 50–59.

Buckland, C. Toward a theory of parent education: family learning centers in the post-industrial society. *Family Coordinator*, 1972, *21*, 151–162.

Carter, H., and W. Hodges. *Self evaluation manual: behavior oriented prescriptive teaching approach.* Atlanta, Ga.: Georgia State University, Department of Early Education, 1972.

Chow, S., and P. Elmore. *Early childhood information unit: resource manual and program descriptions.* New York: Educational Products Information Exchange, 1973.

Colvin, R., and E. Zaffiro. (eds.). *Educating young children: handbook for teacher training and program design in early childhood education.* New York: Springer, 1974, in press.

Cooney, J. G. Sesame Street. *PTA Magazine*, 1970, *64*, 25–26.

Coopersmith, S. *The antecedents of self-esteem.* San Francisco: Freeman, 1968.

Culhane, J. Report card on Sesame Street. *New York Times Magazine*, May 24, 1970.

Davies, D. The emerging third force in education. *Inequality in Education*, 1973, No. 15, 5–12.

Dittman, L. (ed.). *What we can learn from infants.* Washington, D.C.: National Association for the Education of Young Children, 1970.

Dittman, L. The infants we care for. In L. Dittman (ed.), *The infants we care for.*

Washington, D.C.: National Association for the Education of Young Children, 1973, 1–9.

Fowler, W. A developmental learning approach to infant care in a group setting. *Merrill-Palmer Quarterly,* 1972, *18,* 145–175.

Freeberg, N., and D. Payne. Parental influence on cognitive development in early childhood: a review. *Child Development,* 1967, *38,* 65–87.

Freeman, S. W., and C. L. Thompson. Parent-child training for the MR. *Mental Retardation,* 1973, *11,* 8–10.

Friedrich, L., and A. Stein. Aggressive and prosocial television programs and the natural behavior of preschool children. *Monographs of the Society for Research in Child Development,* 1973, *38,* Serial No. 151.

Golden, M., B. Birns, W. Bridger, and A. Moss. Social class differentiation in cognitive development among black preschool children. *Child Development,* 1971, *42,* 37–45.

Gordon, I. J. The young child: a new look. In J. Frost (ed.), *Early childhood education rediscovered.* New York: Holt, Rinehart and Winston, Inc., 1968, 305–314.

Gordon, I. J. *Parent involvement in compensatory education.* Urbana, Ill.: ERIC Clearinghouse on Early Childhood Education, 1970. (a)

Gordon, I. J. Reaching the young child through parent education. *Childhood Education,* 1970, February, 101–106. (b)

Gordon, I. J. (ed.). Parents as teachers. *Theory into Practice,* 1972, *11,* 145–201.

Gray, S., and R. Klaus. The early training project: a seventh-year report. *Child Development,* 1970, *41,* 909–924.

Grotberg, E. (ed.). *Day care: resources for decisions.* Washington, D.C.: Government Printing Office, 1971.

Guttentag, M. Children in Harlem's community controlled schools. *Journal of Social Issues,* 1972, *28* (4), 1–20.

Henderson, R., and A. Garcia. The effects of parent training program on the question-asking behavior of Mexican-American children. *American Educational Research Journal,* 1973, *10,* 193–201.

Hess, R., M. Block, J. Costello, R. Knowles, and Dr. Largay. Parent involvement in early education. In E. Grotberg (ed.), *Day care: resources for decisions.* Washington, D.C.: Government Printing Office, 1971, 265–298.

Holt, J. Big Bird, meet Dick and Jane. *Atlantic Monthly,* 1971, *227,* 72–74.

Honig, A. *Infant development projects: problems in intervention.* Syracuse, N.Y.: Syracuse University Children's Center, 1972.

Honig, A. *Infant education and stimulation: a bibliography.* Urbana, Ill.: ERIC Clearinghouse on Early Childhood Education, 1973.

Honig, A., and S. Brill. A comparative analysis of the Piagetian development of 12 month old disadvantaged infants in an enrichment center with others not in such a center. Syracuse, N.Y.: Syracuse University Children's Center, 1970.

Ingersoll, G. M. Sesame Street can't handle all the traffic. *Phi Delta Kappan,* 1971, *53,* 185–186.

Kagan, J., and R. Klein. Cross-cultural perspectives on early development. *American Psychologist,* 1973, *28,* 947–961.

Karnes, M. *A new role for teachers: involving the entire family in the education of preschool disadvantaged children.* Urbana, Ill.: University of Illinois Press, 1969.

Keister, M. *The "good life" for infants and toddlers: group care of infants.* Washington, D.C.: National Association for the Education of Young Children, 1970.

King, W., and B. Seegmiller. Performance of 14- to 22-month-old black, firstborn male infants on two tests of cognitive development. *Developmental Psychology*, 1973, *8*, 317–326.

Klaus, R., and S. Gray. The early training project for disadvantaged children: a report after five years. *Monographs of the Society for Research in Child Development*, 1968, *53*, Ser. No. 120.

Kliger, S. Fog over Sesame Street. *Teachers College Record*, 1970, *72*, 41–56.

Kowatrakul, S., M. Robinson, and E. Stivers. *Need achievement training for Head Start children and their mothers.* Paper read at the meeting of the American Educational Research Association, New York, February, 1971.

Lally, J. R. *The family development research program: a program for prenatal, infant, and early childhood enrichment. Progress report.* Syracuse, N.Y.: Syracuse University, College for Human Development, 1973.

Levenstein, P. Cognitive growth in preschoolers through verbal interaction with mothers. *American Journal of Orthopsychiatry*, 1970, *40*, 426–432.

Levin, T. Preschool education and the communities of the poor. In J. Hellmuth (ed.), *Disadvantaged Child*, Vol. 1. Seattle: Special Child Publications, 1967, 351–403.

Liebert, R. M., J. M. Neale, and E. S. Davidson. *The early window: effects of television on children and youth.* New York: Pergamon, 1973.

Little, S. Children's television workshop. *Saturday Review*, 1969, *52*, 60–62.

Luterman, D. A parent-oriented nursery program for pre-school deaf children— a follow-up study. *Volta Review*, 1971, *73*, 106–112.

Lyle, J., and H. R. Hoffman. Children's use of television and other media. In *Television and social behavior: reports and papers, Vol. 4. Television in day-to-day life: patterns of use.* Washington, D.C.: Government Printing Office, 1972, 129–256. (a)

Lyle, J. and H. R. Hoffman. Exploration in patterns of television viewing by preschool age children. In *Television and social behavior: reports and papers*, Vol. 4. *Television in day-to-day life: patterns of use.* Washington, D.C.: Government Printing Office, 1972 257–271. (b)

Meichenbaum, D., and L. Turk. Implications of research on disadvantaged children and cognitive training programs for educational television: ways of improving Sesame Street. *Journal of Special Education*, 1972, *6*, 27–42.

Nash, J. The father in contemporary culture and current psychological literature. *Child Development*, 1965, *36*, 261–297.

National Instructional Television. *Television guidelines for early childhood education.* Bloomington, Ind.: National Instructional Television, 1969.

Naylor, A. Some determinants of parent-infant relationships. In L. Dittman (ed.), *What we can learn from infants.* Washington, D.C.: National Association for the Education of Young Children, 1970, 25–48.

Nedler, S. *Parent education and training: literature review.* Austin, Tex.: Southwest Educational Development Laboratory, 1973.

Nimnicht, G., and E. Brown. The toy library: parents and children learning with toys. *Young Children*, 1972, *28*, 110–117.

Painter, G. The effect of a structured tutorial program on the cognitive and language development of culturally disadvantaged infants. *Merrill-Palmer Quarterly*, 1969, *15*, 279–293.

Palmer, E. Can television really teach? *American Education*, 1969, *5*, 2–6.

Palmer, E., and D. Connell. Sesame Street: a lot of off-beat education? *National Elementary Principal*, 1971, *5*, 14–25.

Palmer, F. Socioeconomic status and intellective performance among Negro preschool boys. *Developmental Psychology*, 1970, *3*, 1–9.

Pickarts, E., and J. Fargo. *Parent education: toward parental competence.* Englewood Cliffs, N.J.: Prentice-Hall, 1971.

Pieper, A. Parent and child centers—impetus, implementation, in-depth view. *Young Children,* 1971, *26,* 70–76.

Radin, N. Maternal warmth, achievement motivation, and cognitive functioning in lower-class preschool children. *Child Development,* 1971, *42,* 1560–1565.

Radin, N. Three degrees of maternal involvement in a preschool program: impact on mothers and children. *Child Development,* 1972, *43,* 1355–1364.

Ratliff, A. R., and R. G. Ratliff. Sesame Street: magic or malevolence? *Young Children,* 1972, *27,* 199–204.

Robinson, H., and N. Robinson. Longitudinal development of very young children in a comprehensive day care program: the first two years. *Child Development,* 1971, *42,* 1673–1683.

Rogers, J. A summary of the literature on Sesame Street. *Journal of Special Education,* 1972, *6,* 43–50.

Rosenthal, A. The Sesame Street generation arrives. *Today's Health,* 1970, *48,* 42–45.

Schaefer, E. Need for early and continuing education. In V. Denenberg (ed.), *Education of the infant and young child.* New York: Academic Press, 1970, 61–107.

Schaefer, E. Toward a revolution in education: a perspective from child development research. *National Elementary Principal,* 1971, *50,* 17–25.

Schaefer, E. Parents as educators: evidence from cross-sectional, longitudinal, and intervention research. In W. Hartup (ed.), *The young child.* Vol. 2. Washington, D.C.: National Association for the Education of Young Children, 1972, 184–201.

Schaefer, E. Learning from each other. In J. Frost (ed.), *Revisiting early childhood education.* New York: Holt, Rinehart and Winston, 1973, 76–81.

Scheinfeld, D., D. Bowles, S. Tuck, and R. Gold. Parents' values, family networks, and family development: working with disadvantaged families. *American Journal of Orthopsychiatry,* 1970, *40,* 413–425.

Sigel, I. Language of the disadvantaged: the distancing hypothesis. In C. S. Lavatelli (ed.), *Language training in early childhood education.* Urbana, Ill.: University of Illinois Press, 1971, 60–76.

Sigel, I., A. Secrist, and G. Forman. Psychoeducational intervention beginning at age two: reflections and outcomes. In J. Stanley (ed.), *Compensatory education for children, ages 2 to 8.* Baltimore: The Johns Hopkins Press, 1973, 25-62.

Sprigle, H. A. Can poverty children live on Sesame Street? *Young Children,* 1971, *26,* 202–217.

Sprigle, H. A. Who wants to live on Sesame Street? *Young Children,* 1972, *28,* 91–109.

Staats, A. *Learning, language, and cognition.* New York: Holt, Rinehart and Winston, 1968.

Stanley, J. (ed.). *Compensatory education for children, ages 2 to 8.* Baltimore: The Johns Hopkins Press, 1973.

Stein, A. H. Mass media and young children's development. In I. J. Gordon (ed.), *Early Childhood Education.* Chicago: University of Chicago Press, 1972, 181–202.

Stein, A. H., L. K. Friedrich, and F. Vondracek. Television content and young children's behavior. In *Television and social behavior: reports and papers.* Vol. 2. *Television and social learning.* Washington, D.C.: Government Printing Office, 1972, 202–317.

Stevens, J. H., Jr. Planning for parent involvement. In T. Kaltsounis, E. King,

C. Rubow, and J. H. Stevens, Jr., *A handbook for administrators of child care program: empirical bases for program decisions.* In press.

Stevenson, H. W. Television and the behavior of preschool children. *In Television and social behavior reports and papers.* Vol. 2. *Television and social learning.* Washington, D.C.: Government Printing Office, 1972, 346–371.

Steward, M., and D. Stewart. The observation of Anglo-, Mexican-, and Chinese-American mothers teaching their sons. *Child Development,* 1973, *44,* 329–337.

Streissguth, A., and H. Bee. Mother-child interaction and cognitive development in children. In W. Hartup (ed.), *The young child.* Vol. 2. Washington, D.C.: National Association for the Education of Young Children, 1972, 158–183.

Weikart, D., and D. Lambie. Early enrichment in infants. In V. Denenberg (ed.), *Education of the infant and young child.* New York: Academic Press, 1970, 85–108.

White, B. *Human infants.* Englewood Cliffs, N.J.: Prentice-Hall, 1971.

White, B. Conference address on infant education. National conference of the National Association for the Education of young Children, Seattle, Washington, November 1973.

Yarrow, L., J. Rubenstein, F. Pederson, and J. Jankowski. Dimensions of early stimulation and their differential effects on infant development. *Merrill-Palmer Quarterly,* 1972, *18,* 205–218.

Photograph courtesy of Camera Craft, Seattle, Washington.

major issues in perspective

Throughout the preceding eight chapters it should have been apparent that early childhood education, like education generally, is the result of a complex decision-making process. This process is often marked by systematic and rational thought. But it is sometimes marked by intuitive—even fortuitous—thought. Programs and policies can grow more "like Topsy," than by conscious and empirically based design. Either way, adults continually make decisions about what they think is desirable or true in educating young children. They establish conditions which in theory (formal or naive) they think will lead to desired goals. Hopefully, appropriately designed evaluation research can provide information about any degree of success that has been attained. As we have seen, when such evaluation activity occurs, it often entails a comparison of one approach with another. This method can set the stage for competition among program builders over what program or combination of experiences is best for various children. Definitive data pertinent to this issue cannot yet be cited. Several important variables influence too strongly the question of what is best. Some of these are the nature of goals sought by a program, the particular needs of the children involved, time, and the social context of instruction. Even the most optimistic scholar would probably agree that a definitive answer to the question of what approach to education is best for children will never be answered, certainly not to the satisfaction of everyone.

With this caveat on record, the present writer chooses not to engage in polemics about what currently operative program might be best for all, or even most, children. Nor does he attempt a synthesis for the purpose of advancing a program for the best of all early education worlds. Rather, the intent in this final chapter is to examine in reasonable detail some major components of decision making about early childhood education: goals, content, pedagogical procedures, timing of instructional activities, staffing, and choice of settings for early education. As suggested in Chapter 1, these are the *what, how, when, who,* and *where* issues. This chapter also includes a discussion of research problems in early education, again built upon the foundation established in Chapter 1. Some selected comments about ethics and the immediate future of early childhood education provide a conclusion to this book.

GOALS FOR EARLY CHILDHOOD EDUCATION

With a few exceptions, early childhood education program builders believe that both immediate and long-range objectives must be planned for in developing curricula. In practice, long-range objectives are general and abstract; immediate objectives are usually much more specific. Even so, the interrelationship of short- and long-term objectives is often obscure, although ample mixes of philosophical and psychological thought are invariably reflected in goal statements. Irrespective of specific mixes, there does not seem to be much serious conflict among program builders over long-term goals. For example, few oppose the worthy aim of "education for the development of maximum individual potential." Other related and frequently expressed long-range goals for early education include independence in judgment, critical thinking ability, personal initiative and responsibility, self-respect, and respect for the rights and properties of others. Such listings can be endless and, as will be seen, questions can be raised about their usefulness and appropriateness. Even when they are recognized as legitimate, educators must concern themselves with the foundations of such behavior—the requisites or early approximations which can be established during the early years. This notion of requisites usually is based upon another (poorly tested) assumption that certain events of early childhood are critical in the child's ultimate development. It is here that genuine conflict begins to surface. Debate among educators seems continually to rage over the short-term objectives for young children and the kinds of experiences which may provide a continuity in development from early childhood through the later school years. The importance of an educational and social philosophy for deciding about such objectives and experiences cannot be overemphasized. If early childhood education is placed in a total context of organized developmental education, then one's philosophy is indispensible for seeking answers to many questions. What should be the characteristics of a "good life"? To what extent should different social, ethnic, or ability groups receive different kinds of education? What constitutes a proper balance between individuality and intellectual-social conformity? And should schools encourage children and youth to change (improve) the social order? These are but a few examples (Furth, 1958) of the inescapable "should" or "ought" questions for philosophy.

Whether or not made verbally explicit for public inspection, the answers to such should questions are manifested in the behavior of those who take responsibility for children's educational guidance. Such philosophical decisions have been noted in the present book in reference to whether preschool children should receive formal academic training and the extent to which all children should be required to master given subject matter content within specified time periods. Also noted was a particularly delicate issue involved in so-called compensatory education. Should a forceful intervention policy be applied to children of poverty and, if so, what should be the nature of this intervention? As we have seen, many psychologists and educators have answered both questions, but a consensus is far from near.

For Cronbach (1969), part of the problem of consensus is due to confusion among educators about the two basic ways in which an environmental modification may be helpful to children. One way is to construct an "optimal maintenance environment" so that children's growth can be promoted in the best possible fashion. A second way is to create a "special intervention environment" for the period of time necessary to develop children's readiness for the conventional environment. Once this readiness has been reached, then special treatment can be withdrawn. The major source of current disagreement among educators seems to be the philosophical basis for deciding which kind of environment is most suitable for this or that group of children.

In sum, the basic intervention-or-not question raised above bares two related problems. First, the answer will depend largely upon decisions about what long-term characteristics constitute a desirable adult existence. Called for is a clear definition of an adult role of value both to the individual and society (Cronbach, 1969). Second, the intervention question reveals the intimate relationship of philosophy to psychology. Psychology's role in the selection of worthy and reachable goals for early childhood education is also crucial. Studies of children's learning and development may provide data that can shape reasonable expectations about children's abilities and limitations at various periods and under certain conditions of development. Such studies may also provide information about the efficiency (economy) and effectiveness (permanency) of educational procedures for young children. Psychological questions in education generally ask what are the effects of given manipulations, but once the answers become known, any decision to implement them in educational planning requires value judgments. Thus, philosophy (including ethics), again comes into play.

Given this brief introduction, some approaches to the issue of goals in early education may now be presented. In this way, the reader may better appreciate the complexity of this issue and sharpen his or her own thinking about the matter.

Some Examples of Diverse Outlook about Goals in Early Education

Development as the Aim of Education   In Chapter 1, a long-standing conflict between heritors of naturalistic, indigenous growth theories of development and those who hold the cultural competence of environmental determination viewpoint was summarized. In succeeding chapters, several educational approaches consistent with, if not derived from, these theories were also discussed. But recently both traditions have been challenged as sources for educational goals. According to Kolhberg and Mayer (1972), the romantic, natural growth tradition is inadequate for determining educational goals because of its excessive emphasis upon the "bag-of-virtues" ethic: goal statements which represent arbitrary vague personality traits and are usually couched in a value-laden philosophy of mental health without universal validity. Thus, goals such as spontaneity, curiosity, self-discipline, independence in judgment, and positive social adjustment are difficult to define and constitute arbitrary value statements related to conventional cultural standards. Such goals can create puzzling paradoxes for the educator: what constitutes "independence in judgment" for one teacher may be "dogmatism" or "nonconformity" for another. Conflict also can inhere among the traits included in a set of goal statements. For example, can a consistency of educational practices be achieved in order to develop both "self-discipline" and "spontaneity?" Or "independence" and "getting along with others?" Moreover, does a bag-of-virtues tradition in educational goal setting implicitly cast a teacher in the role of erstwhile psychiatrist or mental health specialist? Kohlberg and Mayer (1972) feel that this can occur most obviously in conventional approaches to affective education, but also in much traditional early childhood education.

The cultural transmission viewpoint is also rejected as a basis for educational planning for three reasons. First, Kohlberg and Mayer (1972) believe that this viewpoint is based upon faulty concepts of learning and motivation. Second, like the bag-of-virtues tradition, the cultural training viewpoint is arbitrary. The only difference is emphasis. Specifically at issue is the rationale for determining *academic content* among those who take the cultural transmission approach. Third, Kohlberg and Mayer argue, this academic content emphasis leads to the widespread use of spurious achievement tests which, in turn, are employed inappropriately to determine the worth of children and their education.

What, then, are the alternatives to these allegedly inadequate bases for educational planning? For Kohlberg and Mayer there is but one genuine option. Educational aims must be conceptualized in terms of both *intellectual and moral development*: the attainment of successively higher stages of development (see Chapter 5) bringing the individual an under-standing of logical and ethical principles which transcend culture and time. In other words, the true course of human development becomes the source of curriculum goals. Stage retardation should be avoided, and so should ill-advised attempts at stage acceleration. Education, then, is essentially a matter of providing stimulation (akin to an optimal maintenance environment) through stages of development considered universal for all children.

In early childhood education, this could mean that every effort would be made to maximize preoperational and then concrete-operational thought (the criteria for which are outlined by Piaget). To this would be added ample experience in moral judgmental activity according to schema and principles described elsewhere (e.g., Kohlberg, 1969). Academic learning, at least of basic skills, ostensibly would be laced throughout the educational process in the spirit of open education.

In sum, Kohlberg and Mayer (1972) advocate that cognitive-developmental theory and the progressivism advanced by Dewey (1916) serve as the sources of educational goals. Ultimately, the development of a "free and powerful character" must be the educational aim for all individuals. This long-range goal dominates the scene, although it is noteworthy that the developmentalist position can provide room for schools to teach reading, writing, and arithmetic—probably not in the early years, however.

Similar views have been offered. Sigel (1973), for example, argues that before any just decision about educational intervention can be made, a more basic problem must be solved: how to achieve a clear understanding of human nature and development. To this end, he calls upon educators and psychologists to focus more sharply upon children's self-regulatory behavior, their adaptive mechanisms, and other behaviors generic to human nature. In this way, Sigel argues, better cues should emerge for determining what contributions education can make to the course of development. Of course, the achievement of a clear understanding of human nature and development is a formidable task, one that has occupied serious students of the human condition for centuries. It seems fair to say that progress toward the completion of this task has been at best modest.

A related yet somewhat different position has been taken by Spodek (1970), who believes that developmental theory is best viewed as a *tool* for curriculum analysis rather than as a source of curriculum. Spodek also suggests that the aim of education inevitably becomes a value statement about what children should be like. His preferred master goal—personal autonomy based on reason—exemplifies a root value of most current school curricula (at least as they are formally stated) and from which curricular experiences theoretically are derived. This goal, of course, is not inconsistent with Kohlberg and Mayer's position; it is just derived from a somewhat different premise about the role of developmental theory in education.

Not much is known about the educability of autonomy behaviors in early childhood. However, this much talked-about issue is central to many early education programs (e.g., the Montessori Method) and experimental techniques for autonomy development increasingly are being tested (see Kuzma and Stern, 1972). It seems fair to say that regardless of the extent to which developmental theory or stage-sequence growth guides curriculum goal selection, the goal of autonomy based on reason is highly general and extends far beyond the immediate objectives of most early education programs.

Early Childhood Education as Preparatory   Other authorities have preferred to concentrate on short-range goals for early childhood education programs. It can be inferred from Smilansky and Smilansky (1970), for example, that preparation for scholastic success is the principal standard for establishing educational priorities in early childhood for most children in advanced societies. Their argument is particularly strong in the case of educationally handicapped young children who are immediately confronted in school with achievement demands that they are ill equipped to meet. This idea of preparation is really in the long tradition of "readiness building" in early childhood education from which a generally consensual curriculum for nursery school through first grade has evolved (Lazarus, 1972; Weber, 1969). This readiness-building approach leads one to think of *short-range goals*—goals attainable within the time available and which provide teachers with specific ideas about what they can (and should) do. Short-range goals are usually formulated in terms of what children need or what they have not learned in the preschool or "natural environment." In contrast, long-range goals are seen as useful only as ideals to which one may aspire (Anderson and Bereiter, 1972).

Even if one takes the preparatory view suggested above, one can ask how short-term goal decisions can be made accurately in the absence of prior decisions about the long-range goals that the more immediate goals are designed to serve. In this regard, Anderson and Bereiter (1972) interpret the Deweyian philosophy differently than have Kohlberg and Mayer (1972):

> [John] Dewey has claimed that short-range educational achievements are valuable insofar as they increase the future options available to the learner. Dewey rejected the whole question of ultimate values and asserted that educational goals should grow out of potentialities discovered in the present situation.
>
> Following Dewey, we tend to reject all such long-range value statements as that—children should develop into creative, expressive individuals, revolutionaries, responsible citizens, competent scholars and the like, simply on the grounds that these goals, if seriously pursued, would lead to limitations on individual freedom and to the forcing of children into some predetermined mold. If it is argued that short-range goals inevitably reflect one's biases with respect to long-range values and purposes, we should reply that this is a potential

source of corruption that should be watched for and guarded against to the best of our abilities. Corruptive biases should be identified and pointed out and goals should be altered so as to remove as much as possible the influence of such biases. This is the proper application of intelligence and reflective thinking to the determination of goals (Anderson and Bereiter, 1972, pp. 349–350).[1]

Anderson and Bereiter use this viewpoint and additional arguments to justify direct instruction in conceptual and academic skills for young children. This issue again highlights the schism in thinking about goals (as well as content and methodology) between the cognitive-developmental and behavioristic orientations to early childhood education. This conflict certainly includes the issue of what is teachable and what is not. The behaviorists Anderson and Bereiter feel education in the schools should be reserved for teachable skills; Kohlberg and Mayer view education much more globally as a catalyst for development, including moral judgment.

The Basic Behavior Repertoire. It seems unlikely that educators will soon give up the idea of preparing children for successful academic progress in the early years of school. Part of the problem in the past has been a lack of specificity in the hierarchical arrangement of curriculum experiences to facilitate basic pre-academic and early academic skills. As we have seen, many of the more dramatic departures from traditional early education practice (e.g., Distar) represent attempts to correct this situation. An even more basic approach to the identification of short-range goal domains for early education can be taken from the concept of a basic behavior repertoire (Staats, 1968). This repertoire concerns fundamentals of the spoken language (including syntax and grammar), attentional responses (including responsiveness to verbal cues), primary discrimination skills, and the various sensory-motor skills required for play and manipulative activities. Its major components are reproduced in the following list, although Staats (1968, pp. 397–469) should be consulted for further details.

The Basic Behavior Repertoire

1. Basic Language Repertoire
   a. Phonemes and phonemic combinations (unit speech responses which comprise the sounds of language; extends to an ability to link phonemes for purposes of word and sentence construction).
   b. Imitative speech responses (the ability to produce imitative sounds; a "fundamental" for reading response acquisition).
   c. Labeling speech repertoire (vocabulary development that makes a child sufficiently capable of responding with appropriate labels to environmental stimuli).
   d. Motor behavior under the control of verbal stimuli (ability to

---

[1] Reproduced by permission of Allyn and Bacon, Inc.

control one's own motor responses by verbal means and follow the verbal instructions of others when appropriate).

   e. Basic set of word meanings (broad comprehension of the semantic properties of words used in daily child-adult interaction).

   f. Word association (a broad scope of grammatical word associations in which standard sentence constructions and verbal sequences assist memory and reasoning).

   g. Number repertoire (basic counting responses where correct orders of verbal responses prevail).

2. Attention:

   a. "Sense placing" responses (e.g., looking, feeling under stimulus control, e.g., verbal instructions, to permit effective sensory stimulation).

   b. Discrimination skills (refined attention which results in differential responding, e.g., attending to critical attributes which differentiate stimuli by form and color through simultaneous and successive comparison).

3. Sensory-motor Skills

   a. General balance and coordinated movement through space.

   b. Eye-hand coordination.

   c. Imitation responses (including the ability to discriminate the actions of other persons, the stimuli that control such actions, and when imitation is appropriate).

4. Motivation (including responsiveness to "natural reinforcers" such as praise and social approach and "self-reinforcers" such as successful task accomplishment which are relied upon in the classroom to maintain attention, persistence, and the like).

Staats (1968) argues that the basic behavior repertoire is a necessary foundation for any child's subsequent learning success (cognitive, social, emotional), especially in formal educational environments as they are presently constituted. In a phrase, he claims that the quality of basic behavior repertoire acquisition will affect a child's ability to profit from later training, specifically the rate and quality of future school learning. Of course, acquisition of the basic behavior repertoire is itself complex and depends heavily upon the systematic application of several principles, including instrumental discrimination learning and reinforcement (see Chapter 3). With this in mind, Staats argues that America's educational system has apparently been built from the assumption that children come to school with a basically sound repertoire. If actual school practice is taken as evidence, educators seem to believe that parents have successfully managed to prepare their children for success. Staats, however, seriously questions this implicit belief or premise. He maintains that parents, whose abilities to teach children vary greatly, have rarely encountered systematic training in techniques for successful preparation of their children. Staats further maintains that society has generally expected that parents will deal with a great variety of training problems, some of which are very difficult (e.g., mentally and physically handicapped children). The problem, as Staats sees it, is that parents have typically not been provided with sufficient knowledge, skills, and materials to help solve these training problems. Staats concludes that our current educational system reflects little regard for the foundation upon which it rests, namely, early childhood learning.

Many implications flow from this line of thought; for example, the possible extension of compulsory public education downward so that a child's basic repertoire can be earlier assessed and refined. More likely and probable, however, is the use of the repertoire as one source of cues for the development of parent education programs and behavioral criteria for analyzing any given early education program for children themselves. Certainly the repertoire may be an appealing source of goal selection in designing preschool programs. If so, early education would be partly conceived as skill training, something strongly resisted by purveyors of the romantic tradition in early childhood circles. The repertoire, of course, has nothing concretely to say about the ideal, long-range outcomes of education except by implication: the best indicator of long-range learning effectiveness is success with present learning. Nor does the repertoire necessarily suggest anything about the weighty relationship of educational goals to national (political-social) goals. It is questionable, of course, whether educators should be involved, except as citizens, in making decisions about this relationship.

A Final Word about Goals

In Chapter 1 and again in the foregoing discussion we have seen that psychology may contribute to early childhood education priority-setting in terms of developmental theory and learning psychology. Still other terms can be advanced. For example, the well-known "developmental task" approach can be useful in thinking about educational objectives, cues for timing and sequencing learning activities, and how to evaluate children's educational progress (Havighurst, 1972). Psychological constructs identified through psychological research, such as the self-concept, intellectual achievement responsibility, divergent thinking abilities, cognitive style, and delay of gratification also can help educators to hone their conceptualizations of educational goals. Both these constructs and the development task approach are discussed in some detail in the first edition of this book (Evans, 1971). There is little reason to repeat that discussion here except to ask an important question. Is the task of determining educational goals best done by marshaling a set of value-related psychological constructs? If so, one needs to make a thoroughgoing analysis of these constructs' theoretical and empirical features in order to achieve a rational integration, if this is possible. Otherwise, such a practice can easily fall prey to the bag-of-virtues criticism already discussed. The developmental task approach is heavily culturally bound, although many tasks also have their source in biological maturation. Interested readers are encouraged to study the updated version of developmental tasks and education offered by Havighurst, 1972. This approach purports to occupy a middle ground between two polarized educational theories: the theory of freedom, which permits the child to develop in his own way in his own time for his own purposes, and the theory of constraint, which relies upon social restraints to achieve the child's conformity to a "responsible" adult role. Havighurst views developmental tasks as being midway between individual needs and societal demands. These tasks call for active learning within a dynamic social environment. And, finally, they require an explicit examination of the relationship between human development and the process of education.

Another, albeit related, approach has been suggested by Kagan (1972). He correctly recognizes as value statements any profile of psychological characteristics which serves as an educational objective. In consideration of contemporary societal circumstances. Kagan's most basic value is *adaptability*. Among other things, adaptability emphasizes autonomy and self-reliance. It also gives continued emphasis to most, and probably all, children's development of reading competence, quantitative skills, the ability to write coherently, and skill in discriminating effective from ineffective arguments. Admittedly, these goals are not fully developed or crystallized in the early childhood years, but their precursors presumably should be. For Kagan, the dominant thrust at the preschool level should be to cultivate in children certain basic motivational characteristics: a wish to be intellectually competent, a positive expectancy for achieving intellectual competence, and a strong personal identity.

Apart from some independent criteria which can be applied across the full range of early childhood education curriculum development, a discussion of the goals issue must be limited to idiosyncratic programs. Goal emphases *do* vary. The major goals of most programs discussed in this book have been described and need not be reiterated. But any serious student of early childhood education should routinely look carefully at goals and their sources as a part of general evaluation. In addition to some thoughts in the present section, the conceptual analysis procedures first discussed in Chapter 1 may be useful for this purpose.

Finally, it should be clear that the authorities referred to thus far in our discussion are concerned with *universalistic goals*, i.e., goals thought desirable for all children to attain (Lesser, 1971). Much less specific attention has been given by leaders in early childhood education to the matter of young children's *particularistic goals*, i.e., goals or objectives that children should (and can) achieve on the basis of special personal characteristics (Lesser, 1971). Among other things, this matter also calls for priority planning and criteria for judging the importance of objectives, both universalistic and particularistic.

One helpful approach for this purpose has been provided by Stake (1972). Within this approach priorities in goals and objectives can be established first in relation to three kinds of information: the needs of

*A persistent theme in goal statements for early education concerns the develop-
ment of autonomy and self-reliance. To this end, it is presumed that children
should be helped to develop a desire to be intellectually competent and a strong
sense of personal identity. Surprisingly little is yet known, however, about the
impact of early schooling on such patterns of behavior. Photo by Peter Rinearson.*

children who may benefit from a given school program, the available
resources, and knowledge about the probable payoffs of various resource
deployments and instructional strategies. To these types of information
can be added three kinds of "special conditions," or circumstances which
often require change in instructional procedures. One condition, "in-out
criteria," refers to the basis for deciding when work on a given objective
should start and stop. A second set of special conditions involves a
consideration of essential resources; the success of some objectives
may depend on unique or special requirements not readily available.
Individual student differences provide the third special condition for determining educational objectives: a study of the relationship between
personal characteristics and objectives selection so that children with

particular "needs, histories, readiness, interests, talents, and aspirations [can be provided with] personally relevant learning opportunities" (Stake, 1972, p. 18).

OTHER MAJOR ISSUES

Program Content

The issue of goals for early childhood education cannot be divorced from the medium of content through which these goals are sought. It should be clear that the content of many early childhood education programs varies along such dimensions as specific concepts to be taught and materials to be used. In Chapter 1 the move to cognitive enrichment as the "essential content" was discussed. Recently, this trend has been subject to intense criticism, particularly by protagonists of affective education. Too often, the rhetoric appears in adversarial terms, i.e., cognitive versus affective education. This easily leads to a false dichotomy in which one educates either for intellectual-academic or emotional development. To be sure, emphasis may vary, but these two contents are never mutually exclusive. A more sensible distinction may serve to illustrate the content issue. In one authority's terms, it is the issue of academic versus intellectual content (Katz, 1970); in another's, it is skills proficiency versus subject matter proficiency (Rohwer, 1970). Both authorities seem to converge upon a useful distinction. An emphasis upon academics involves the mastery of certain quantities of predetermined factual material along traditional subject matter lines. This stands in contrast to intellectual content, which is intended to foster inquiry, question asking, and problem-solving skills are fostered. It is commonly charged that academic goals, in the narrowest sense, too often become ends in themselves at the expense of genuine intellectual growth.

Admittedly, the distinction is a fine one. Yet an intellectual skills approach actually can be free of any given content. Content, in other words, is only a means to a higher end. The problem is that a commitment to intellectual growth often deteriorates into an obsession with performance: number of addition and subtraction facts correctly written, number of words spelled correctly, and so on.

To discuss fully the content of early childhood programs throughout the United States is not feasible in these few pages. What is important in the content issue is a reëmphasis of the widespread differences among programs. Content varies, even though the reasons for this variation are often obscure. Program goals may provide one set of criteria for the selection of content; but goals cannot tell the whole, or sometime even part, of the story. To use an earlier example, what directions for content selection are provided by the goal of "personal autonomy based on reason"? Clearly, additional criteria are needed. And this gives further cause for debate. Chapter 7 presented the open education view that children's interests should dominate the process of selecting content.

Those with the scholastic preparatory view, of course, are less likely to leave this important matter in the hands of children.

At best, early childhood education is beset with a confusing state of affairs about content. It would be nice if data were available to show that certain program contents are "best" at successive levels of educational development. From the psychology of task analysis, of course, we know that certain things must be known before certain other things can be learned (e.g., a mastery of basic arithmetical operations is necessary to learn fractions). Educators also generally avoid the introduction of content which is beyond the normative capabilities of children in general to master (e.g., attempting to teach the scientific method to three-year-olds). But apart from very broad guidelines, content selection will probably continue to reflect what adults think is important for children to learn. The reader is encouraged to re-examine more deeply the content dimensions of various programs discussed in this book from the standpoint of conceptual analysis (Parker and Day, 1972). At this time sound rationales for content selection in early childhood programs appear sorely lacking. Aside from a "survival skills" approach, cues for content selection derived from developmental theory (see Chapter 5, for example) seem most promising. The cognitive process orientation of developmental theory eventually may be utilized for better solutions to the problem of the match in early childhood education (see Chapter 6).

Program Methodology

Equally problematical in terms of consensus among the experts is the matter of *how* instruction should be prosecuted. Extant approaches are perhaps most diverse in the general degree of structure involved in educational programming and the specific principles used to sequence instructional material. Behavioral analysis procedures, for example, do not demand for their application a given body of content, but they do require the sequencing principle of successive approximations. Sequencing principles are also basic to the Montessori Method, Distar, and certain interpretations of Piagetian psychology for classroom learning. In contrast, careful attention to sequencing is not always apparent in conventional programs, even when they are executed in the spirit of compensatory education. Again, sequencing depends in part upon the theoretical foundations of a curriculum. The basis upon which content is organized is often adult logic, as in Distar, rather than child psychology, as in Piagetian formulations. Whether children learn content best when it is organized according to adult concepts of knowledge structure still is debated and most strongly by supporters of open education.

The overall amount of external organization, sequencing, and teacher-centered methods of instruction can be taken as a broad measure of program structure (Bissell, 1973). And perhaps no other aspect of early childhood education provokes stronger emotion and discord among teachers and parents than program structure. In practice, *structure* can mean many things. The term therefore requires some differentiation. One can think, for example, about general structure in terms of low to moderate to high along several dimensions including time, program content and materials, nature of teacher-child interactions (including degree of preplanned encounters), and the general learning environment (including space and equipment). Programs may be high in some aspects of structure and low in others. For instance, the Montessori Method is based on a moderate to highly structured learning environment (especially materials), but children are generally free to pursue activities at their own rate and for self-determined amounts of time (low structure). Piagetian curricula are generally structured in cognitive objectives but not in informational content, as would be Distar. The Bank Street approach exemplifies comparatively low structure across all dimensions, although teachers purportedly structure their spontaneous interactions with children in the interests of developmental learning.

Many other examples of variations in structure could be explicated from the program descriptions in this book. It may be more instructive, however, to consider the general contribution of structure to program effectiveness as measured by children's cognitive gains. The three following generalizations are supported by empirical data, although these data were admittedly gathered more systematically in compensatory (versus regular) preschool programs (Bissell, 1973):

1. Preschool programs with general objectives of fostering cognitive growth, with specific emphasis on language development, and with teacher-directed strategies that provide highly structured experiences for disadvantaged children are more effective in producing cognitive gains than programs lacking these characteristics.
2. Preschool programs high on the dimension of quality control, having well-trained staff, a high degree of supervision, and a low pupil-teacher ratio, are the most effective programs in producing cognitive gains.
3. Directive, highly structured preschool programs tend to be more effective with the *more* disadvantaged of lower-class children or to be equally effective with all lower-class children. In contrast, nondirective, less structured programs tend to be more effective with the *less* disadvantaged of lower-class children (Bissell, 1973, p. 238).

If structure is an important mediator of program effectiveness, one may look for reasons for this phenomenon. Most simply, the importance of structure may be a function of ensuring that what one intends to occur actually occurs during the course of instruction. As one authority has put it, "If you don't plan for it, it won't happen" (Karnes, 1971). Further plausible reasons can be advanced for the comparatively greater measured effectiveness of structured programs for many children (Cazden, 1972). First, the possible artifact of measurement must be accounted for. In many programs—especially those designed to promote mastery of specified skills—the content of tests is taught. Gains, then, may refer only to specific skills not necessarily generalizable to broader competencies. Additionally, the setting for testing in structured programs has more in common with the setting for original learning than is true in more loosely structured programs. In fact, children whose learning environment includes more testing have a better opportunity to develop advantageous test-taking skills than do their test-inexperienced peers.

But testing artifacts cannot explain program effectiveness fully. Program components themselves are involved in four possible ways (Cazden, 1972). First, structured programs may provide for a more equal distribution of teacher attention and teacher-child interaction than do low-structure approaches. Second, structured programs often provide a greater variety of settings for conversations wherein communications are more clear about what activities are valued in school. This may help children to feel more secure in knowing what is expected of them and to enjoy a greater familiarity with classroom activities. Third, the greater continuity and consistency characteristic of teacher-child interactions in more structured programs can lead to more content-rich conversations. This is because such interactions often build upon cumulative interpersonal knowledge and teachers can become more familiar with idiosyncrasies in language and learning styles of children. Finally, loosely organized programs may go too far in the direction of creativity—to the point where chaos prevails. If so, the teacher-child interactions may become oriented more toward the control of social behavior than toward the imparting of intellectual ideas. That is, important conditions for talking out ideas—orderliness, predictability, and leisure—may disappear in the melee of a tempestuous classroom.

These losses need not occur in loosely structured classrooms. Individual teacher skill and children's self-management skills are the issues here. Unfortunately, not many teachers seem capable of handling the complexities of low-structured educational programs with more than just a handful of children. It should be re-emphasized that the discussion about structure pertains largely to cognitive outcomes (including language) among economically under-privileged preschool children. Nevertheless, this discussion does illustrate the need for deep thought about the role of different kinds of structure in implementing programs for different kinds of purposes.

Other, less global, aspects of early education programs can be mentioned to reinforce the methodological controversy. For example, data have recently appeared to challenge several popular assumptions about children's learning. Devor and Stern (1970) have shown that children do not necessarily learn concepts better when they can manipulate real objects; in fact, these investigators have shown that the manipulative approach is often less efficient in terms of time. A comparison of environmentally enriched to austere classroom experience has shown no real advantage for the former in terms of disadvantaged children's overall cognitive development (Busse et al., 1972). Neither has a comparative study of heterogeneous and homogeneous classroom grouping along social class lines shown any advantage for the former grouping method in improving children's social interactions (Feitelson, Weintraub, and Michaeli, 1972). These data, combined with reviews of similar studies (Stephens, 1967), call into question the efficacy of a search for magic combinations of gross methodological and administrative arrangements to improve the learning process. We are left with the rather insipid ideas that (1) different things work for different children and (2) a child's social class and a teacher's repertoire of specific teaching techniques and interpersonal skills are the principal mediators of learning effectiveness. More will be said about these conclusions later. In the meantime, readers interested in a rough means for assessing the teacher control aspect of program structure can consult Webster (1972).

Timing Considerations in Early Education

Even less certainty surrounds the issue of timing educational experiences. This uncertainty, most apparent in relation to the sequential aspects of child development and learning, is partly due to a lack of firm empirical data about the total and cumulative effects of certain kinds of learning experiences at particular ages. In practice, then, attempts to resolve this *when* issue involve tradition, economics, social attitudes, logical reasoning, necessity, and the like. In Chapter 8, for instance, a general resistance in American society to the placement of children in extra-home settings earlier than age 3 was noted. The phenomenon of the working mother is now contributing to changes in such thinking. And increasing numbers of research workers and educators have argued that "compensatory" education delayed until age 4 or 5 is probably too late for lasting and possibly even immediate results. Of course there may exist better compensatory strategies than are currently practiced. But it may also be more productive to think in terms of preventive rather than remedial education. Clearly, the timing issue cannot be divorced from that of goals and content; the more encompassing question is, What forms of stimulation are most effective for what purposes and what points in the developmental process?

In Chapter 1, much was said about the rationale for early intervention and the gradual trend toward progressively earlier ages for intervention. Implicit in this trend is the idea that the earlier one intervenes, the better. Or as the assumption has also been phrased, "if academic achievement is good, early achievement is best." (Kohlberg and Mayer, 1972, p. 283). Not all early interventionists are committed to this extreme viewpoint. But only in the past few years have serious questions even been raised about the possible hazards of intervention during infancy and the preschool years. Among the most volatile of these challenges to early childhood educators is that of Moore and Moore (1972). Their challenge consists of three basic arguments. One involves the notion that, neurological growth patterns and sensory development are normally not completed until age 7 or 8. From this premise Moore and Moore argue that children probably should not experience formal schooling until that age. In other words, the premature introduction of complex sensory activities like reading may be not only inefficient but possibly adverse for normal development.

A second argument advanced by Moore and Moore against early intervention is that schemes for preschool education have failed to show any lasting advantage. Why, they ask, should we continue something that at best does not work well and at worst may undermine a child's development? Their third main charge is leveled at educators whom they believe have fallaciously assumed that the school is a better environment for children's learning than are the home and neighborhood. Moore and Moore themselves presume that young children who are thrust too early into a formal group setting apart from their mothers are vulnerable to emotional disorder. This assumption provides a link to the issue of where forms of early education should occur (discussed in Chapters 1 and 8). Additional comment about this issue will be forthcoming.

It is not surprising that the widely publicized Moore and Moore critique had two immediate effects. First, it seemed to shake thoroughly, if temporarily, the hallowed psychological and philosophical foundations of early childhood education. Second, it added much fuel to the already burning fires of skepticism, reluctance, and apprehension about early education among parents and also among legislators, who make important programs funding decisions. Even educators previously tentative or unconvinced about the needs and values of early childhood education seemed moved to join in the chorus of Moore and Moore's "heresy."

This heresy has probably had a constructive effect in that it forced even the staunchest early childhood educators to re-examine their thinking and actions. Still, the Moore and Moore critique about timing (and content) in early education is problematical on several grounds. First, the critique too easily generates several versions of the either-or fallacy: either one has early childhood education or one does not; early education takes place either in the home or in the school. Second, educators reacted to the critique as an indictment of early education, although it is more accurately a criticism of "premature" formal, highly structured, academic training for young children. For example, even if the neurological growth necessary for certain activities is incomplete until age 7 or 8, it seems illogical to deduce that schooling before that time is necessarily bad for children. Educational experiences can be geared to children's developmental status; and, very little convincing evidence can be marshaled to demonstrate that children show less attachment to their mothers or become emotionally unstable in early day care or preschool settings. It must be said, however, that certain forms of education could conceivably be disadvantageous for certain groupings of children. According to Meyer (1972), for example, some children develop representational skills earlier than do others. For the later developers, he suggests that certain intensely cognitive activities (including formal reading instruction) be (1) delayed

The timing of formal instruction in basic literacy skills is among the most complex of the major issues in early childhood education. Photo by Peter Rinearson.

through the primary grades and (2) replaced by a program based more on a continuity of a development through enrichment. Otherwise, Meyer believes that the emotional costs of education can outweigh its benefits.

Moore and Moores' second argument (1972)—that early schooling schemes have failed—is only partially true. The implementation phase of large-scale intervention programs such as Head Start has not produced impressive gains in children's achievement; but many smaller-scale controlled experimental programs have shown impressive results. This leaves much room for hope. A second counterargument to Moore and Moore is that even large-scale intervention programs have realized important benefits for children in other areas than children's achievement (see Chapter 2, for example).

To Moore and Moores' third charge—that educators arrogantly have assumed the school as superior to the home for children's learning and development—two things can be said. First, there is little sound evidence for this criticism, even though it may be true in some communities. To this writer, early education seems based more on educators' presuming the school to be a better place for certain *kinds* of learning which parents are either unable or unwilling to foster. Hence, parents expect and financially support the schools to accomplish certain objectives. Perhaps, a better criticism would be that the schools often fail in their basic functions (for reasons which could easily supply material for a separate book).

For data and arguments relevant to the timing issue in early education, this writer has found other accounts both more carefully developed and constructive. Rohwer (1971), for example, uses solid research findings to suggest that the years of late childhood and early adolescence represent a much more efficient period for many skill learnings now attempted in most early education programs. To illustrate:

> consider the sacred cow of reading proficiency. Reading instruction generally begins with the onset of formal schooling, usually at age five, and the child's progress in reading typically becomes the major desideratum for judging his success in school. Yet there is no compelling evidence that delaying the onset of reading instruction by one or even several years would retard the rate at which the component skills are acquired. Furthermore, there is no persuasive evidence that reading is the principal means by which the student can acquire the other kinds of information that might be useful to learning during the first five years of schooling; even given current schooling practices, the evidence is thin. The evidence on whether or not the presentation of information in text form is optimal for learning is thinner still (Rohwer, 1971, p. 321).[2]

Rohwer applies the same pattern of analysis to the issue of age of formal school entry. Essentially, the question is one of the evidence that one can compile to justify a progressive lowering of required school entrance. As Rohwer correctly indicates, the empirical data that show a positive effect (or *any* effect) of early school entrance on later school achievement are meager indeed. We are again faced with the stark reality that unexamined values and untested or poorly tested assumptions provide the basis for many important decisions about timing.

For Rohwer, decisions about timing would be better made on the basis of the degree to which given school tasks assist a child toward greater adaptability in *extra-school* tasks. Rohwer (1971) uses an analogy to the well-known psychometric distinction between concurrent and predictive validity:

> an instructional practice should be judged valid for implementation at the second-grade (or any) level either because it assists the students in meeting extra-school demands placed on second graders (concurrent) or because it is necessary or, at the very least, helpful in the acquisition of other skills required in the extra-school tasks which students face in later life (predictive). No instructional practice should be implemented unless its validity in one of these two senses, concurrently or predictive, can be demonstrated empirically. And in no case should a student's school attainments be evaluated by a standard that does not have demonstrable concurrent and/or predictive validity for extra-school demands (p. 320).

Some readers may dismiss these recommendations too quickly as excessively pragmatic or constraining in mass education. Certainly, a careful specification of extra-school tasks—an activity seldom undertaken by

---

[2] Reproduced by permission of Teachers College Press.

educators—is a necessary first step in acting upon these suggestions. But Rohwer extends his argument to suggest that a postponement of certain schooling practices poorly validated for early childhood education (e.g., early reading and mathematics achievement and memory work in discipline-oriented academic content) can have two advantages. First, he believes that equal, if not better, results in general achievement (especially extra-school achievement) could be attained; and, second, that much of the frustration-failure load presently endured by many (and particularly marginal) students could be reduced. The latter effect would result from increased efficiency and meaningfulness in better-timed learning. This argument is strengthened by Rohwer's own learning experiments. His data suggest that direct training for the autonomous use of "effective learning skills" is considerably more effective with older children (ages 10 to 14) than with younger ones (ages 5 to 7). Ultimately, then, Rohwer joins with others (such as Sigel, 1972) who argue that future research and educational planning in relation to the nature of children's intellectual functioning and learning capabilities should be made from a developmental perspective. Rohwer (1971) also raises the sticky question of whether formal schooling even is necessary prior to early adolescence. Piaget-oriented researchers, among others, seemingly agree in the sense that delaying formal (highly structured academic) instruction theoretically will increase the period of a child's developmental plasticity. This, in turn, will supposedly set the stage for ultimately higher levels of achievement (Elkind, 1969).

But, as Rohwer argues, the answer is not to abandon formal schooling prior to adolescence, but to change it radically. To this end, Rohwer (1971, 1972) has suggested both a direction for educational changes and a program of research that hopefully will resolve the basic instructional issues inherent in his proposal. Interested readers will find both sets of suggestions enlightening and provocative. By implication, Rohwer seems unconvinced about the efficacy, and certainly the developmental suitability of structured early academic education for children. Thus, his suggestions for change largely contradict one of the few reliable generalizations about early education to date: where program impact can be observed, it is generally a function of well-planned and firmly executed structured intellectual-academic activities.

A more careful examination of what and how young children learn and are taught in formal preschool-kindergarten settings may be needed. It seems clear that much of the content is verbal. Nolan (1973) has presented evidence that younger children are less adept at organizing verbal information in ways to increase their learning rate and aid their retention of the material. In a word, the younger child is more likely to "chunk" than to categorize his experience in conceptual terms. *Chunking* consists of grouping things together according to temporal or spatial relationships; *categorizing* involves grouping on the basis of common attributes. Both chunking and categorizing imply organization. Younger children's problem is that they have greater difficulty organizing material on their own. Compared to older children and adults, young children have more to learn. Thus, they may be slower in their learning. And because their experience is not as interrelated, their retention of material learned may be less effective. In Nolan's terms, chunking is akin to rote learning but is not all that bad: it is from little chunks that big concepts grow.

An important implication for education can be drawn from this analysis. If younger children more characteristically form chunks than concepts, the way in which teachers present material is critical. The quality of learning will depend upon how well material is organized. Since younger children also have more data to process, classroom presentations should be slower and more repetitious (Nolan, 1973). If this analysis is valid, it can be taken as support for more carefully structured learning experiences during the early childhood years. Few professional educators are likely to champion the traditional hickory stick approach to school learning. But if direct, well-organized, and appropriately paced instruction can be made fun, responsive to children's needs, and successful in the early years of school, then alternative approaches may have to be championed primarily on philosophical grounds.

Yet, Rohwer's analysis (1971) of timing problems, much of which is addressed to questions of content and methodology, has some strong empirical features. The rational arguments which can be built to justify competing educational policies will perpetuate debate about timing for years to come. Among the brightest possibilities for progress is a continued nurturance of genuine alternatives in early (and later) education not apart from but *within* the system of public education. Neither should we lose sight of the interactive effects of goals, content, instructional methods, and timing. A study of timing, in other words, cannot occur in isolation from the ways in which certain objectives are sought.

Finally, most educators and many researchers are likely to continue to focus their energies on the more traditional aspect of timing known as "readiness" for school or instruction. However, such research is not likely to be productive unless two factors are accounted for: the specific response demands of any learning task and the precise assessment of an individual learner's relevant response repertoire (motivation included). In fact, from a synthesis of several authoritative statements about readiness can be extracted a set of questions useful for educators (Ausubel, 1958; Gagné, 1970; Tyler, 1964). This set of questions implies a conception of educational readiness not in terms of school generally or broad subject matter areas, but in terms of specific requirements which vary with teaching methods and learning materials. These requirements are four in number:

1. What, exactly, must the child know or be capable of doing in order to learn whatever it is I plan to teach and in the manner I plan to teach it? (task analysis)
2. To what degree does the child have at his command these prerequisite or subordinate skills and knowledge? (assessment)

3. Is this child capable of attending sufficiently to this task so that he may master it? (motivation)
4. Can efficient learning be accomplished at this time? (economy)

As Tyler (1964) has observed, the criterion of efficient accomplishment (number 4) is significant for those who reject the notion that a child's "mere capacity" to perform at some ineffective level is sufficient justification to initiate formal instruction. For this writer, a more defensible position is to delay such instruction until the child can reap greater benefits.

Personnel for Early Education

During the earlier discussion of mainstream nursery-kindergarten education, the issue of *who* conducts and is accountable for an early education was examined. This issue gives us pause to consider a number of factors including teacher role models, characteristics of the effective teacher, staff requirements, and certification. Role models, for example, clearly vary according to the objectives and basic pedagogy of programs. There currently seems to be little support for a simple maternal-surrogate role model in early childhood education, although the therapeutic model persists in situations characterized by strong affective education where children's needs for self-expression and understanding are emphasized. More basic conflict occurs between two other role models: the "instructional" and "facilitator" models (Katz, 1970). The former model prescribes a comparatively high degree of directive teaching, including transmitting information, setting goals for learning, and supervising skill drills. Such is the preferred and necessary role in many more structured academic programs such as Distar and behavior analysis classrooms. In contrast is the facilitator role, deftly illustrated in the Montessori method and perhaps even more in exemplary open education classrooms. This role requires a difficult combination of being encouraging, responsive, and skilled in the exacting process of individualized instruction.

Role models, in other words, are an integral part of any well-defined curriculum model. And much of the teacher role model problem in early education concerns the degree to which an individual believes in and feels comfortable in his or her role in a given program. As indicated in Chapter 5, this factor of belief—together with constructive in-service training and supervision—seems to be fundamental to the success of any program. In the final analysis, few would argue that teacher quality can make or break a program. Inevitably, this recognition leads to the question of what constitutes the effective or successful teacher. Unfortunately, neither professional educators nor researchers who study teacher behavior agree on the criteria for effective instruction. This writer feels that teaching effectiveness should be assessed largely in terms of how well children (learners) achieve the objectives of a program (assuming the objectives are valid and realistic). The acceptance of this criterion obviously requires systematic research into the kind and degree of behavior changes among the learners in a given program. Two general outcomes, by no means mutually exclusive, are perhaps most relevant: learner *competence* in terms of cognitive and psychomotor skills "where applicable" and learner *sentiment*, including attitude development and satisfaction with self-progress (Anderson, 1959).

Research about teaching effectiveness across educational levels generally suggests that teachers who are perceived by others as most effective (in terms of the criteria above) rate high in enthusiasm and communication skill (Evans, 1969). Similarly, other important variables include skill in (1) adapting teaching objectives, content, and method *in process* (in response to the reactions, learning problems, and needs of pupils); and (2) activating student interest and personal involvement (through teacher flexibility and motivational skill). Other research workers have pointed to the importance of empathy, nurturance, and a secure self-image for teachers of young children (Hogan, 1969; O'Leary and Becker, 1968–1969). These qualities—together with the characteristics of enthusiasm, communication skill, flexibility, and ability to involve children actively in the learning process—can be said to be desirable among all teachers involved in early childhood education.

The argument that teachers should possess selected desirable personality characteristics must be made essentially on humanistic grounds. The research evidence is insufficient to indicate that persons who love and enjoy working with children are necessarily better teachers than those who do not (Spodek, 1972). Of course, kindly and attentive teachers are usually better liked by children and this should count for something. In this writer's judgment, teacher educators should at least examine their selection and training procedures in relation to these important human characteristics.[3] However, one can too easily overlook the notion that different teaching styles and certain personal characteristics may be perceived differently by children and even affect their learning in different ways. An increasing number of studies (e.g., St. John, 1971) indicates that the ethnic, social class, and personal characteristics can interact with teacher characteristics and style to produce different outcomes. It is therefore most difficult to synthesize a description of the "effective teacher" apart from the context in which instruction occurs and the characteristics of the children involved (Turner, 1970).

Strong arguments also have been offered for the importance of child workers serving as models of rational authority for children (Baumrind, 1973). Such authority is based upon a competence or expertise which enables an adult to interact intentionally and thoughtfully with children

---

[3] Recommendations concerning the preparation of nursery and kindergarten teachers have recently been made through the National Education Association's Commission on Teacher Education and Professional Standards (Haberman and Persky, 1969). One principal recommendation is that teachers of young children should be evaluated in terms of demonstrated competence and personal suitability as well as in terms of the usual criterion of academic preparation.

and "to designate a behavioral alternative for another where the alternatives are perceived by both" (Baumrind, 1973, p. 161). Indecisiveness, passivity, overprotectiveness, and punitiveness are all inconsistent with an attitude of rational authority. This authority has perhaps too often been abdicated under the guise of a permissiveness which in reality becomes a de facto laissez-faire approach to character development. Baumrind extrapolates from impressive research about patterns of parental authority to suggest that teachers and day care personnel should be capable of self-assertion and self-sufficiency in accord with self-defined standards of conduct and values. It is remarkable how little attention has been given to this issue in early childhood education teacher training and supervision.

Apart from general personal attributes and degree of commitment to one's teaching task, instructional effectiveness is a function of program-specific knowledge and abilities. The application of behavioral analysis procedures, for example, involves more advanced skills in contingency management and data taking than are developed in most teacher education programs. A teacher in a Piaget-based program must, among other things, be thoroughly conversant with Piagetian theory and the *méthode-clinique.* A successful Montessori teacher must be an extraordinary observer of children and extraordinarily adept in the demonstration and arrangement of learning activities. The same holds for teachers in any program where a child-centered approach prevails. These skills are not likely to be developed without intensive training. This writer, for one, flatly rejects the contention so often heard in lay circles that "Anyone can teach!" or the popular view that parenthood qualifies one as a teacher of young children.

Issues of teacher training, the assessment of teacher effectiveness, and general professionalization are made even more salient by the trend toward differentiated staffing in early childhood education: adults working together in different roles and in different relationships with one another and children (Spodek, 1972). This differentiation includes a much greater acceptance and use of auxiliary personnel (e.g., teacher aides) and team teaching arrangements. The research base for differentiated staffing and the use of paraprofessionals is still weak. Consequently, not much can be said about the impact of these phenomena except that a low adult-child ratio in the classroom is generally a positive factor. Data lacks notwithstanding, strong positions about training paraprofessionals for work with infants and toddlers have been taken (e.g., Lally, Honig, and Caldwell, 1973). The federal Child Development Associate Project, designed to provide competent personnel for early child care and education, is also being conducted as this book goes to press (see Williams and Ryan, 1972). This project bears watching, as it is bound to have implications for future staffing policies in early childhood education.

The concern for quality control in staffing is perhaps best symbolized by the trend toward more thorough certification standards in early childhood education. Yet at least two serious problems exist. First, and as indicated in Chapter 2, many states still have no licensing standards for nursery school and day care center personnel. Or the standards that exist are so loose and general that little is accomplished by their presence. Public support for the removal of conditions which contribute to teaching failures (for example, faulty teacher training procedures, inappropriate and insufficient learning materials, and tolerance of mediocre or incompetent school personnel) is sorely needed. Second, procedures for monitoring the extent to which even minimum standards are maintained are woefully lacking. Further complications can be traced to the primitive state of knowledge about what constitutes effective training procedures in the helping professions generally. In teacher education, for example, the familiar "course model" approach continues to be applied in the absence of any firm evidence that the accumulation of college credits per se has any relationship whatsoever to teaching effectiveness. Procedures for selecting persons for teacher education also seem dominated by the revered grade-point average criterion, with too little attention paid to the important human characteristics mentioned earlier. Such issues must be faced and dealt with decisively in view of the proliferation of early childhood and day care programs in America. Staff needs are sure to intensify, both in terms of the range and number of workers required (including parents, Spodek, 1972).

Finally, the concern for providing a better balance of male and female sex role models for preschool and early school-age children has increased measurably over the past few years (Lee, 1973). It is no secret that early childhood education has been dominated by women throughout its history in America. Concerns about the undue feminization of young male children are frequently expressed. Equally strong concerns are now apparent in regard to restrictive and excessively biased sex role conditioning for young females. Theorizing far exceeds definitive research findings about the singular effect of a teacher's sex upon children of either sex. It seems sensible, however, to work for change in the traditional ratio of male to female teachers and day care workers. The beginnings of a case for change are documented elsewhere (Lee, 1973).

The Setting for Early Education

A final issue to be discussed here concerns *where* early education programs are conducted. In the past, educational authorities have not dealt explicitly and extensively with this significant issue. Possibly this is because education has traditionally been equated with formalized activity. Many educators and parents have assumed, perhaps with good reason, that formal educational activities are best executed in special environments outside the home. A tradition of formal schooling in group settings by age 5 or 6 seems so firmly established within American society that a significant shift from this pattern is unlikely. It seems equally unlikely that a majority of Americans will support a downward extension of compulsory education to include children as young as age 3.

Educational opportunities for children age 3 and younger are a different matter. Aside from home-based teaching programs here and there (see Chapter 8), education and developmental day care for children surely will continue as extra-home functions. Even so, many parents, educators, and psychologists harbor a certain uneasiness, if not fear, about the effect of early and prolonged group experiences away from the home. Of course, the question may become moot if the trend toward maternal employment continues at its present pace. Further implications of this trend are discussed elsewhere (e.g., Poznanski, Maxey, and Marsden, 1970). To pit the home and family against the schools and day care centers, however, misses the real point. The variable of initial quality in parent-child relationships seems more at issue. A growing body of evidence indicates that normal development can be, and usually is, maintained under "good" conditions of early group care as measured against home care (e.g., Goldman, 1971; Moyles and Wolins, 1971). Preferably, *premium*, not just good, conditions should be guaranteed in all institutional settings. Presently, United States children often have much less than this (Caldwell, 1973). Joint home-school and day care center collaboration and mutual support for child advocacy and welfare are needed, especially where developmental and learning problems of children are involved (Scott, 1971). Obstacles of various kinds—financial, ideological, and inevitable shortcomings of institutional settings in meeting children's many needs—are sure to persist (Baumrind, 1973). But group activity for children away from the home as early as infancy seems here to stay. For younger children, in particular, groups should remain small and be supported by ample numbers of qualified adult caregivers or teachers. And the thrust should be toward strengthening, not diluting, nuclear family relationships.

Again, the issue of where cannot be separated from the other major issues discussed, notably timing, content, and staffing. Where and when should what kinds of experiences be provided and by whom for a given child or group of children? Every architect of a program of caregiving or education should be able to specify a psychological-philosophical rationale when answering this question.

RESEARCH IN EARLY EDUCATION

A major theme throughout this book has been that evidence of behavior change is (and should be) instrumental in determining the merits of a program or procedure. This determination can be a matter of policy without undue emphasis on specific behavioral outcomes. The point is that empirical data are an important aspect of the final authority for decision making in education. Sadly, this authority is difficult to reach. So many problems inhere in early childhood education research and evaluation that one wonders if a definitive statement about anything will ever be made. In Chapter 1, many of these problems were introduced under the topics of evaluation criteria, measurement, internal validity, and external validity. That earlier discussion can now be embellished by references to several important commentaries on research and evaluation functions in early childhood education. Glick (1968), for example, has warned against several pitfalls, including the common failure to differentiate between (1) a child's actual performance and his ability to perform, (2) a child's achievement and the process or structure underlying it, and (3) the potential positive *and* negative effects of early education (intervention) in terms of longer-term developmental change. Skager and Broadbent (1968) have expressed concern over the tendency for programs to be evaluated too narrowly, that is, without the application of criteria sufficiently broad in scope or with an assessment strategy that represents only the value system of the evaluator.[4] Similarly, Sroufe (1970) has stressed that value judgments may subtly and negatively influence the objectivity necessary for a scientific interpretation of research.[5] He also decries the not so subtle tendency of researchers to discuss correlational data as if they represented cause-effect relationships. For example, a positive correlation between teacher warmth and pupil creativity or between social class and intelligence cannot stand as "proof" of an antecedent-consequent relationship. Finally, in respect to measurement problems, Sroufe (1970) is critical of the failure in many quarters to maintain the distinction between a construct and the procedure used to measure that construct: that is, a failure to qualify one's data in terms of the validity and reliability of the procedures utilized to gather them. Thus, instead of speaking of the effects of intervention on intelligence (implying total adaptive capacity), it would be more appropriate to speak of "intelligence" as measured by whatever instrument one has used. This problem inheres in any psychometric approach to the study of behavior and can be avoided in many respects by the measurement procedures set forth for the experimental or applied analysis of behavior (Chapter 3). Such procedures have not been used much in other than university research settings.

Other research and evaluation difficulties congruent with the Chapter 1 discussion can be identified (Grotberg, 1969; Payne, Mercer, Payne, and Davison, 1973; Sigel, 1973). A clear rationale both for predicting outcomes and formulating testable hypotheses is needed. It is mandatory, for example, to distinguish the philosophical from the psychological (empirical) aspects of a question. This involves the basic "should" and "what" aspects of a question. A legitimate intervention research question must be formulated in terms of, What are the effects of this treatment?, as opposed to the philosophical question, Should this treatment be applied? Such judgmental aspects of research require careful attention before and after an experiment but cannot be researched in an empirical sense. As an example, the question, What are the effects of language programs X, Y, and Z

---

[4] This criticism is echoed in specific terms by Margolin (1969), who is critical of those who make an "artifical" distinction between intellectualism and exploratory workplay and the widespread lack of attention to the study of aesthetic development in children.

[5] As an example, Sroufe (1970) refers to the value-based problems involved when lower-class black parents and children are observed and evaluated by middle-class white research workers.

upon the development of children's vocabulary and syntax?, is empirical. In contrast, the question, Should language program X, Y, Z, be used with kindergarten-age children?, is philosophical. One may be assisted toward an answer to the should question if he first answers the empirical question. An answer to the empirical question depends, however, on the skill with which a researcher specifies precisely the components of each language program (antecedents) and his criteria for evaluating each program (consequents, or behavioral outcomes). Perhaps too frequently, global programs (such as "kindergarten experience") have been "evaluated" with global measures (such as teacher's ratings of language development) where the results have limited value for the practitioner. Rarely are teacher-pupil interactions examined in method-comparison studies for the purpose of specifying which teacher behaviors affect which pupil behaviors and vice versa. Similarly, gross and delayed evaluation such as end-of-year achievement or IQ gain scores based upon groups (versus individual children) often is extremely limited in its value for helping teachers teach or providing clues for program improvement. Called for are both immediate and more individualized evaluation procedures to provide a better "feedback loop" for teachers regarding their effectiveness with each and every child. Again, applied behavior analysis procedures and other methods of formative evaluation can be helpful for this purpose.

As suggested in Chapter 1, further methodological problems include sampling techniques (means of selecting children for study), limitations in measurement procedures, and the statistical analysis of data. For example, research projects frequently involve comparisons of extremely small numbers of children where background factors such as socio-economic status and measured intelligence are insufficiently controlled. Valid and reliable measures are not plentiful, especially for measuring young children's affective characteristics. Frequently, decisions regarding how data gathered from children will be analyzed seem to be made after the data are in, rather than having been made in advance of study. A related problem is that statistical analyses may violate the fundamental assumptions about sampling upon which the analysis procedure is based. For example, many analyses which may culminate in a statement of statistical significance depend upon the premise that a random sample of children has been selected for study. In practice, truly random samples are rare. This must be considered a serious limitation of early education research, particularly when the study involves simultaneous comparisons of two or more programs.

Another set of problems, logistical in nature, can illustrate how events often impede and unduly complicate research progress (Grotberg, 1969). Examples include the frequent loss of subjects (children) from a study because of illness or change in residence; extensive time periods mandatory for certain types of testing, interviewing, and observing; and the occasional inability or unwillingness of parents and teachers or children to cooperate in a research program. In addition to the time problem, research

— 4 sorts of progs — p 16
— evaluation p 21 Problems p 27

assumptions of early intervention

① Bereiter & Engel
  (of Head Start)
② Engelmann
③ Bushell?
  Bijou
④ Bijou
⑤ Skinner?
⑥ Bijou...
⑦ Evans
Summary

97-105

— extensive explication
  (of Head Start)

— role of objectives,
  evaluation (including
  Piaget's)
— sequence readings

G. McK
733-4447
33 Bill Ave.

MEMORANDUM

To ..... Faculty

Graduate Students

From ..... J. Jaap Tuinman
Director Graduate Programs
Faculty of Education

Subject ..... Assistance on Computer Work/
Statistical Analysis

Date ..... May 13, 1980

    In order for John Walsh, the newly appointed Lab Instructor
to function effectively it's important that he is allowed
adequate turn-around time on the work you are asking him to do.

    I urge you therefore to plan your research in such a
fashion that you can allow 2-3 weeks for a specific job. If
this request inconveniences you, I'll be glad to discuss the
matter with you.

J. Jaap Tuinman

can be very expensive in terms of materials, data analysis, and research workers' salaries. Unquestionably, such logistical problems have prevented otherwise promising research projects from getting off the ground.

Problems of interpretation also pervade much early childhood intervention research. These problems usually are based in differences among theoreticians regarding the nature and process of child development and education, including compensatory education. We have seen, for example, how differently psychologists and educators who align themselves with cognitive-developmental theory, structural pedagogy, and behavioral analysis conceptualize research strategies and interpret research data. In addition, conflicting findings have resulted even when investigators employ similar techniques to study similar problems among similar groups of children. The sources of these conflicting data are generally difficult to pinpoint, and research workers' attempts to identify these sources often result in speculation. This speculation often takes the form of interpretations based upon diverse theoretical preferences which result in contradictory "explanations." This situation can unduly confuse the practitioner who is unfamiliar with the conceptual intricacies and abstractions characteristic of psychological theories. The complex interactions between instructional, content, and personal variables which frequently occur in method-comparison research create equally complex interpretational problems. We have seen examples of this type of problem in both Montessori-based and Piaget-based research—to name only two areas of study discussed in this book. Finally, a problem of interpretation commonly associated with research to produce normative data is a tendency to confuse what children can learn with what they have learned at a given point in time (Martin, 1965).

To summarize briefly, research in early childhood education involves a number of conceptual, methodological, logistical, and interpretational problems (Grotberg, 1969). Comparative analyses of alternatives to early childhood education are therefore extremely complex. This complexity is perhaps increased by a tendency to reify a method or curriculum model because that method or model has a label (Banta, 1966). That is, most early education strategies are labeled, and this label often leads us to believe that the strategy is something unique and to an emphasis on components that clearly and uniformly differentiate one approach from another. Even if reification is deserved, there is the likelihood that components described on paper will not be translated fully into actual practice. Thus, if one's purpose is a realistic analysis of any program, one must observe firsthand what is taught and how it is taught. Only through systematic observation are the distinguishing features of an early education environment likely to be identified. A telling question is whether such features, even if unique, make a real difference in the educational development of children.

Attempts to "prove" the superiority of one approach over another will probably continue, although they can easily be misguided. The traditional method-comparison type of research typically results only in data that reflect group averages. In other words, the "advantage" of one method over another is usually reported in terms of average gain for all the children in that group. In some broad cases, the average gain may be of minor importance, even though it is statistically significant. For example, a comparison of two methods for reading instruction involving large numbers of children might result in an "advantage" for one group as measured by a reading achievement test. The test score advantage could be statistically significant yet only involve two or three points of difference, between the two groups. Such a finding could hardly be represented as making a major breakthrough in the technique of reading instruction. Further, researchers who report data in terms of group averages rarely examine the extent to which a "treatment" may have increased (or decreased) the range of individual differences in classroom-based performance or whether a given method, while generally advantageous, has no positive effect on certain children within a given group. Thus, intragroup analyses are needed, as well as more attention to combinations of experiences suitable for *individual children*.

The suggestion that educators should focus more sharply on the behavior of individual children can be related to the concept of gene-environment interaction (Caspari, 1968). That is, all aspects of behavioral development depend upon some combination of genetic and environmental factors. Applied to educational practice, this means that different children will respond differently to any given educational method to the extent that their genetic makeup and past environmental experiences differ. While some educational approaches may be better than others for larger numbers of children, a singularly optimal method for all children is not possible, at least in principle. This leads us again to the value of individualization in education. In terms of research, it is possible that Piaget's *méthode clinique* and applied behavior analysis techniques, though vastly different in concept, can contribute in unique ways to better individualization practices.

Research and the Teacher

Thus far, our discussion about research problems and issues has been largely technical. But the role of research in early childhood education can be further analyzed for teachers at a more personal level. Hartup (1970), for example, has written that much early education research may be more valuable to teachers as a source of "educational innovations" rather than "specific prescriptions" for instruction. As an illustration, current experimental research about the role of play in learning and development may provide broad cues for program changes in early education curricula. On the other hand, we have seen that some very specific ideas about instruction can be gleaned from well-designed and conducted evaluation research. Some teachers, for instance, may interpret the tutorial techniques developed by Blank and Solomon (Chapter 4) as being close to a prescriptive model—at least in the form of a set of hypotheses about language training which can be further tested.

In any case, an attitude of critical inquiry among teachers is important.

If research is to make any difference in educational practice, the classroom teacher is the final arbiter of change. In other words, it is the practicing teacher who eventually translates research findings into action. One problem with this, unfortunately, has been a frequent gap between the technical research enterprise and real children. Another problem, at least in this writer's experience, is that teachers are often intimidated by the technicalities and ambiguity of much research. They also rarely are constructively trained to interpret and draw implications from research, much less to view themselves as important members of a collective educational research team. Both teachers and specialized research workers must work together and share certain responsibilities if research is ever to be more than academic. According to Scott (1972), for example, research can be meaningful in education if certain conditions can be met:

. . . if teachers can clearly specify what they want to help learn. They will then know more clearly what knowledge they need and will probably be more likely to want it. This applies whether the goal is a particular kind of social behavior, knowledge, feeling or physical skills, creative expression, or the capacity to learn.

. . . if research workers keep clear the links between their research questions and real life issues, and communicate these in reporting findings. Then the applications of research, when appropriate, will be more evident.

. . . if teachers understand something of the process of research, how current studies extend or question a systematically gathered body of knowledge, and why certain questions may not yet have been asked. They will then not expect to apply findings from a single study and be met with contradictions from another. This experience is often responsible for the attitude of "research gets nowhere."

. . . if researchers acknowledge that complex questions not necessarily dealt with in testing theoretical principles appear at the point of application, and try to study the additional issues which these attempts to apply research results make evident. The artificial status of "pure" research will be less likely to be perpetuated and the separation between theory and practice might be reduced. The responsibilities of teachers will more readily be recognized.

. . . if teachers distinguish between knowledge of human development (provided by research) and the working out of its applications to their own teaching program (the task of education). They are unlikely then to equate understanding children with teaching them. Hopefully, they will see such knowledge as a prerequisite for teaching, and will give recognition to the specialized research fields contributing to education as existing in their own right.

. . . if personal contact is established between research workers and practicing teachers. Research will then be less in danger of becoming stereotyped. It will have the stimulus of knowing what current knowledge is being used, the results of attempts to apply it, and areas where additional study is needed. Teaching practices may be more open to the influence of research findings conveyed personally with the opportunity for discussion. (Scott, 1972, pp. 21–22)[6]

Similarly, a helpful list of questions for teachers concerned with testing the applicability of research materials for their own classroom practices has been proposed (Hartup, 1970). These questions fit nicely with the emphasis upon formative, as well as summative, evaluation discussed in Chapter 1:

1. Does the research-based procedure work? If so, are there other side effects of procedures?
2. Did the new procedure produce mixed consequences; that is, were there negative side effects accompanying positive results?
3. Did the procedure totally fail? Why?
4. Did the extension of the procedure used in the classroom omit significant details of the original research procedure?
5. Did classroom conditions change or dilute in any way the effects of an experimental procedure that was otherwise accurately reproduced?
6. Did the procedure work with some children and not with others?
7. Are differences in outcome between the experiment and the classroom possibly related to characteristics of children? (Hartup, 1970, p. 31).

Teacher Evaluation of Prepackaged Materials   Teachers not only can take an active role in the implementation or further field testing of experimental instructional techniques; they are key figures in the selection and evaluation of prepackaged learning materials as well. Several examples of materials prepackaged for school use have appeared in this book—Distar, Peabody Language Development Kit, Lavatelli's Piaget-based kindergarten program, and Bessell's human development program, to name only a few. An aura of authenticity or validity seems to accompany such prepackaged programs merely because of the fact that they are published by commercial firms for widespread distribution. The attractive displays of such materials at meetings of professional education organizations are well known. At issue is how extensively and carefully such programs have been formulated, tested revised, retested, and the like. As a matter of course, it is good and professional practice to examine packaged materials in terms of selected evaluation criteria prior to their classroom use. Mini-

---

[6] Reprinted with permission from *The Young Child, Reviews of Research,* Vol. 2, 1972, edited by Willard W. Hartup. National Association for the Education of Young Children, 1834 Connecticut Avenue, N.W., Washington, D.C. 20009.

mal guidelines useful for this purpose have been offered by Bugelski (1971):[7]

1. Does a publisher or commercial distributor of a new method or set of materials describe in precise terms the content areas or skills they purport to cover? Very broad, often vague, terms such as *language* or *intellectual development* occasionally are used by educational hucksters when a very narrow range of content or skills is actually involved. It is important that explicit information about learning goals, content domains, costs (or savings) of money and instructional time, and teacher training needs be available for inspection. In this way, goals and cost factors can be compared for decision-making purposes with a teacher's present instructional approach.

2. Is the nature of the population for whom the program is intended clearly specified? Prepackaged programs often are designed for different levels of learning; some can be used in a variety of different ways. Either way, it is desirable to have the prerequisites or program entry requirements specified better to match program levels with individual children's needs and capabilities. It is also desirable to consider the relationship of a prospective program to the overall developmental curriculum within an educational setting. Degree of integration consistency and continuity with other aspects of the school curriculum are often important concerns.

3. What evaluative research data about the program's use are available for close inspection? Generally speaking, the more extensive the evaluation component of a program is, the better. Both the internal and external validity of a program should be examined (see Chapter 1).

These would seem to be among the most basic questions to ask about any prepackaged program, educational kit, or learning materials designed for classroom use. Fortunately, even more extensive guidelines for the selection and evaluation of programs and materials are available for use by teachers and administrators and their study can be highly beneficial (e.g., Educational Products Information Exchange, 1972a, 1972b; Smith and Giesy, 1972).

Looking Ahead

Much has been learned since the early childhood renaissance of the 1960s. As Sigel (1973) has observed, we have a much better data base from which to plan, conceptualize, and evaluate intervention strategies. We are perhaps less inclined to expect that early education will be the ultimate and lasting force in influencing the course of children's development. But with a broadened set of social services made possible through the early intervention movement, many children and their families hopefully have enjoyed improved life circumstances and expanded avenues of opportunity.

---

[7] This matter also concerns the general component of program exportability first discussed in Chapter 1.

As we have learned and profited in many ways from the intervention movement, so have we confronted additional problems and questions which can not be readily solved or answered. Many fundamental aspects of early childhood education continue to demand serious thinking and re-thinking: these include the truth about child growth and development, valid and appropriate methods of child study, and suitable goals and methods for early education. Concerning early education strategies there is the persistent and largely unanswered question of how substantial can be the effects of early intervention on children's "learning capacity" and general motivation. With increasing numbers of children attending preschools, many of which are academically oriented, there is the question of what transformations should occur in public school kindergarten–primary curricula across the country. Community action ideas originally associated with Project Head Start are bound to have an even broader and more profound impact on school-related matters. It is now important to examine schools in terms of how well they respond to the needs of *all* the clientele they exist to serve. This means, at least, a much broader range of provisions for culturally and linguistically different children and their families.

Still other developments of interest to early childhood educators can be identified. Concentrated efforts are under way to provide specialized educational services to variously handicapped preschool-age children. For example, eight programs—exemplary in their notable and important

A clear trend in education and child care for the 1970s concerns more comprehensive and long overdue preschool services for children with various developmental handicaps. As these services are delivered, remarkable progress in early behavior development can be achieved. These active and alert youngsters are members of a special preschool class for Down's Syndrome children. Photo courtesy of Media Services, Experimental Education Unit, University of Washington.

features—have recently been showcased by the federal government (Abt Associates, 1973). An emergent trend of the 1970s involves the idea of "children teaching children" (e.g., Gartner, Kohler, and Reissman, 1971). That is, much is now being said about the values or advantages of supervised programs where children become teachers of other, usually younger, children. The underlying idea—that a good, if not the best way to learn something is to teach it yourself—is not new. But its serious and broad-scale application in this century has not been apparent in early education, especially in the public schools. It should also be noted that more extensive developments in children's educational television seem likely throughout the 1970s. One intriguing possibility is home viewing via cable television. Cable television has the capacity to deliver signals to the home as well as carry back information from the home to a central source. This capacity, known as "interactive" or "two-way" service, has great potential for the education of children and parents alike (Morrisett, 1973).

Any success that may be achieved through mass communication ventures will, of course, depend heavily upon the parents of preschool children. And this issue is related to the still larger challenge of establishing more productive interaction between home and school, parents and teachers (Biber, 1969). But it is not simply a matter of home-school interchange. Also to be dealt with is the growing issue of coordinating educational and developmental day care services for children. The responsibilities and procedures of these services have not yet been satisfactorily clarified. Promising new patterns of continuing service, beginning with maternal prenatal care and extending through infant care and preschool education have been conceived on a pilot basis and may possibly serve as guideposts for progress (Balzer, 1973).

The conceptual fabric for these new patterns comes neither easily nor cheaply. Enormous amounts of resources usually are expended for even the slightest new insight. The federal government has, of course, been instrumental in much of the social action program development within early childhood education circles. But political winds can shift quickly and with them go sources of program funding. As this book is written it cannot even be said that programs like Head Start are safe from the axes of austerity and reordered priorities. Surely, the future of the various federally supported early intervention programs can be influenced by concerned parents and educators working together for the overall welfare of America's children. At the same time, it is probably unwise to depend too strongly upon the federal government for early education support; state and local governmental resources are badly in need of coordination for better and more responsive action in the world of young children (Goodlad, Klein, and Novotney, 1973).

In this book, many changes in the theory and practice of early education have been noted. Often, change can mean progress. Yet the wheels of progress turn slowly. Despite the conceptual advances and general ferment in early childhood education triggered during the early 1960s, there are clear indications that the typical American preschool is a rather pedestrian operation, albeit a generally comfortable place for children to be (Goodlad, Klein, and Novotney, 1973). From an impressive observational study of 201 representative American nursery schools, it has been concluded that the personnel of such schools still operate in isolation from the professional and intellectual activity within the early education field. Also reported is a frequent lack of critical self-evaluation and continual efforts at program improvement among staff, even though staff are dedicated to child care. Stated goals and program emphases often are incongruent as well. This has the net result of a seemingly narrow homogeneity among preschool programs, certainly more than may be desirable in terms of children's capabilities, the value of genuine alternatives for parents and their children, and the need for precision in instruction required by some children to benefit from the preschool experience (Goodlad, Klein, and Novotney, 1973).

As we move into the 1980s, the communication network for early education must become less hampered; much of the responsibility for this development rests with the early childhood education leadership. Research workers, teachers, parents, and public officials together should profit from more open and systematic interchange at all levels of program development and implementation. But effective communication is not enough. Also needed are the creative problem-solving efforts of professionals and lay persons to sustain the momentum of the early intervention movement.

REFERENCES

Abt Associates, Inc. *Exemplary programs for the handicapped.* Vol. 3. *Early childhood education.* Washington, D.C.: U.S. Department of Health, Education, and Welfare, 1973.

Anderson, R. Learning in discussion: a résumé of the authoritarian–democratic studies. *Harvard Educational Review*, 1959, *29*, 201–215.

Anderson, V., and C. Bereiter. Extending direct instruction to conceptual skills. In R. Parker (ed.), *The preschool in action.* Boston: Allyn and Bacon, 1972, 339–352.

Ausubel, D. *Theory and problems in child development.* New York: Grune and Stratton, 1958.

Balzer, F. What about tomorrow? Directions for the future. In L. Dittman (ed.), *The infants we care for.* Washington, D.C.: National Association for the Education of Young Children, 1973, 102–108.

Banta, T. Is there really a Montessori method? Cincinnati, Ohio: University of Cincinnati, Department of Psychology, 1966.

Baumrind, D. Will a day care center be a child development center? *Young Children*, 1973, *28*, 154–159.

Biber, B. *Challenges ahead for early childhood education.* Washington, D.C.: National Association for the Education of Young Children, 1969.

Bissell, J. The cognitive effects of preschool programs for disadvantaged children. In J. Frost (ed.), *Revisiting early childhood education.* New York: Holt, Rinehart and Winston, 1973, 223–240.

Bugelski, B. R. *The psychology of learning applied to teaching.* Indianapolis: Bobbs-Merrill, 1971.

Busse, T., M. Ree, M. Gutridge, T. Alexander, and L. Powell. Environmentally enriched classrooms and the cognitive and perceptual development of Negro preschool children. *Journal of Educational Psychology*, 1972, *63*, 15–21.

Caldwell, B. Can young children have a quality life in day care? *Young children*, 1973, *28*, 197–208.

Caspari, E. Genetic endowment and environment in the determination of human behavior: biological viewpoint. *American Educational Research Journal*, 1968, *5*, 43–55.

Cazden, C. The issue of structure. In C. Cazden (ed.), *Language in early childhood education.* Washington, D.C.: National Association for the Education of Young Children, 1972, 23–34.

Cicirelli, V. The effects of sibling relationships on concept learning of young children taught by child-teachers. *Child Development*, 1972, *43*, 282–287.

Cronbach, L. Heredity, environment, and educational policy. *Harvard Educational Review*, 1969, *39*, 338–347

Devor, G., and S. Stern. Objects versus pictures in the instruction of young children. *Journal of School Psychology*, 1970, *8*, 77–81.

Dewey, J. *Democracy and education.* New York: The Macmillan Co., 1916.

Educational Products Information Exchange. *Early childhood education: how to select and evaluate materials.* New York: Educational Products Information Exchange Institute, 1972. (a)

Educational Products Information Exchange. *Early childhood education: evaluation of kits for early learning.* New York: Educational Products Information Exchange Institute, 1972. (b)

Elkind, D. Preschool education: enrichment or instruction? *Childhood Education*, 1969, *46*, 321–328.

Evans, E. Student activism and teaching effectiveness: survival of the fittest? *Journal of College Student Personnel*, 1969, March, 102–108.

Evans, E. D. *Contemporary influences in early childhood education.* New York: Holt, Rinehart and Winston, 1971.

Feitelson, D., S. Weintraub, and O. Michaeli. Social interactions in heterogeneous preschools in Israel. *Child Development*, 1972, *43*, 1249–1259.

Furth, E. *Constructing evaluation instruments.* New York: McKay, 1958.

Gagné, R. *The conditions of learning*, 2d ed. New York: Holt, Rinehart and Winston, 1970.

Gartner, A., M. Kohler, and F. Reissman. *Children teach children.* New York: Harper & Row, 1971.

Getzels, J. Preschool education. *Teachers College Record*, 1966, 68, 219–228.

Glick, J. Some problems in the evaluation of pre-school intervention programs. In R. Hess and R. Bear (eds.), *Early education.* Chicago: Aldine, 1968, 215–221.

Goldman, R. Psychosocial development in cross-cultural perspective: a new look at an old issue. *Developmental Psychology*, 1971, *5*, 411–419.

Goodlad, J., M. Klein, and J. Novotney. *Early schooling in the United States.* New York: McGraw-Hill, 1973.

Grotberg, E. *Review of research: 1965 to 1969.* Washington, D.C.: Project Head Start, Office of Economic Opportunity, 1969.

Haberman, M., and B. Persky, *Preliminary report of the ad hoc joint committee on the preparation of nursery and kindergarten teachers.* Washington, D.C.: National Education Association, 1969.

Harris, B., and R. Fisher. Distortions in the kindergarten. *Young Children*, 1969, *24*, 279–284.

Hartup, W. Early childhood education and research-significance and needs. *Journal of Teacher Education,* 1970, *21,* 23–33.

Haskett, G. Research and early education. *American Psychologist,* 1973, *28,* 248–256.

Havighurst, R. *Developmental tasks and education.* New York: McKay, 1972.

Hogan, R. Development of an empathy scale. *Journal of Consulting and Clinical Psychology,* 1969, *33,* 307–316.

Kagan, J. *Preschool enrichment and learning.* Fort Lee, N.J.: Sigma Information, Inc. Behavioral Sciences Tape Library, 1972.

Karnes, M. Personal communication, April 30, 1971.

Katz, L. *Four questions on early childhood education.* Urbana, Ill.: ERIC Clearinghouse on Early Childhood Education, 1970.

Kohlberg, L. Stage and sequence: the cognitive-developmental approach to socialization. In D. Goslin (ed.), *Handbook of socialization theory and research.* Skokie, Ill.: Rand McNally, 1969, 347–480.

Kohlberg, L., and R. Mayer. Development as the aim of education. *Harvard Educational Review,* 1972, *42,* 449–496.

Kuzma, K., and C. Stern. The effects of three preschool intervention programs on the development of autonomy in Mexican-American and Negro children. *Journal of Special Education,* 1972, *6,* 197–206.

Lally, J., A. Honig, and B. Caldwell. Training paraprofessionals for work with infants and toddlers. *Young Children,* 1973, *28,* 173–182.

Lazarus, M. The historical antecedents of early childhood education. In I. Gordon (ed.), *Early childhood education.* Chicago: University of Chicago Press, 1972, 33–54.˙

Lee, P. Male and female teachers in elementary schools: an ecological analysis. *Teachers College Record,* 1973, *75,* 79–98.

Lesser, G. Matching instruction to student characteristics. In G. Lesser (ed.), *Psychology and educational practice.* Glenview, Ill.: Scott, Foresman, 1971, 530–550.

Margolin, E. Crucial issues in contemporary early childhood education. *Childhood Education,* 1969, *45,* 500–504.

Martin, J. Montessori after 50 years. *Teachers College Record,* 1965, *67,* 552–554.

McCandless, B. Personal correspondence, January 13, 1970.

Meacham, M. L., and A. E. Wiesen. *Changing Classroom Behavior.* Scranton, Pa.: International Textbooks, 1969.

Meyer, W. *Cognitive performance: process or product.* Fort Lee, N.J.: Sigma Information, Inc. Behavioral Sciences Tape Library, 1972.

Moore, R., and D. Moore. The dangers of early schooling. *Harper's,* June-July 1972, *245,* 58–62.

Morrisett, L. Television technology and the culture of childhood. *Educational Researcher,* 1973, *2* (12), 3–5.

Moyles, E., and M. Wolins. Group care and intellectual development. *Developmental Psychology,* 1971, *4,* 370–380.

Nolan, J. Conceptual and rote learning in children. *Teachers College Record,* 1973, *75,* 251–258.

O'Leary, K., and W. Becker. The effects of the intensity of a teacher's reprimands on children's behavior. *Journal of School Psychology,* 1968–1969, *7* (1), 8–11.

Parker, R., and M. Day. Comparisons of preschool curricula. In R. Parker (ed.), *The preschool in action.* Boston: Allyn and Bacon, 1972, 466–508.

Payne, J., C. Mercer, R. Payne, and R. Davison. *Head Start: a tragicomedy with epilogue.* New York: Behavioral Publications, 1973.

Poznanski, E., A. Maxey, and G. Marsden. Clinical implications of maternal employment: a review of research. *Journal of the American Academy of Child Psychiatry*, 1970, *9*, 741–761.

Quellmalz, E., and J. Hylton. *The training of kindergarten children as instructional tutors*. Austin, Tex.: Southwest Educational Development Laboratory, 1971.

Rohwer, W. D., Jr. Prime time for education: early childhood or adolescence? *Harvard Educational Review*, 1971, *41*, 316–341.

Rohwer, W. D., Jr. Decisive research: a means for answering fundamental questions about instruction. *Educational Researcher*, 1972, *1* (7), 5–11.

Schmitthausler, C. The professionalization of teaching in early childhood education. *Journal of Teacher Education*, 1969, *20*, 188–190.

Scott, P. About research. In W. Hartup (ed.), *The young child*. Vol. 2. Washington, D.C.: National Association for the Education of Young Children, 1972, 1–23.

Scott, R. School and home: not either-or. *Merrill-Palmer Quarterly*, 1971, *17*, 335–346.

Sigel, I. Developmental theory: its place and relevance in early intervention programs. *Young Children*, 1972, *27*, 364–372.

Sigel, I. Where is preschool education going: or are we en route without a road map? In *Proceedings of the 1972 Invitational Conference on Testing Problems*. Princeton, N.J.: Educational Testing Service, 1973, 99–116.

Sigel, I. Contributions of psychoeducational intervention programs in understanding of preschool children. Unpublished manuscript, State University at Buffalo, 1973.

Skager, R., and L. Broadbent. *Cognitive structures and educational evaluation*. Berkeley: University of California Press, 1968.

Smilansky, S., and M. Smilansky. The role and program of preschool education for socially disadvantaged children. *International Review of Education*, 1970, *16*, 45–64.

Smith, M., and R. Giesy. A guide for collecting and organizing information on early childhood programs. *Young Children*, 1972, *27*, 264–271.

Spodek, B. What are the sources of early childhood curriculum? *Young Children*, 1970, *26*, 48–56.

Spodek, B. Staff requirements in early childhood education. In I. J. Gordon (ed.), *Early childhood education*. Chicago: University of Chicago Press, 1972, 339–366.

Sroufe, L. A methodological and philosophical critique of intervention-oriented research. *Developmental Psychology*, 1970, *2*, 140–145.

Staats, A. *Learning, language, and cognition*. New York: Holt, Rinehart and Winston, 1968.

Stake, R. *Priorities planning*. Los Angeles: Instructional Objectives Exchange, 1972.

Stephens, J. *The process of schooling*. New York: Holt, Rinehart and Winston, 1968.

St. John, N. Thirty-six teachers: their characteristics and outcomes for black and white pupils. *American Educational Research Journal*, 1971, *8*, 635–648.

Turner, R. Good teaching and its contexts. *Phi Delta Kappan*, 1970, *52*, 155–158.

Tyler, F. Issues related to readiness to learn. In E. Hilgard (ed.), *Theories of learning and instruction*. Chicago: University of Chicago Press, 1964, 210–239.

Weber, E. *The kindergarten*. Belmont, Calif.: Wadsworth, 1969.

Webster, P. R. The teacher structure checklist: a possible tool for communication. *Young Children*, 1972, *27*, 149–153.

Williams, C., and T. Ryan. Competent professionals for quality child care and early education: the goal of CDA. *Young Children*, 1972, *28*, 71–74.

index